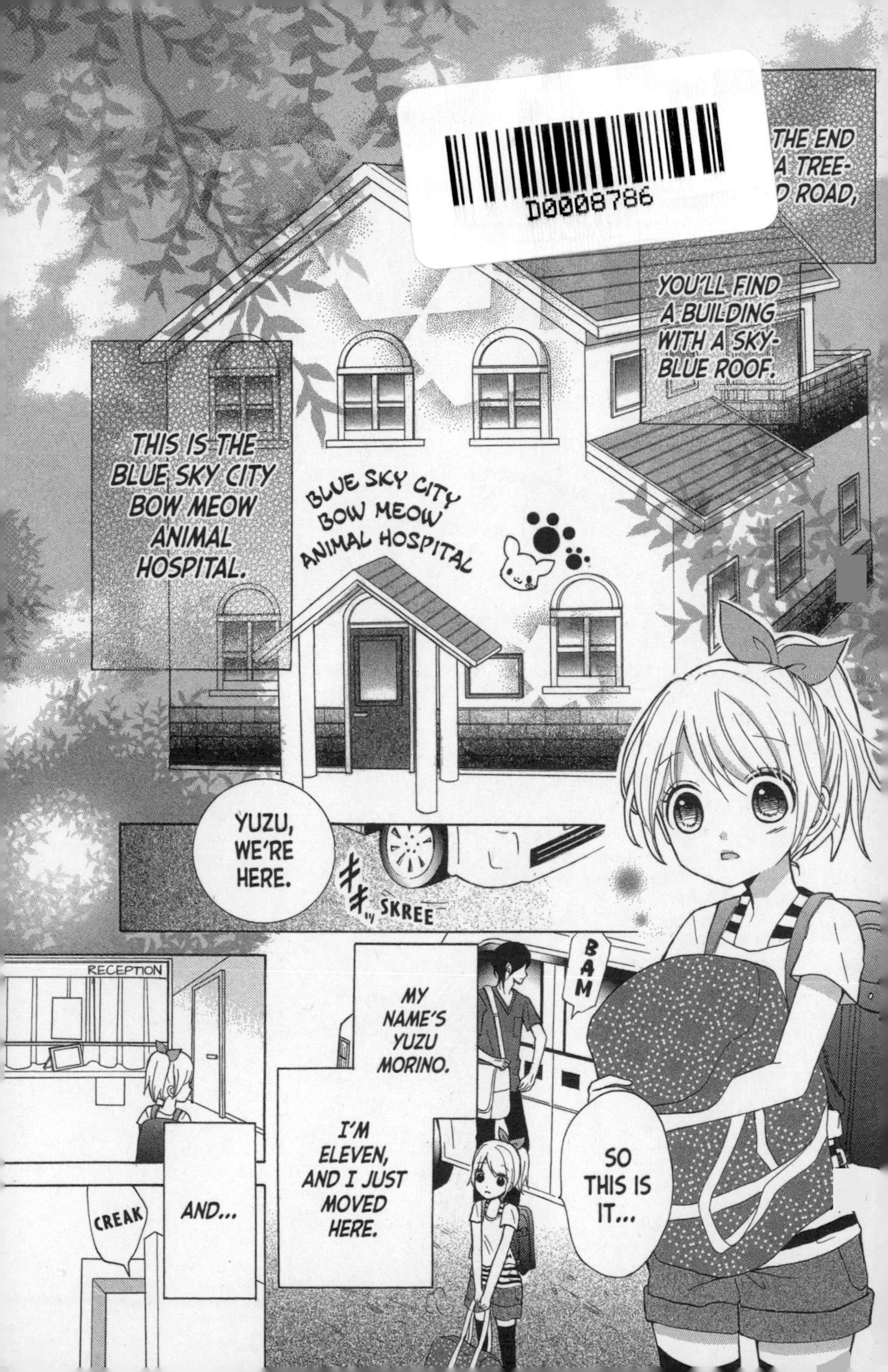
THE END
A TREE-
D ROAD,
YOU'LL FIND A BUILDING WITH A SKY-BLUE ROOF.
THIS IS THE BLUE SKY CITY BOW MEOW ANIMAL HOSPITAL.
BLUE SKY CITY BOW MEOW ANIMAL HOSPITAL
YUZU, WE'RE HERE.
SKREE
BAM
SO THIS IS IT...
MY NAME'S YUZU MORINO.
I'M ELEVEN, AND I JUST MOVED HERE.
AND...
CREAK
RECEPTION

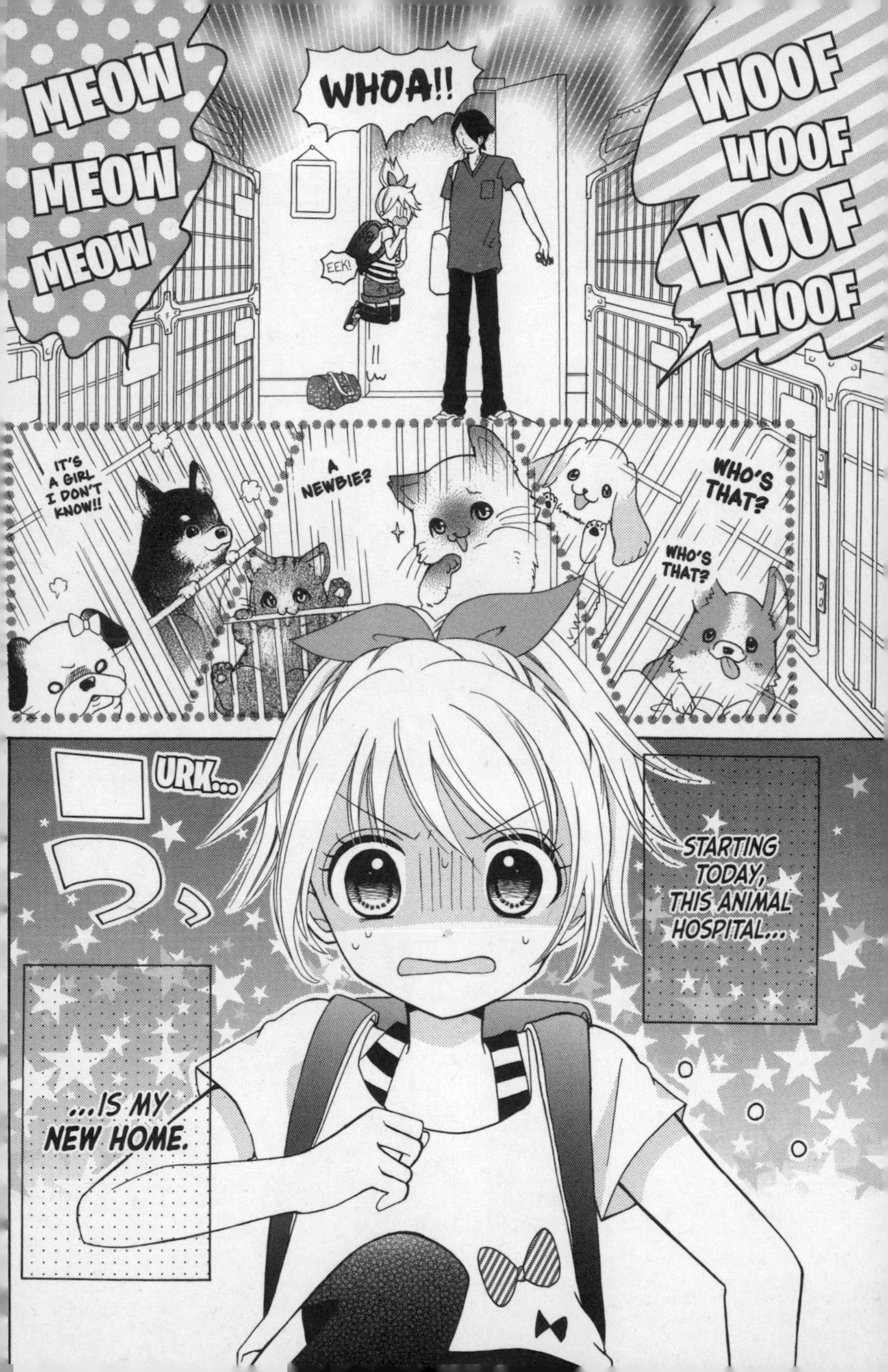
WOOF WOOF WOOF WOOF
WHOA!!
MEOW MEOW MEOW
EEK!
WHO'S THAT?
WHO'S THAT?
A NEWBIE?
IT'S A GIRL I DON'T KNOW!!
STARTING TODAY, THIS ANIMAL HOSPITAL...
URK...
...IS MY NEW HOME.

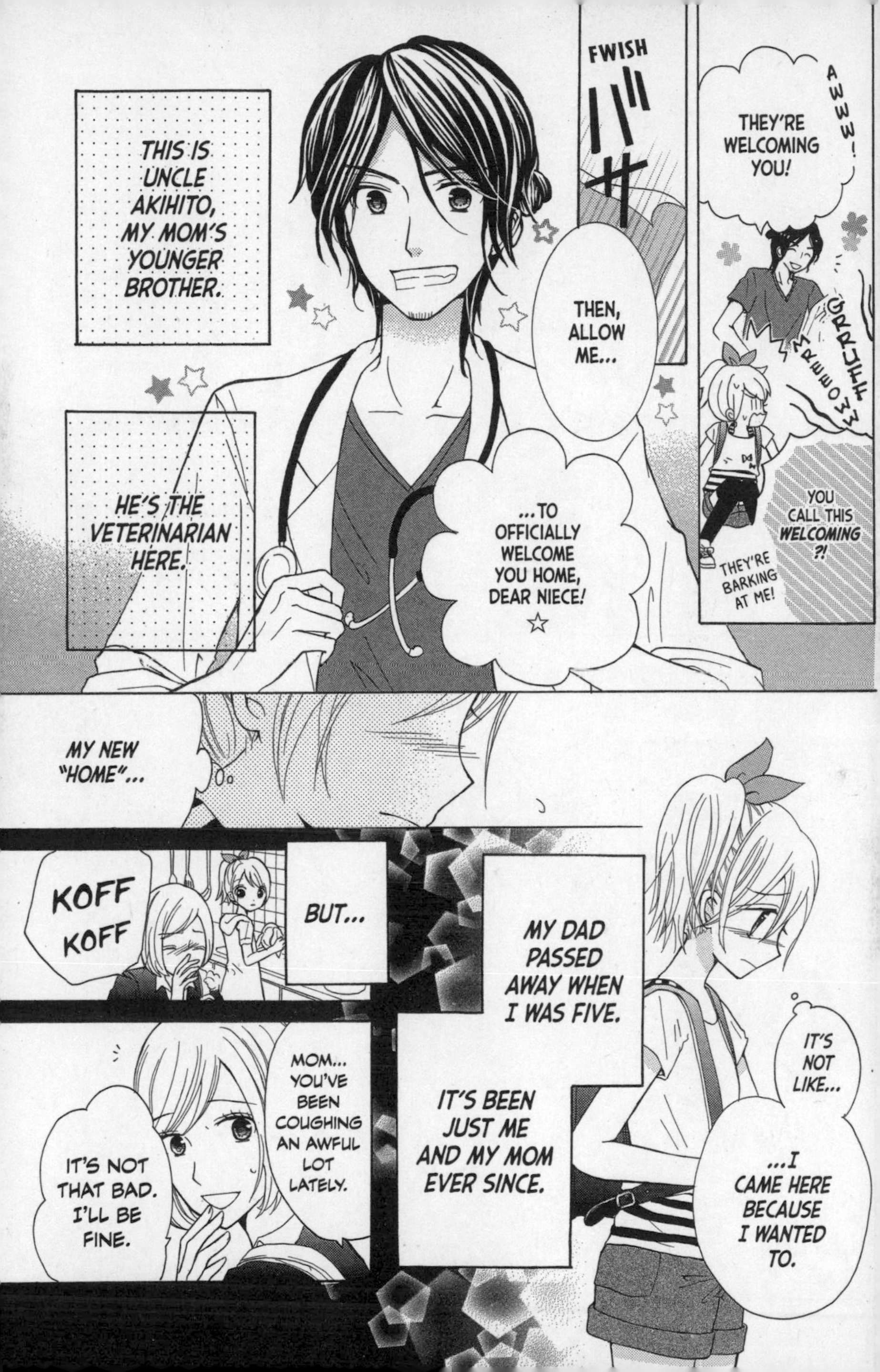
AWWW!
THEY'RE WELCOMING YOU!
GRRRUFF
MREEOWW
YOU CALL THIS WELCOMING?!
THEY'RE BARKING AT ME!
FWISH
THEN, ALLOW ME...
...TO OFFICIALLY WELCOME YOU HOME, DEAR NIECE! ☆
THIS IS UNCLE AKIHITO, MY MOM'S YOUNGER BROTHER.
HE'S THE VETERINARIAN HERE.
MY NEW "HOME"...
IT'S NOT LIKE...
...I CAME HERE BECAUSE I WANTED TO.
MY DAD PASSED AWAY WHEN I WAS FIVE.
IT'S BEEN JUST ME AND MY MOM EVER SINCE.
BUT...
KOFF KOFF
MOM... YOU'VE BEEN COUGHING AN AWFUL LOT LATELY.
IT'S NOT THAT BAD. I'LL BE FINE.

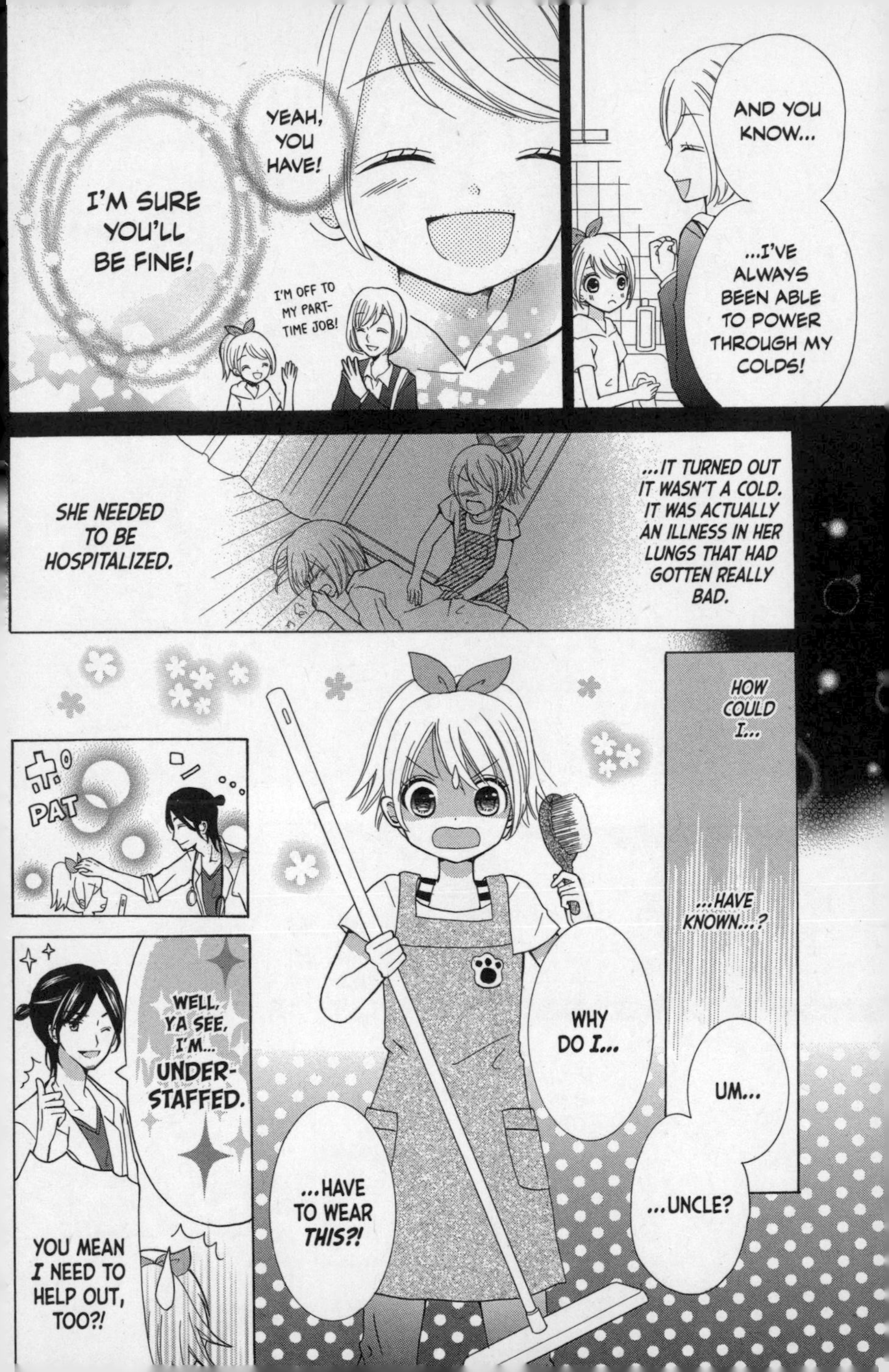
AND YOU KNOW...
...I'VE ALWAYS BEEN ABLE TO POWER THROUGH MY COLDS!
YEAH, YOU HAVE!
I'M SURE YOU'LL BE FINE!
I'M OFF TO MY PART-TIME JOB!
...IT TURNED OUT IT WASN'T A COLD. IT WAS ACTUALLY AN ILLNESS IN HER LUNGS THAT HAD GOTTEN REALLY BAD.
SHE NEEDED TO BE HOSPITALIZED.
HOW COULD I...
...HAVE KNOWN...?
UM...
...UNCLE?
WHY DO I...
...HAVE TO WEAR THIS?!
PAT
WELL, YA SEE, I'M... UNDER-STAFFED.
YOU MEAN I NEED TO HELP OUT, TOO?!

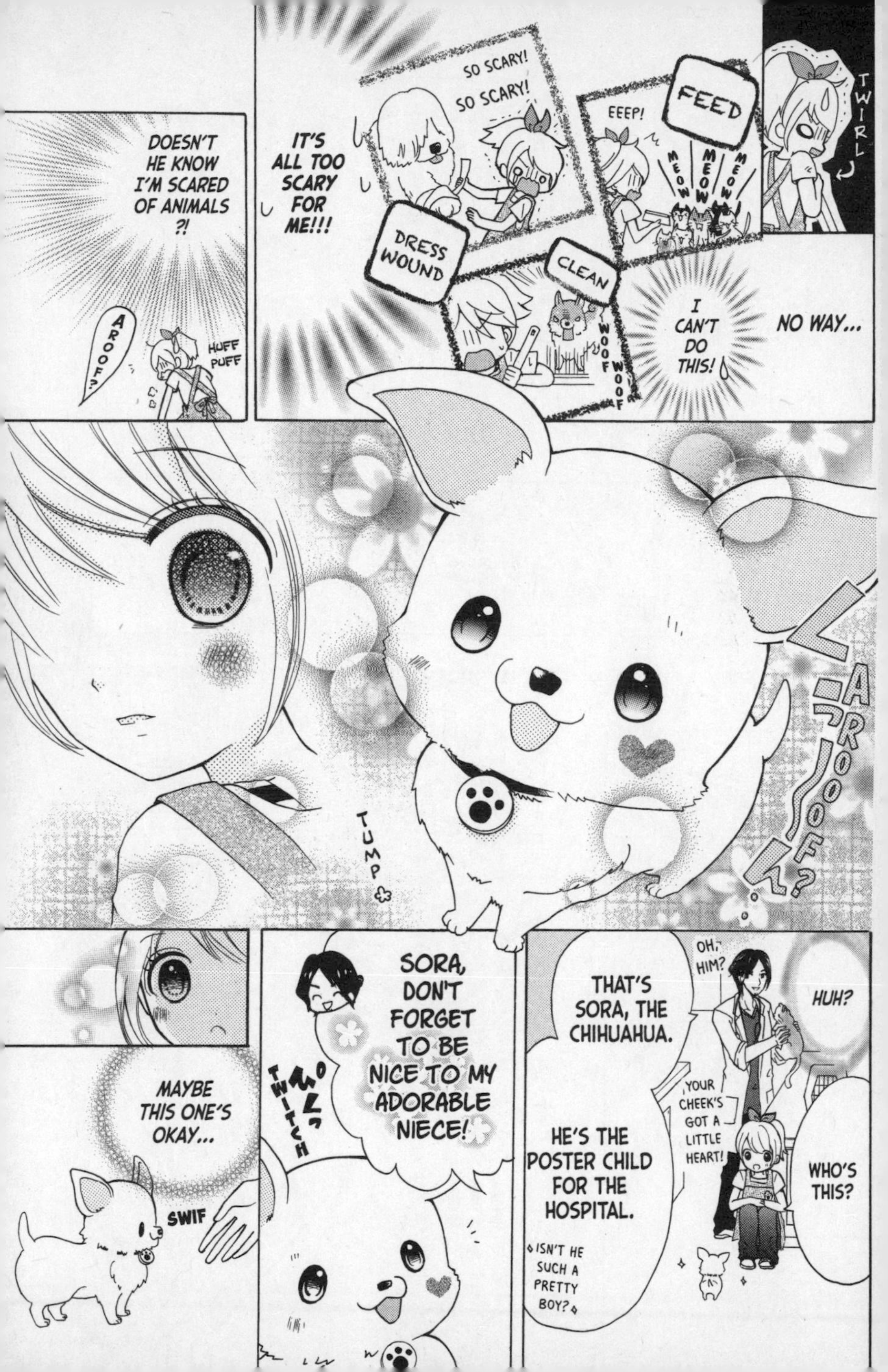
TWIRL
FEED
EEEP!
MEOW MEOW MEOW
SO SCARY!
SO SCARY!
CLEAN
WOOF WOOF WOOF
DRESS WOUND
NO WAY...
I CAN'T DO THIS!
IT'S ALL TOO SCARY FOR ME!!!
DOESN'T HE KNOW I'M SCARED OF ANIMALS ?!
HUFF PUFF
AROOF?!
AROOOOF?
TUMP
HUH?
WHO'S THIS?
OH, HIM?
YOUR CHEEK'S GOT A LITTLE HEART!
THAT'S SORA, THE CHIHUAHUA.
HE'S THE POSTER CHILD FOR THE HOSPITAL.
ISN'T HE SUCH A PRETTY BOY?
SORA, DON'T FORGET TO BE NICE TO MY ADORABLE NIECE!
TWITCH
MAYBE THIS ONE'S OKAY...
SWIF

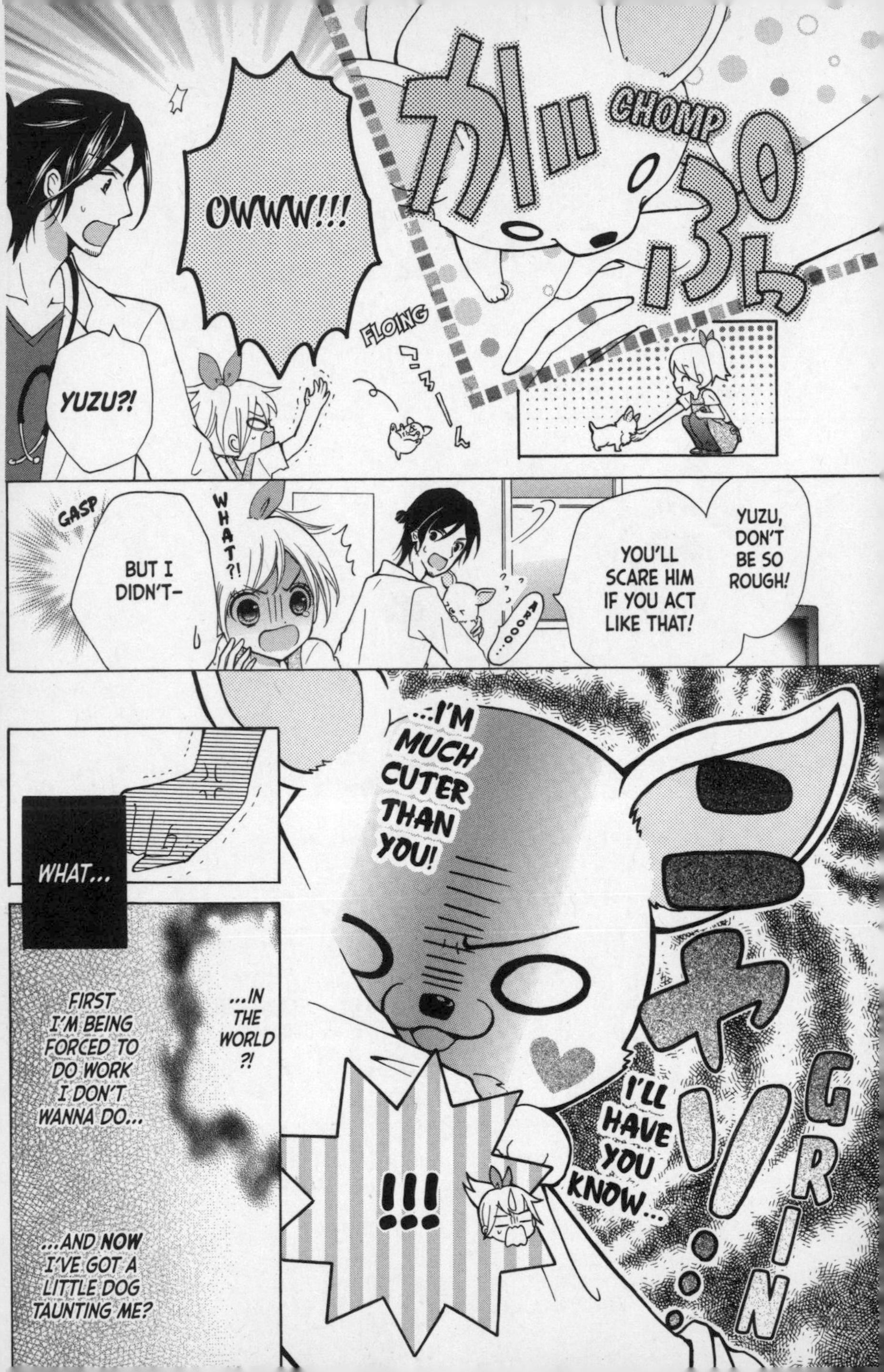
CHOMP
FLOING
OWWW!!!
YUZU?!
YUZU, DON'T BE SO ROUGH!
YOU'LL SCARE HIM IF YOU ACT LIKE THAT!
WHAT?!
GASP
BUT I DIDN'T-
GRIN
I'LL HAVE YOU KNOW...
...I'M MUCH CUTER THAN YOU!
!!!
WHAT...
...IN THE WORLD?!
FIRST I'M BEING FORCED TO DO WORK I DON'T WANNA DO...
...AND NOW I'VE GOT A LITTLE DOG TAUNTING ME?

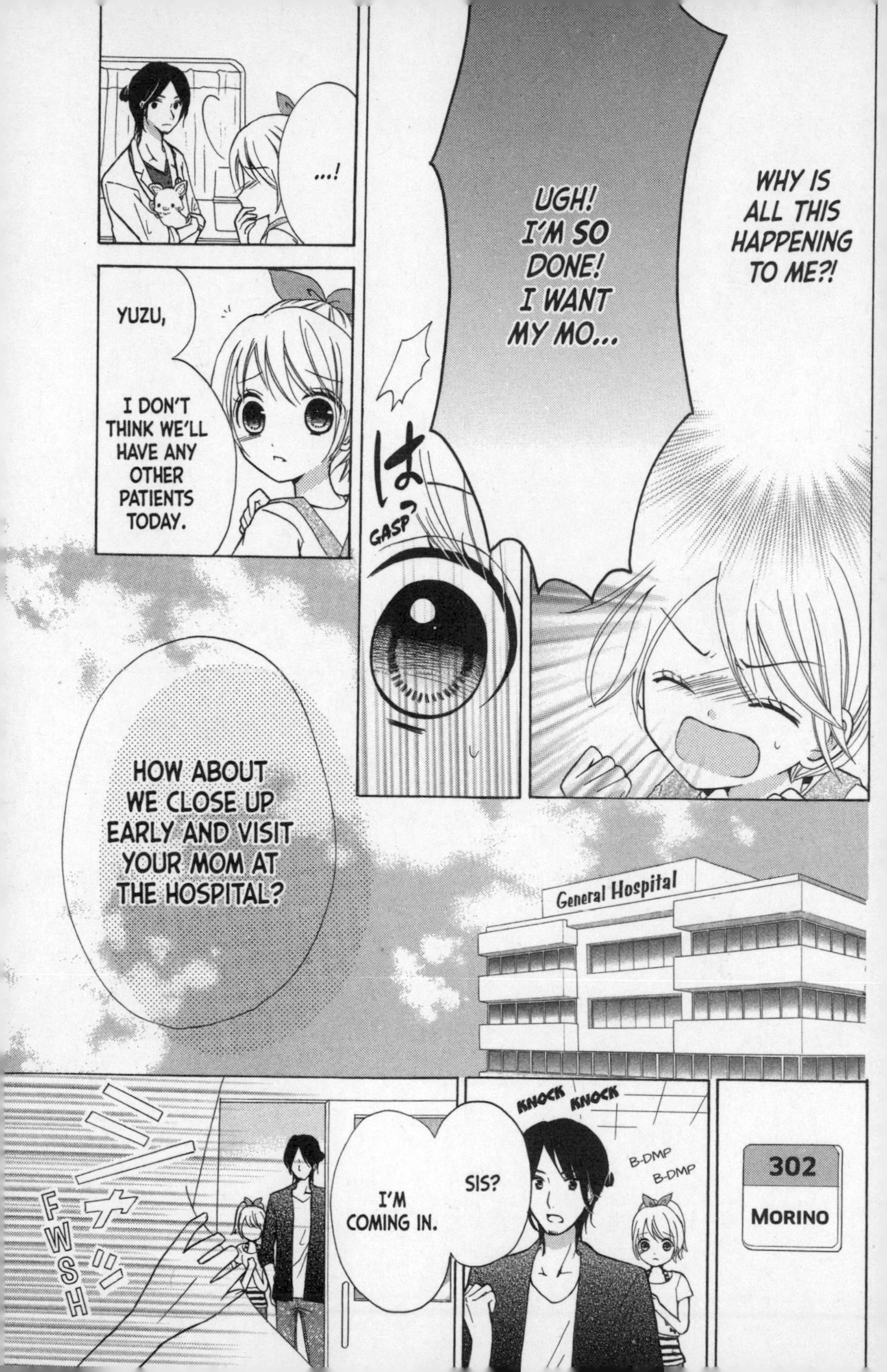
WHY IS ALL THIS HAPPENING TO ME?!
UGH! I'M SO DONE! I WANT MY MO...
GASP
...!
YUZU,
I DON'T THINK WE'LL HAVE ANY OTHER PATIENTS TODAY.
HOW ABOUT WE CLOSE UP EARLY AND VISIT YOUR MOM AT THE HOSPITAL?
General Hospital
302
MORINO
KNOCK KNOCK
B-DMP B-DMP
SIS?
I'M COMING IN.
FWSH

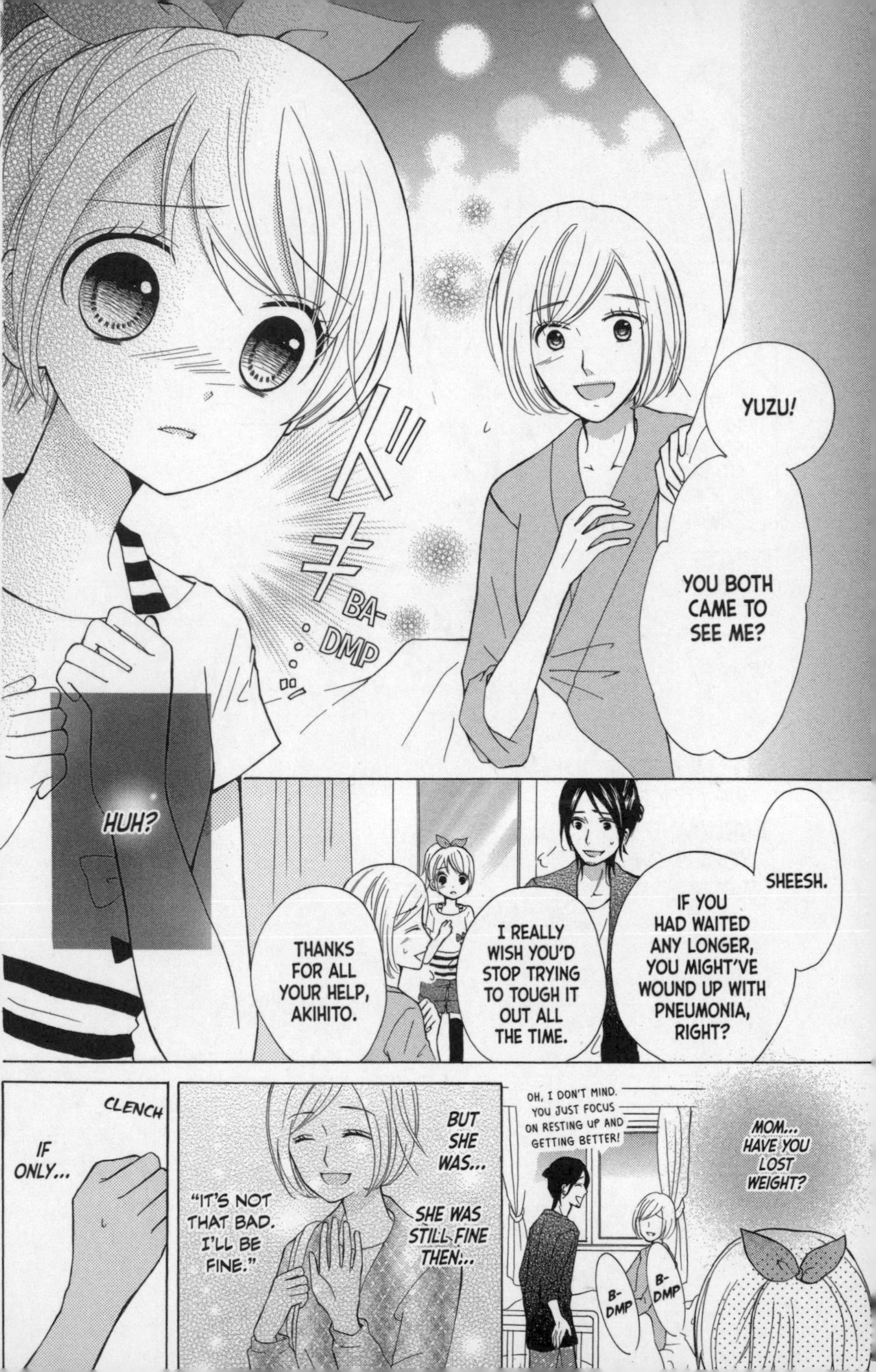
YUZU!
YOU BOTH CAME TO SEE ME?
ドキ
BA-DMP
HUH?
SHEESH.
IF YOU HAD WAITED ANY LONGER, YOU MIGHT'VE WOUND UP WITH PNEUMONIA, RIGHT?
I REALLY WISH YOU'D STOP TRYING TO TOUGH IT OUT ALL THE TIME.
THANKS FOR ALL YOUR HELP, AKIHITO.
OH, I DON'T MIND. YOU JUST FOCUS ON RESTING UP AND GETTING BETTER!
MOM... HAVE YOU LOST WEIGHT?
B-DMP
B-DMP
BUT SHE WAS...
"IT'S NOT THAT BAD. I'LL BE FINE."
SHE WAS STILL FINE THEN...
CLENCH
IF ONLY...

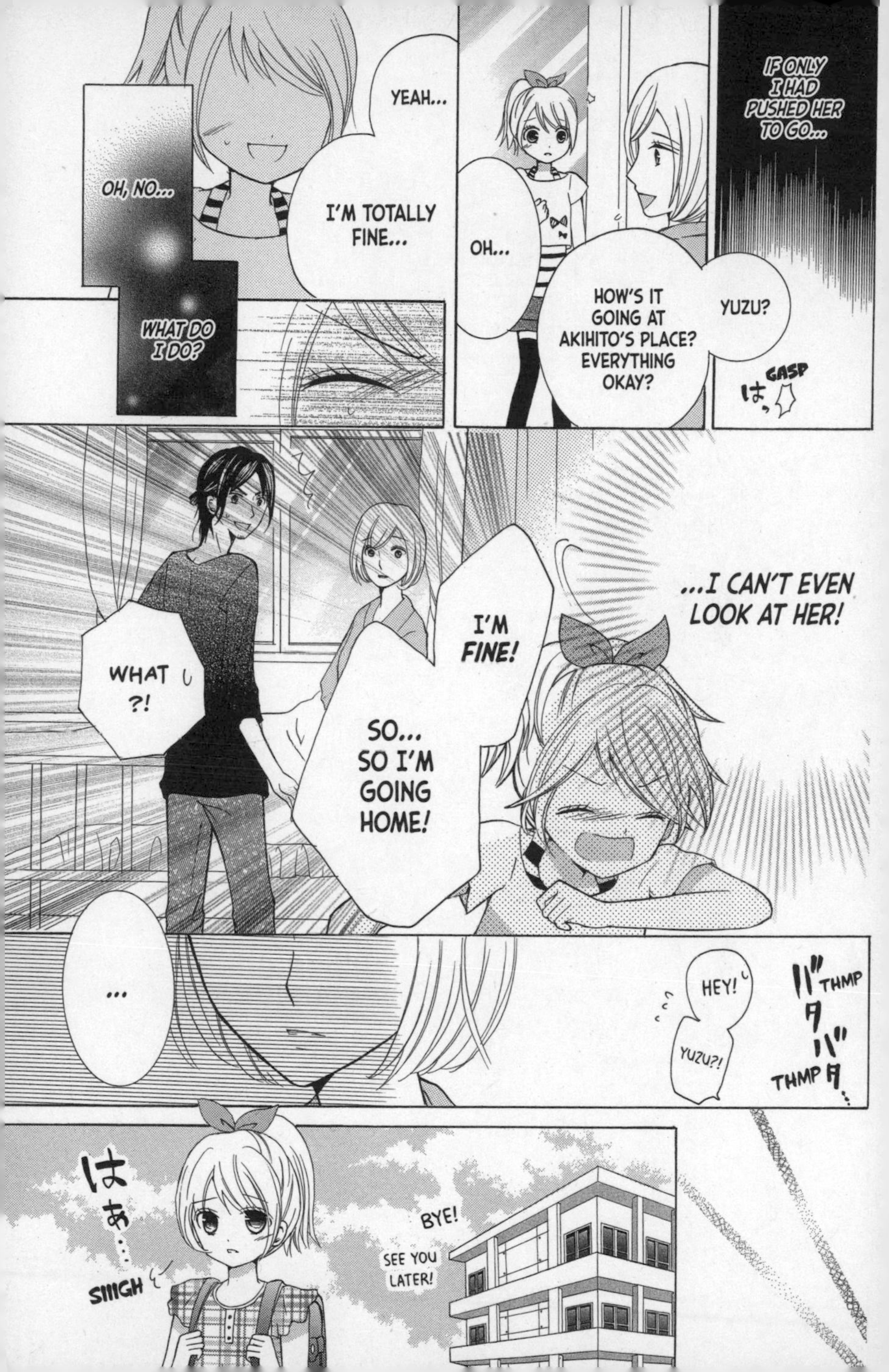
IF ONLY I HAD PUSHED HER TO GO...
YUZU?
はっ GASP
HOW'S IT GOING AT AKIHITO'S PLACE? EVERYTHING OKAY?
OH...
YEAH...
I'M TOTALLY FINE...
OH, NO...
WHAT DO I DO?
...I CAN'T EVEN LOOK AT HER!
I'M FINE!
SO... SO I'M GOING HOME!
WHAT ?!
バタバタ THMP THMP
HEY!
YUZU?!
...
BYE!
SEE YOU LATER!
はぁ… SIIIGH

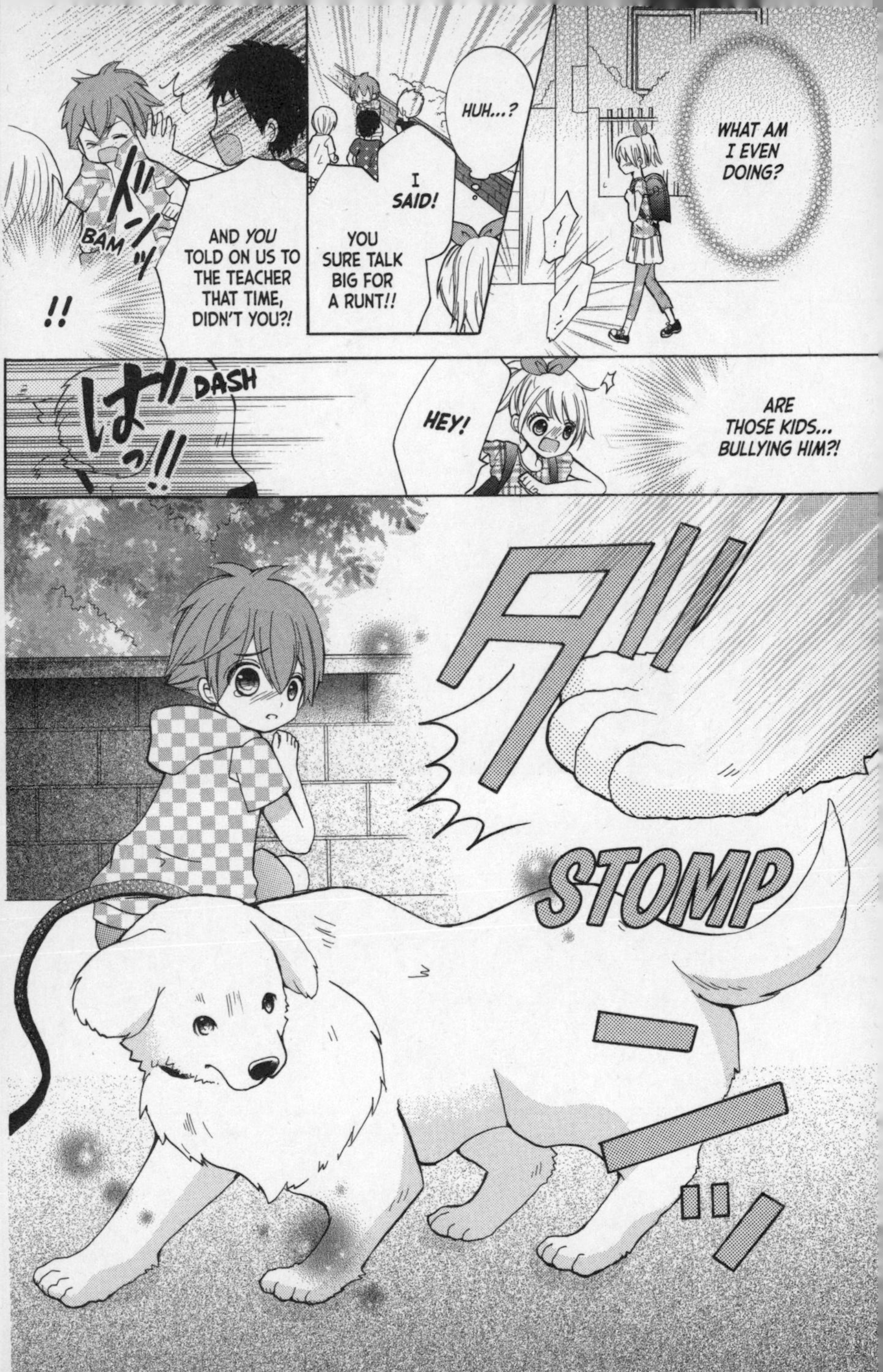
WHAT AM I EVEN DOING?
HUH...?
I SAID!
YOU SURE TALK BIG FOR A RUNT!!
AND YOU TOLD ON US TO THE TEACHER THAT TIME, DIDN'T YOU?!
BAM
!!
ARE THOSE KIDS... BULLYING HIM?!
HEY!
DASH
STOMP

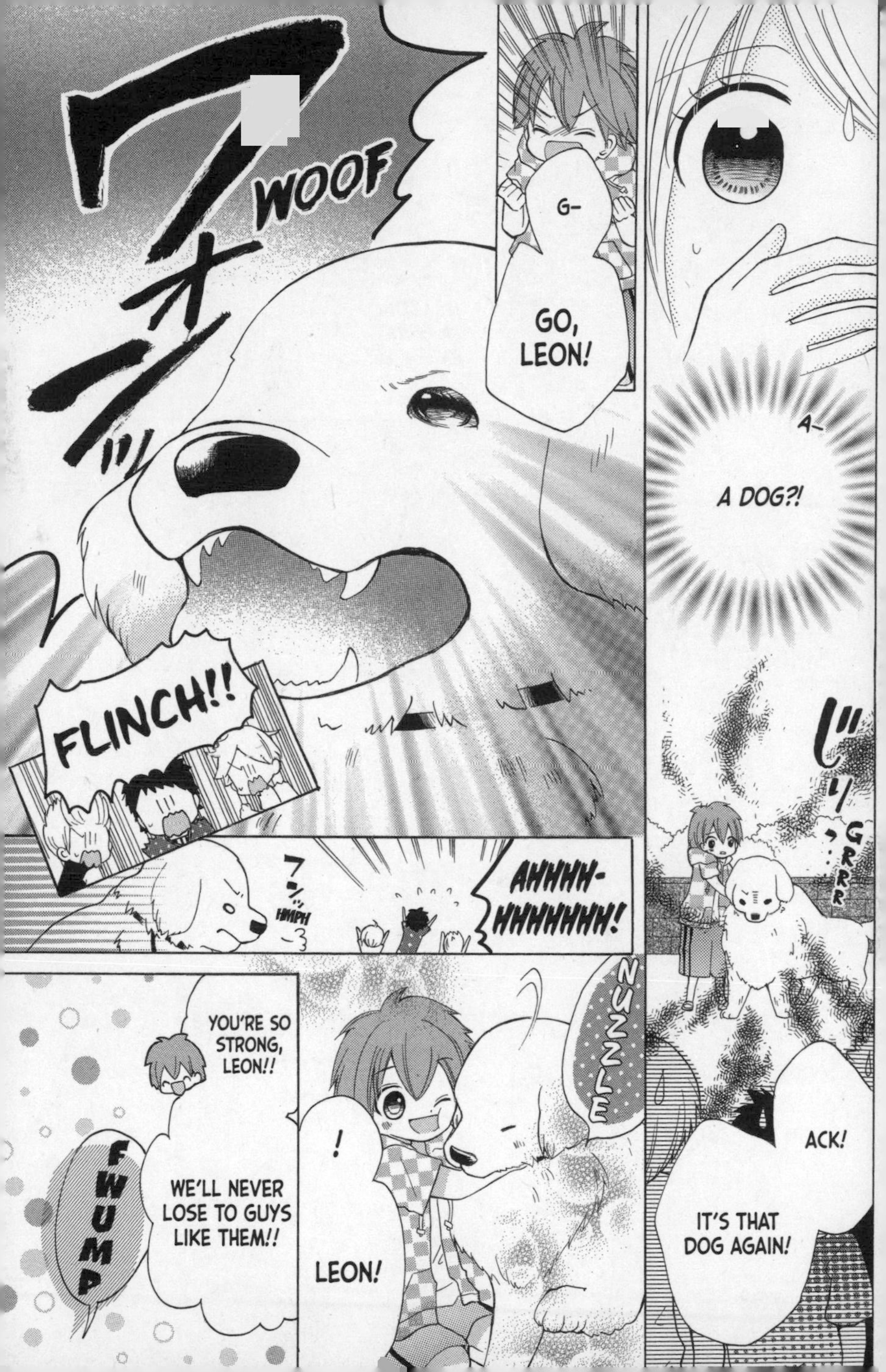
A–
A DOG?!
GRRR
ACK!
IT'S THAT DOG AGAIN!
G–
GO, LEON!
WOOF
FLINCH!!
AHHHH-HHHHHHH!
HMPH
!
LEON!
NUZZLE
YOU'RE SO STRONG, LEON!!
WE'LL NEVER LOSE TO GUYS LIKE THEM!!
FWUMP

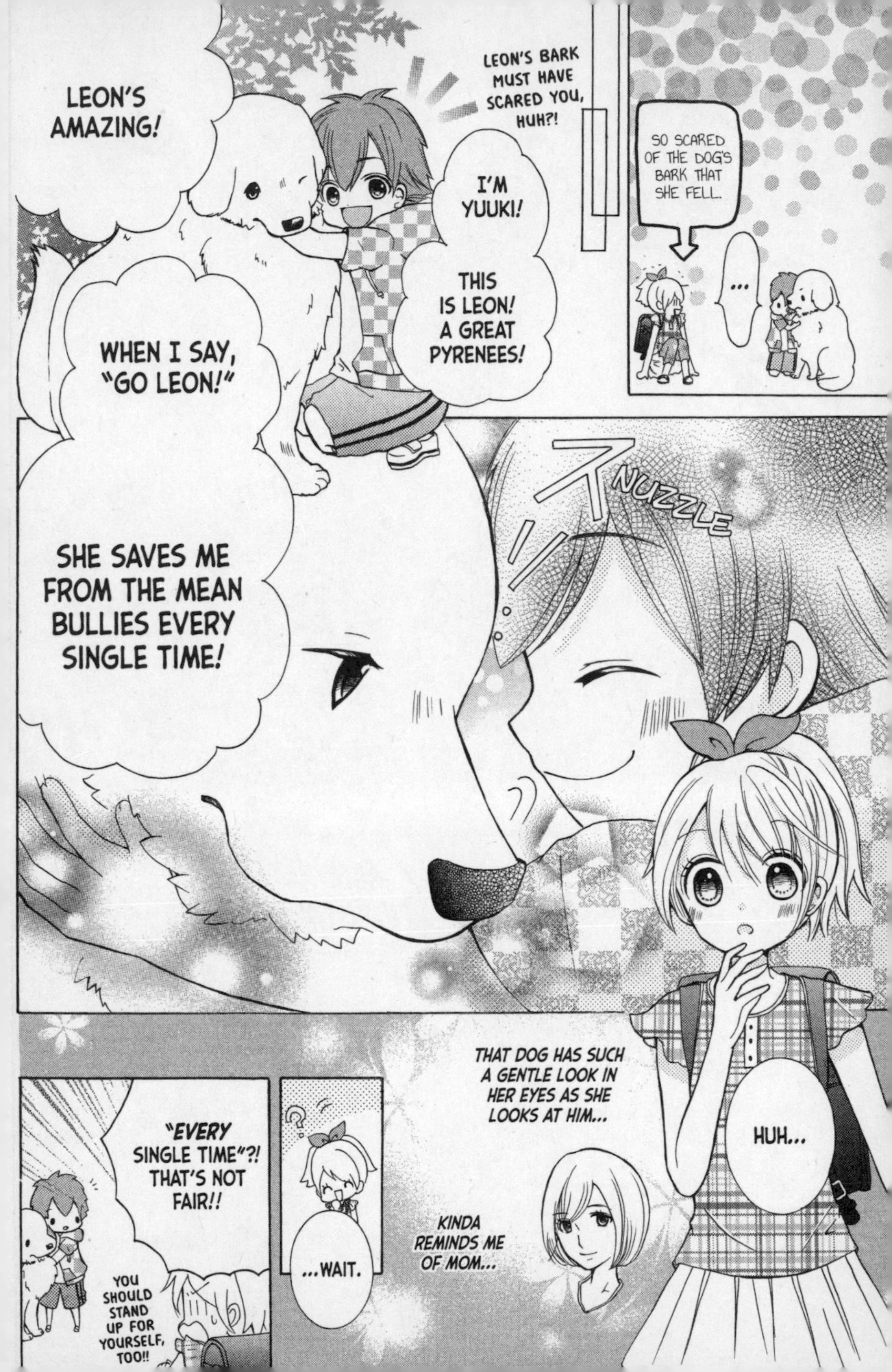
SO SCARED OF THE DOG'S BARK THAT SHE FELL.
...
LEON'S BARK MUST HAVE SCARED YOU, HUH?!
I'M YUUKI!
THIS IS LEON! A GREAT PYRENEES!
LEON'S AMAZING!
WHEN I SAY, "GO LEON!"
SHE SAVES ME FROM THE MEAN BULLIES EVERY SINGLE TIME!
NUZZLE
THAT DOG HAS SUCH A GENTLE LOOK IN HER EYES AS SHE LOOKS AT HIM...
HUH...
KINDA REMINDS ME OF MOM...
...WAIT.
"EVERY SINGLE TIME"?! THAT'S NOT FAIR!!
YOU SHOULD STAND UP FOR YOURSELF, TOO!!

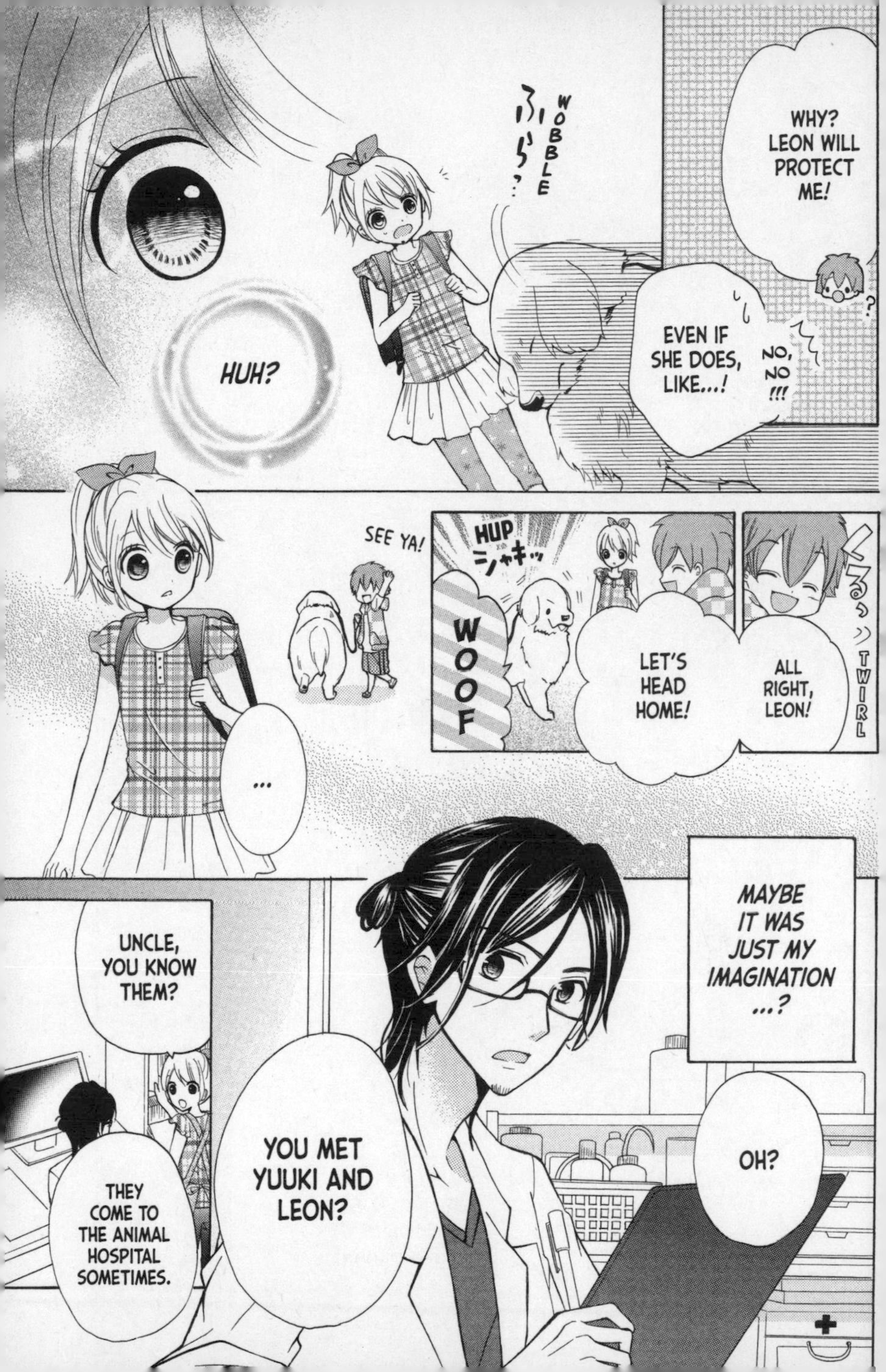

WHY? LEON WILL PROTECT ME!
?
EVEN IF SHE DOES, LIKE...!
NO, NO !!!
ふらっ
WOBBLE
HUH?
くるっ
TWIRL
ALL RIGHT, LEON!
LET'S HEAD HOME!
HUP
シャキッ
WOOF
SEE YA!
...
MAYBE IT WAS JUST MY IMAGINATION ...?
OH?
YOU MET YUUKI AND LEON?
UNCLE, YOU KNOW THEM?
THEY COME TO THE ANIMAL HOSPITAL SOMETIMES.

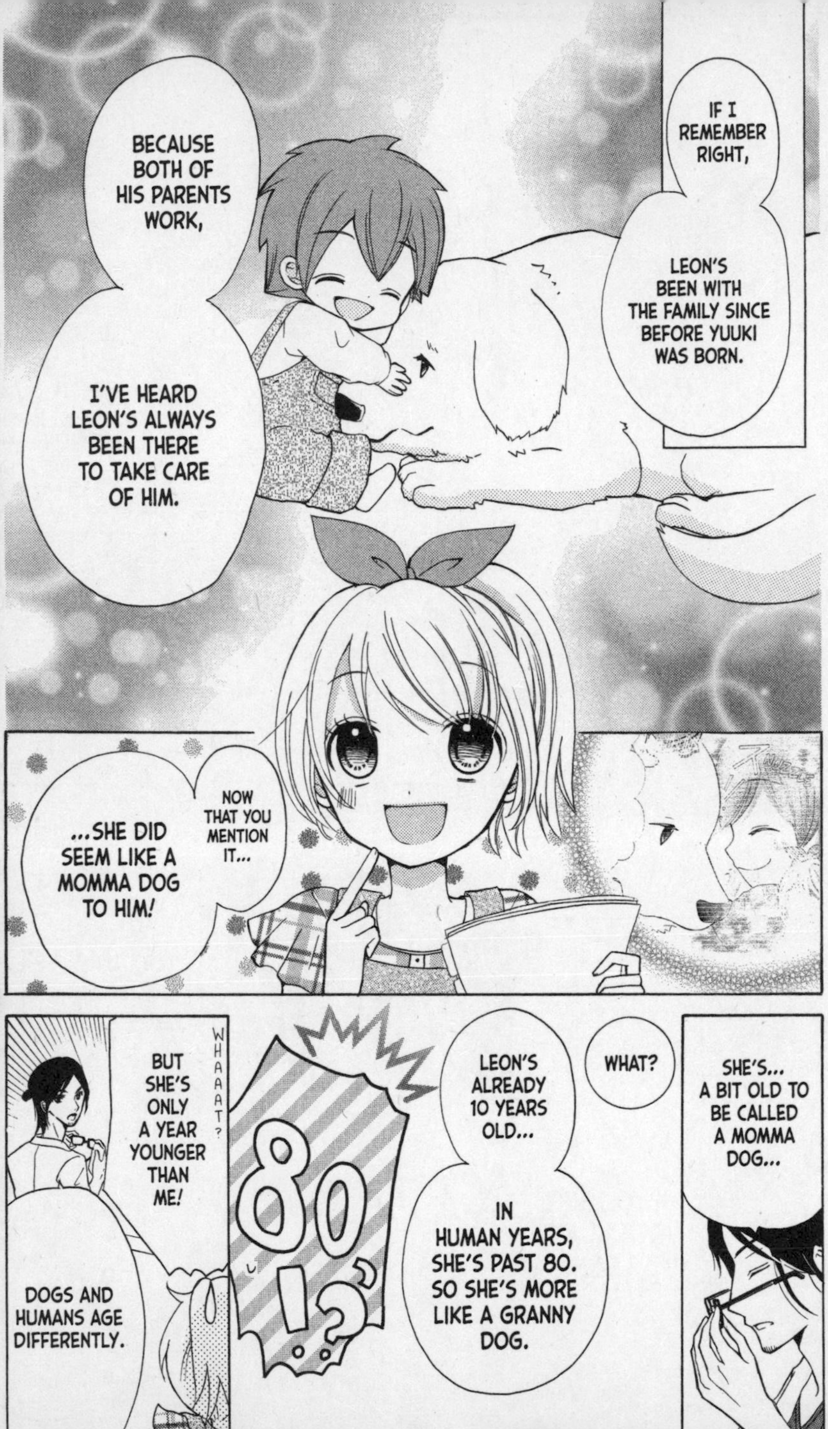

IF I REMEMBER RIGHT,
LEON'S BEEN WITH THE FAMILY SINCE BEFORE YUUKI WAS BORN.
BECAUSE BOTH OF HIS PARENTS WORK,
I'VE HEARD LEON'S ALWAYS BEEN THERE TO TAKE CARE OF HIM.
NOW THAT YOU MENTION IT...
...SHE DID SEEM LIKE A MOMMA DOG TO HIM!
SHE'S... A BIT OLD TO BE CALLED A MOMMA DOG...
WHAT?
LEON'S ALREADY 10 YEARS OLD...
IN HUMAN YEARS, SHE'S PAST 80. SO SHE'S MORE LIKE A GRANNY DOG.
80!?
WHAAAT?
BUT SHE'S ONLY A YEAR YOUNGER THAN ME!
DOGS AND HUMANS AGE DIFFERENTLY.

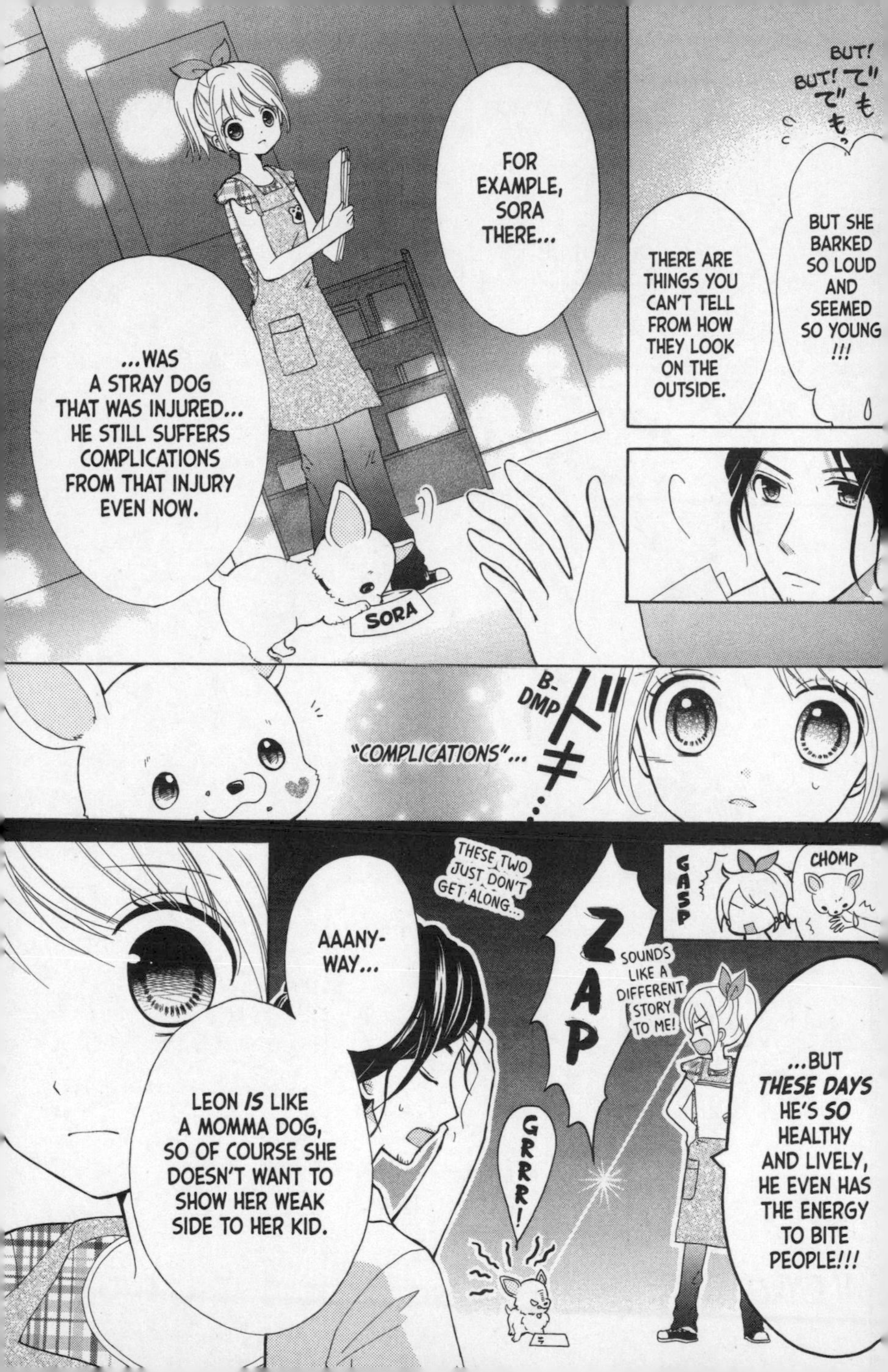

BUT! BUT!
でも でも
BUT SHE BARKED SO LOUD AND SEEMED SO YOUNG!!!
THERE ARE THINGS YOU CAN'T TELL FROM HOW THEY LOOK ON THE OUTSIDE.
FOR EXAMPLE, SORA THERE...
...WAS A STRAY DOG THAT WAS INJURED... HE STILL SUFFERS COMPLICATIONS FROM THAT INJURY EVEN NOW.
SORA
B-DMP
ドキ…
"COMPLICATIONS"...
CHOMP
GASP
...BUT *THESE DAYS* HE'S *SO* HEALTHY AND LIVELY, HE EVEN HAS THE ENERGY TO BITE PEOPLE!!!
SOUNDS LIKE A DIFFERENT STORY TO ME!
ZAP
GRRR!
THESE TWO JUST DON'T GET ALONG...
AAANY-WAY...
LEON *IS* LIKE A MOMMA DOG, SO OF COURSE SHE DOESN'T WANT TO SHOW HER WEAK SIDE TO HER KID.

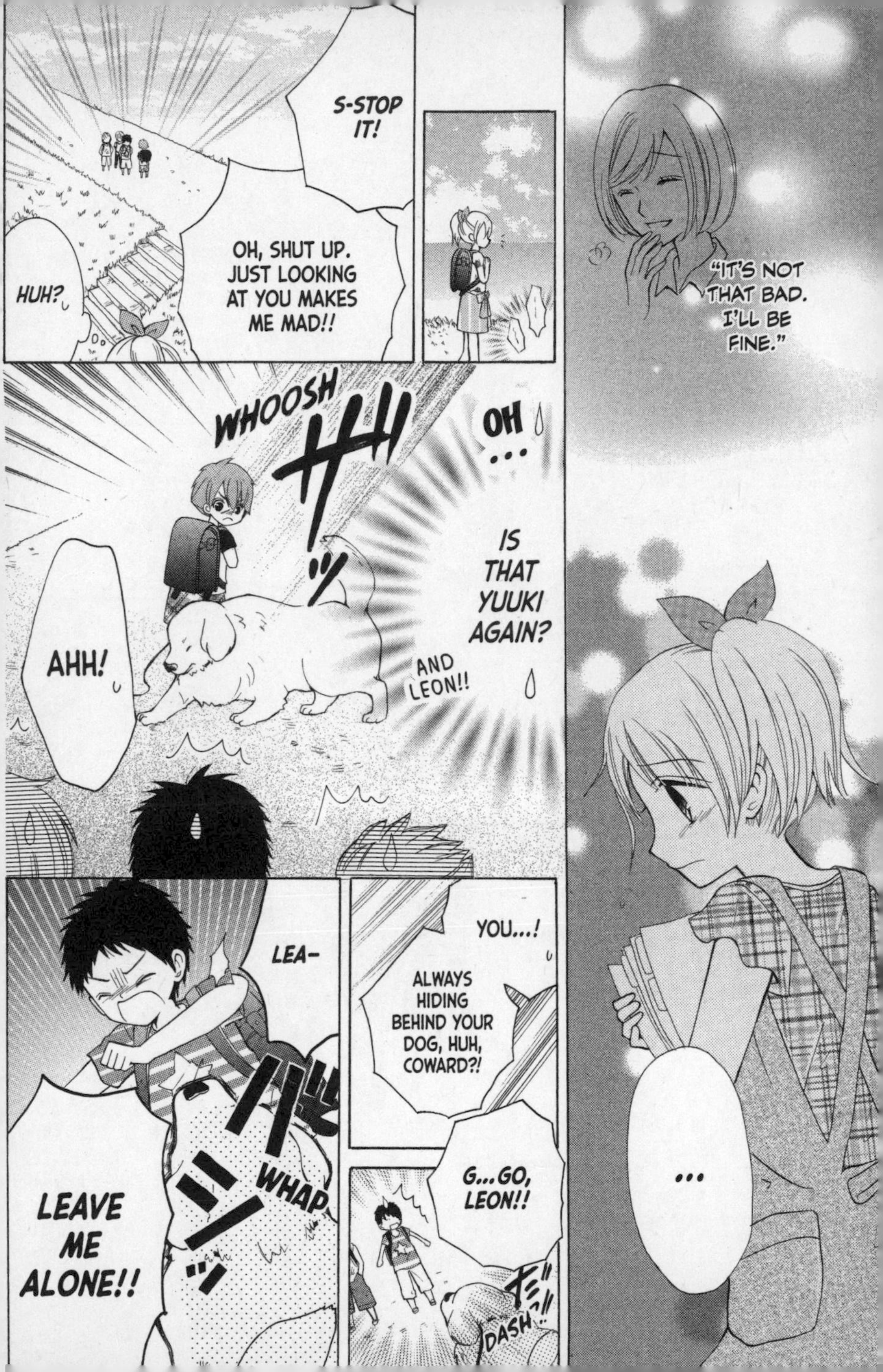
"IT'S NOT THAT BAD. I'LL BE FINE."
...
S-STOP IT!
OH, SHUT UP. JUST LOOKING AT YOU MAKES ME MAD!!
HUH?
WHOOSH
OH...
IS THAT YUUKI AGAIN?
AND LEON!!
AHH!
YOU...!
ALWAYS HIDING BEHIND YOUR DOG, HUH, COWARD?!
G...GO, LEON!!
DASH
LEA-
WHAP
LEAVE ME ALONE!!

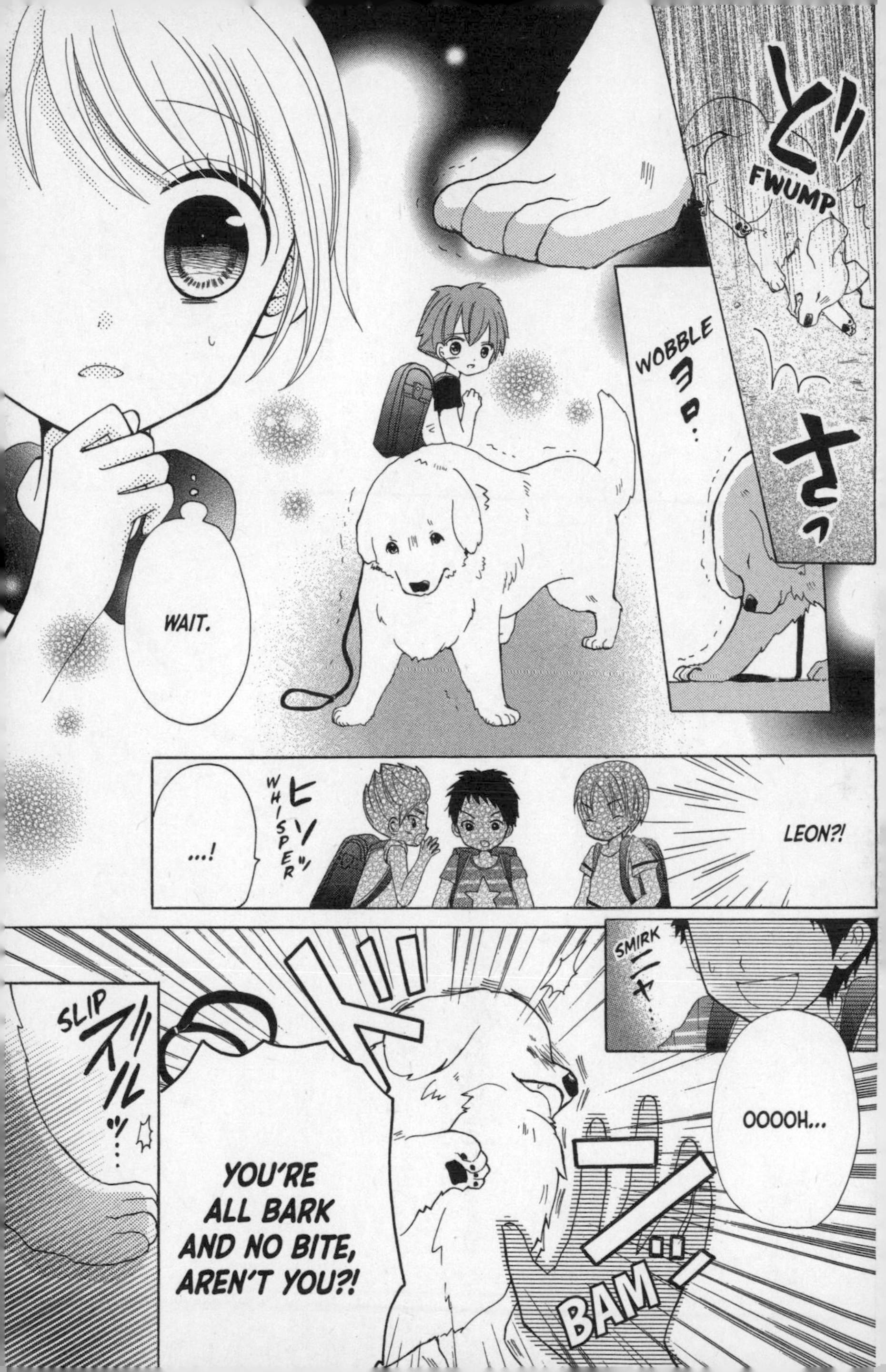
とッ
FWUMP
WOBBLE ヨロ..
さっ
WAIT.
LEON?!
WHISPER ヒソッ
...!
SMIRK ニヤ...
OOOOH...
BAM
SLIP ズルッ...
YOU'RE ALL BARK AND NO BITE, AREN'T YOU?!

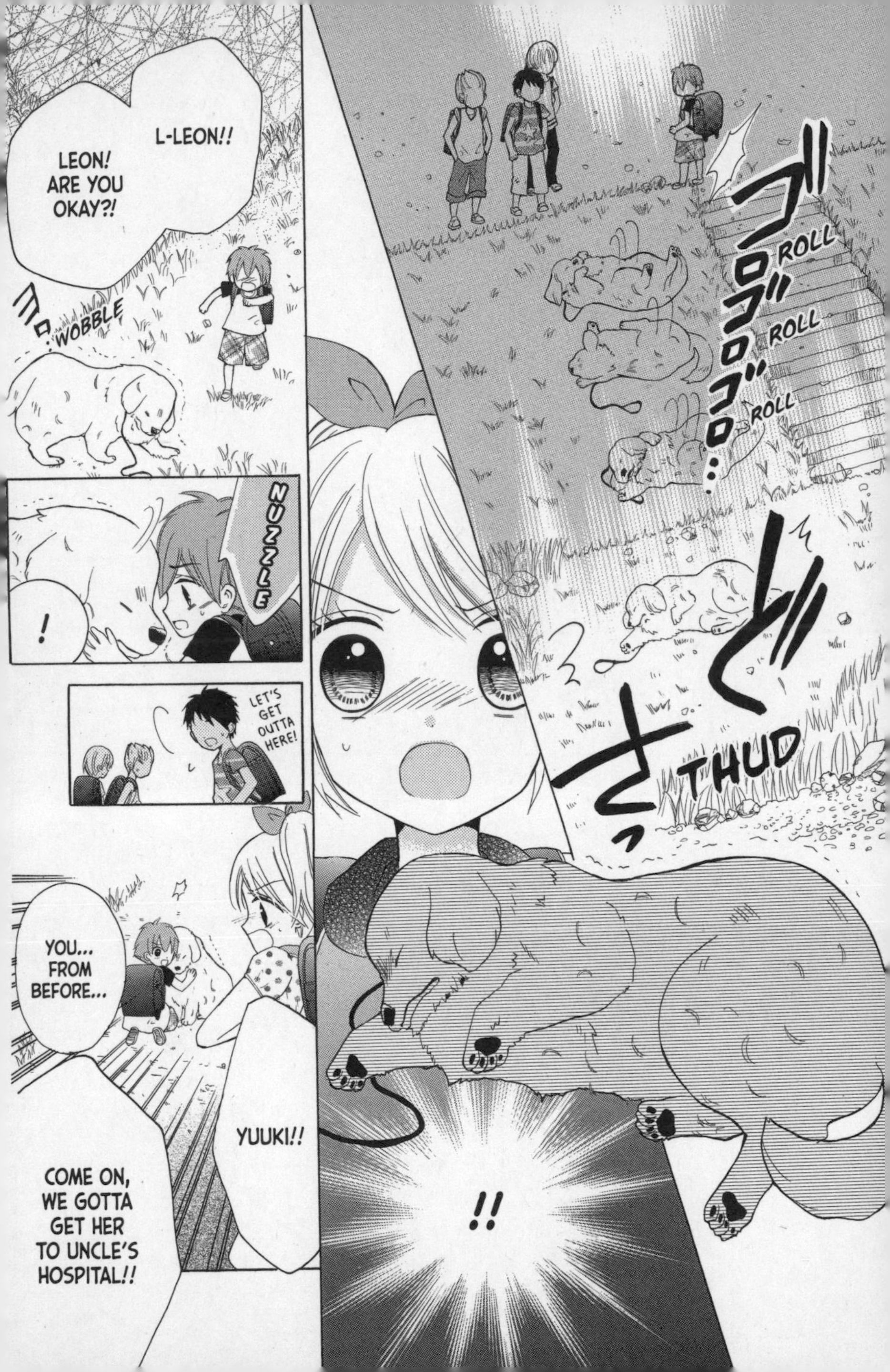
ゴロゴロゴロ…
ROLL
ROLL
ROLL
どさっ
THUD
!!
L-LEON!!
LEON! ARE YOU OKAY?!
ヨロ
WOBBLE
NUZZLE
!
LET'S GET OUTTA HERE!
YOU... FROM BEFORE...
YUUKI!!
COME ON, WE GOTTA GET HER TO UNCLE'S HOSPITAL!!

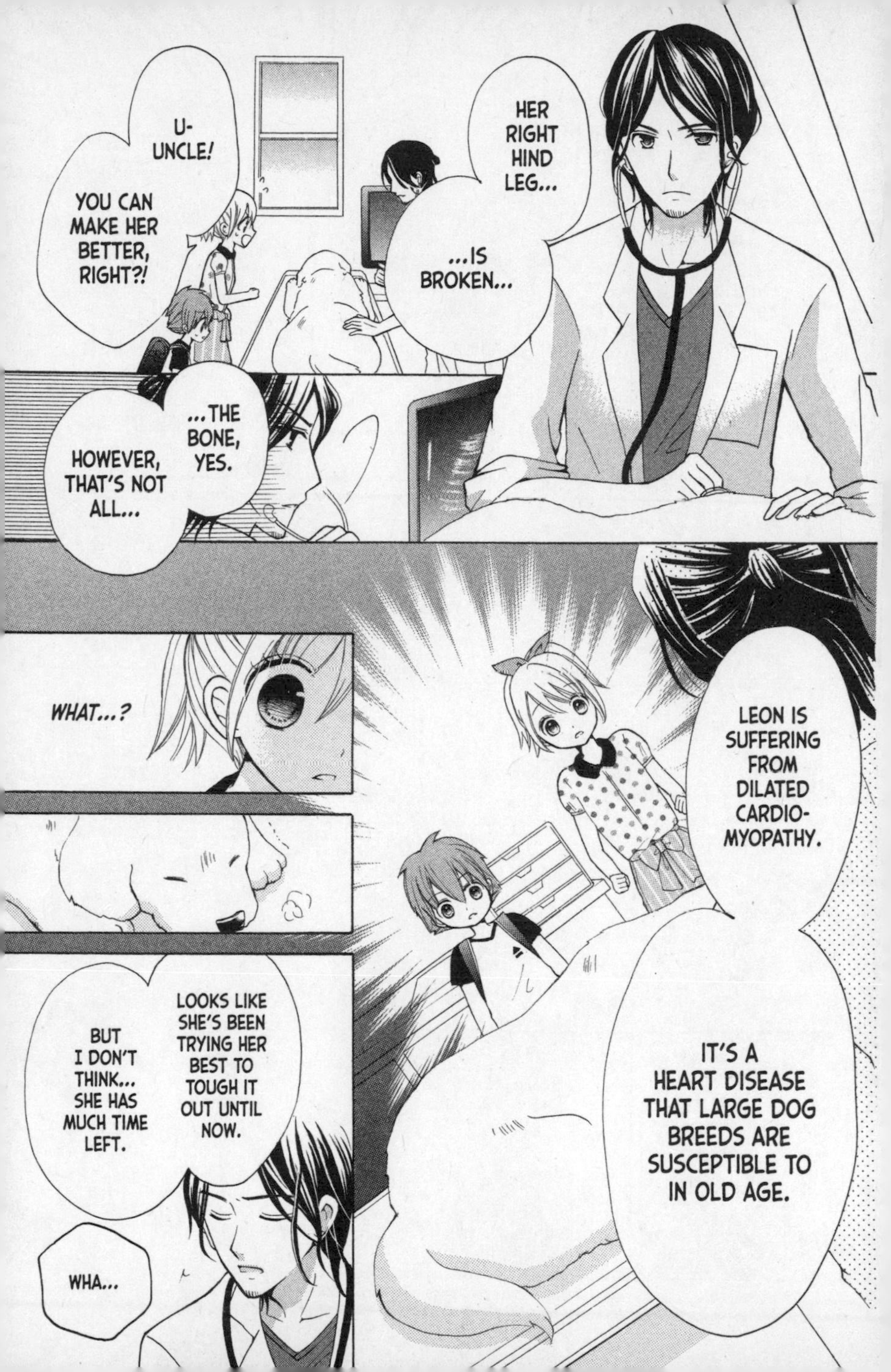
HER RIGHT HIND LEG...
...IS BROKEN...
U-UNCLE!
YOU CAN MAKE HER BETTER, RIGHT?!
...THE BONE, YES.
HOWEVER, THAT'S NOT ALL...
LEON IS SUFFERING FROM DILATED CARDIO-MYOPATHY.
IT'S A HEART DISEASE THAT LARGE DOG BREEDS ARE SUSCEPTIBLE TO IN OLD AGE.
WHAT...?
LOOKS LIKE SHE'S BEEN TRYING HER BEST TO TOUGH IT OUT UNTIL NOW.
BUT I DON'T THINK... SHE HAS MUCH TIME LEFT.
WHA...

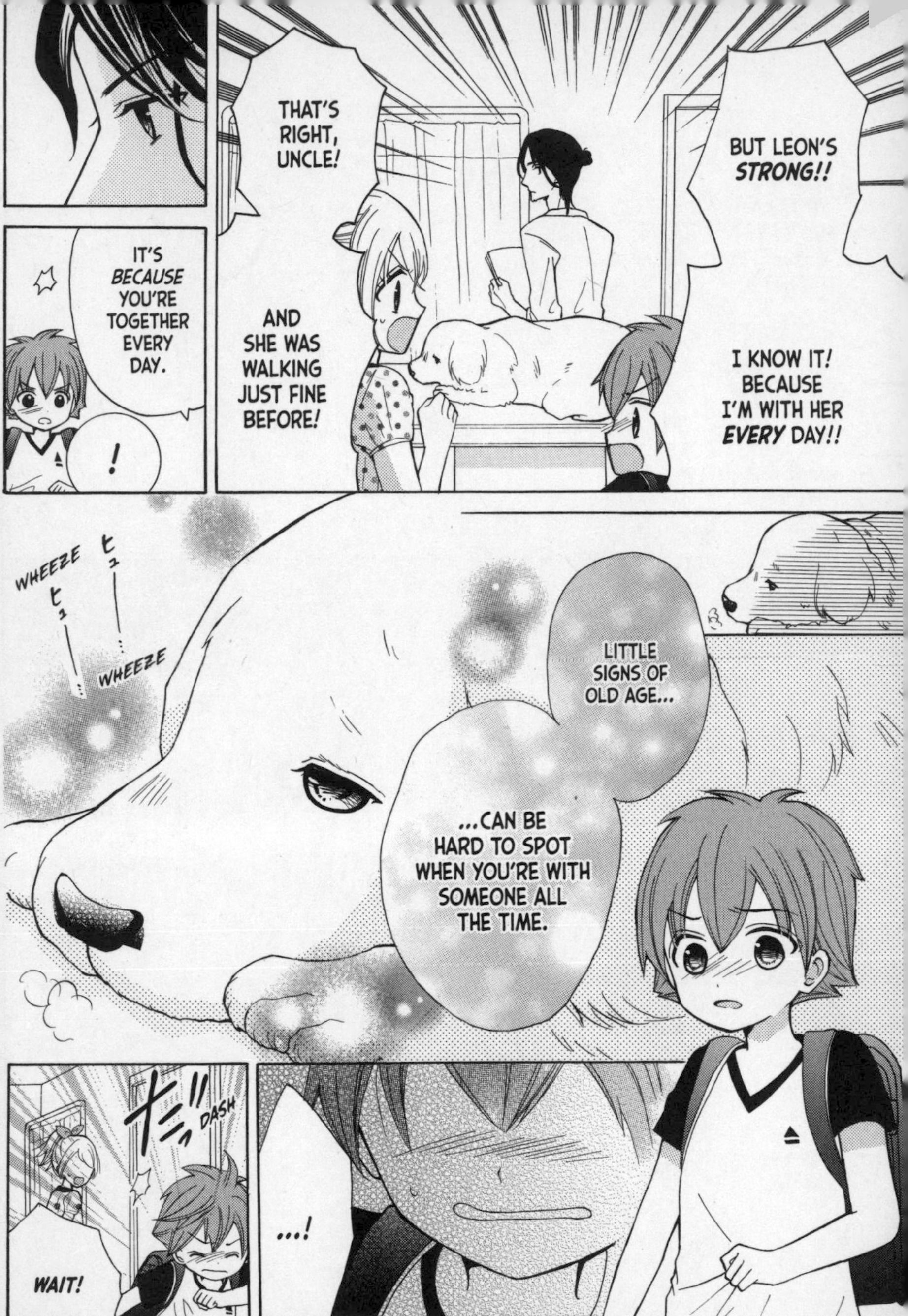
BUT LEON'S STRONG!!
I KNOW IT! BECAUSE I'M WITH HER EVERY DAY!!
THAT'S RIGHT, UNCLE!
AND SHE WAS WALKING JUST FINE BEFORE!
IT'S BECAUSE YOU'RE TOGETHER EVERY DAY.
!
LITTLE SIGNS OF OLD AGE...
...CAN BE HARD TO SPOT WHEN YOU'RE WITH SOMEONE ALL THE TIME.
WHEEZE
WHEEZE
...!
DASH
WAIT!

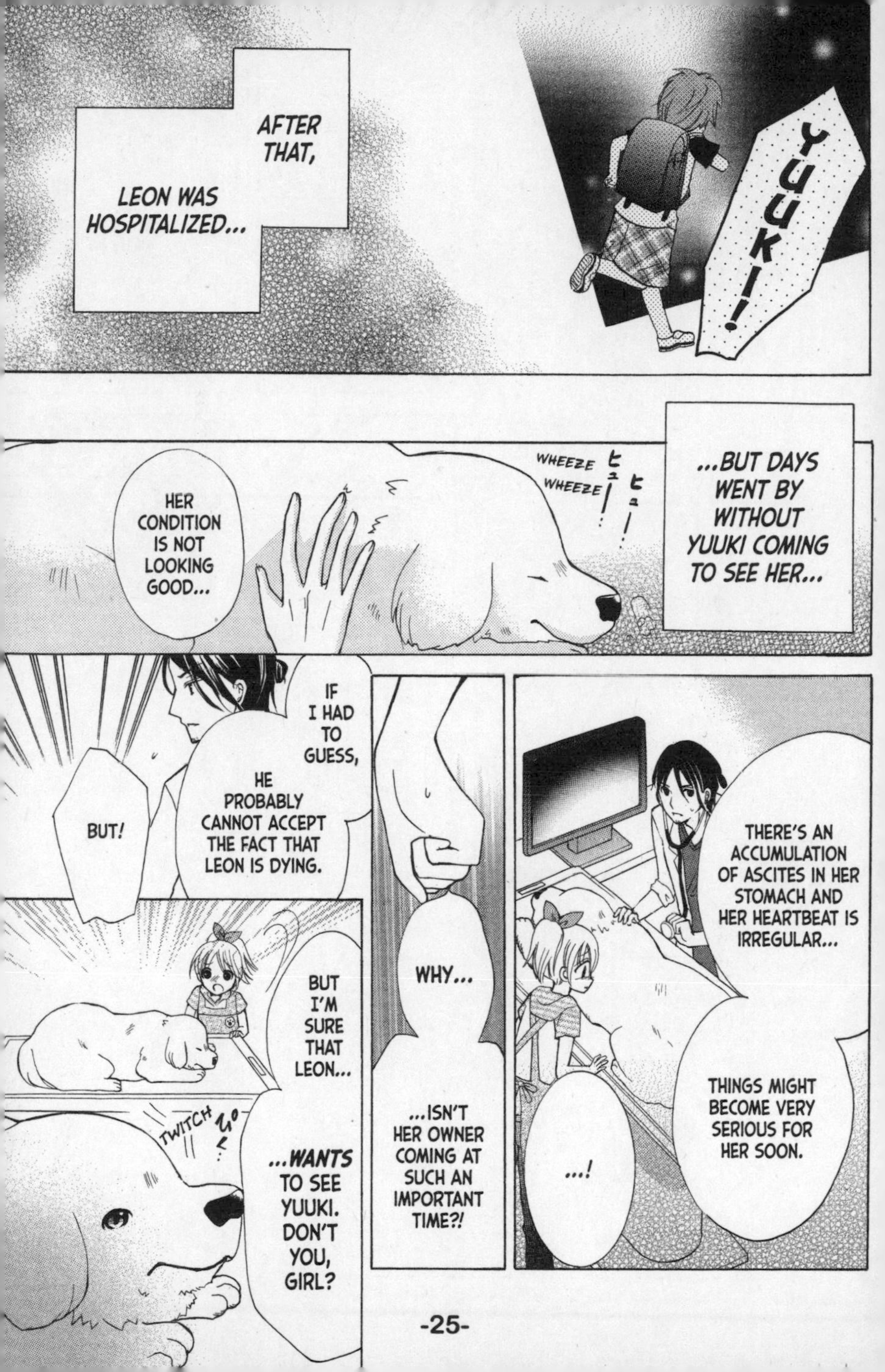
YUUKI!
AFTER THAT, LEON WAS HOSPITALIZED...
...BUT DAYS WENT BY WITHOUT YUUKI COMING TO SEE HER...
WHEEZE WHEEZE
HER CONDITION IS NOT LOOKING GOOD...
THERE'S AN ACCUMULATION OF ASCITES IN HER STOMACH AND HER HEARTBEAT IS IRREGULAR...
THINGS MIGHT BECOME VERY SERIOUS FOR HER SOON.
...!
WHY...
...ISN'T HER OWNER COMING AT SUCH AN IMPORTANT TIME?!
IF I HAD TO GUESS,
HE PROBABLY CANNOT ACCEPT THE FACT THAT LEON IS DYING.
BUT!
BUT I'M SURE THAT LEON...
TWITCH
...**WANTS** TO SEE YUUKI. DON'T YOU, GIRL?

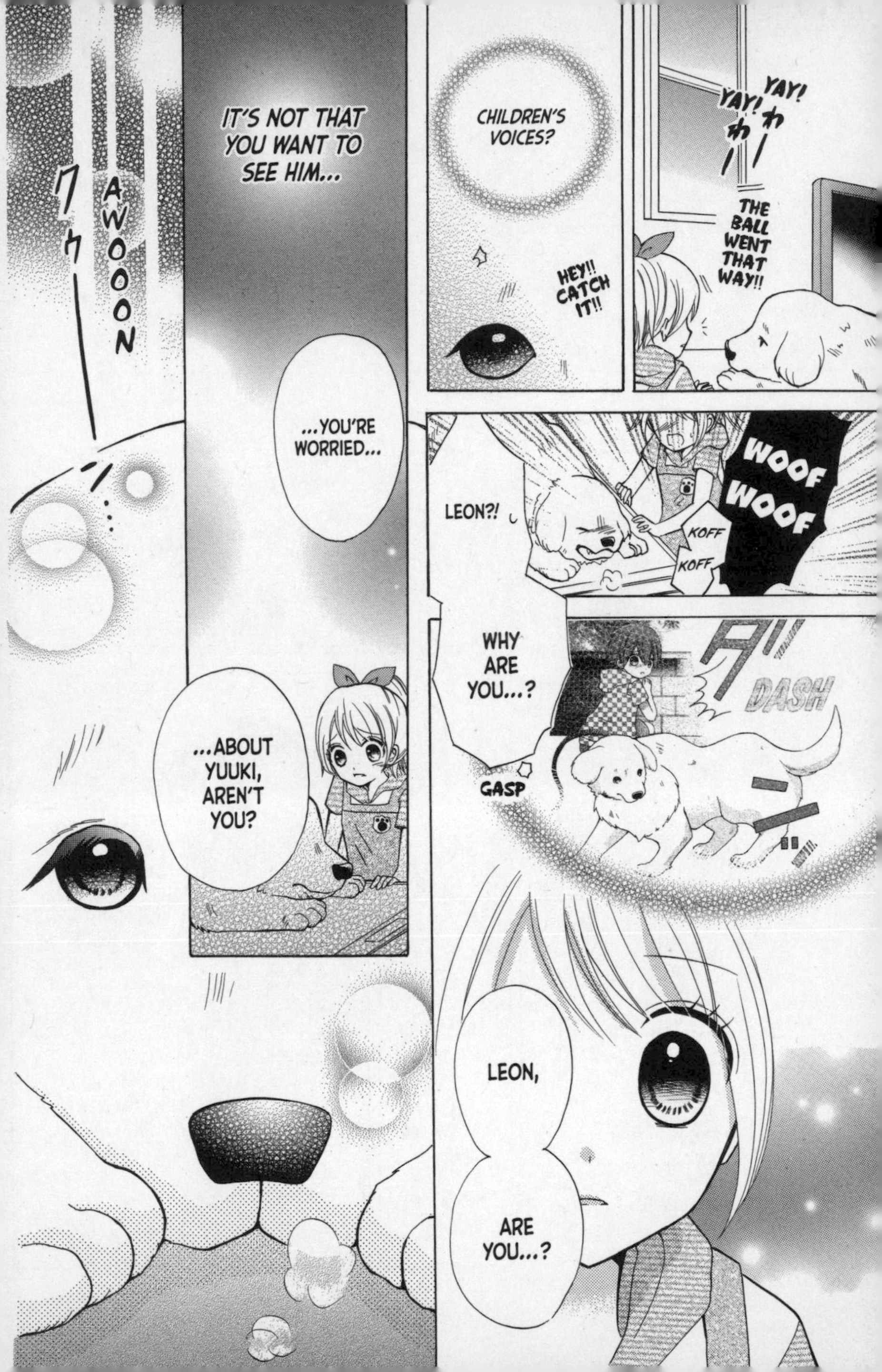
YAY! わー
YAY! わー
THE BALL WENT THAT WAY!!
CHILDREN'S VOICES?
HEY!! CATCH IT!!
WOOF WOOF
KOFF KOFF
LEON?!
ダッ DASH
WHY ARE YOU...?
GASP
LEON,
ARE YOU...?
IT'S NOT THAT YOU WANT TO SEE HIM...
...YOU'RE WORRIED...
...ABOUT YUUKI, AREN'T YOU?
ワゥー
AWOOON

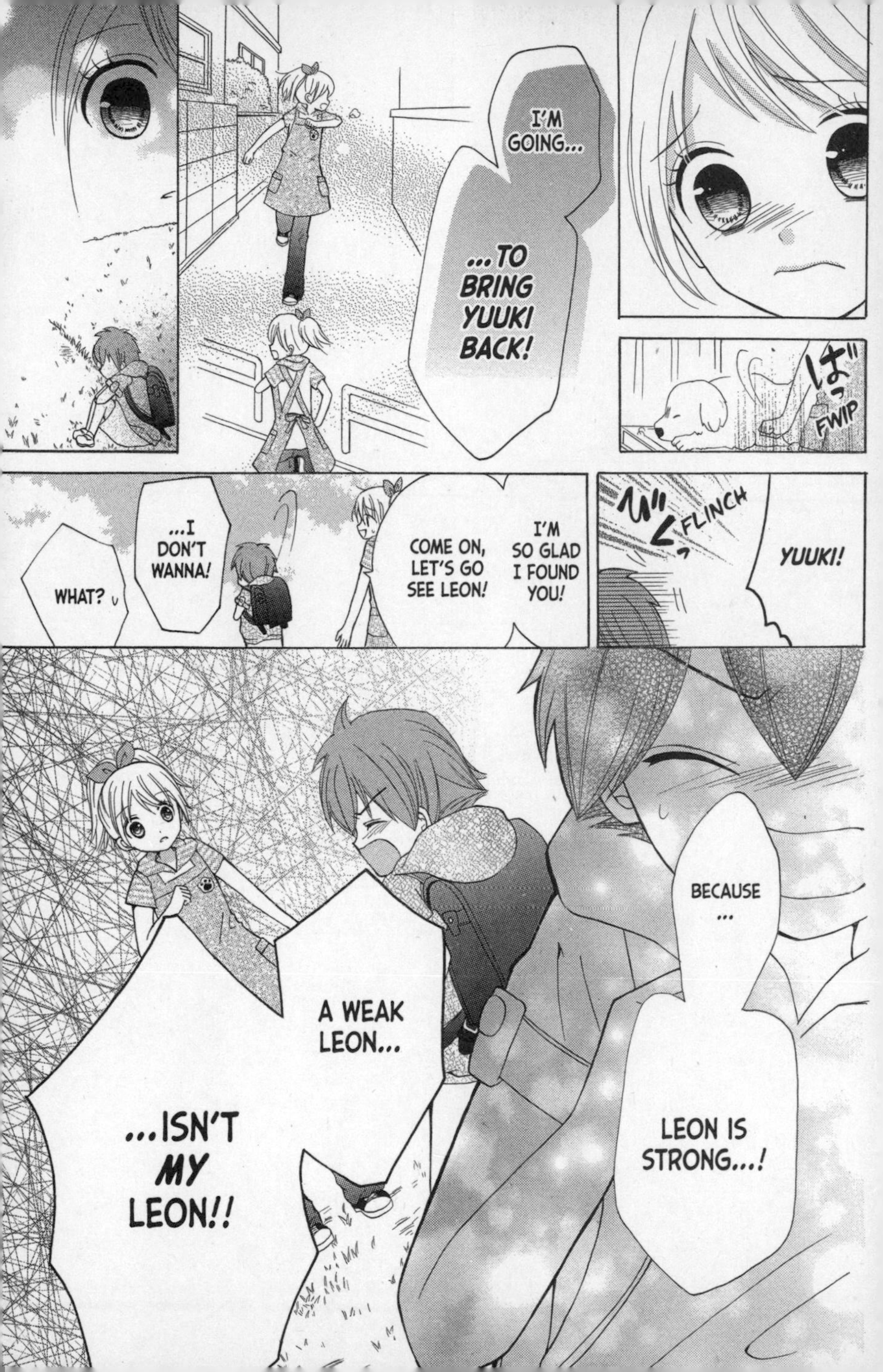
ばっ
FWIP
I'M GOING...
...TO BRING YUUKI BACK!
びくっ
FLINCH
YUUKI!
I'M SO GLAD I FOUND YOU!
COME ON, LET'S GO SEE LEON!
...I DON'T WANNA!
WHAT?
BECAUSE...
LEON IS STRONG...!
A WEAK LEON...
...ISN'T *MY* LEON!!

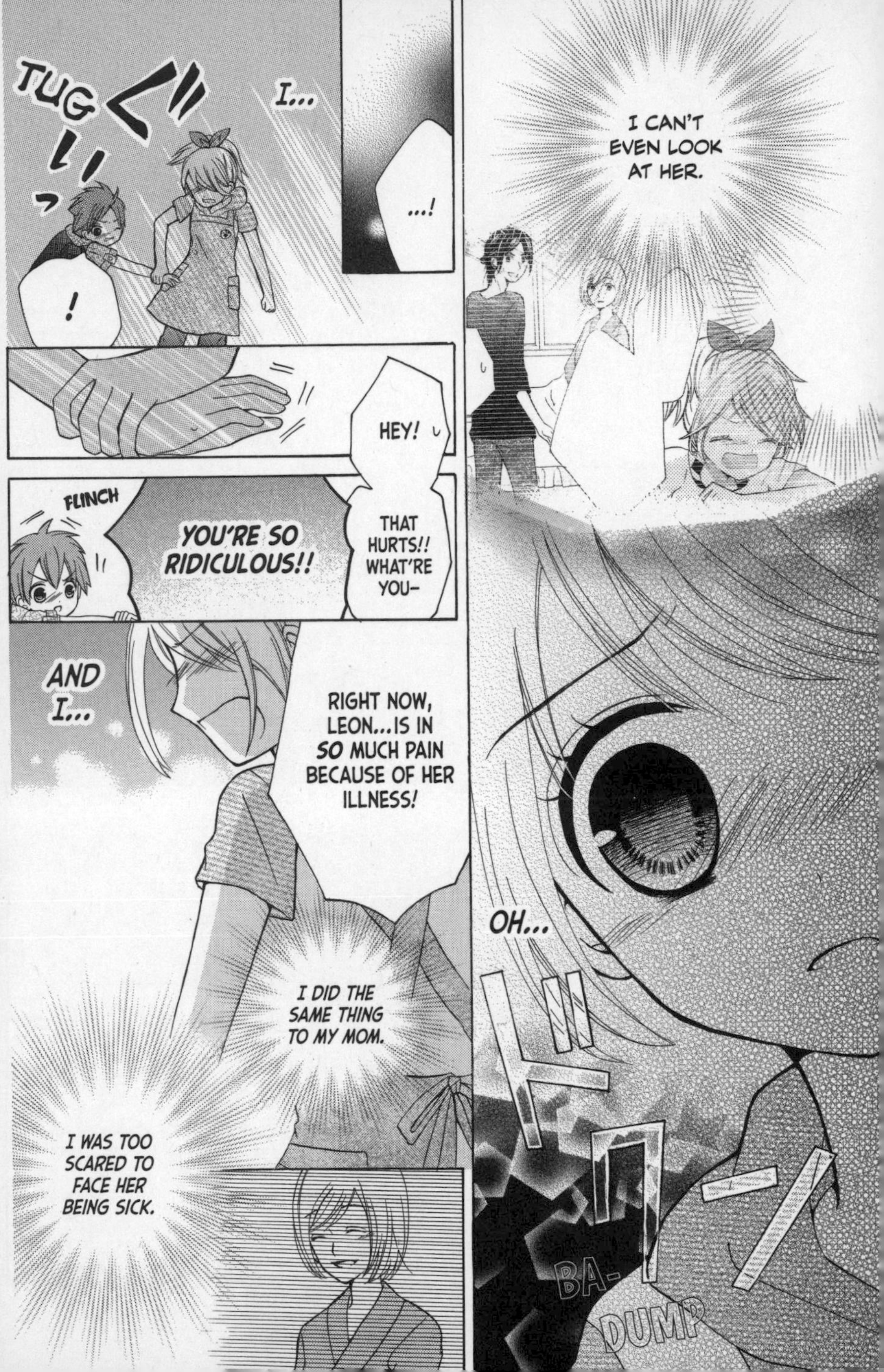
I CAN'T EVEN LOOK AT HER.
OH...
BA-DUMP
...!
I...
TUG
!
HEY!
THAT HURTS!! WHAT'RE YOU-
YOU'RE SO RIDICULOUS!!
FLINCH
RIGHT NOW, LEON...IS IN SO MUCH PAIN BECAUSE OF HER ILLNESS!
AND I...
I DID THE SAME THING TO MY MOM.
I WAS TOO SCARED TO FACE HER BEING SICK.

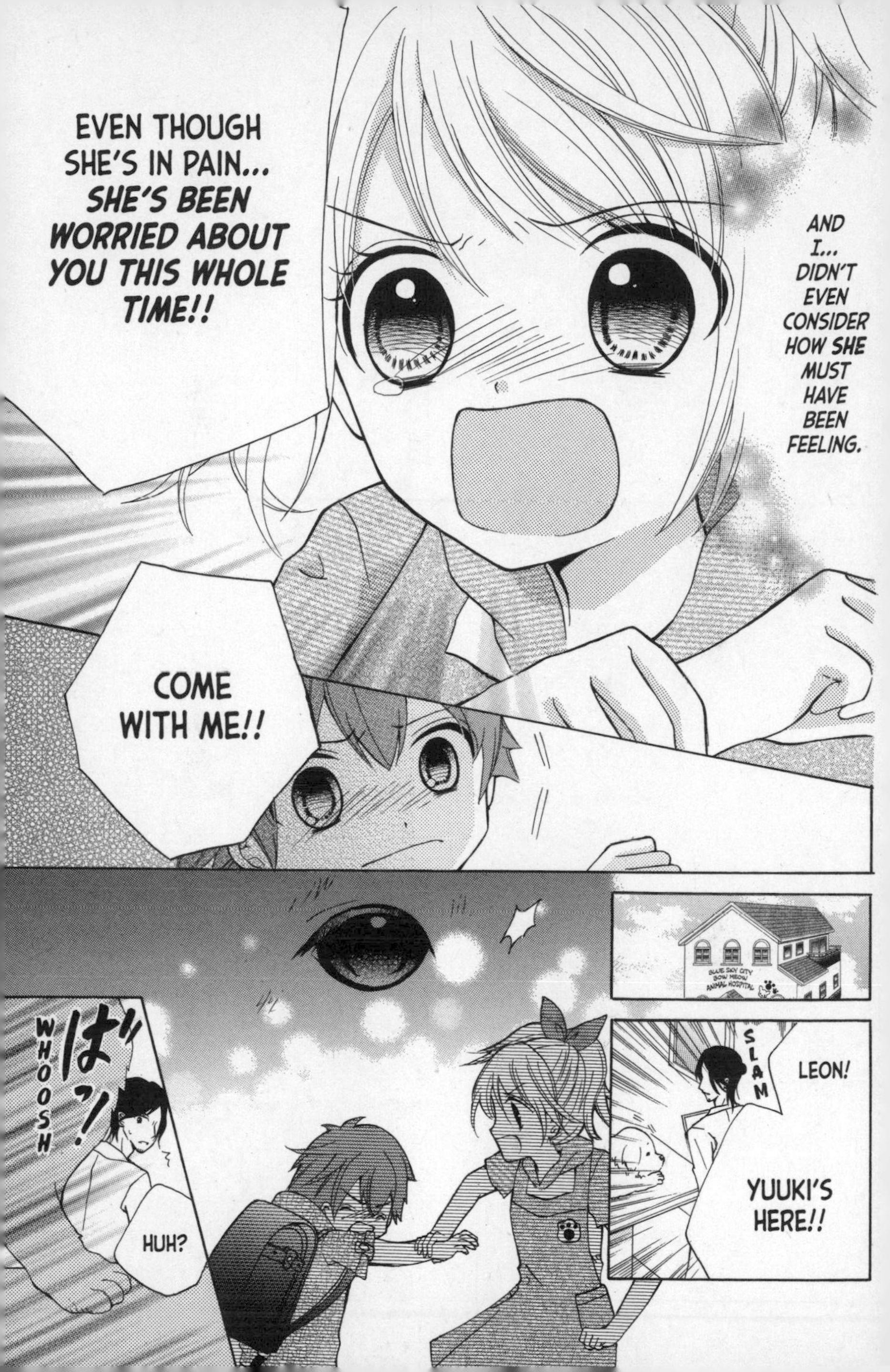
EVEN THOUGH SHE'S IN PAIN... SHE'S BEEN WORRIED ABOUT YOU THIS WHOLE TIME!!
AND I... DIDN'T EVEN CONSIDER HOW SHE MUST HAVE BEEN FEELING.
COME WITH ME!!
BLUE SKY CITY BOW MEOW ANIMAL HOSPITAL
SLAM
LEON!
YUUKI'S HERE!!
ばっ!
WHOOSH
HUH?

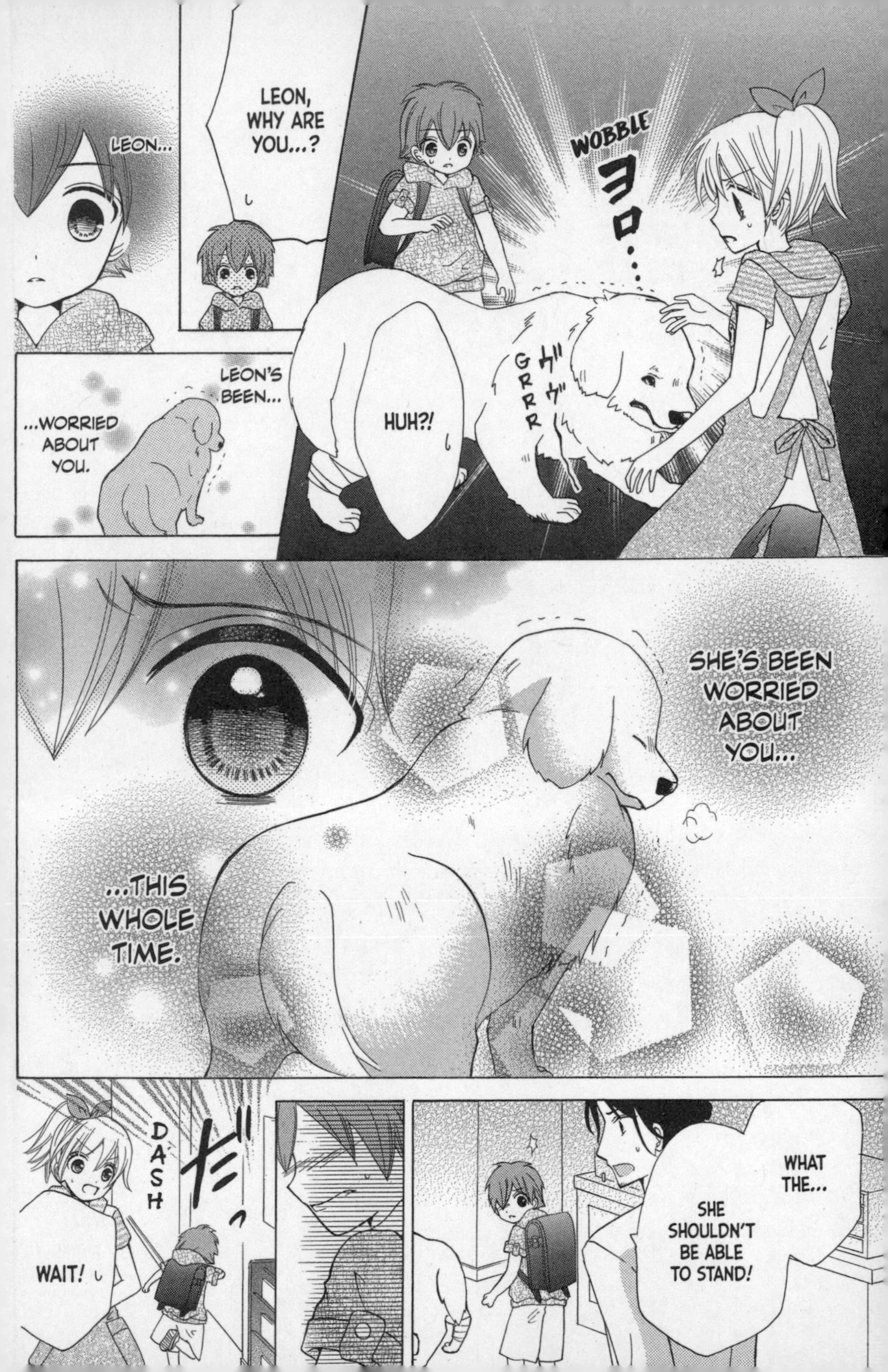
WOBBLE
ヨロ…
GRRR
ヴヴ
HUH?!
LEON, WHY ARE YOU...?
LEON...
LEON'S BEEN...
...WORRIED ABOUT YOU.
SHE'S BEEN WORRIED ABOUT YOU...
...THIS WHOLE TIME.
WHAT THE...
SHE SHOULDN'T BE ABLE TO STAND!
DASH
ダッ
WAIT!

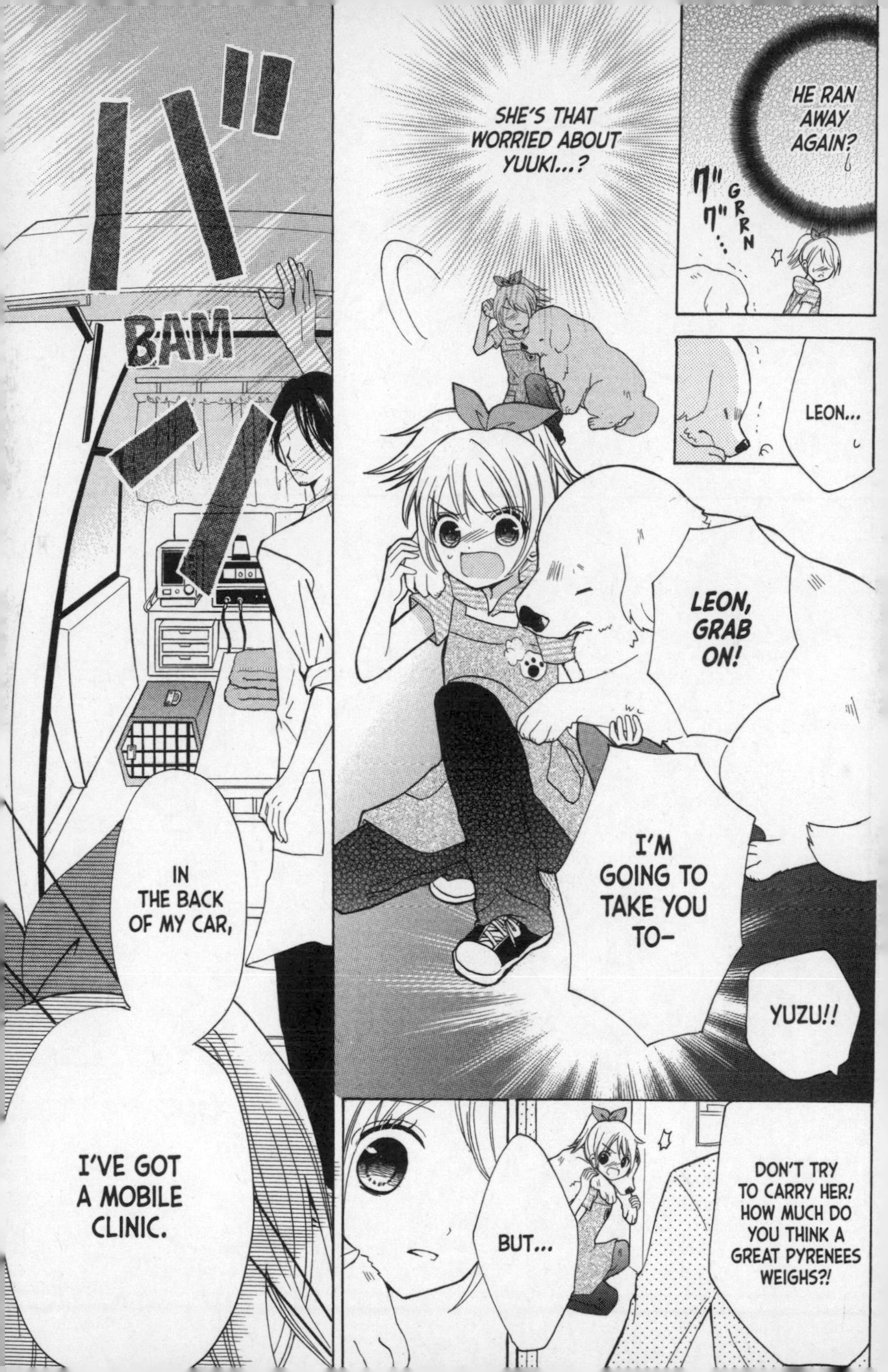
HE RAN AWAY AGAIN?
GRRN
LEON...
SHE'S THAT WORRIED ABOUT YUUKI...?
LEON, GRAB ON!
I'M GOING TO TAKE YOU TO–
YUZU!!
DON'T TRY TO CARRY HER! HOW MUCH DO YOU THINK A GREAT PYRENEES WEIGHS?!
BUT...
BAM
IN THE BACK OF MY CAR,
I'VE GOT A MOBILE CLINIC.

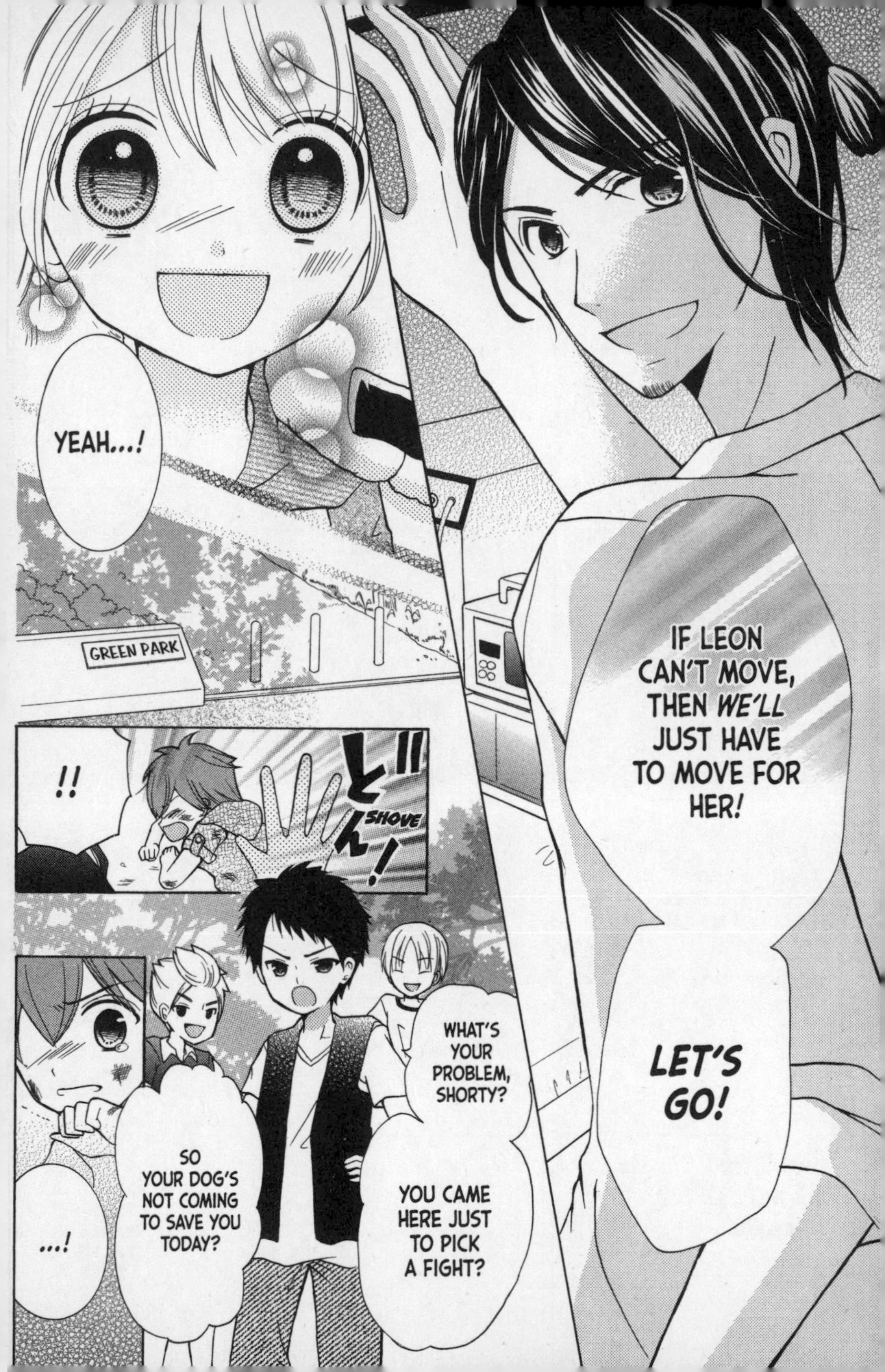
IF LEON CAN'T MOVE, THEN *WE'LL* JUST HAVE TO MOVE FOR HER!
LET'S GO!
YEAH...!
GREEN PARK
!!
とん
SHOVE
!
WHAT'S YOUR PROBLEM, SHORTY?
YOU CAME HERE JUST TO PICK A FIGHT?
SO YOUR DOG'S NOT COMING TO SAVE YOU TODAY?
...!

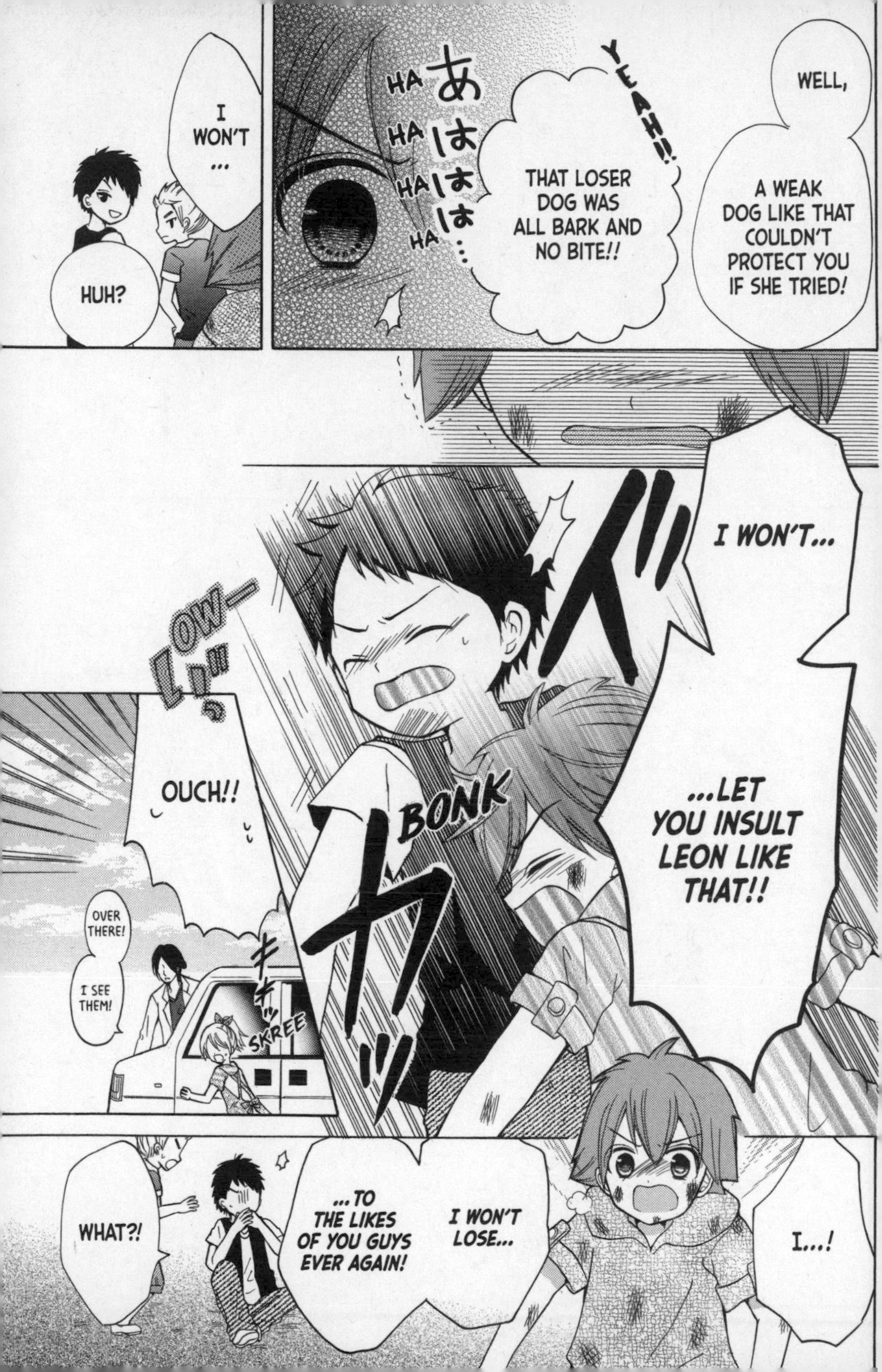
WELL,
A WEAK DOG LIKE THAT COULDN'T PROTECT YOU IF SHE TRIED!
YEAH!!
THAT LOSER DOG WAS ALL BARK AND NO BITE!!
あははは…
HA HA HA HA
I WON'T ...
HUH?
I WON'T...
...LET YOU INSULT LEON LIKE THAT!!
ズ
BONK
ガッ
OW—
OUCH!!
キキッ
SKREE
OVER THERE!
I SEE THEM!
I...!
I WON'T LOSE...
...TO THE LIKES OF YOU GUYS EVER AGAIN!
WHAT?!

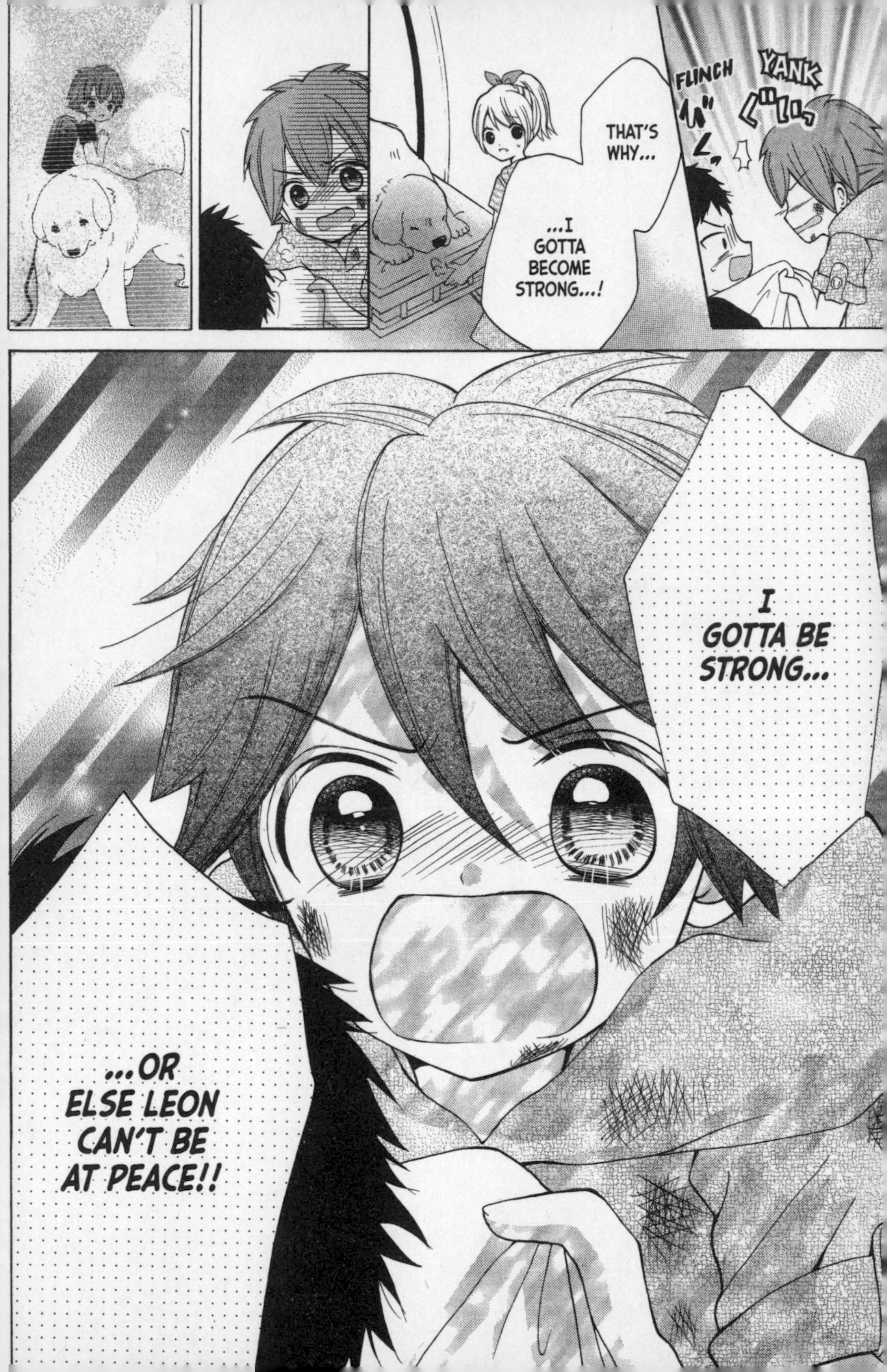
YANK
FLINCH
THAT'S WHY...
...I GOTTA BECOME STRONG...!
I GOTTA BE STRONG...
...OR ELSE LEON CAN'T BE AT PEACE!!

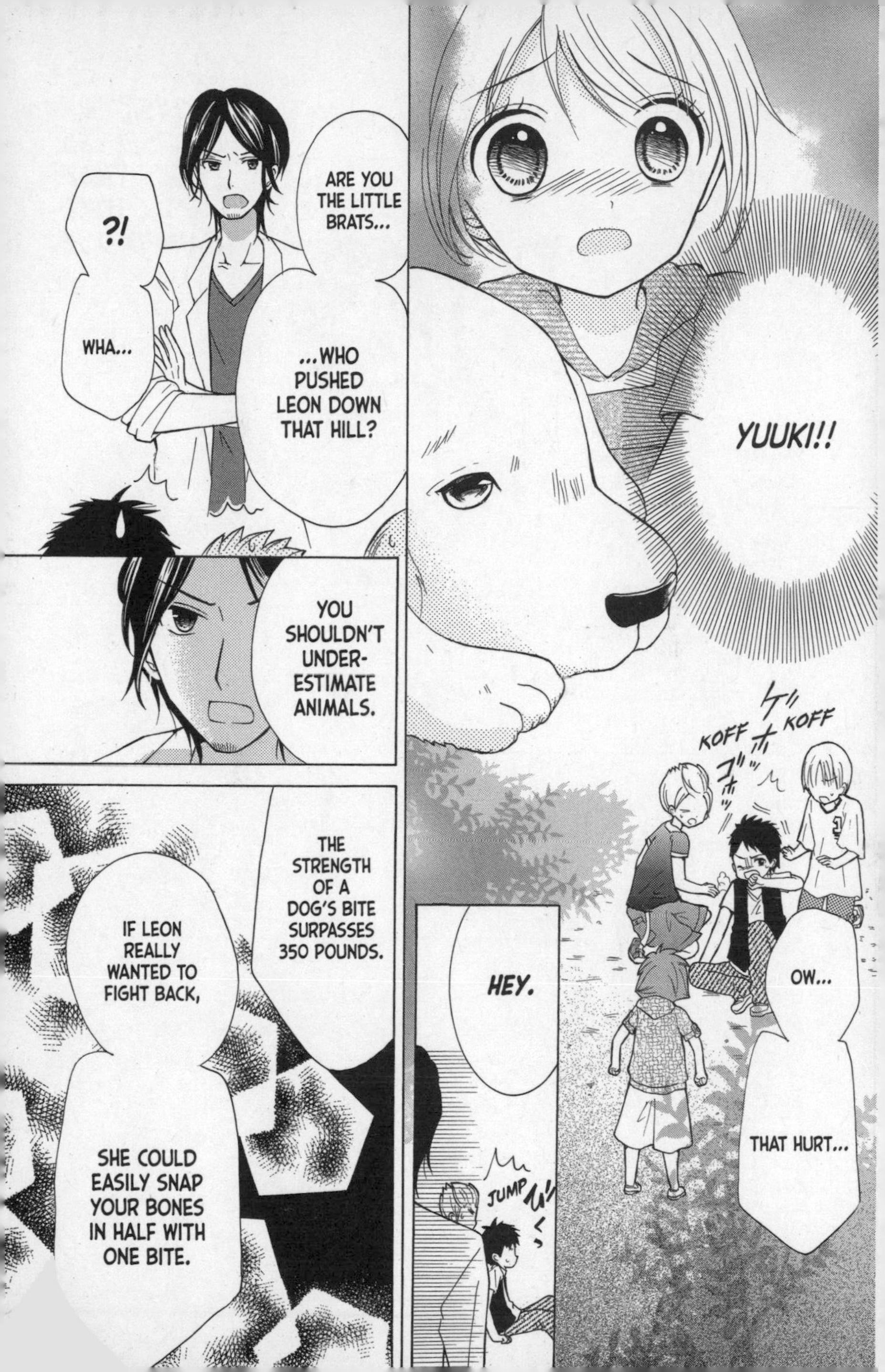
YUUKI!!
KOFF
KOFF
OW...
THAT HURT...
HEY.
JUMP
ARE YOU THE LITTLE BRATS...
...WHO PUSHED LEON DOWN THAT HILL?
?!
WHA...
YOU SHOULDN'T UNDER-ESTIMATE ANIMALS.
THE STRENGTH OF A DOG'S BITE SURPASSES 350 POUNDS.
IF LEON REALLY WANTED TO FIGHT BACK,
SHE COULD EASILY SNAP YOUR BONES IN HALF WITH ONE BITE.

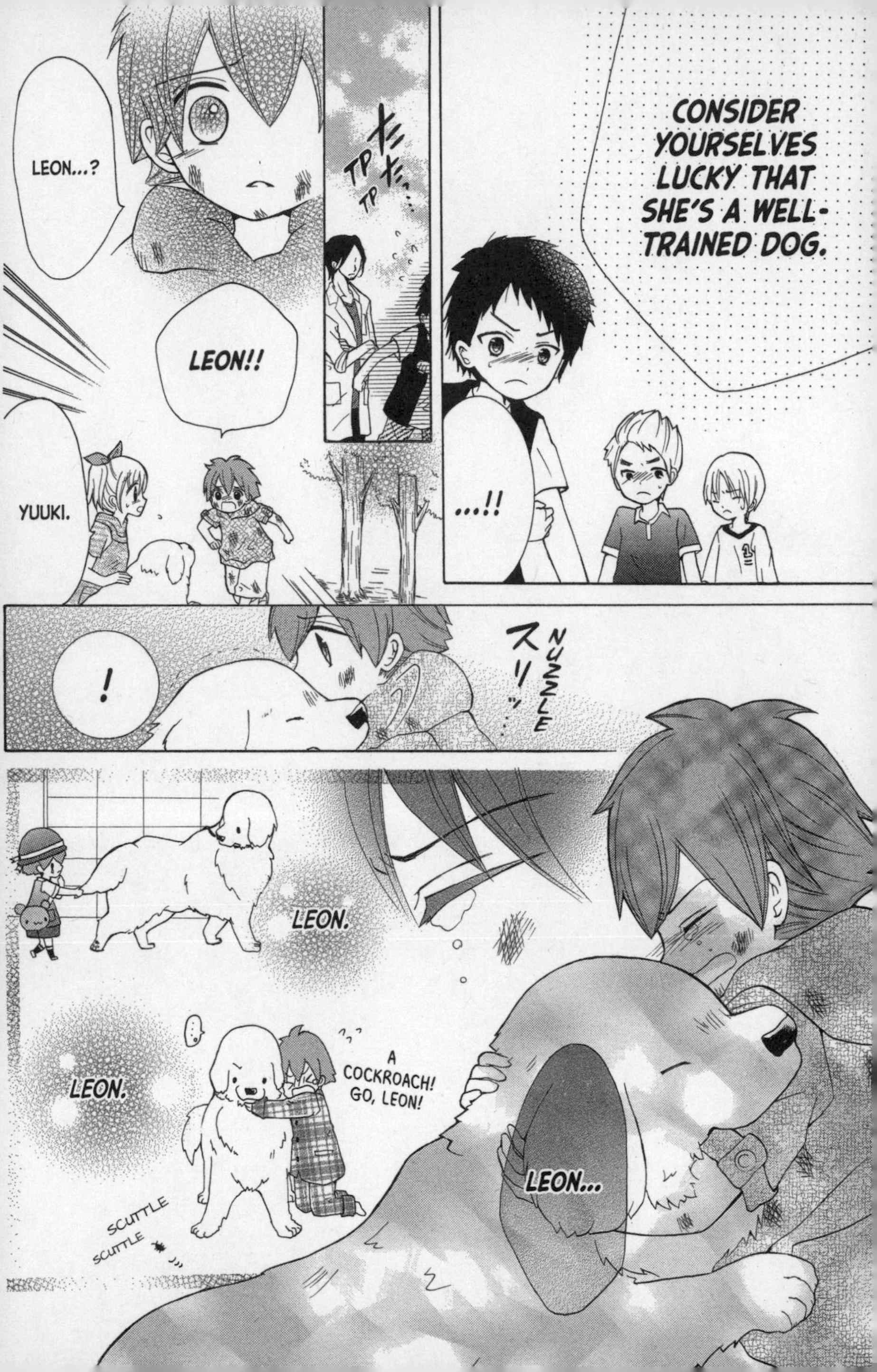
CONSIDER YOURSELVES LUCKY THAT SHE'S A WELL-TRAINED DOG.
...!!
TP TP
LEON...?
LEON!!
YUUKI.
スリッ NUZZLE
!
LEON.
A COCKROACH! GO, LEON!
LEON.
SCUTTLE SCUTTLE
LEON...

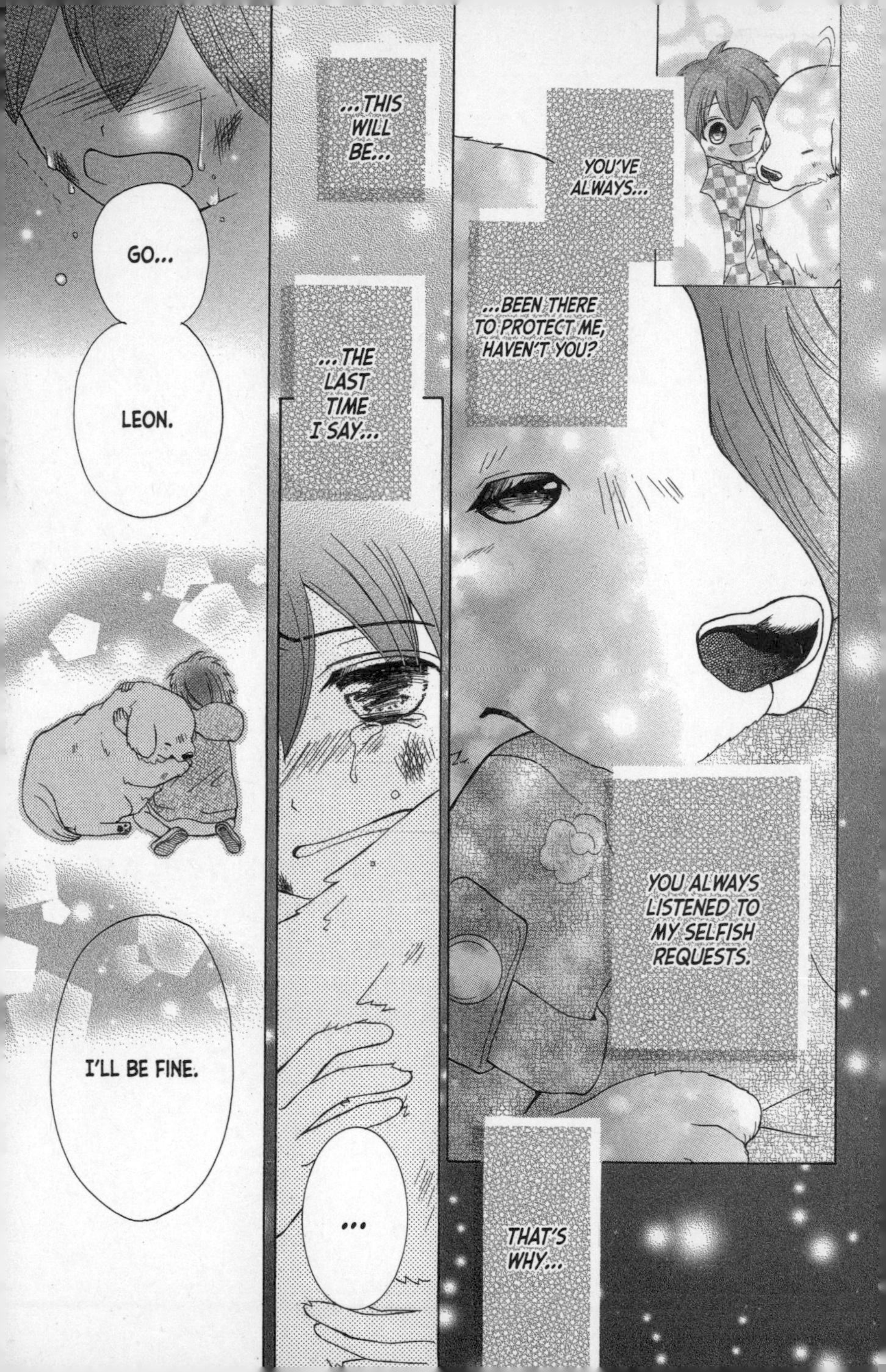
YOU'VE ALWAYS...
...BEEN THERE TO PROTECT ME, HAVEN'T YOU?
YOU ALWAYS LISTENED TO MY SELFISH REQUESTS.
THAT'S WHY...
...THIS WILL BE...
...THE LAST TIME I SAY...
...
GO...
LEON.
I'LL BE FINE.

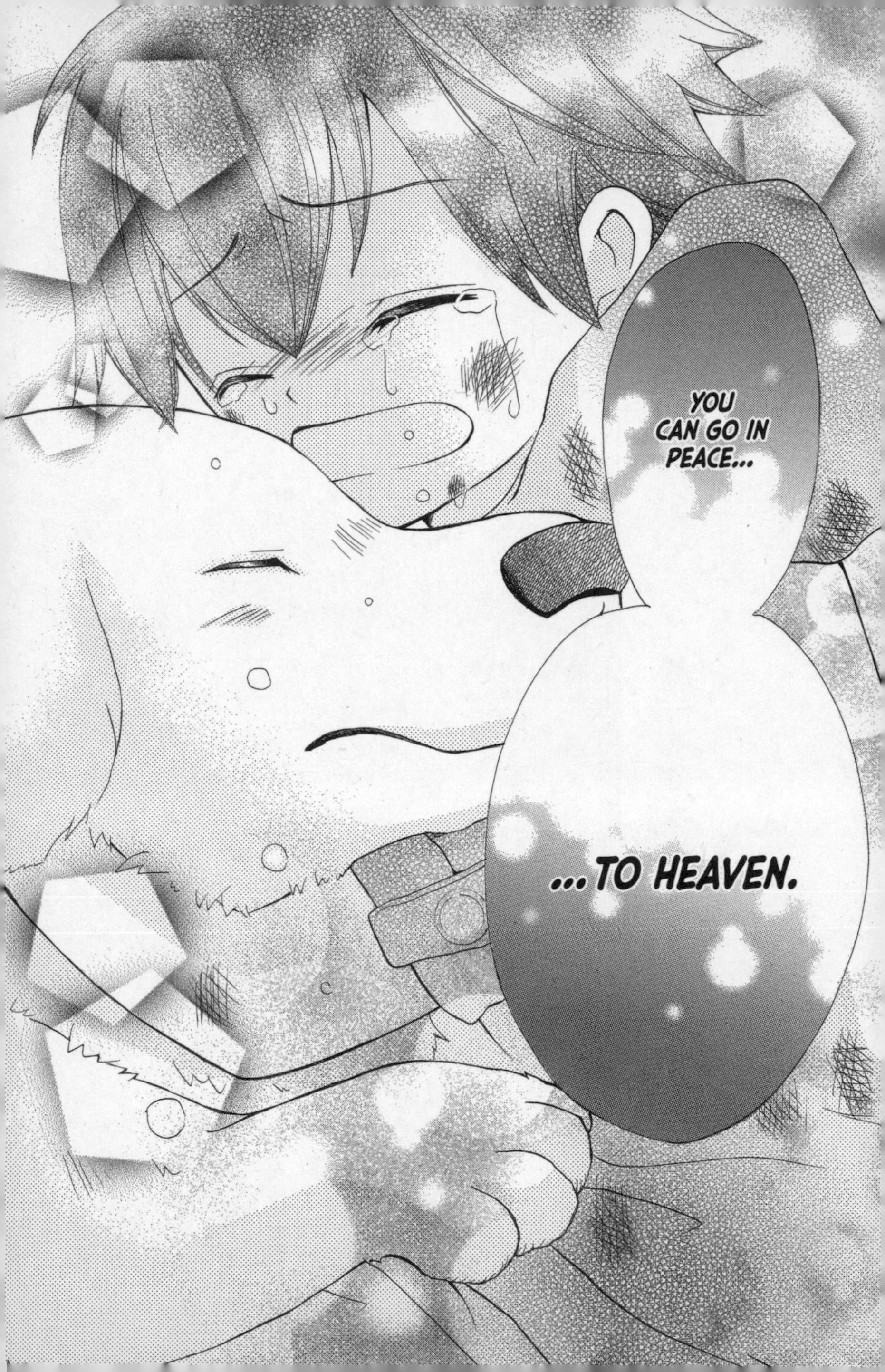
YOU CAN GO IN PEACE...
...TO HEAVEN.

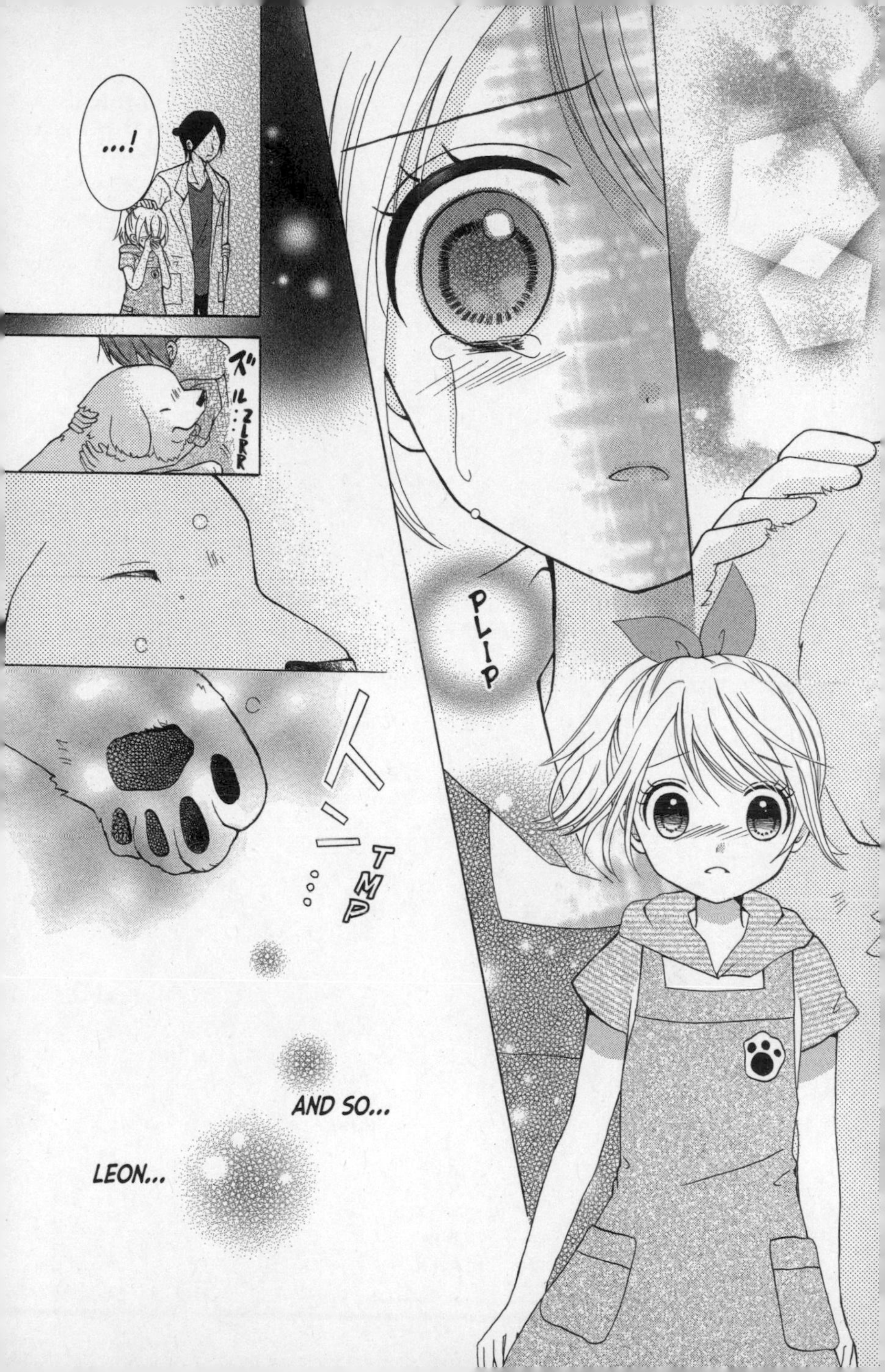
PLIP
...!
ズル... ZLRR
トー... TMP
AND SO...
LEON...

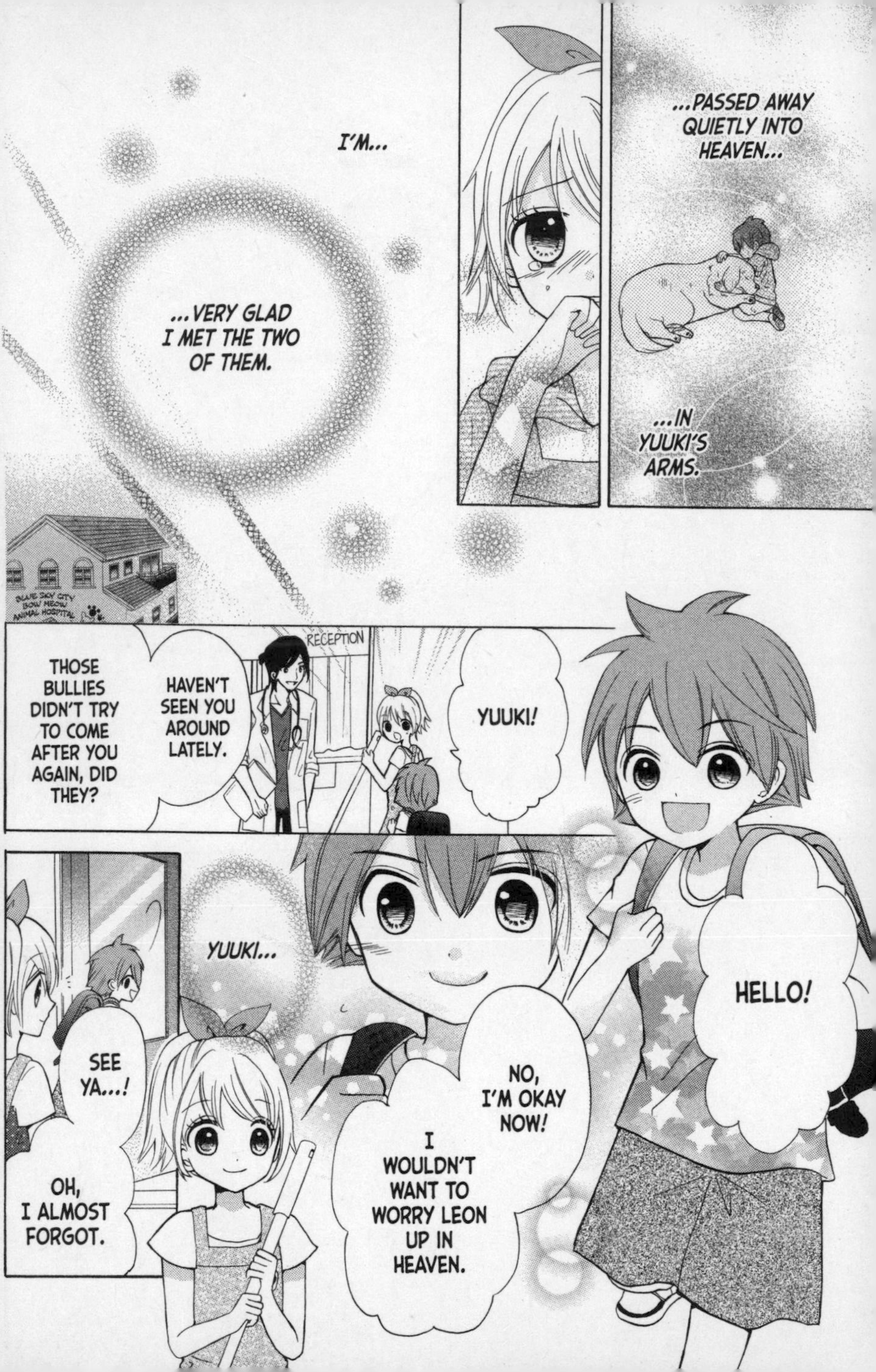
...PASSED AWAY QUIETLY INTO HEAVEN...
...IN YUUKI'S ARMS.
I'M...
...VERY GLAD I MET THE TWO OF THEM.
BLUE SKY CITY BOW MEOW ANIMAL HOSPITAL
YUUKI!
HELLO!
RECEPTION
HAVEN'T SEEN YOU AROUND LATELY.
THOSE BULLIES DIDN'T TRY TO COME AFTER YOU AGAIN, DID THEY?
NO, I'M OKAY NOW!
I WOULDN'T WANT TO WORRY LEON UP IN HEAVEN.
YUUKI...
SEE YA...!
OH, I ALMOST FORGOT.

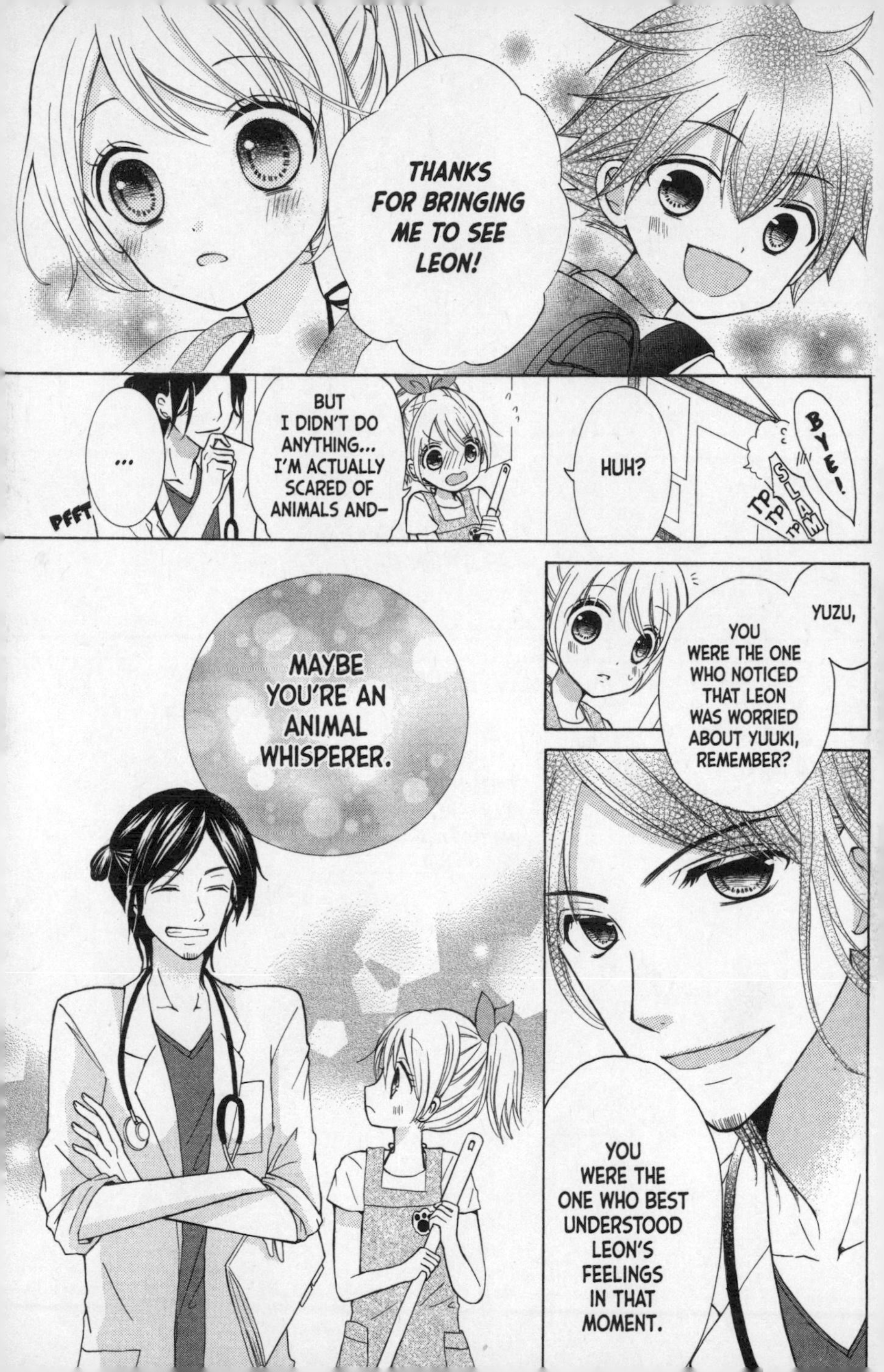
THANKS FOR BRINGING ME TO SEE LEON!
BYE!
TP TP TP
SLAM
HUH?
BUT I DIDN'T DO ANYTHING... I'M ACTUALLY SCARED OF ANIMALS AND–
...
PFFT
YUZU,
YOU WERE THE ONE WHO NOTICED THAT LEON WAS WORRIED ABOUT YUUKI, REMEMBER?
YOU WERE THE ONE WHO BEST UNDERSTOOD LEON'S FEELINGS IN THAT MOMENT.
MAYBE YOU'RE AN ANIMAL WHISPERER.

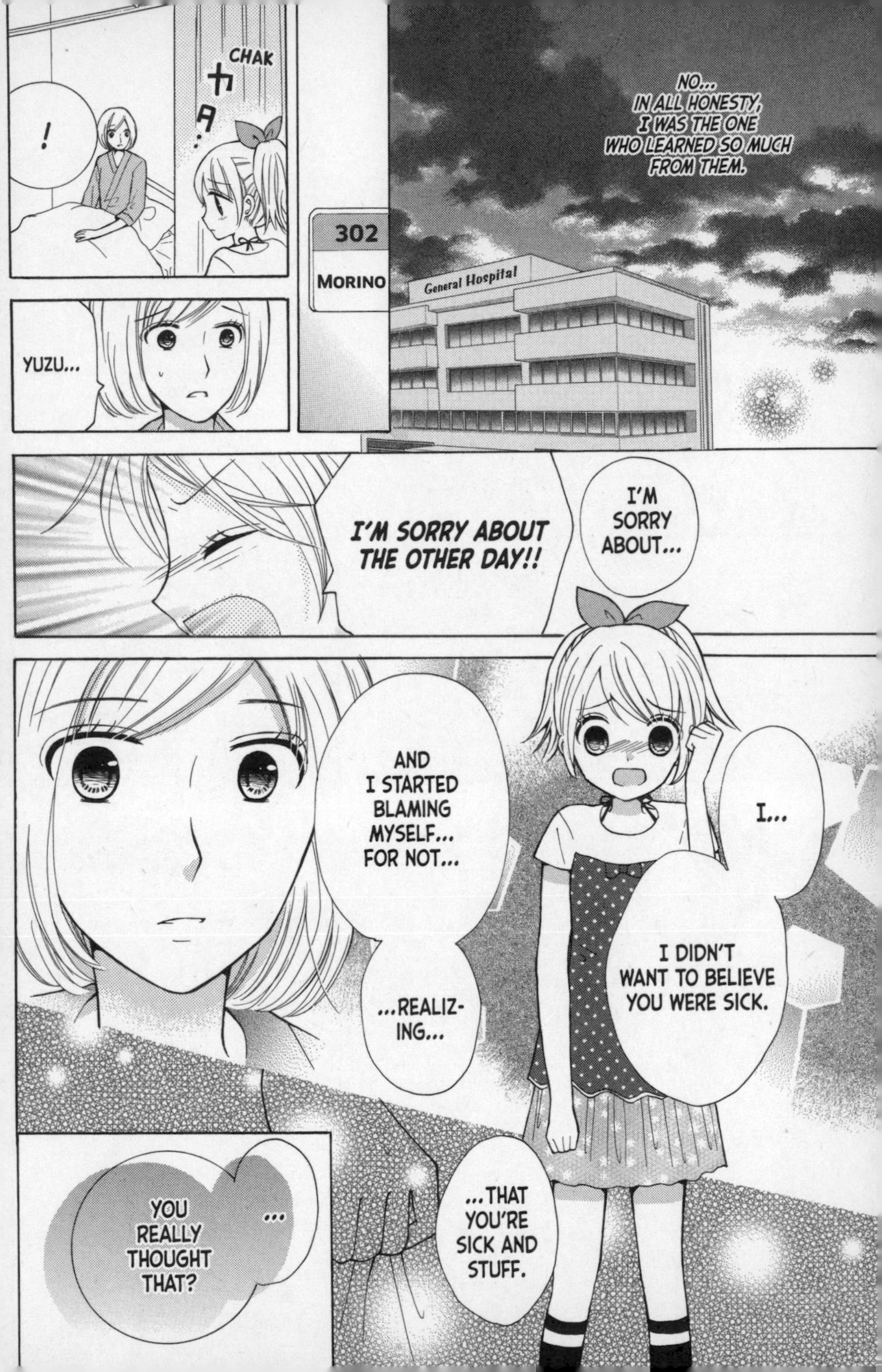
NO... IN ALL HONESTY, I WAS THE ONE WHO LEARNED SO MUCH FROM THEM.
General Hospital
302
MORINO
CHAK
カタ
!
YUZU...
I'M SORRY ABOUT...
I'M SORRY ABOUT THE OTHER DAY!!
I...
I DIDN'T WANT TO BELIEVE YOU WERE SICK.
AND I STARTED BLAMING MYSELF... FOR NOT...
...REALIZ-ING...
...THAT YOU'RE SICK AND STUFF.
...
YOU REALLY THOUGHT THAT?

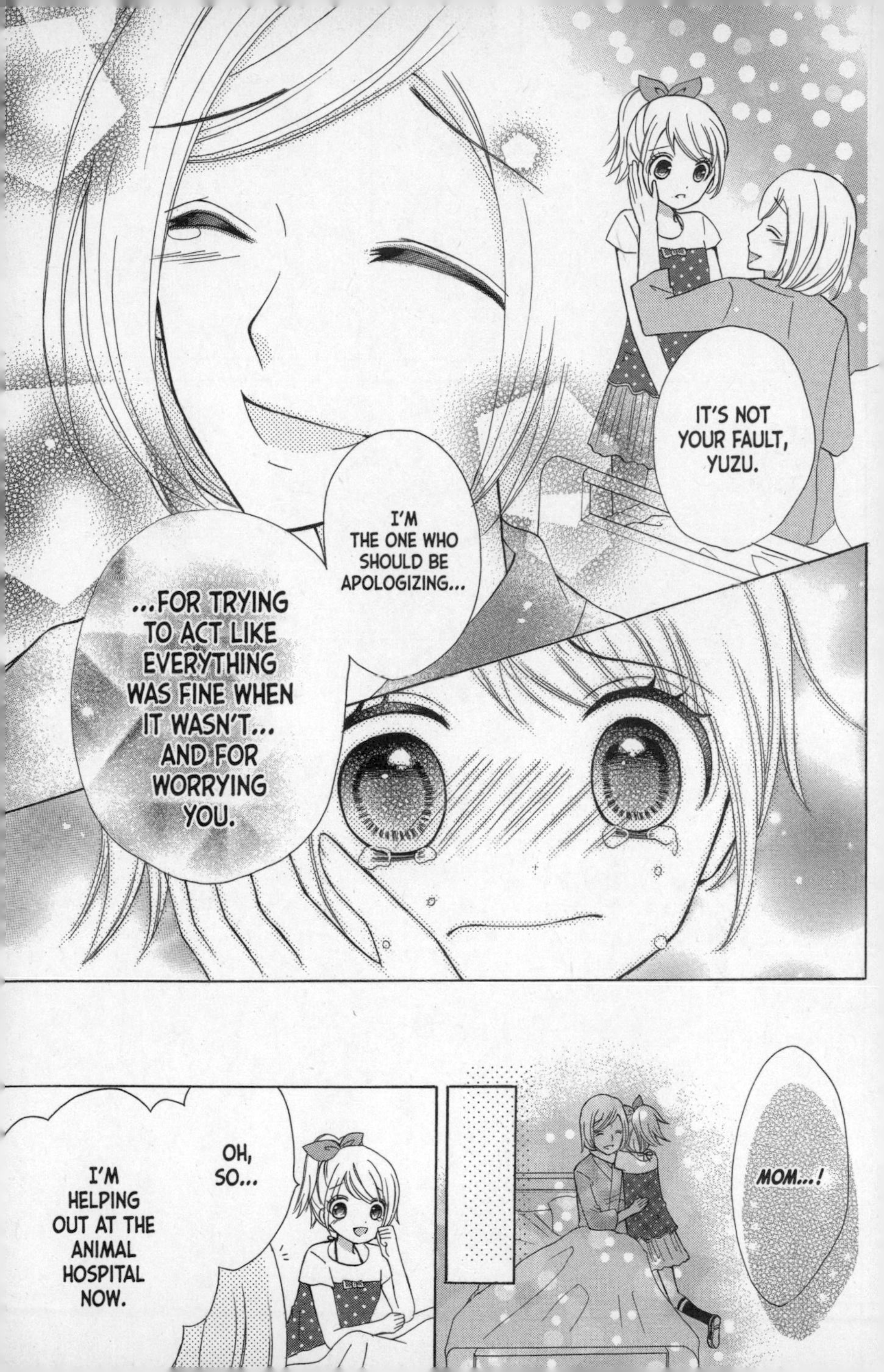
IT'S NOT YOUR FAULT, YUZU.
I'M THE ONE WHO SHOULD BE APOLOGIZING...
...FOR TRYING TO ACT LIKE EVERYTHING WAS FINE WHEN IT WASN'T... AND FOR WORRYING YOU.
MOM...!
OH, SO...
I'M HELPING OUT AT THE ANIMAL HOSPITAL NOW.

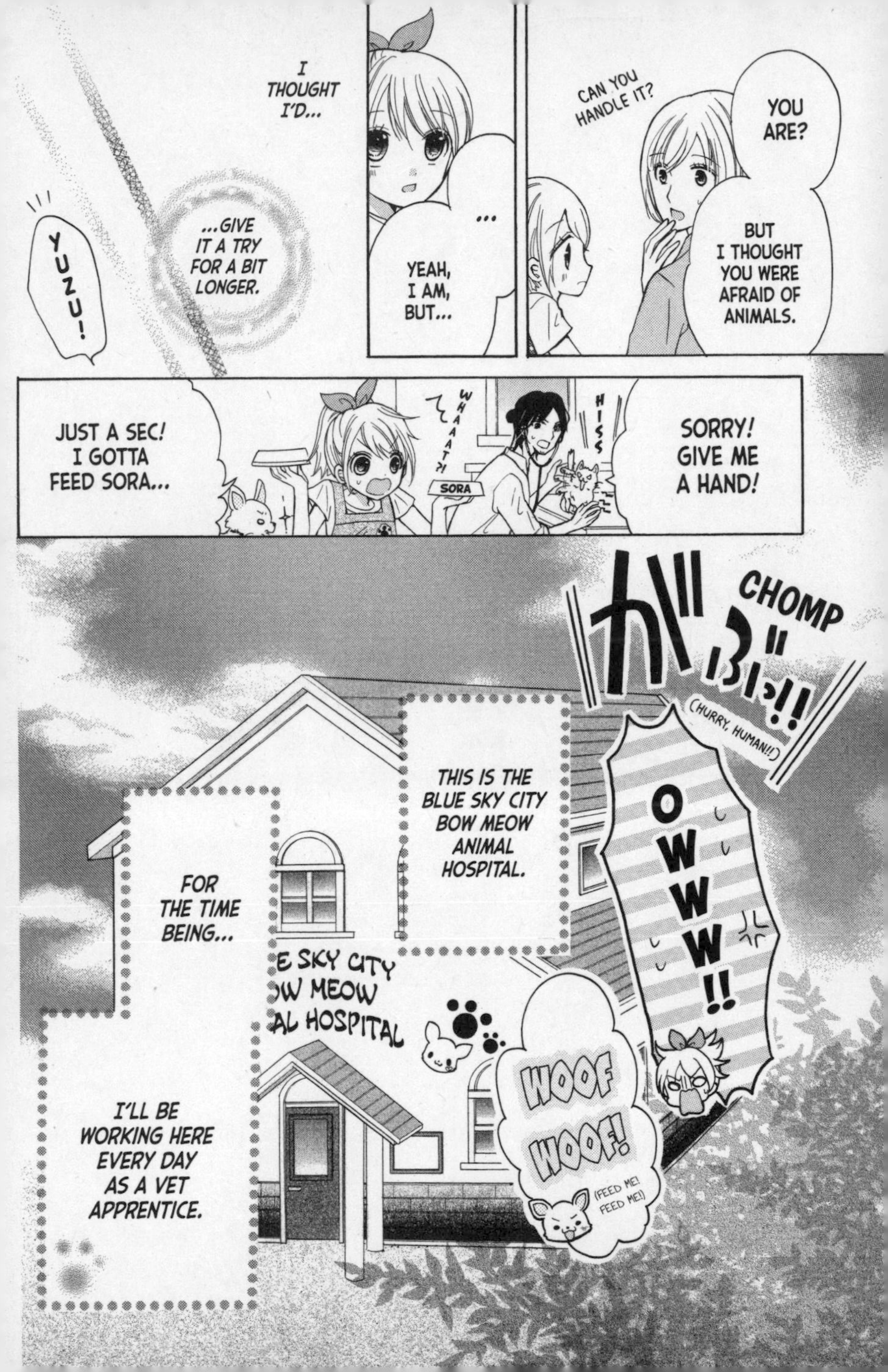
YOU ARE?
CAN YOU HANDLE IT?
BUT I THOUGHT YOU WERE AFRAID OF ANIMALS.
...
YEAH, I AM, BUT...
I THOUGHT I'D...
...GIVE IT A TRY FOR A BIT LONGER.
YUZU!
SORRY! GIVE ME A HAND!
HISS
WHAAAT?!
SORA
JUST A SEC! I GOTTA FEED SORA...
がぶっ!!
CHOMP
(HURRY, HUMAN!!)
OWWW!!
THIS IS THE BLUE SKY CITY BOW MEOW ANIMAL HOSPITAL.
E SKY CITY
OW MEOW
AL HOSPITAL
WOOF WOOF!
(FEED ME! FEED ME!)
FOR THE TIME BEING...
I'LL BE WORKING HERE EVERY DAY AS A VET APPRENTICE.

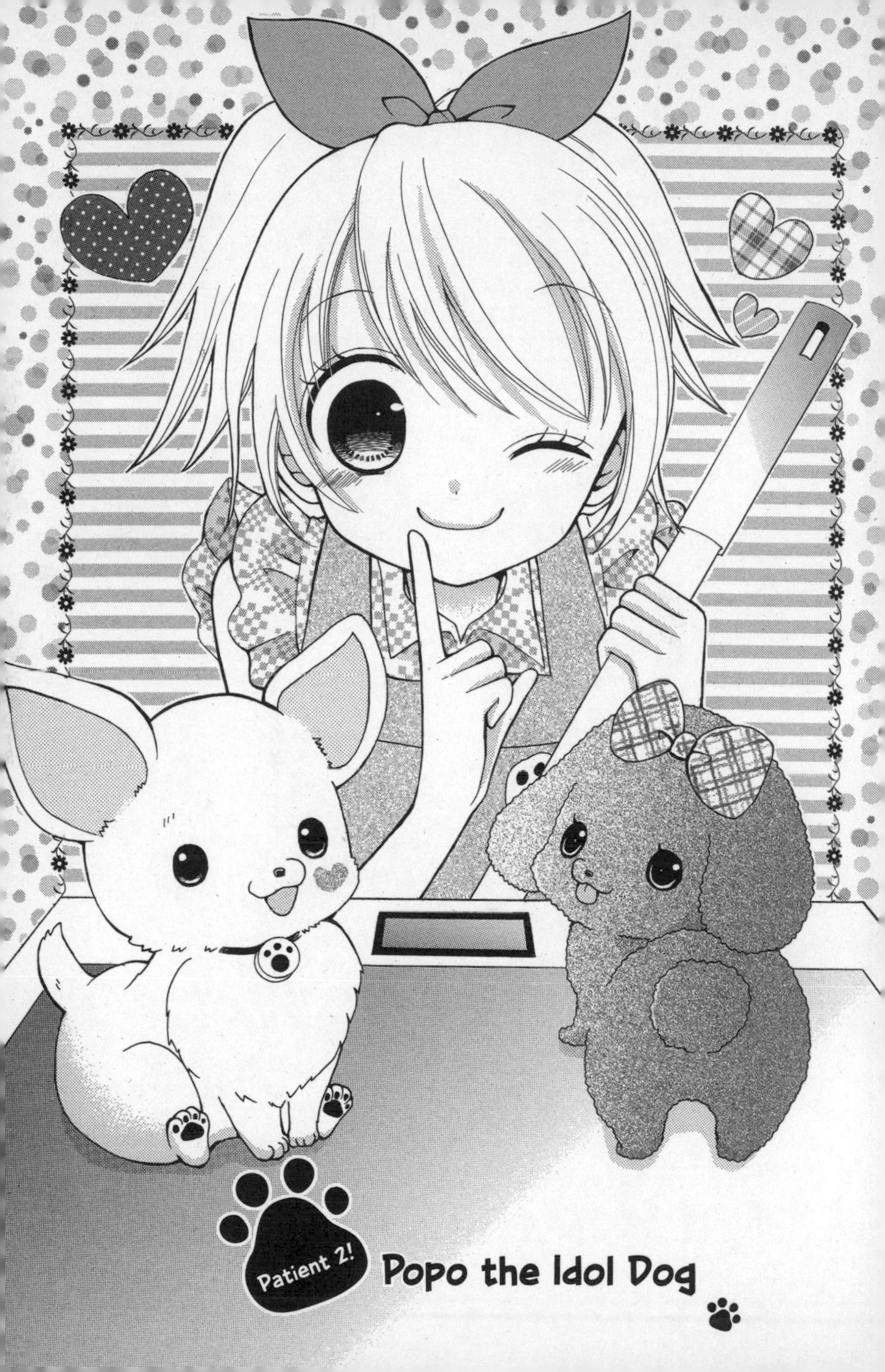
Patient 2!
Popo the Idol Dog

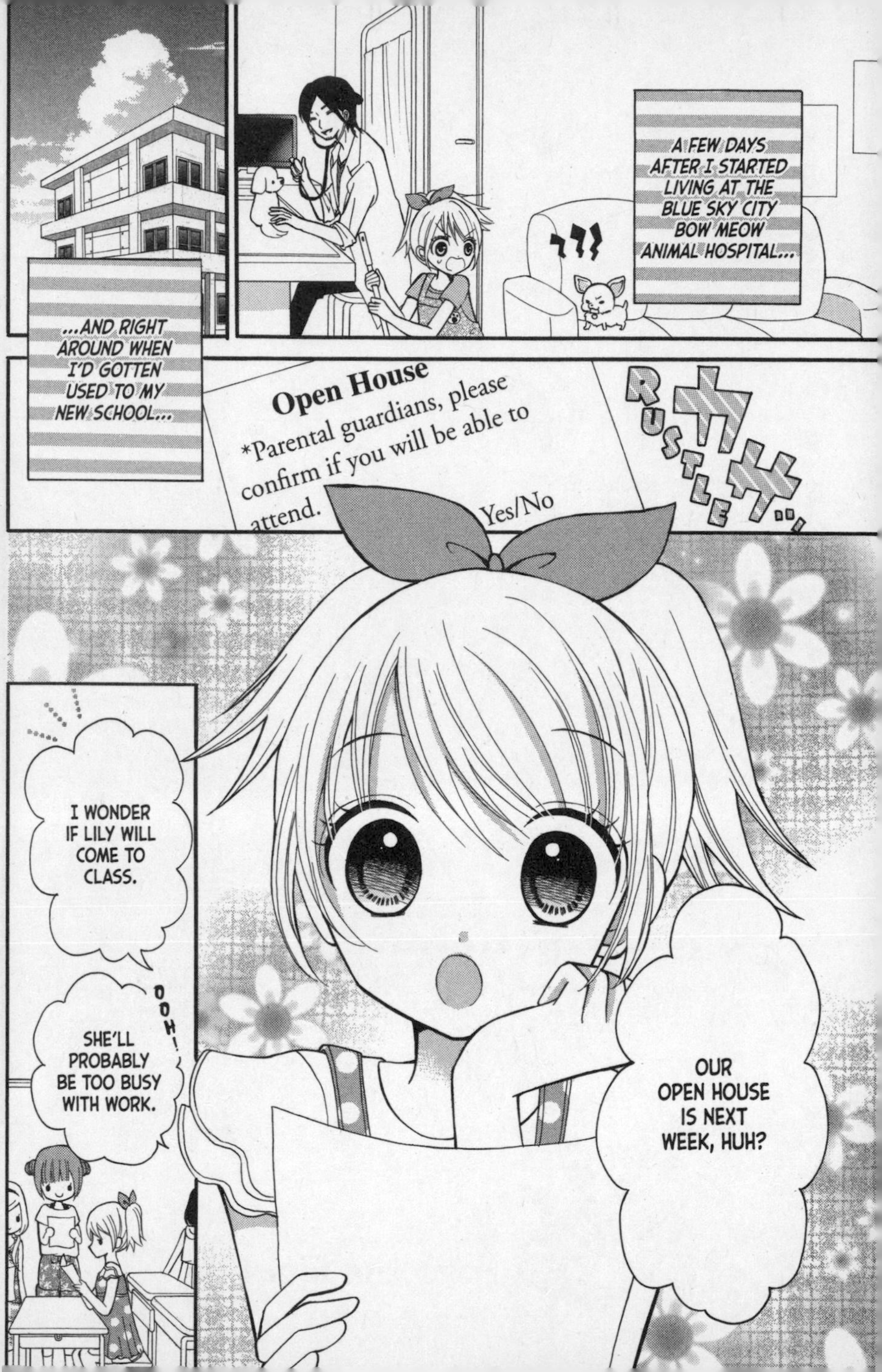
A FEW DAYS AFTER I STARTED LIVING AT THE BLUE SKY CITY BOW MEOW ANIMAL HOSPITAL...
...AND RIGHT AROUND WHEN I'D GOTTEN USED TO MY NEW SCHOOL...
RUSTLE...
Open House
*Parental guardians, please confirm if you will be able to attend. Yes/No
OUR OPEN HOUSE IS NEXT WEEK, HUH?
I WONDER IF LILY WILL COME TO CLASS.
OOH!
SHE'LL PROBABLY BE TOO BUSY WITH WORK.

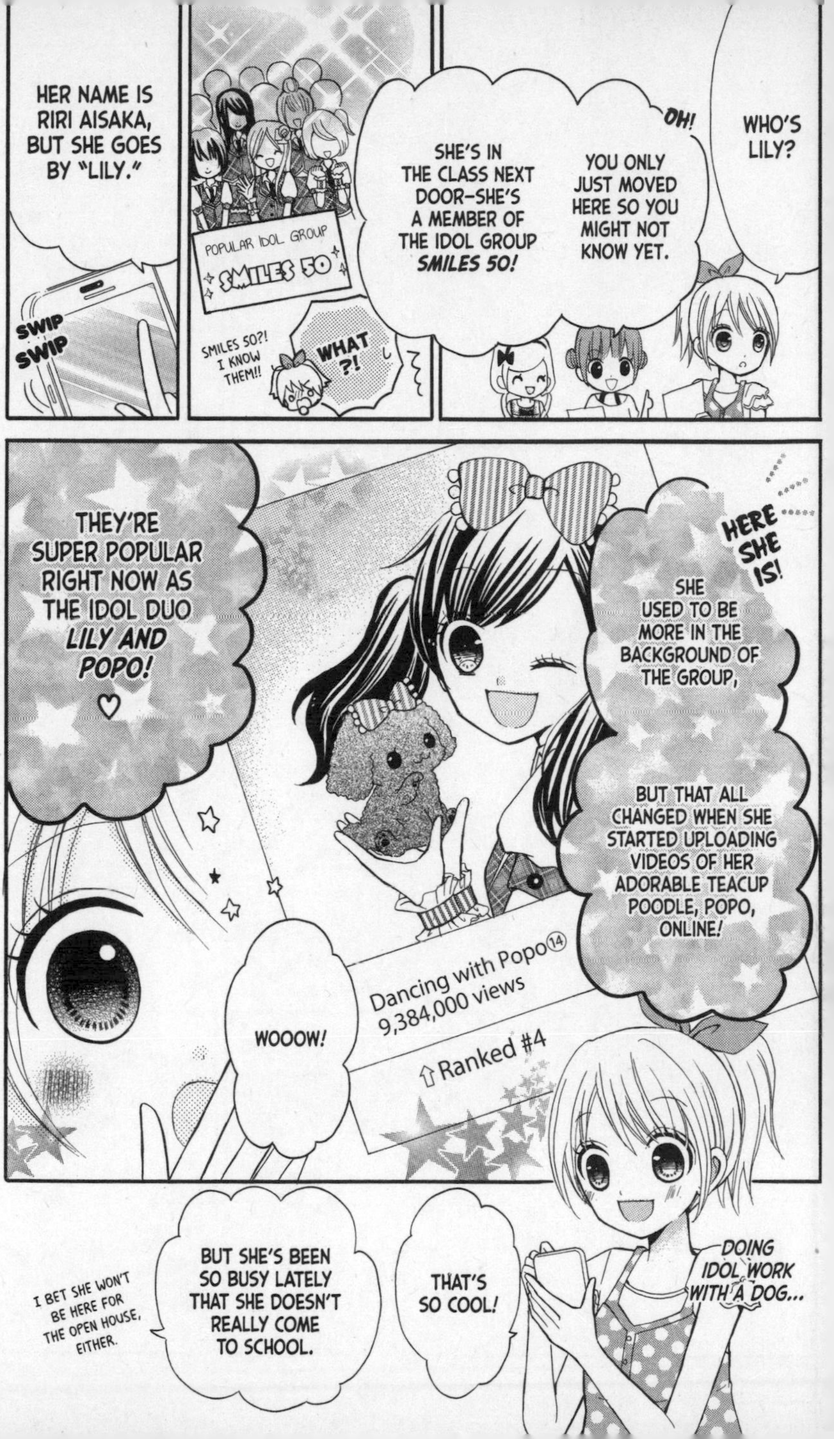
WHO'S LILY?
OH!
YOU ONLY JUST MOVED HERE SO YOU MIGHT NOT KNOW YET.
SHE'S IN THE CLASS NEXT DOOR—SHE'S A MEMBER OF THE IDOL GROUP SMILES 50!
POPULAR IDOL GROUP
SMILES 50
WHAT?!
SMILES 50?! I KNOW THEM!!
HER NAME IS RIRI AISAKA, BUT SHE GOES BY "LILY."
SWIP
SWIP
HERE SHE IS!
SHE USED TO BE MORE IN THE BACKGROUND OF THE GROUP,
BUT THAT ALL CHANGED WHEN SHE STARTED UPLOADING VIDEOS OF HER ADORABLE TEACUP POODLE, POPO, ONLINE!
THEY'RE SUPER POPULAR RIGHT NOW AS THE IDOL DUO LILY AND POPO! ♡
Dancing with Popo⑭
9,384,000 views
⇧Ranked #4
WOOOW!
DOING IDOL WORK WITH A DOG...
THAT'S SO COOL!
BUT SHE'S BEEN SO BUSY LATELY THAT SHE DOESN'T REALLY COME TO SCHOOL.
I BET SHE WON'T BE HERE FOR THE OPEN HOUSE, EITHER.

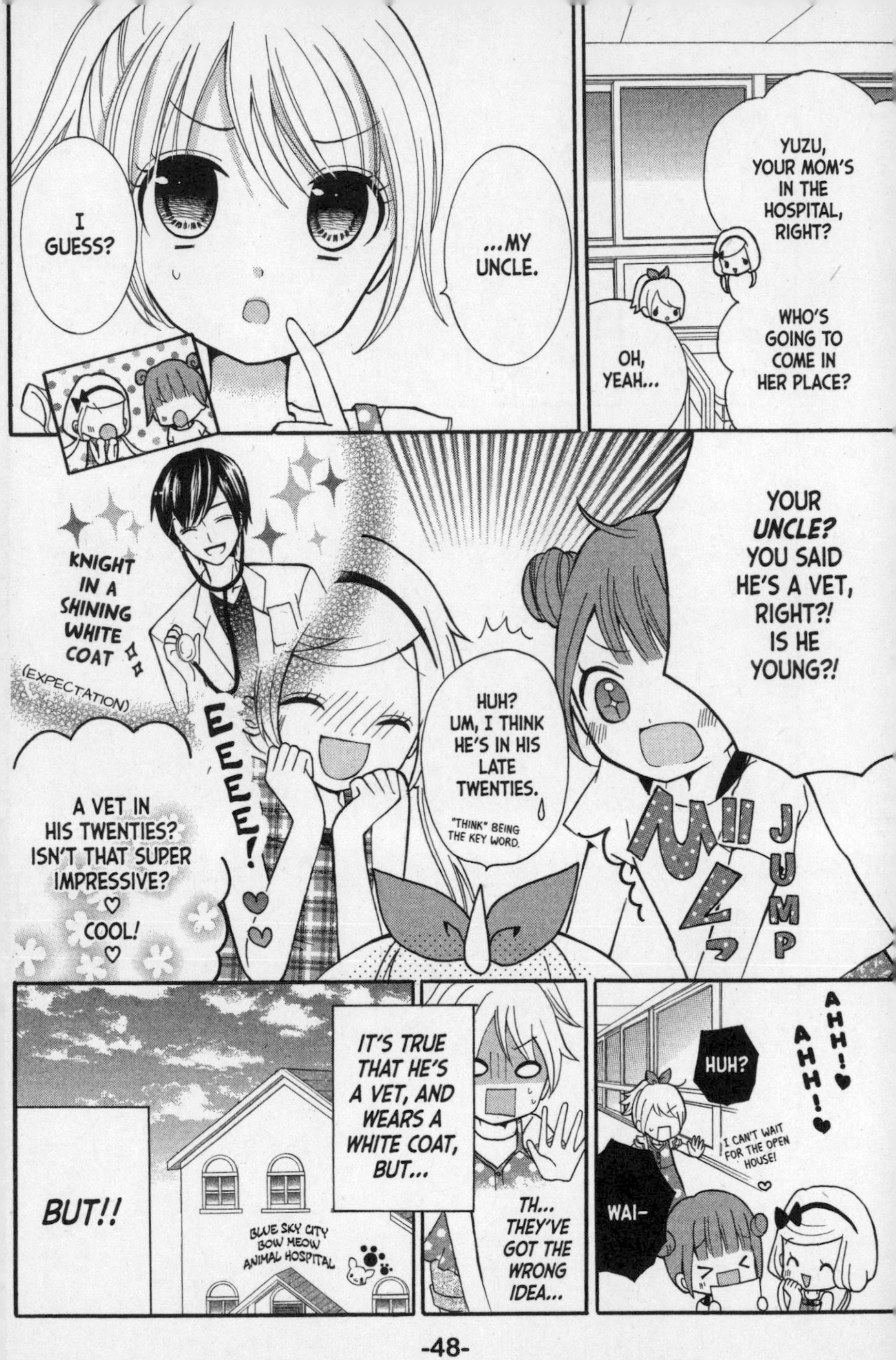
YUZU, YOUR MOM'S IN THE HOSPITAL, RIGHT?
WHO'S GOING TO COME IN HER PLACE?
OH, YEAH...
...MY UNCLE.
I GUESS?
YOUR *UNCLE?* YOU SAID HE'S A VET, RIGHT?! IS HE YOUNG?!
JUMP
HUH? UM, I THINK HE'S IN HIS LATE TWENTIES.
"THINK" BEING THE KEY WORD.
EEEE!
KNIGHT IN A SHINING WHITE COAT
(EXPECTATION)
A VET IN HIS TWENTIES? ISN'T THAT SUPER IMPRESSIVE? ♡
COOL! ♡
AHH! AHH! ♥
HUH?
I CAN'T WAIT FOR THE OPEN HOUSE! ♡
WAI-
IT'S TRUE THAT HE'S A VET, AND WEARS A WHITE COAT, BUT...
TH... THEY'VE GOT THE WRONG IDEA...
BUT!!
BLUE SKY CITY BOW MEOW ANIMAL HOSPITAL

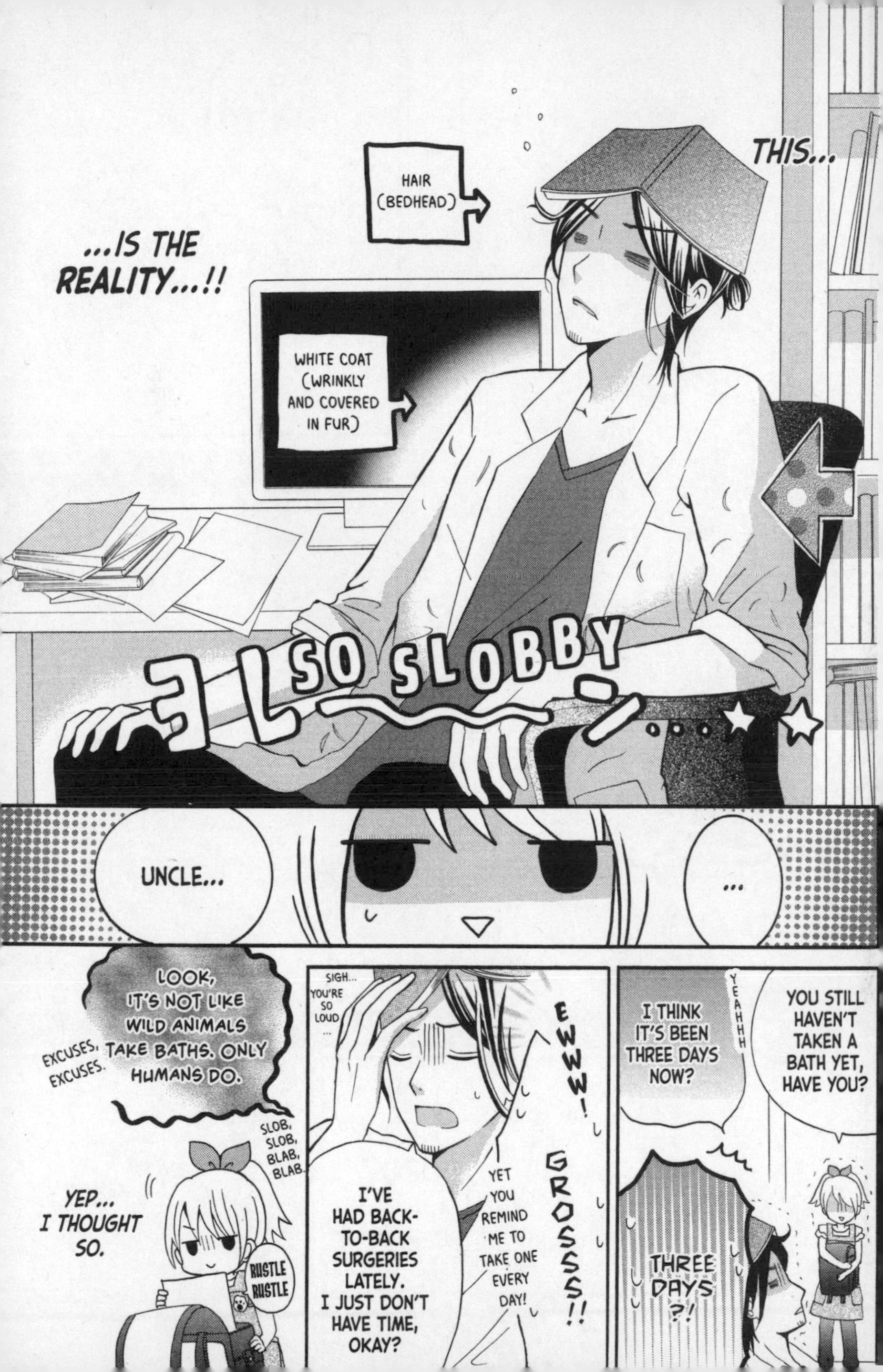
THIS...
...IS THE REALITY...!!
HAIR (BEDHEAD)
WHITE COAT (WRINKLY AND COVERED IN FUR)
SO SLOBBY
...
UNCLE...
YOU STILL HAVEN'T TAKEN A BATH YET, HAVE YOU?
YEAHHH
I THINK IT'S BEEN THREE DAYS NOW?
THREE DAYS?!
EWWW!
GROSSS!!
SIGH... YOU'RE SO LOUD...
I'VE HAD BACK-TO-BACK SURGERIES LATELY. I JUST DON'T HAVE TIME, OKAY?
YET YOU REMIND ME TO TAKE ONE EVERY DAY!
LOOK, IT'S NOT LIKE WILD ANIMALS TAKE BATHS. ONLY HUMANS DO.
EXCUSES, EXCUSES.
SLOB, SLOB, BLAB, BLAB.
YEP... I THOUGHT SO.
RUSTLE RUSTLE

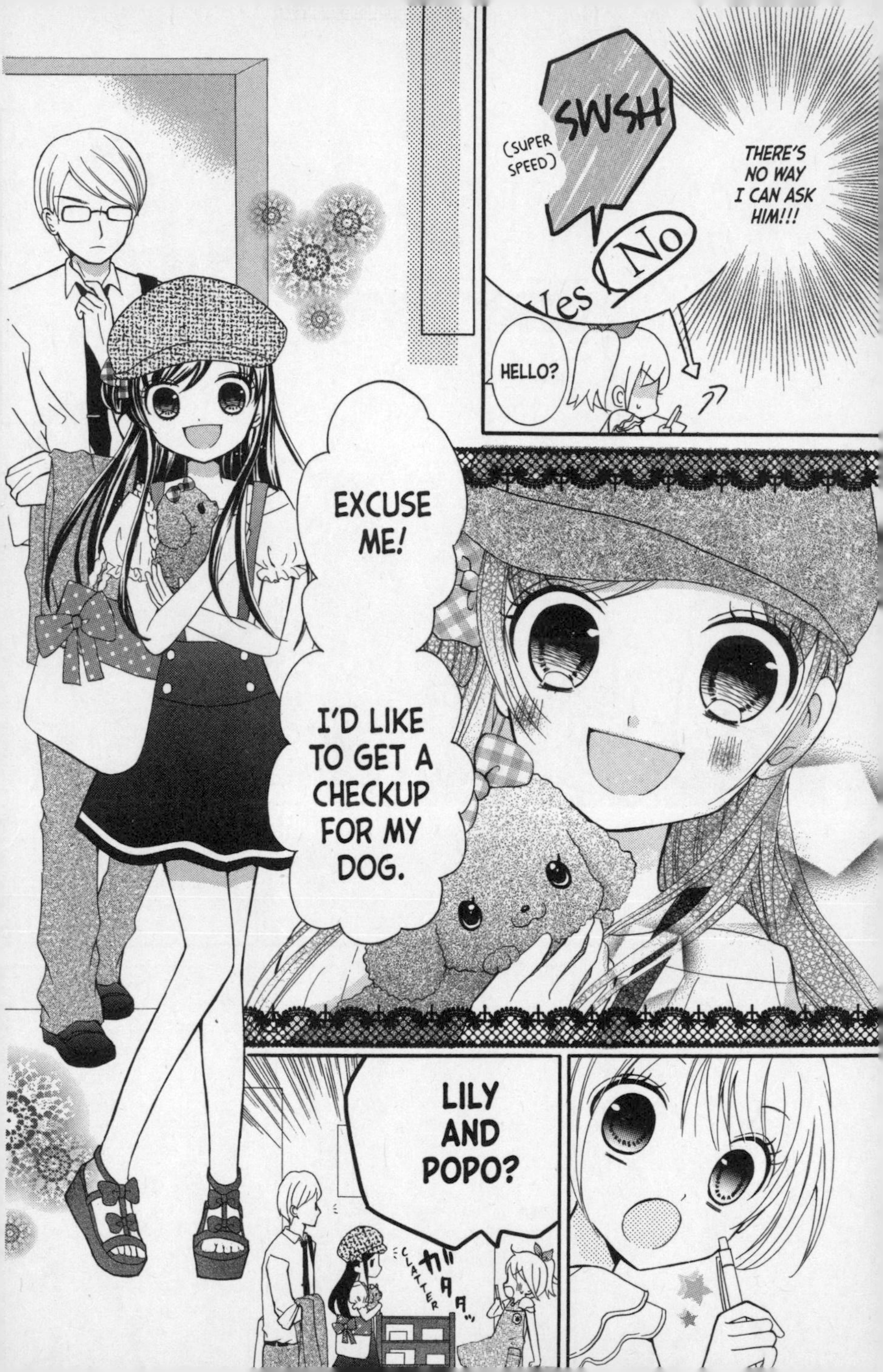
SWSH
(SUPER SPEED)
THERE'S NO WAY I CAN ASK HIM!!!
Yes No
HELLO?
EXCUSE ME!
I'D LIKE TO GET A CHECKUP FOR MY DOG.
LILY AND POPO?
CLATTER

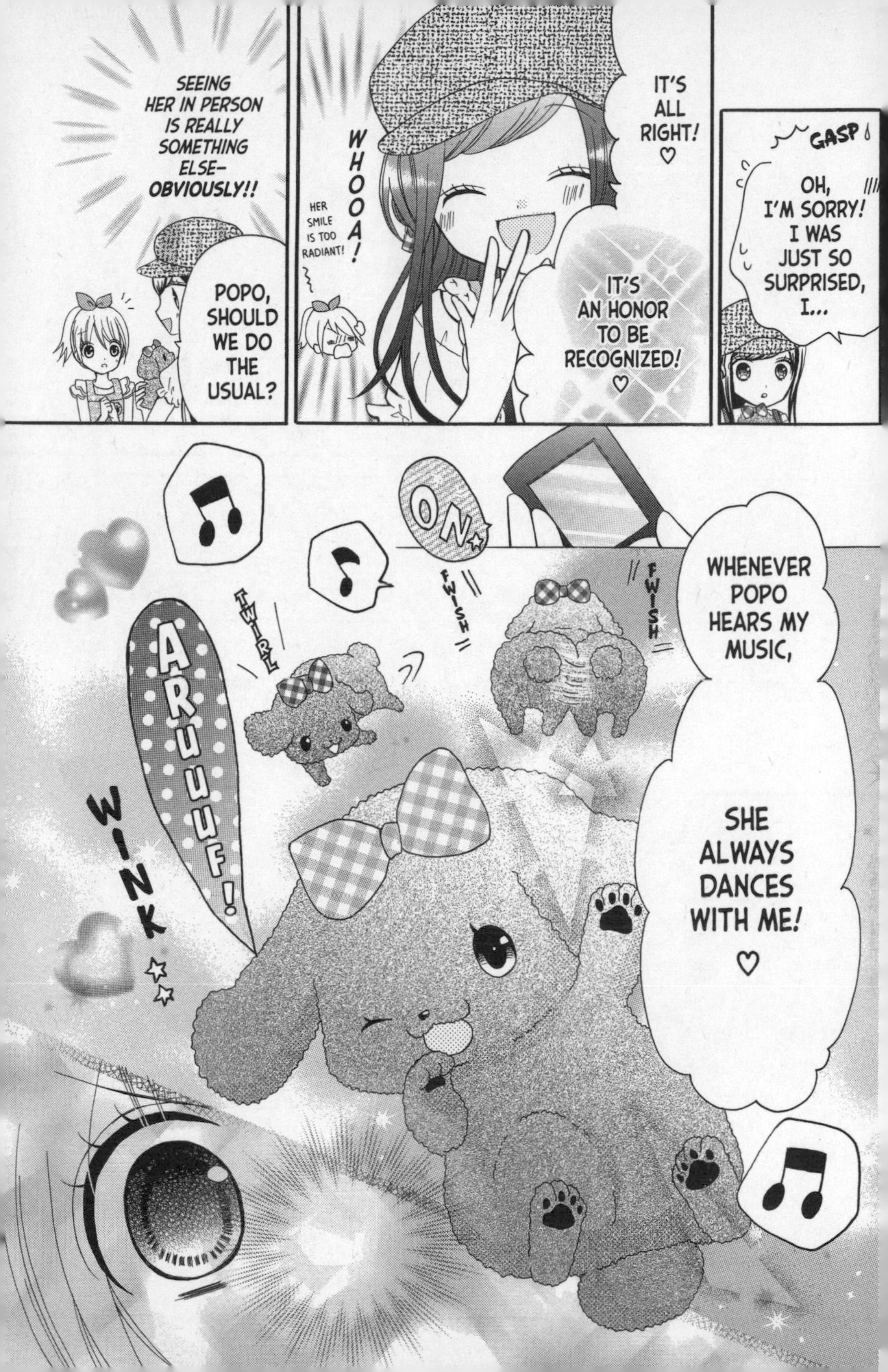
GASP
OH, I'M SORRY! I WAS JUST SO SURPRISED, I...
IT'S ALL RIGHT! ♡
IT'S AN HONOR TO BE RECOGNIZED! ♡
WHOOOA!
HER SMILE IS TOO RADIANT!
SEEING HER IN PERSON IS REALLY SOMETHING ELSE—OBVIOUSLY!!
POPO, SHOULD WE DO THE USUAL?
ON
WHENEVER POPO HEARS MY MUSIC,
SHE ALWAYS DANCES WITH ME! ♡
FWISH
FWISH
TWIRL
ARUUUF!
WINK

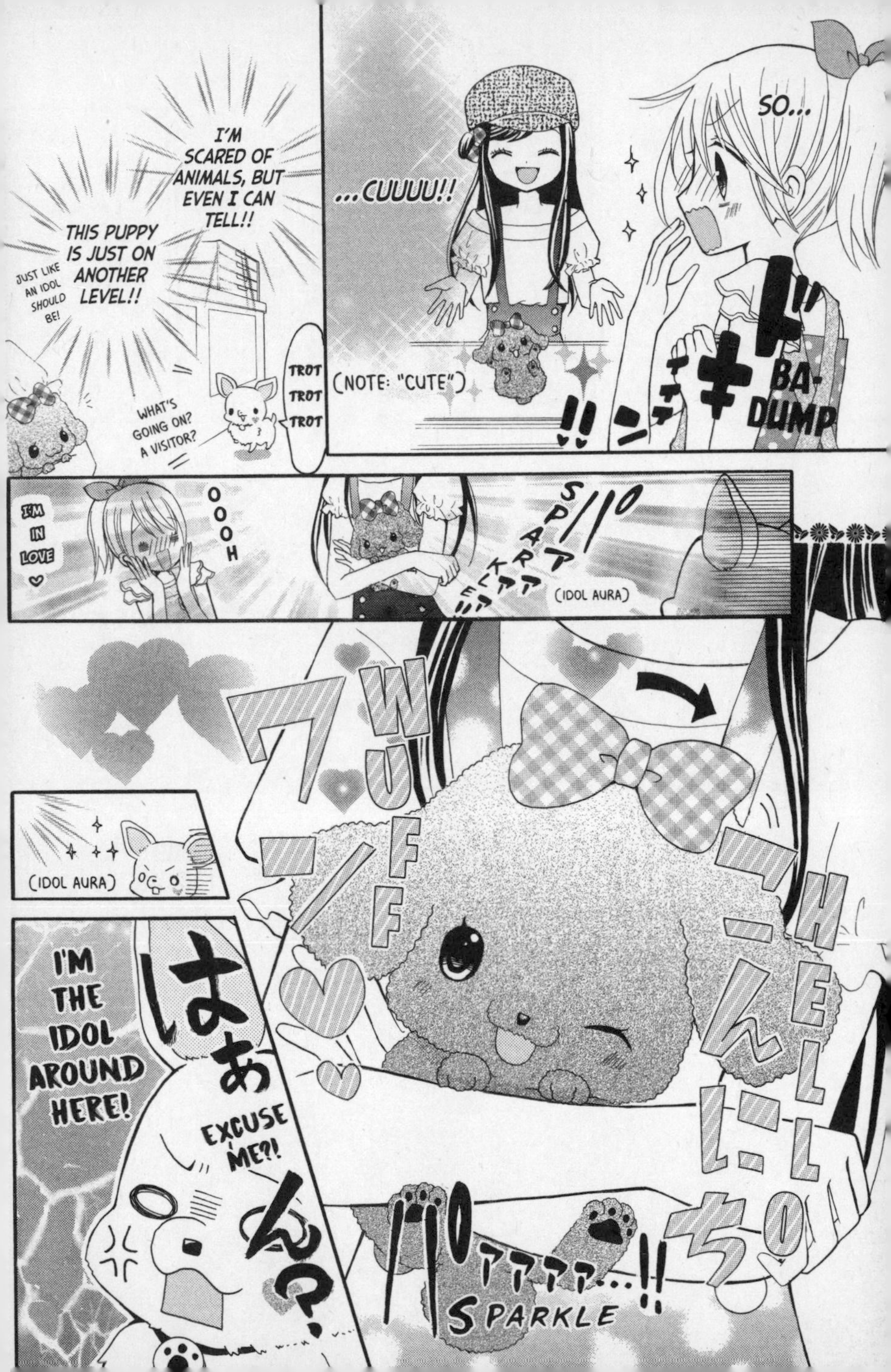
SO...
BA-DUMP
...CUUUU!!
(NOTE: "CUTE")
TROT TROT TROT
WHAT'S GOING ON? A VISITOR?
I'M SCARED OF ANIMALS, BUT EVEN I CAN TELL!!
THIS PUPPY IS JUST ON ANOTHER LEVEL!!
JUST LIKE AN IDOL SHOULD BE!
SPARKLE
(IDOL AURA)
OOOH
I'M IN LOVE
HELLO
WUFF
SPARKLE
(IDOL AURA)
EXCUSE ME?!
I'M THE IDOL AROUND HERE!

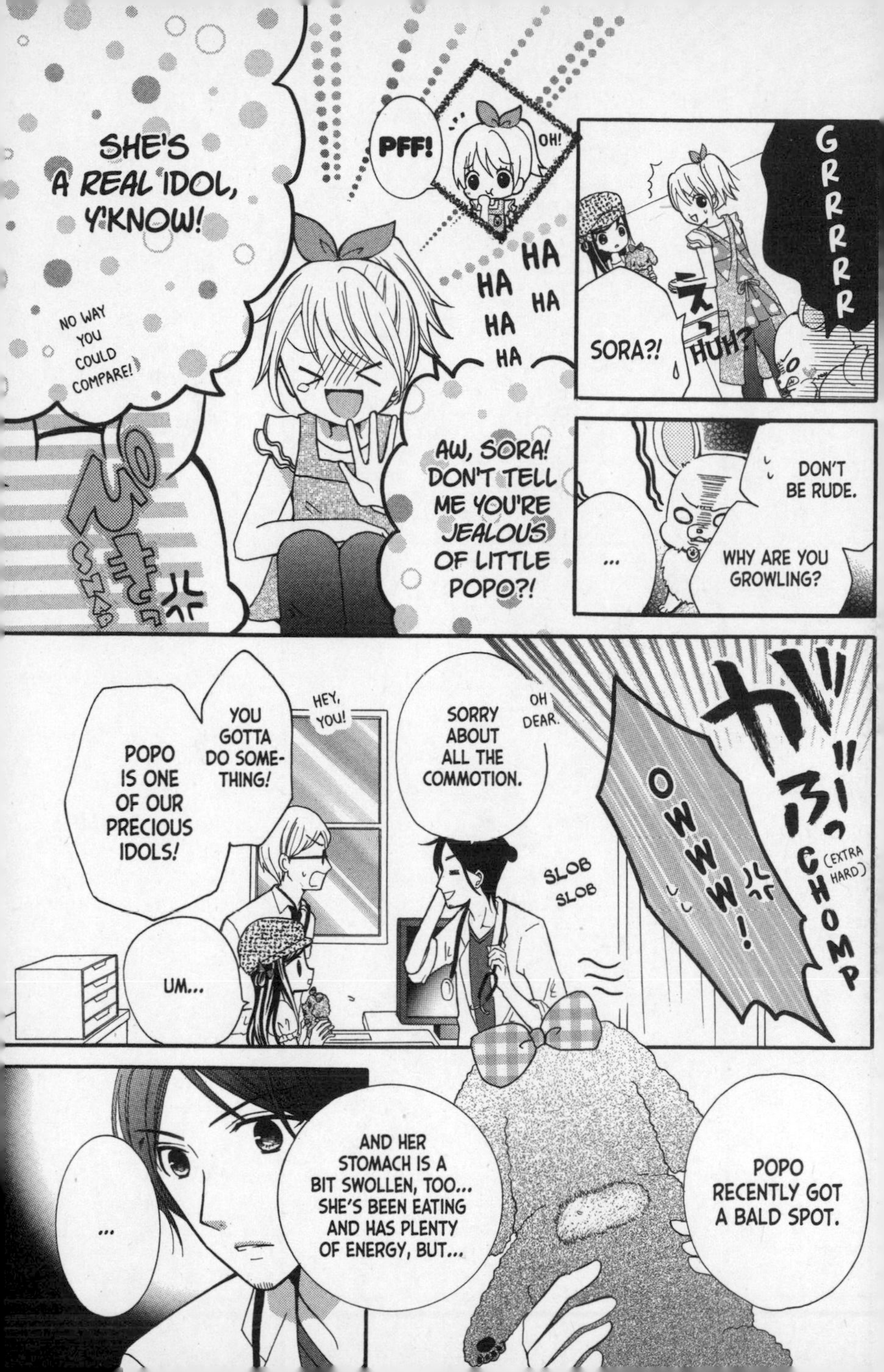
GRRRRR
HUH?
SORA?!
DON'T BE RUDE.
WHY ARE YOU GROWLING?
...
OH!
PFF!
SHE'S A REAL IDOL, Y'KNOW!
HA HA HA HA HA HA
AW, SORA! DON'T TELL ME YOU'RE JEALOUS OF LITTLE POPO?!
NO WAY YOU COULD COMPARE!
CHOMP
(EXTRA HARD)
OWWW!
OH DEAR.
SORRY ABOUT ALL THE COMMOTION.
SLOB SLOB
HEY, YOU!
YOU GOTTA DO SOMETHING!
POPO IS ONE OF OUR PRECIOUS IDOLS!
UM...
POPO RECENTLY GOT A BALD SPOT.
AND HER STOMACH IS A BIT SWOLLEN, TOO... SHE'S BEEN EATING AND HAS PLENTY OF ENERGY, BUT...
...

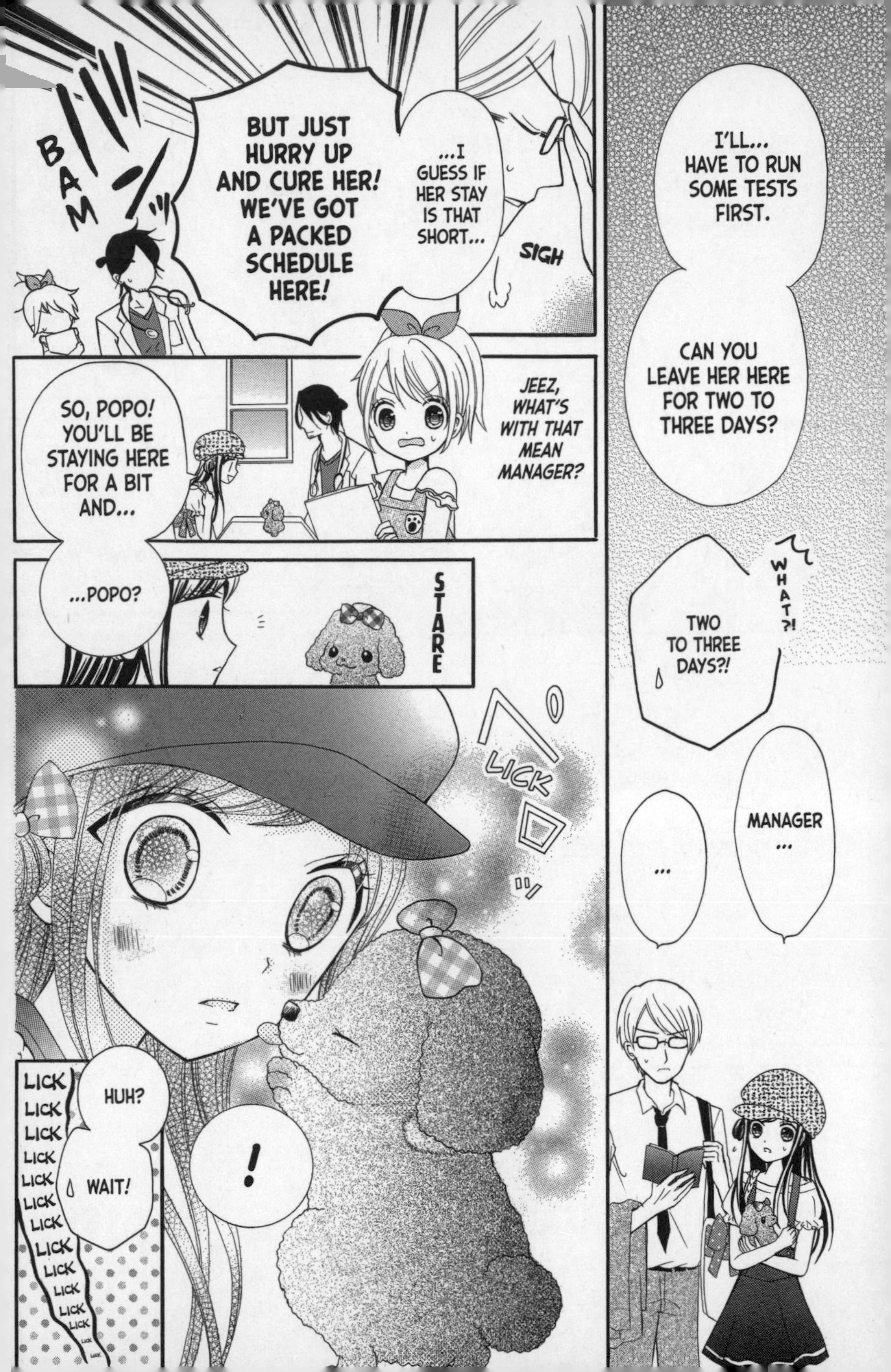

I'LL... HAVE TO RUN SOME TESTS FIRST.
CAN YOU LEAVE HER HERE FOR TWO TO THREE DAYS?
WHAT?!
TWO TO THREE DAYS?!
MANAGER...
...
SIGH
...I GUESS IF HER STAY IS THAT SHORT...
BUT JUST HURRY UP AND CURE HER! WE'VE GOT A PACKED SCHEDULE HERE!
BAM
JEEZ, WHAT'S WITH THAT MEAN MANAGER?
SO, POPO! YOU'LL BE STAYING HERE FOR A BIT AND...
STARE
...POPO?
LICK
!
HUH?
WAIT!
LICK LICK LICK LICK LICK LICK LICK LICK LICK LICK LICK LICK

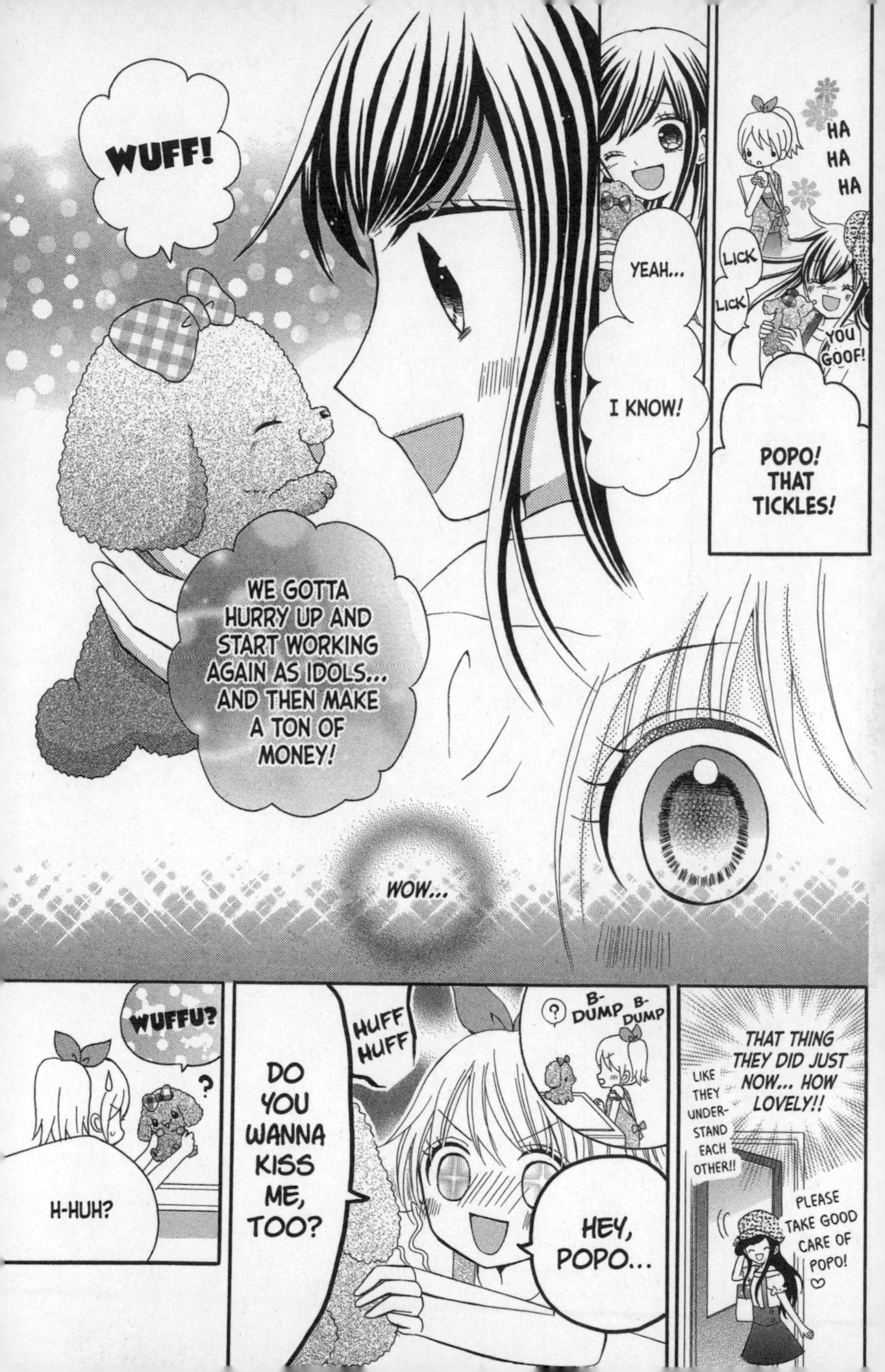
HA HA HA
LICK LICK
YOU GOOF!
POPO! THAT TICKLES!
YEAH... I KNOW!
WUFF!
WE GOTTA HURRY UP AND START WORKING AGAIN AS IDOLS... AND THEN MAKE A TON OF MONEY!
WOW...
THAT THING THEY DID JUST NOW... HOW LOVELY!!
LIKE THEY UNDERSTAND EACH OTHER!!
PLEASE TAKE GOOD CARE OF POPO! ♡
?
B-DUMP B-DUMP
HUFF HUFF
HEY, POPO...
DO YOU WANNA KISS ME, TOO?
WUFFU?
?
H-HUH?

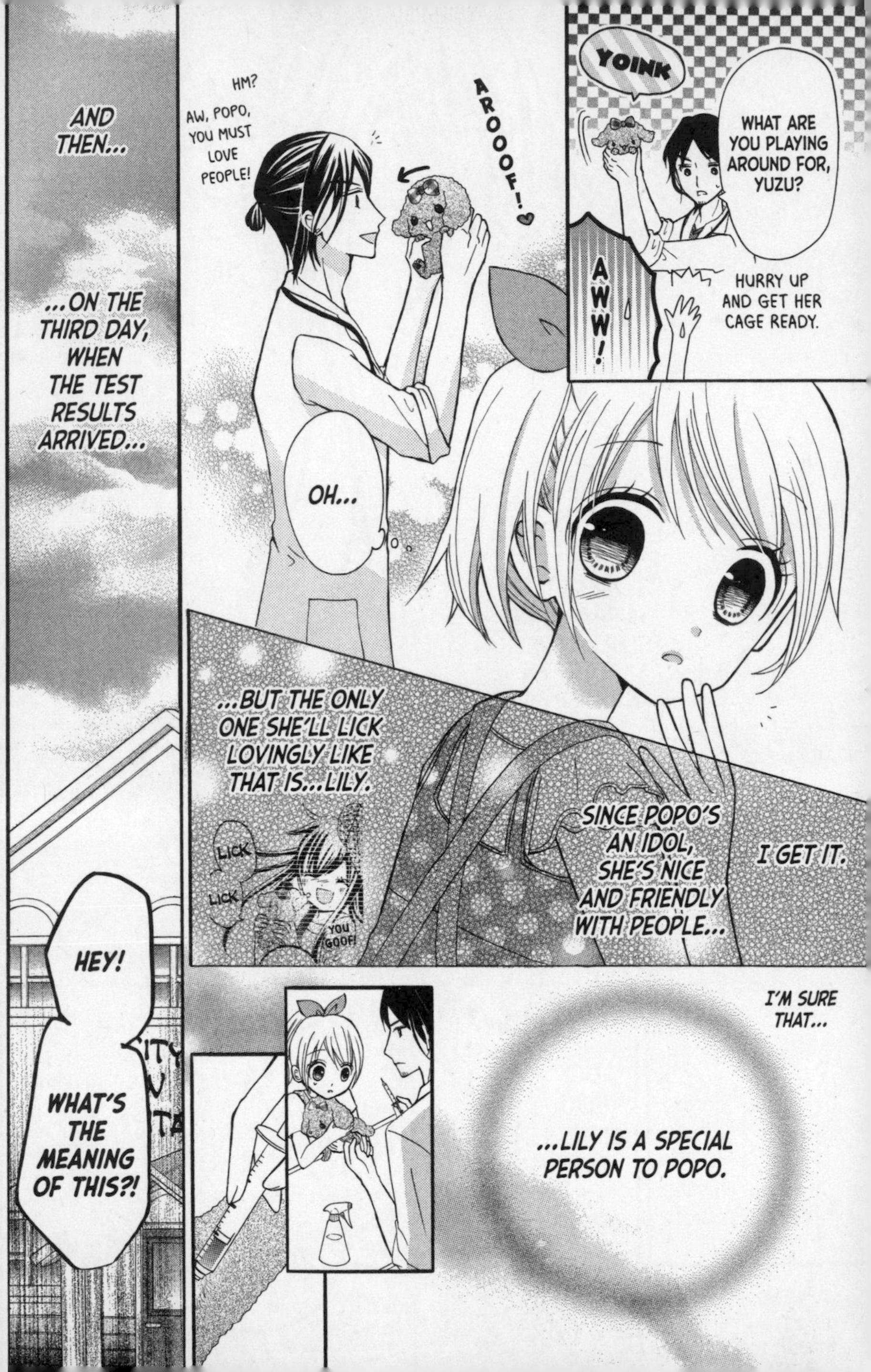
YOINK
WHAT ARE YOU PLAYING AROUND FOR, YUZU?
AWW!
HURRY UP AND GET HER CAGE READY.
AROOOF!♥
HM?
AW, POPO, YOU MUST LOVE PEOPLE!
OH...
I GET IT.
SINCE POPO'S AN IDOL, SHE'S NICE AND FRIENDLY WITH PEOPLE...
...BUT THE ONLY ONE SHE'LL LICK LOVINGLY LIKE THAT IS...LILY.
LICK
LICK
YOU GOOF!
I'M SURE THAT...
...LILY IS A SPECIAL PERSON TO POPO.
AND THEN...
...ON THE THIRD DAY, WHEN THE TEST RESULTS ARRIVED...
HEY!
WHAT'S THE MEANING OF THIS?!

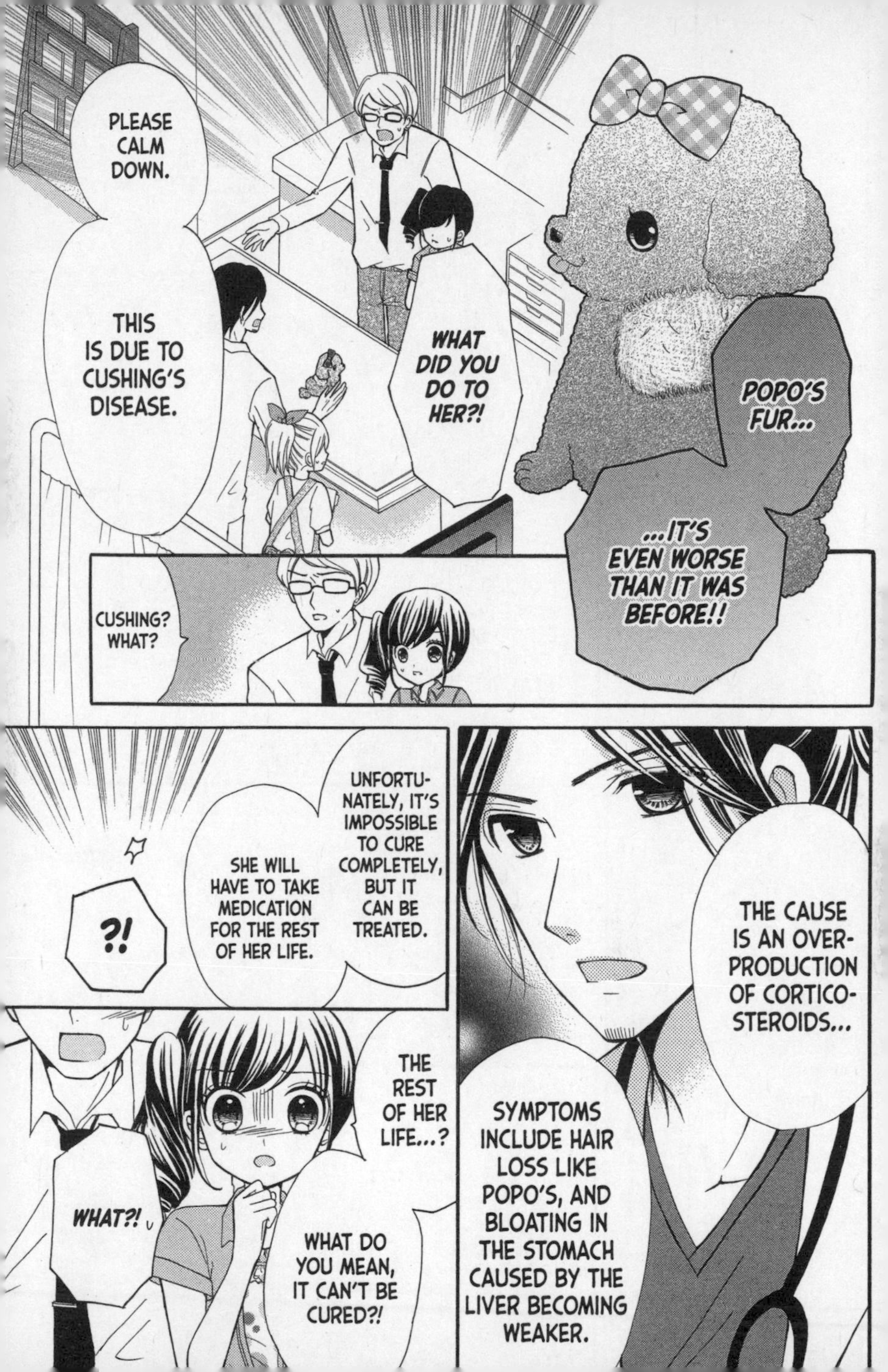
POPO'S FUR...
...IT'S EVEN WORSE THAN IT WAS BEFORE!!
WHAT DID YOU DO TO HER?!
PLEASE CALM DOWN.
THIS IS DUE TO CUSHING'S DISEASE.
CUSHING? WHAT?
THE CAUSE IS AN OVER-PRODUCTION OF CORTICO-STEROIDS...
SYMPTOMS INCLUDE HAIR LOSS LIKE POPO'S, AND BLOATING IN THE STOMACH CAUSED BY THE LIVER BECOMING WEAKER.
UNFORTU-NATELY, IT'S IMPOSSIBLE TO CURE COMPLETELY, BUT IT CAN BE TREATED.
SHE WILL HAVE TO TAKE MEDICATION FOR THE REST OF HER LIFE.
?!
THE REST OF HER LIFE...?
WHAT DO YOU MEAN, IT CAN'T BE CURED?!
WHAT?!

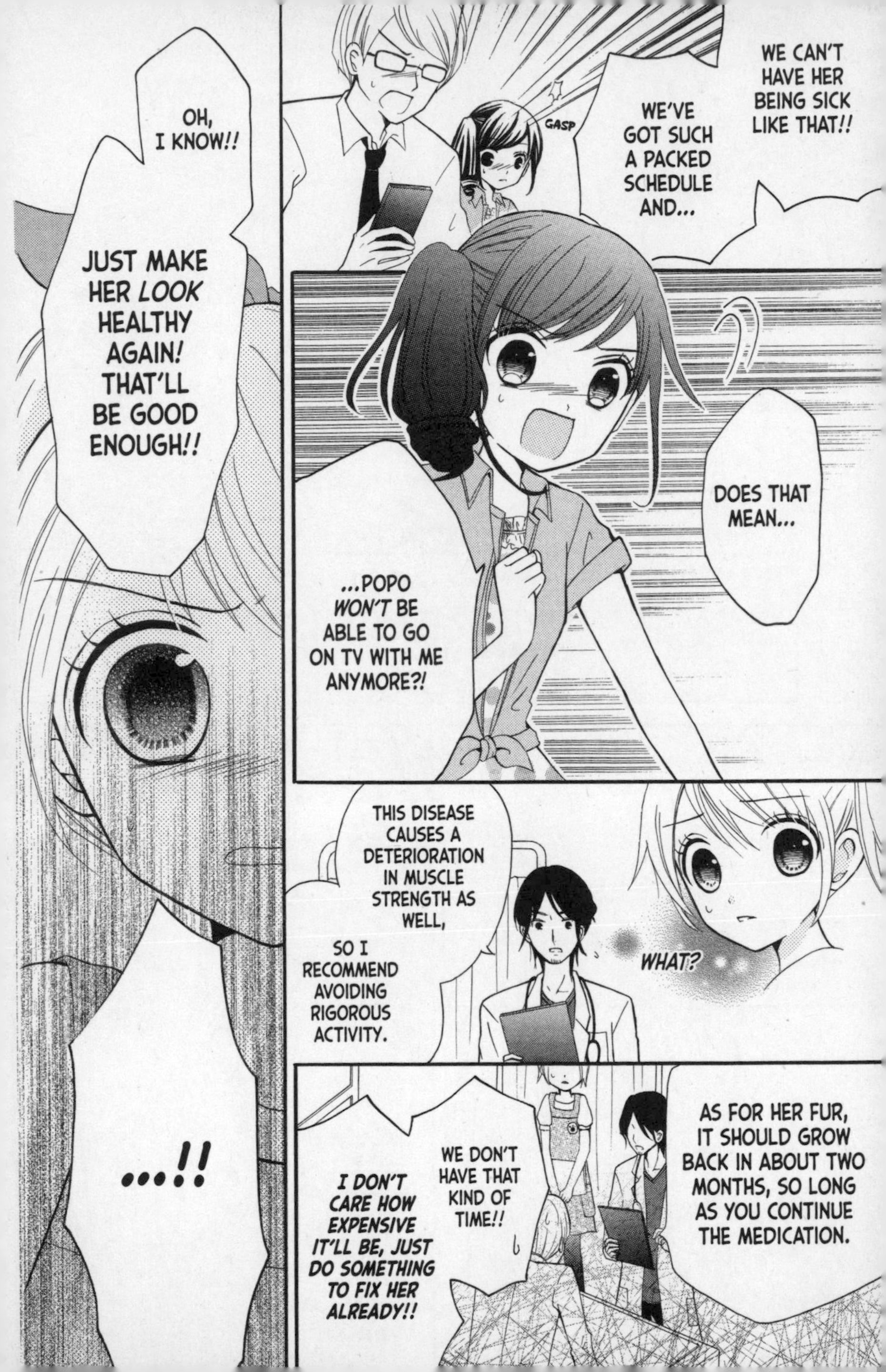
WE CAN'T HAVE HER BEING SICK LIKE THAT!!
WE'VE GOT SUCH A PACKED SCHEDULE AND...
GASP
DOES THAT MEAN...
...POPO *WON'T* BE ABLE TO GO ON TV WITH ME ANYMORE?!
THIS DISEASE CAUSES A DETERIORATION IN MUSCLE STRENGTH AS WELL,
SO I RECOMMEND AVOIDING RIGOROUS ACTIVITY.
WHAT?
AS FOR HER FUR, IT SHOULD GROW BACK IN ABOUT TWO MONTHS, SO LONG AS YOU CONTINUE THE MEDICATION.
WE DON'T HAVE THAT KIND OF TIME!!
I DON'T CARE HOW EXPENSIVE IT'LL BE, JUST DO SOMETHING TO FIX HER ALREADY!!
OH, I KNOW!!
JUST MAKE HER *LOOK* HEALTHY AGAIN! THAT'LL BE GOOD ENOUGH!!
...!!

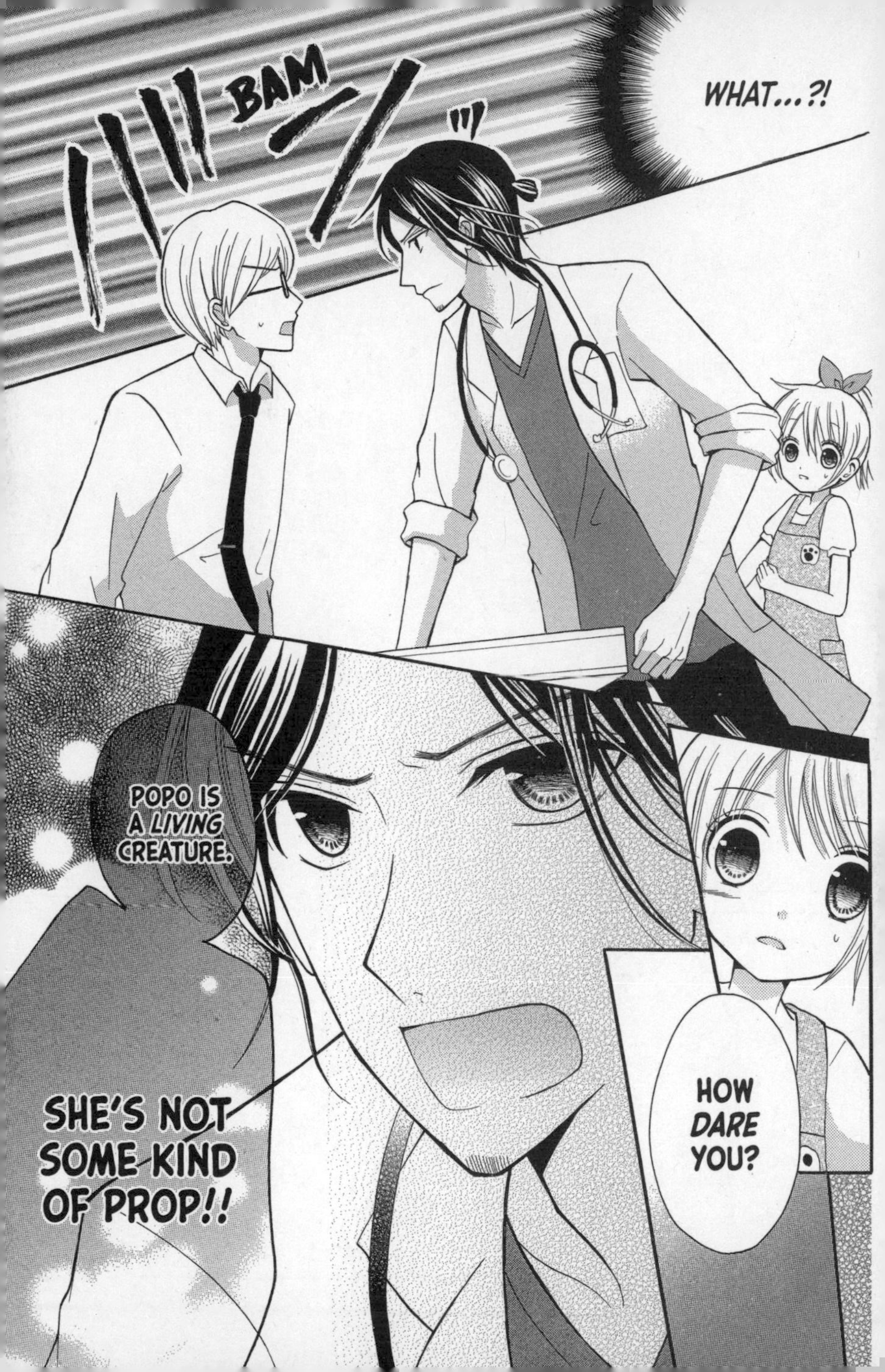
WHAT...?!
BAM
HOW DARE YOU?
POPO IS A *LIVING* CREATURE.
SHE'S NOT SOME KIND OF PROP!!

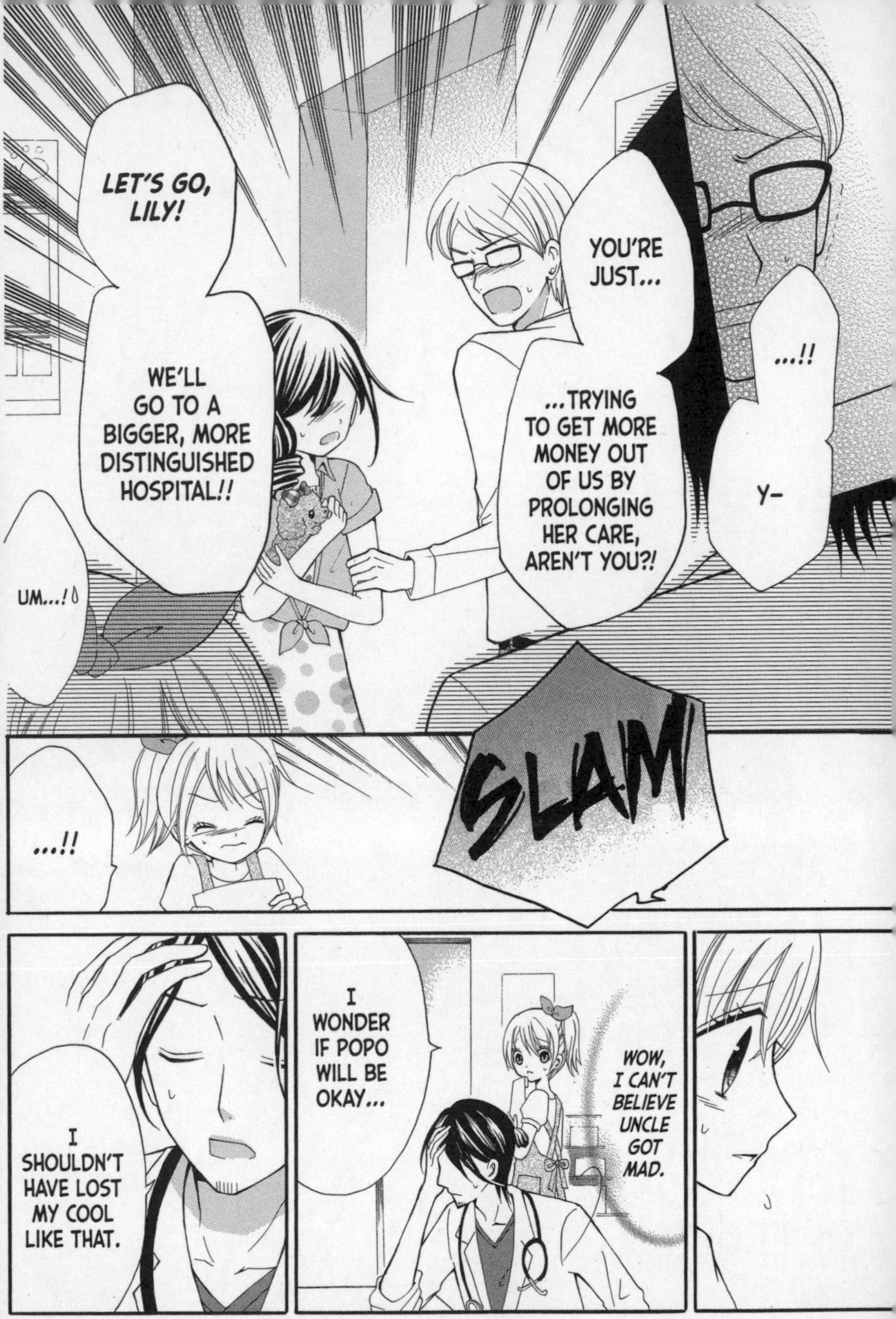
...!!
Y-
YOU'RE JUST...
...TRYING TO GET MORE MONEY OUT OF US BY PROLONGING HER CARE, AREN'T YOU?!
LET'S GO, LILY!
WE'LL GO TO A BIGGER, MORE DISTINGUISHED HOSPITAL!!
UM...!
SLAM
...!!
WOW, I CAN'T BELIEVE UNCLE GOT MAD.
I WONDER IF POPO WILL BE OKAY...
I SHOULDN'T HAVE LOST MY COOL LIKE THAT.

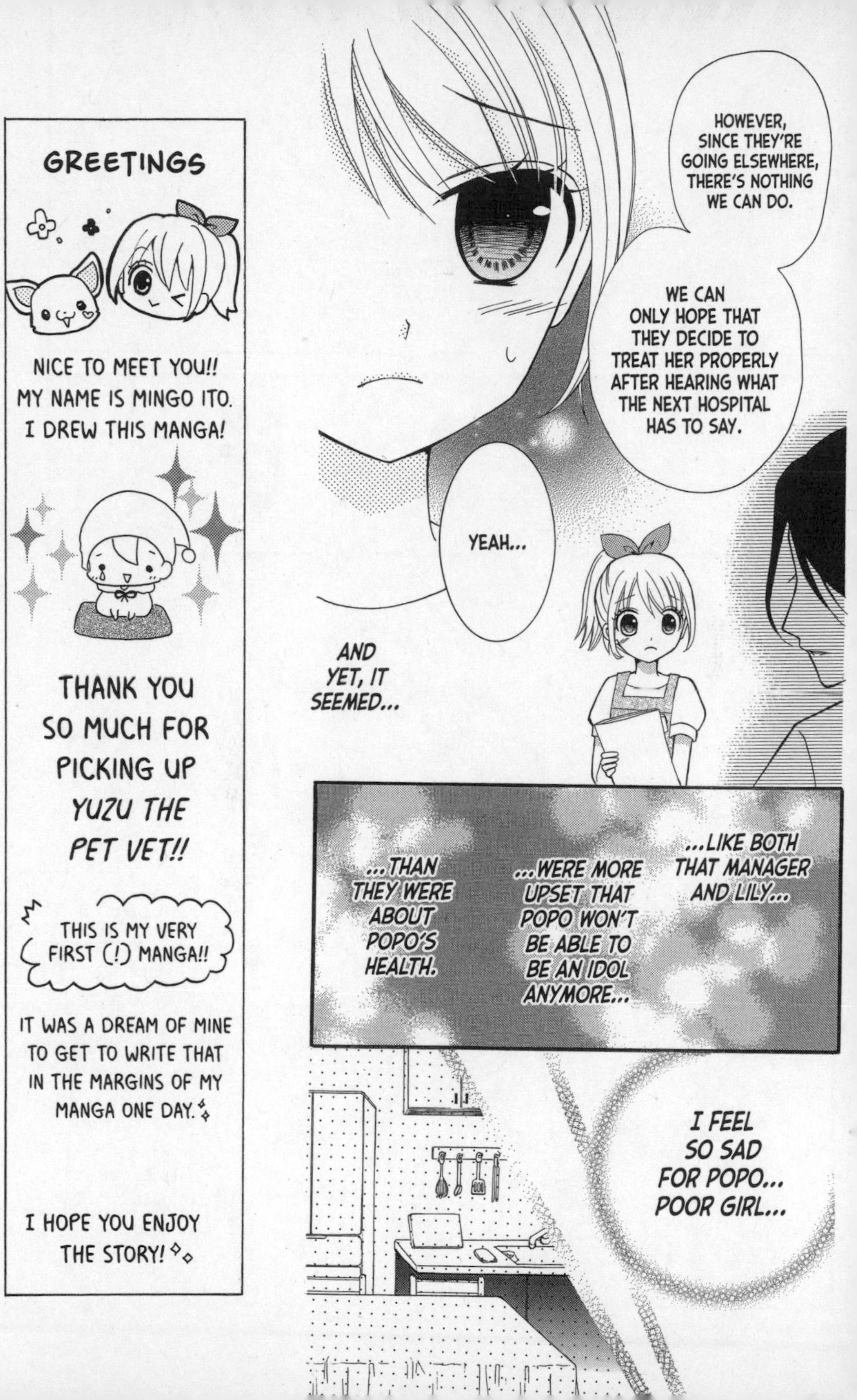
HOWEVER, SINCE THEY'RE GOING ELSEWHERE, THERE'S NOTHING WE CAN DO.
WE CAN ONLY HOPE THAT THEY DECIDE TO TREAT HER PROPERLY AFTER HEARING WHAT THE NEXT HOSPITAL HAS TO SAY.
YEAH...
AND YET, IT SEEMED...
...LIKE BOTH THAT MANAGER AND LILY...
...WERE MORE UPSET THAT POPO WON'T BE ABLE TO BE AN IDOL ANYMORE...
...THAN THEY WERE ABOUT POPO'S HEALTH.
I FEEL SO SAD FOR POPO... POOR GIRL...

GREETINGS

NICE TO MEET YOU!! MY NAME IS MINGO ITO. I DREW THIS MANGA!

THANK YOU SO MUCH FOR PICKING UP *YUZU THE PET VET*!!

THIS IS MY VERY FIRST (!) MANGA!!

IT WAS A DREAM OF MINE TO GET TO WRITE THAT IN THE MARGINS OF MY MANGA ONE DAY.

I HOPE YOU ENJOY THE STORY!

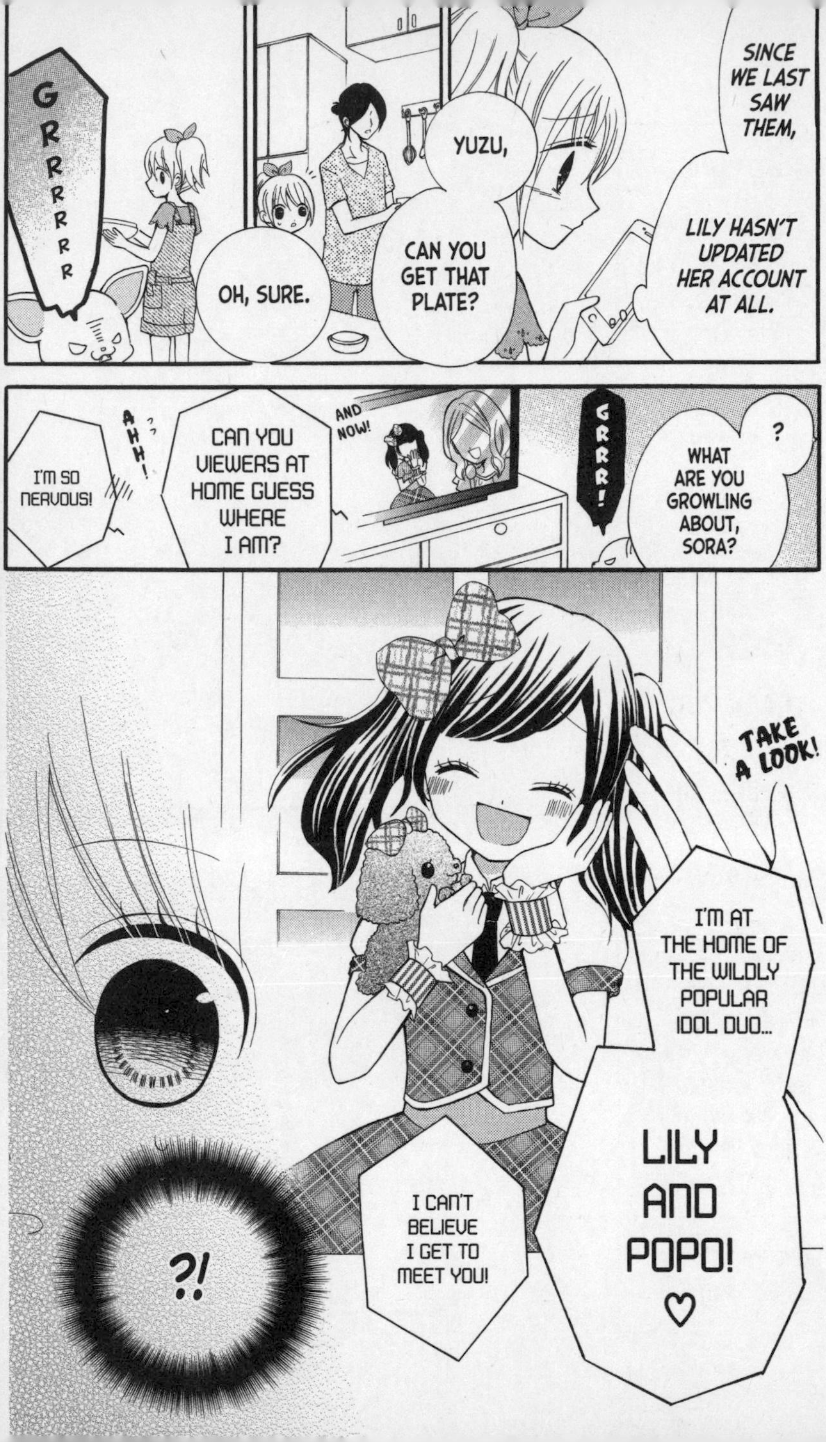

SINCE WE LAST SAW THEM,
LILY HASN'T UPDATED HER ACCOUNT AT ALL.
YUZU,
CAN YOU GET THAT PLATE?
OH, SURE.
GRRRRRR
?
WHAT ARE YOU GROWLING ABOUT, SORA?
GRRR!
AND NOW!
CAN YOU VIEWERS AT HOME GUESS WHERE I AM?
AHH!
I'M SO NERVOUS!
TAKE A LOOK!
I'M AT THE HOME OF THE WILDLY POPULAR IDOL DUO...
LILY AND POPO! ♡
I CAN'T BELIEVE I GET TO MEET YOU!
?!

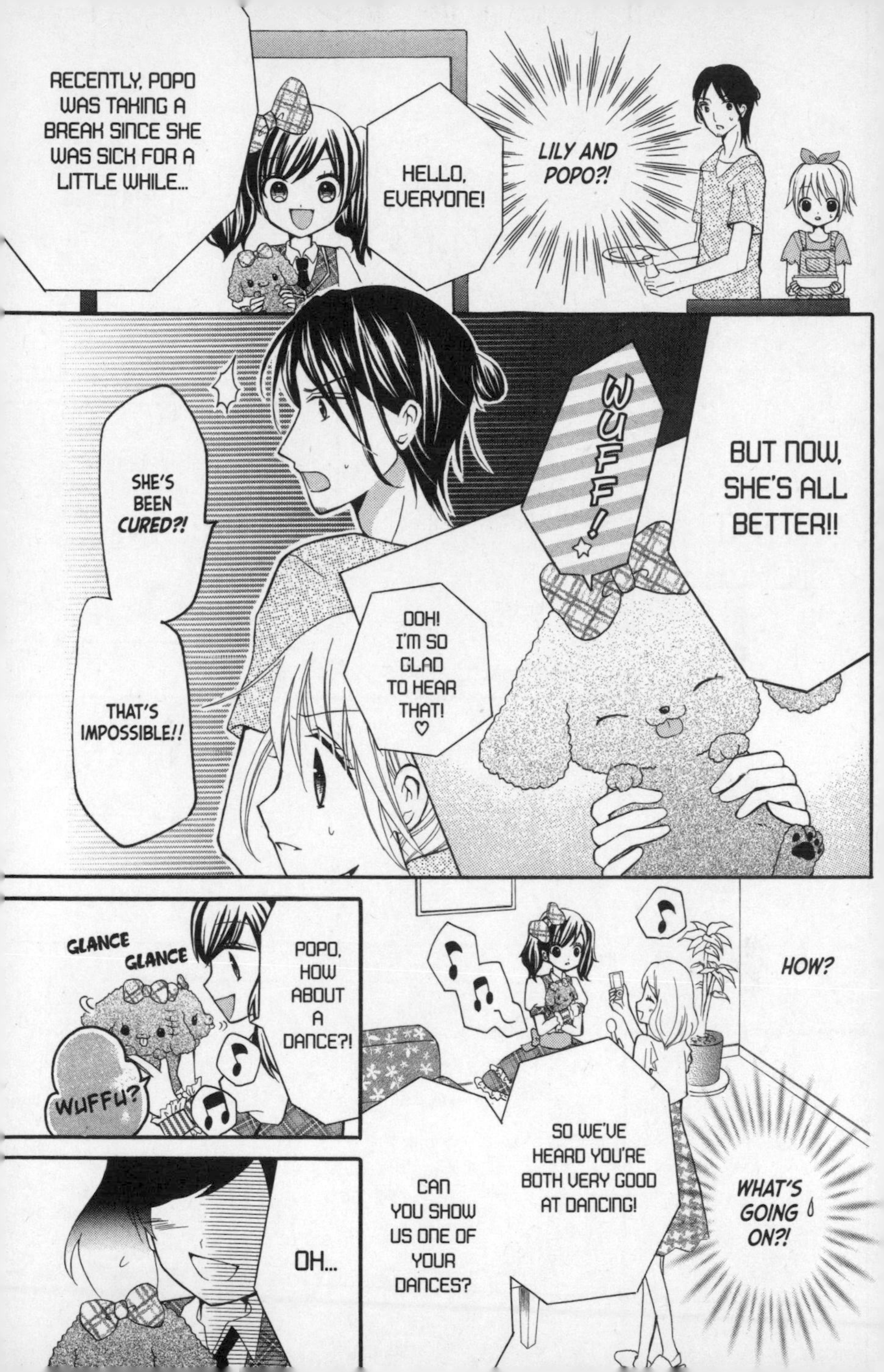
LILY AND POPO?!
HELLO, EVERYONE!
RECENTLY, POPO WAS TAKING A BREAK SINCE SHE WAS SICK FOR A LITTLE WHILE...
BUT NOW, SHE'S ALL BETTER!!
WUFF!
OOH! I'M SO GLAD TO HEAR THAT! ♡
SHE'S BEEN CURED?!
THAT'S IMPOSSIBLE!!
HOW?
SO WE'VE HEARD YOU'RE BOTH VERY GOOD AT DANCING!
WHAT'S GOING ON?!
CAN YOU SHOW US ONE OF YOUR DANCES?
POPO, HOW ABOUT A DANCE?!
GLANCE GLANCE
WUFFU?
OH...

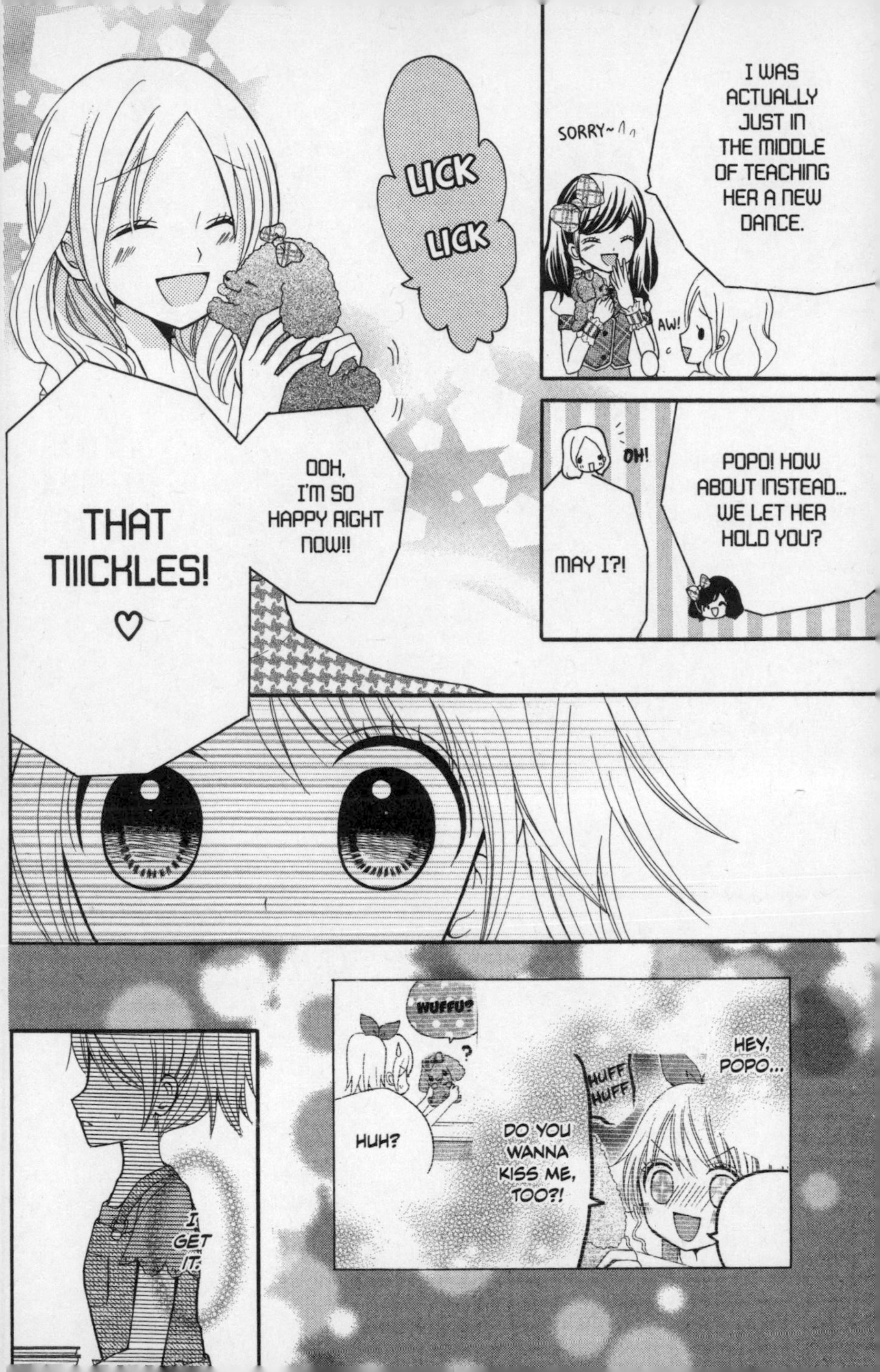
I WAS ACTUALLY JUST IN THE MIDDLE OF TEACHING HER A NEW DANCE.
SORRY~
AW!
POPO! HOW ABOUT INSTEAD... WE LET HER HOLD YOU?
OH!
MAY I?!
LICK LICK
OOH, I'M SO HAPPY RIGHT NOW!!
THAT TIIICKLES! ♡
HEY, POPO...
HUFF HUFF
DO YOU WANNA KISS ME, TOO?!
WUFFU?
HUH?
I GET IT.

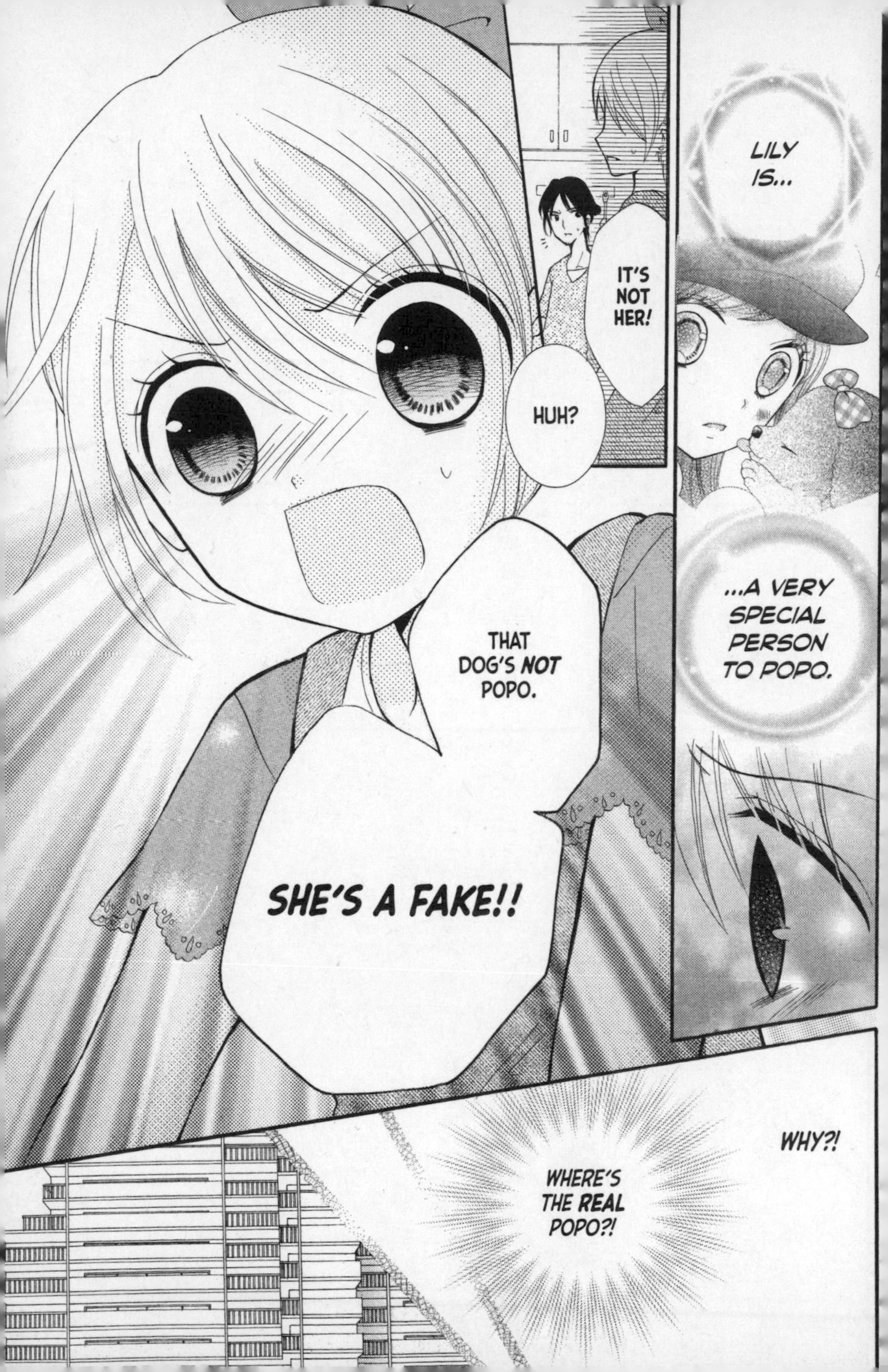
LILY IS...
...A VERY SPECIAL PERSON TO POPO.
IT'S NOT HER!
HUH?
THAT DOG'S *NOT* POPO.
SHE'S A FAKE!!
WHY?!
WHERE'S THE *REAL* POPO?!

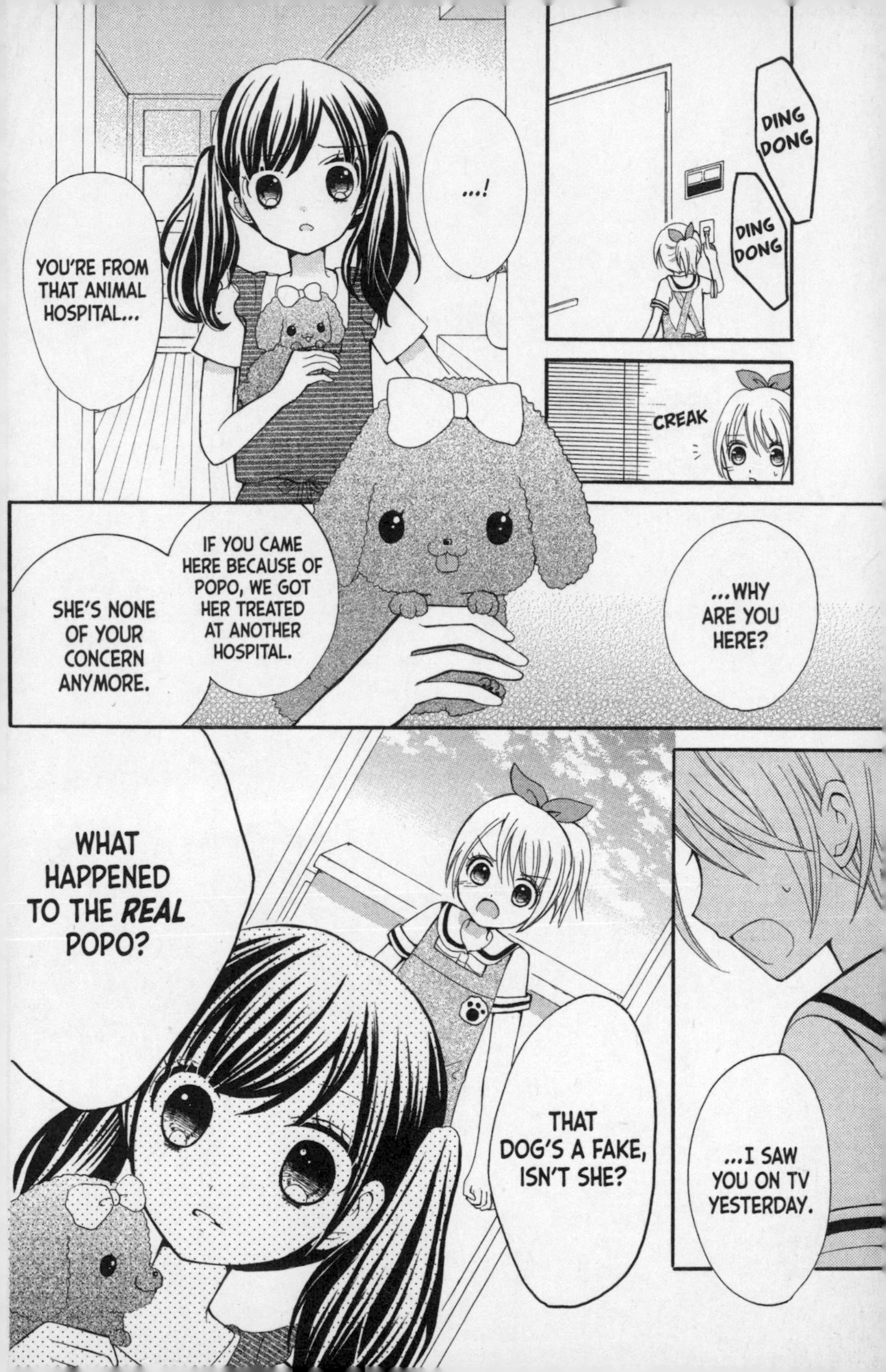
DING DONG
DING DONG
CREAK
...!
YOU'RE FROM THAT ANIMAL HOSPITAL...
...WHY ARE YOU HERE?
IF YOU CAME HERE BECAUSE OF POPO, WE GOT HER TREATED AT ANOTHER HOSPITAL.
SHE'S NONE OF YOUR CONCERN ANYMORE.
...I SAW YOU ON TV YESTERDAY.
THAT DOG'S A FAKE, ISN'T SHE?
WHAT HAPPENED TO THE *REAL* POPO?

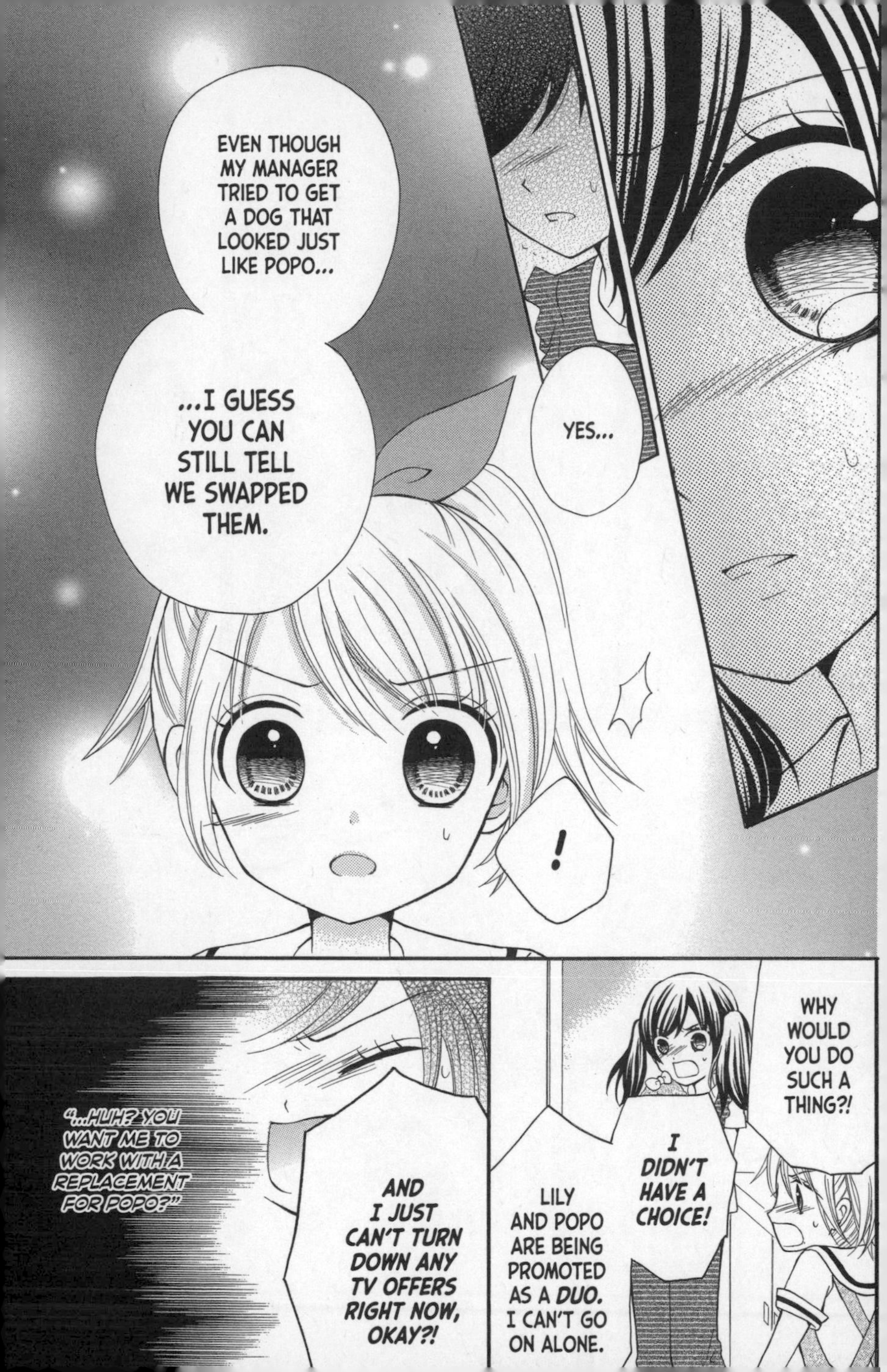
EVEN THOUGH MY MANAGER TRIED TO GET A DOG THAT LOOKED JUST LIKE POPO...
...I GUESS YOU CAN STILL TELL WE SWAPPED THEM.
YES...
!
WHY WOULD YOU DO SUCH A THING?!
I DIDN'T HAVE A CHOICE!
LILY AND POPO ARE BEING PROMOTED AS A DUO. I CAN'T GO ON ALONE.
AND I JUST CAN'T TURN DOWN ANY TV OFFERS RIGHT NOW, OKAY?!
"...HUH? YOU WANT ME TO WORK WITH A REPLACEMENT FOR POPO?"

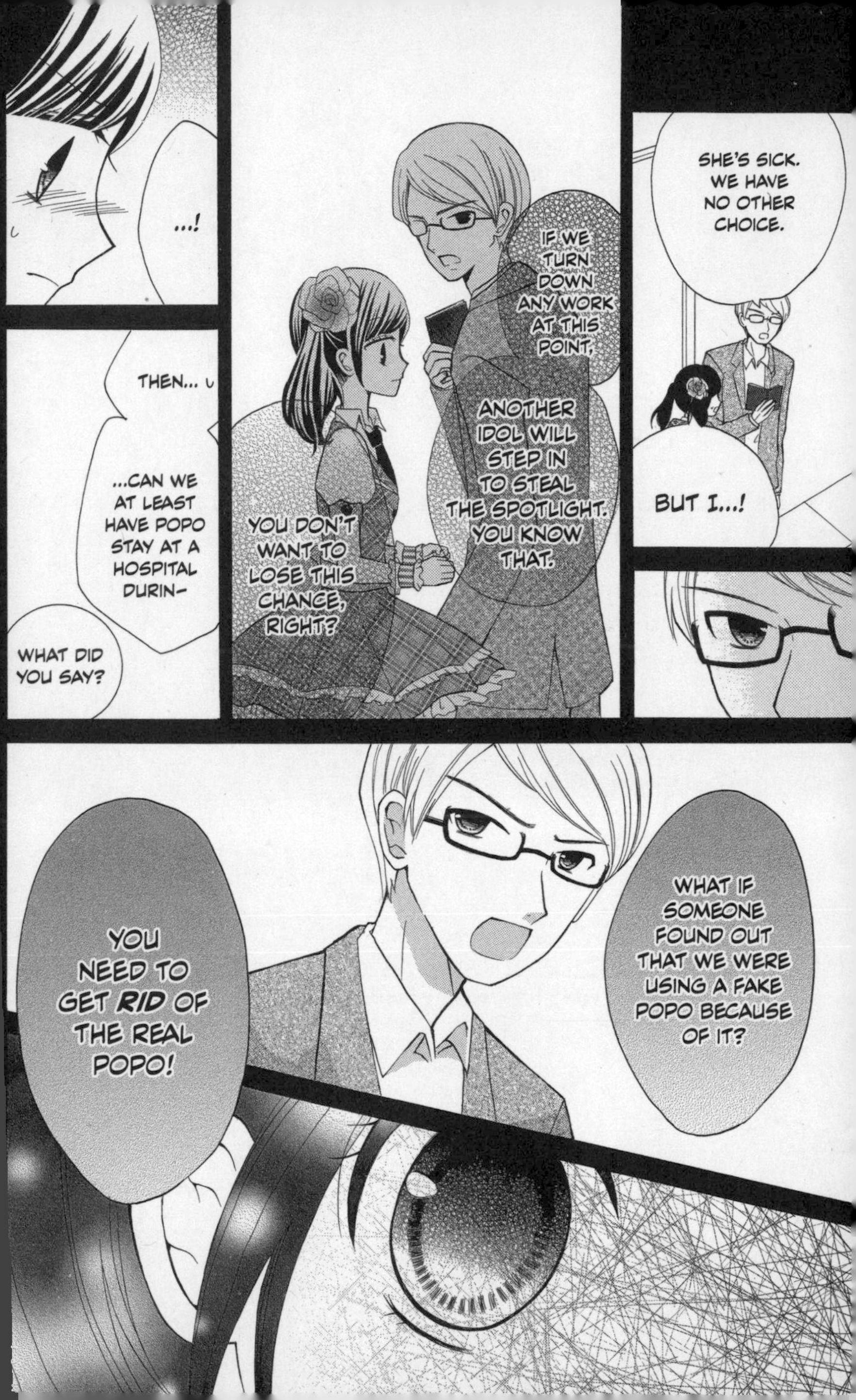
SHE'S SICK. WE HAVE NO OTHER CHOICE.
BUT I...!
IF WE TURN DOWN ANY WORK AT THIS POINT,
ANOTHER IDOL WILL STEP IN TO STEAL THE SPOTLIGHT. YOU KNOW THAT.
YOU DON'T WANT TO LOSE THIS CHANCE, RIGHT?
...!
THEN...
...CAN WE AT LEAST HAVE POPO STAY AT A HOSPITAL DURIN-
WHAT DID YOU SAY?
WHAT IF SOMEONE FOUND OUT THAT WE WERE USING A FAKE POPO BECAUSE OF IT?
YOU NEED TO GET *RID* OF THE REAL POPO!

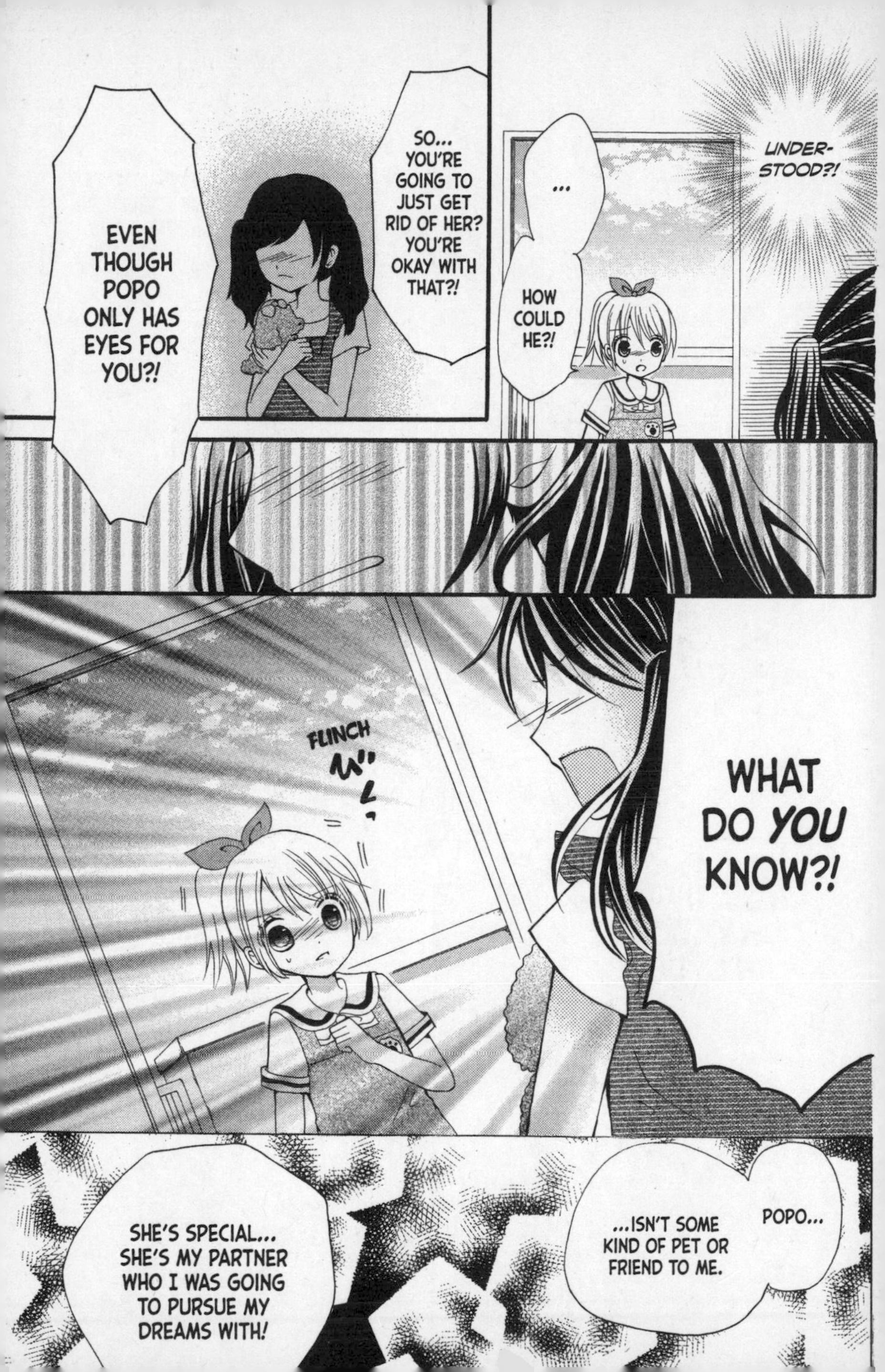
UNDER-STOOD?!
...
HOW COULD HE?!
SO... YOU'RE GOING TO JUST GET RID OF HER? YOU'RE OKAY WITH THAT?!
EVEN THOUGH POPO ONLY HAS EYES FOR YOU?!
WHAT DO YOU KNOW?!
FLINCH
POPO...
...ISN'T SOME KIND OF PET OR FRIEND TO ME.
SHE'S SPECIAL... SHE'S MY PARTNER WHO I WAS GOING TO PURSUE MY DREAMS WITH!

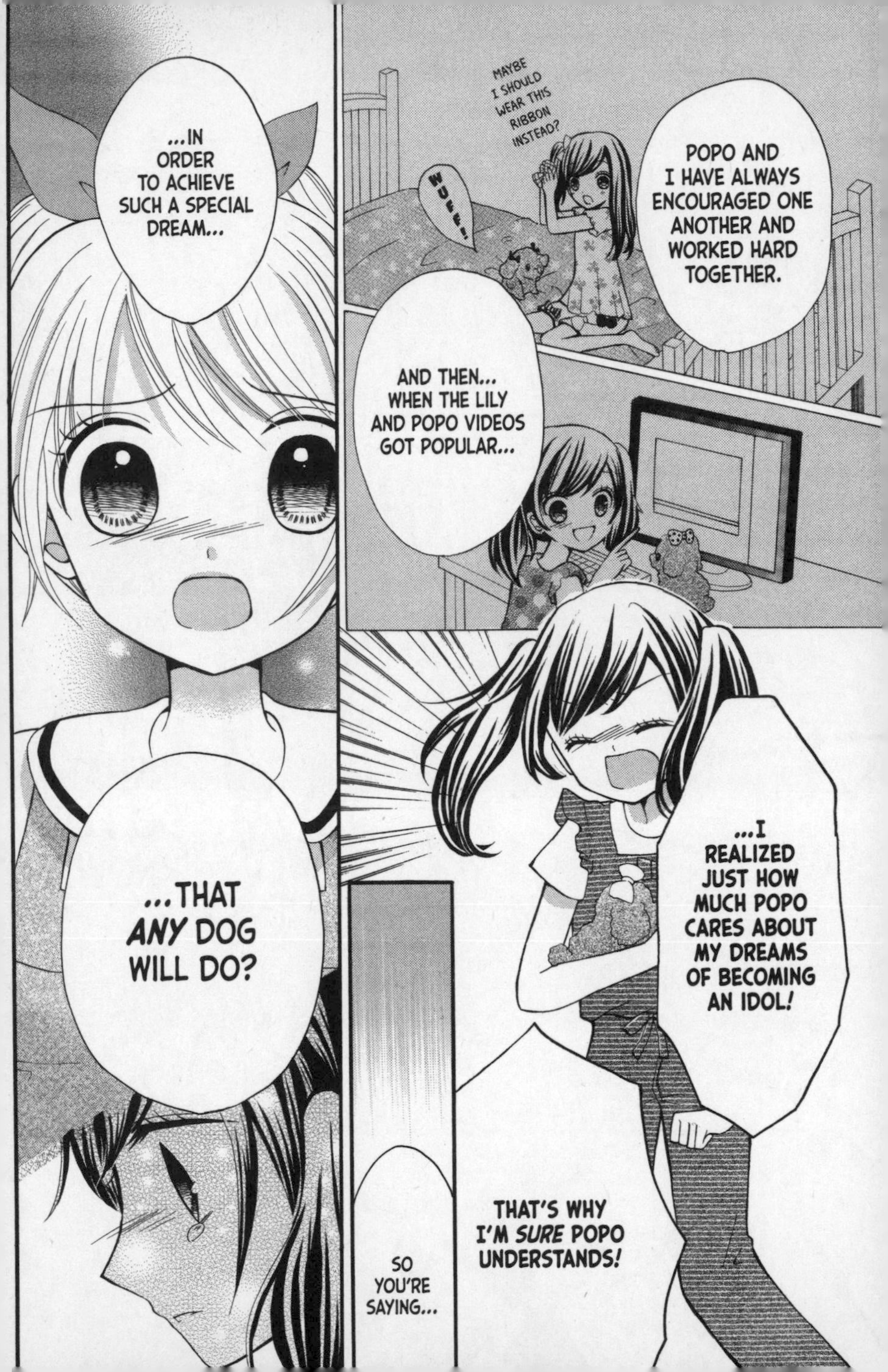
POPO AND I HAVE ALWAYS ENCOURAGED ONE ANOTHER AND WORKED HARD TOGETHER.
MAYBE I SHOULD WEAR THIS RIBBON INSTEAD?
WUFF!
AND THEN... WHEN THE LILY AND POPO VIDEOS GOT POPULAR...
...I REALIZED JUST HOW MUCH POPO CARES ABOUT MY DREAMS OF BECOMING AN IDOL!
THAT'S WHY I'M *SURE* POPO UNDERSTANDS!
SO YOU'RE SAYING...
...IN ORDER TO ACHIEVE SUCH A SPECIAL DREAM...
...THAT *ANY* DOG WILL DO?

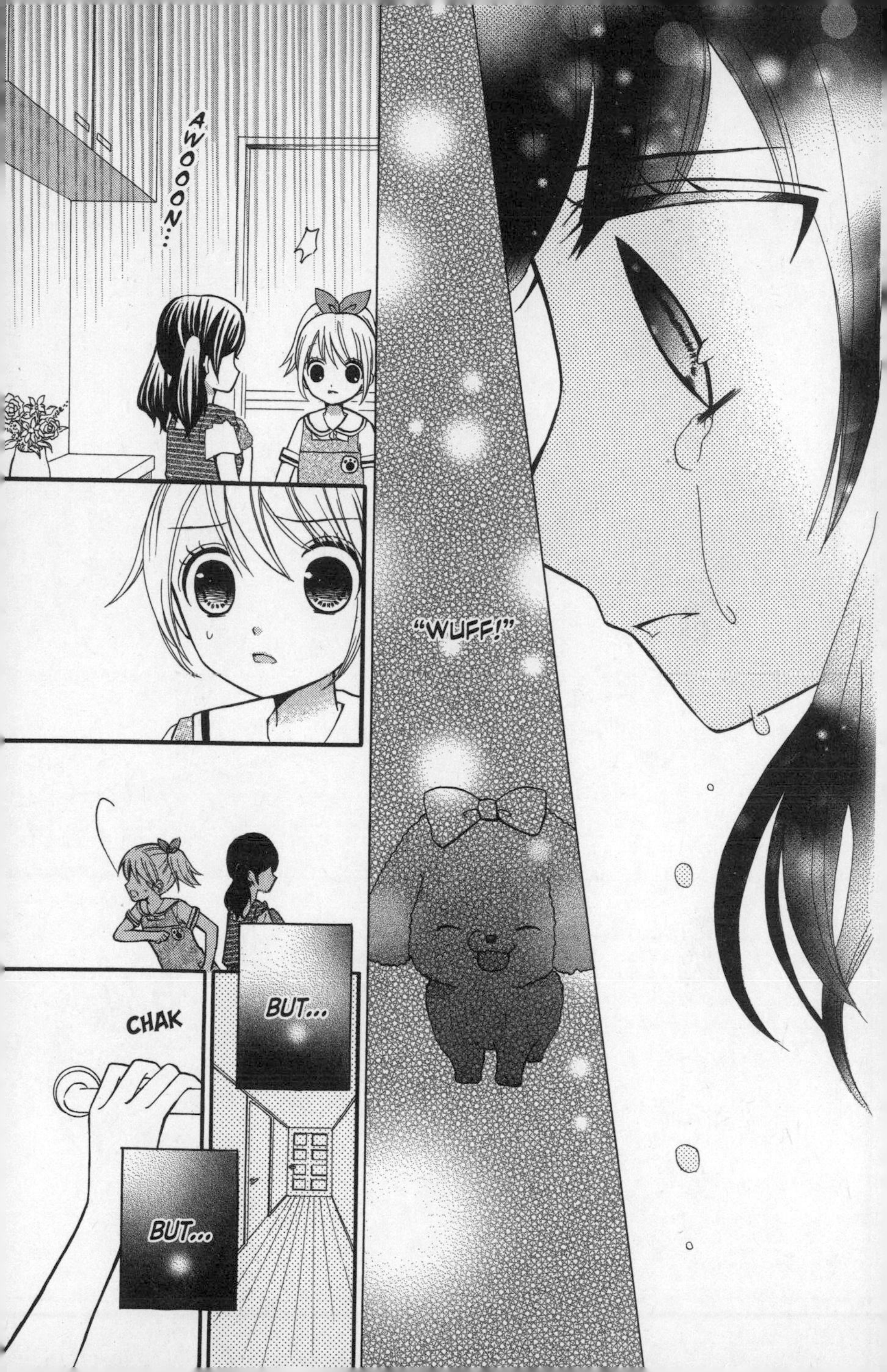
"WUFF!"
AWOOOON...
BUT...
CHAK
BUT...

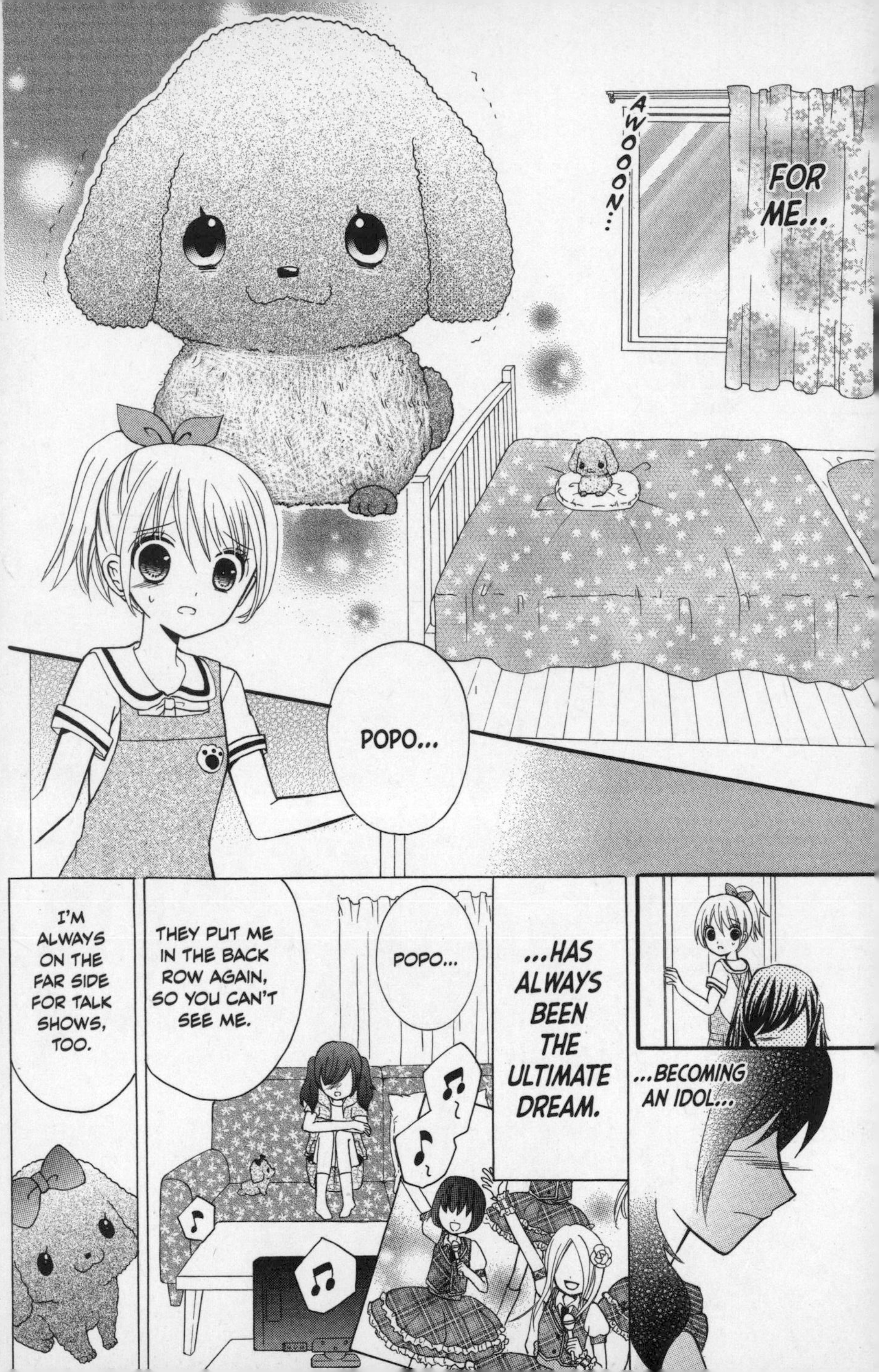
FOR ME...
AWOOON...
POPO...
...BECOMING AN IDOL...
...HAS ALWAYS BEEN THE ULTIMATE DREAM.
POPO...
THEY PUT ME IN THE BACK ROW AGAIN, SO YOU CAN'T SEE ME.
I'M ALWAYS ON THE FAR SIDE FOR TALK SHOWS, TOO.

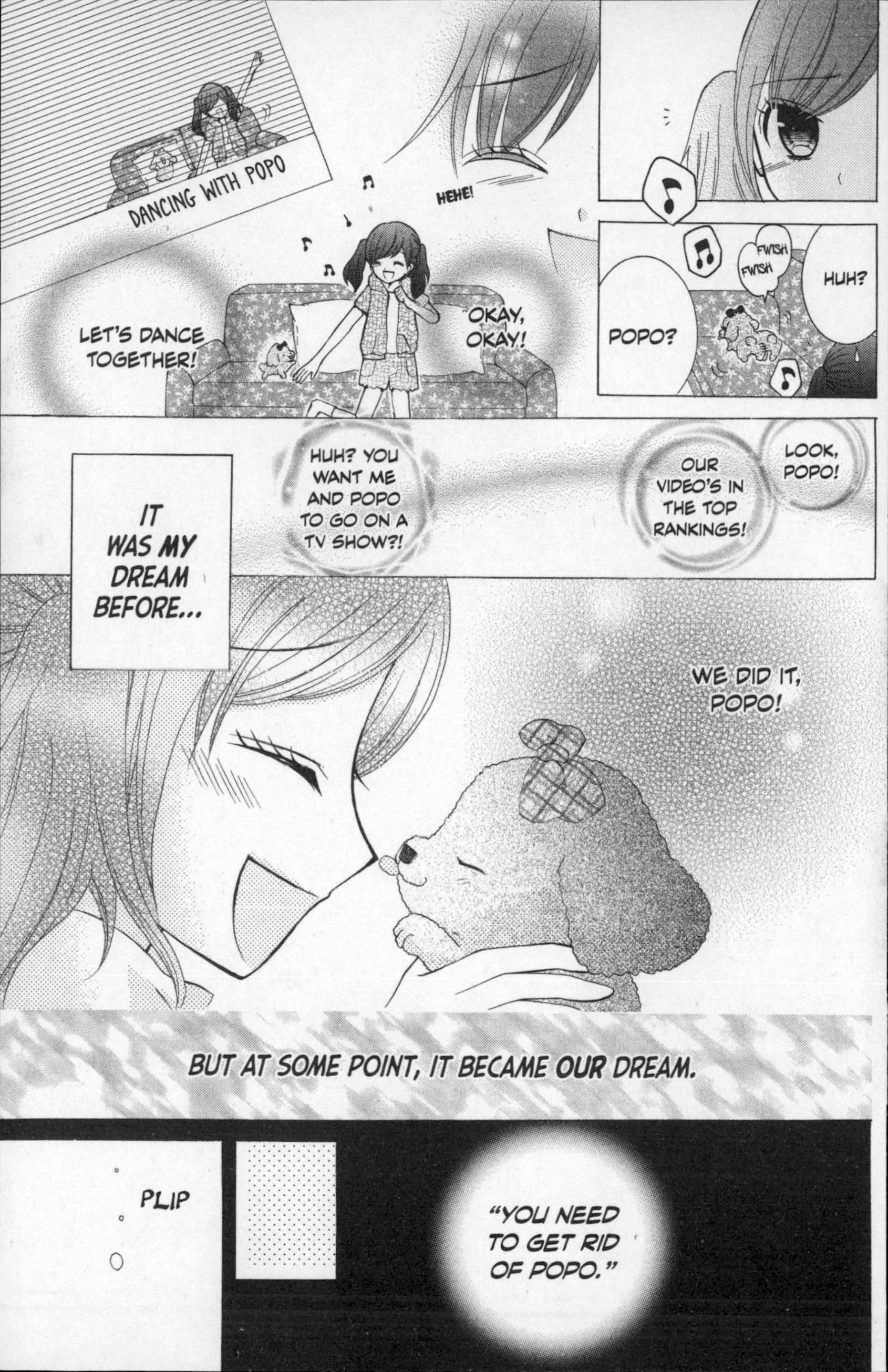
HUH?
FWISH
FWISH
POPO?
HEHE!
DANCING WITH POPO
OKAY, OKAY!
LET'S DANCE TOGETHER!
LOOK, POPO!
OUR VIDEO'S IN THE TOP RANKINGS!
HUH? YOU WANT ME AND POPO TO GO ON A TV SHOW?!
IT WAS MY DREAM BEFORE...
WE DID IT, POPO!
BUT AT SOME POINT, IT BECAME OUR DREAM.
"YOU NEED TO GET RID OF POPO."
PLIP

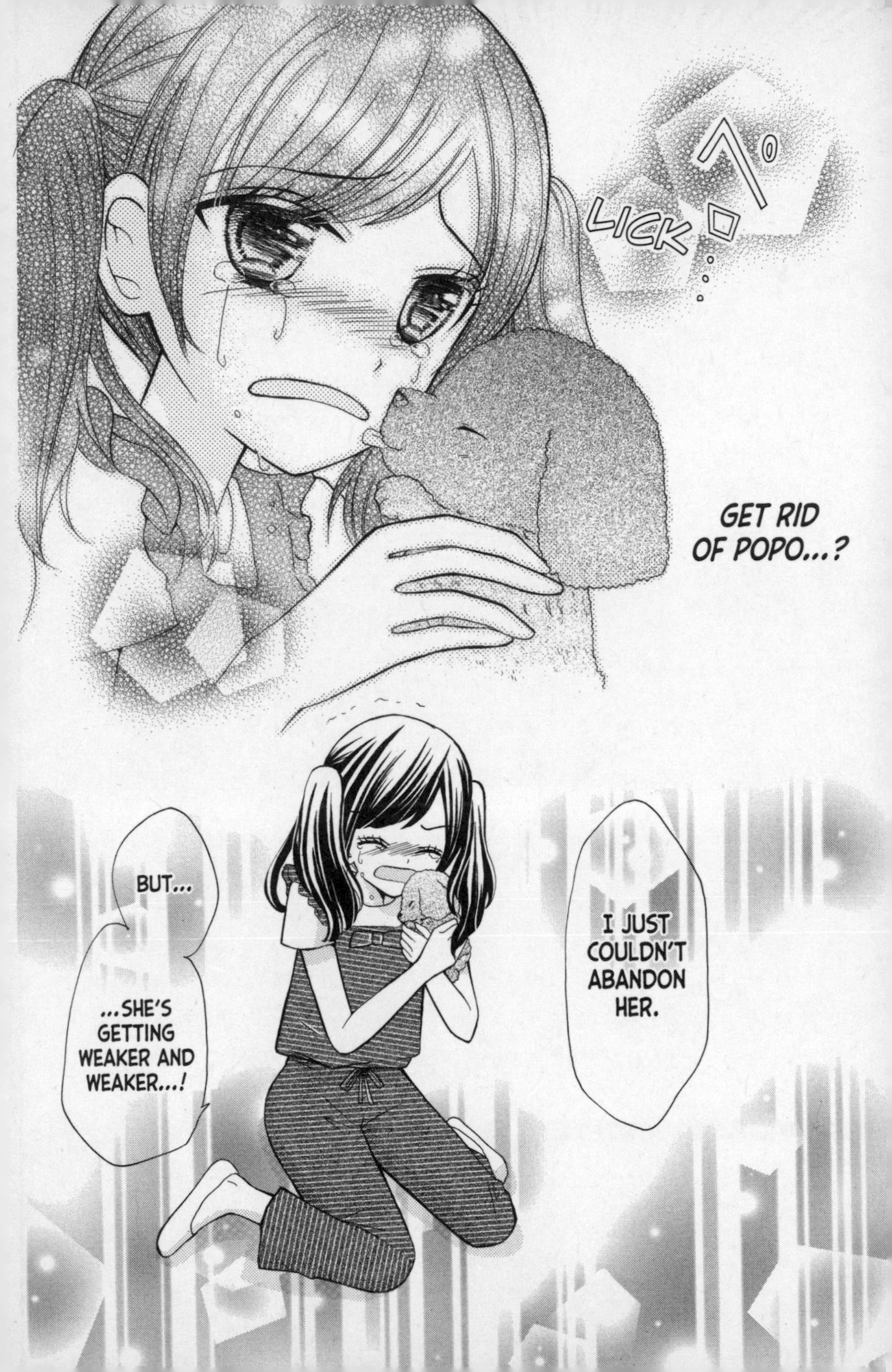
LICK
GET RID OF POPO...?
I JUST COULDN'T ABANDON HER.
BUT...
...SHE'S GETTING WEAKER AND WEAKER...!

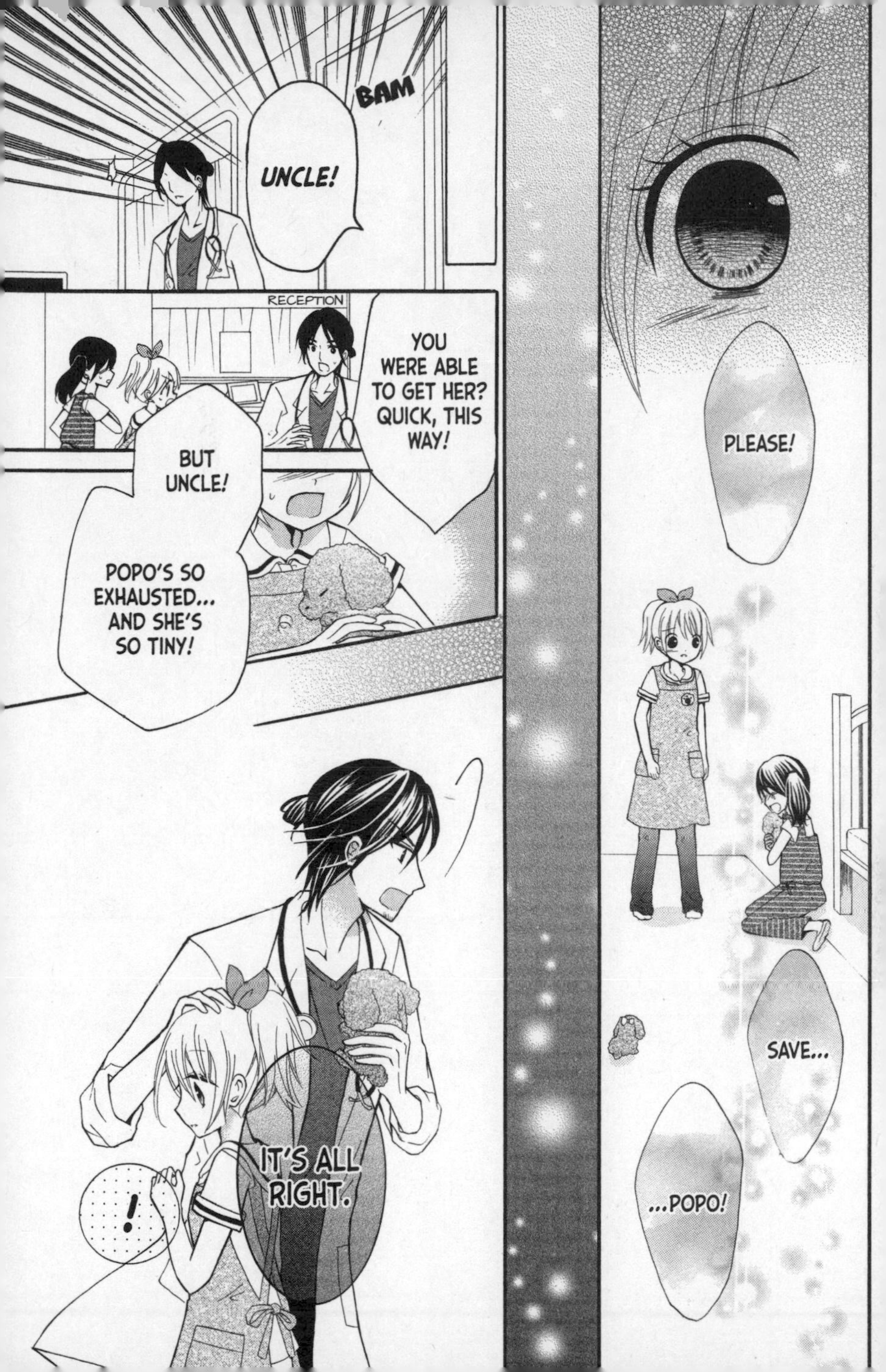
PLEASE!
SAVE...
...POPO!
BAM
UNCLE!
RECEPTION
YOU WERE ABLE TO GET HER? QUICK, THIS WAY!
BUT UNCLE!
POPO'S SO EXHAUSTED... AND SHE'S SO TINY!
IT'S ALL RIGHT.
!

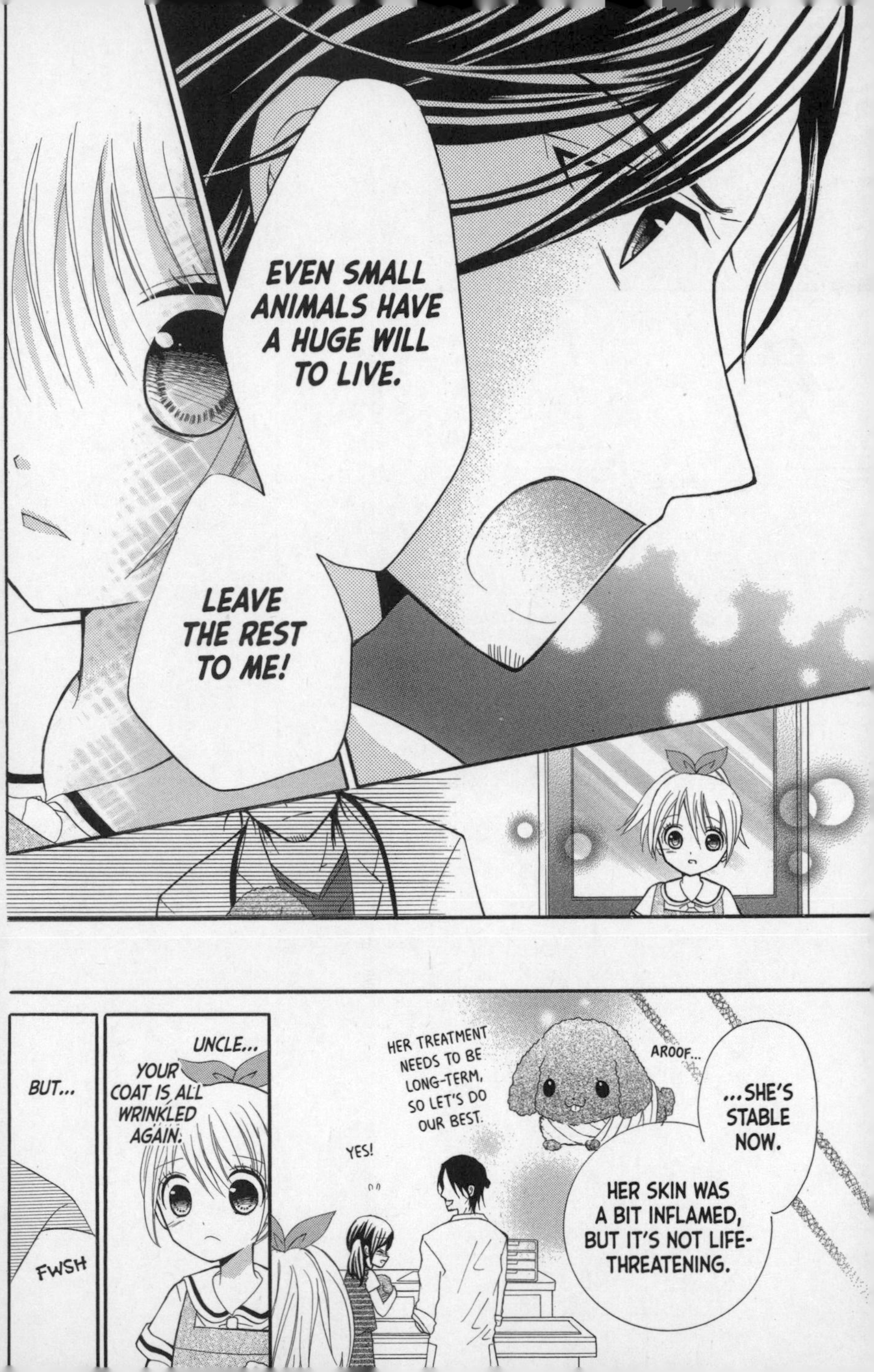
EVEN SMALL ANIMALS HAVE A HUGE WILL TO LIVE.
LEAVE THE REST TO ME!
...SHE'S STABLE NOW.
HER SKIN WAS A BIT INFLAMED, BUT IT'S NOT LIFE-THREATENING.
AROOF...
HER TREATMENT NEEDS TO BE LONG-TERM, SO LET'S DO OUR BEST.
YES!
UNCLE...
YOUR COAT IS ALL WRINKLED AGAIN.
BUT...
FWSH

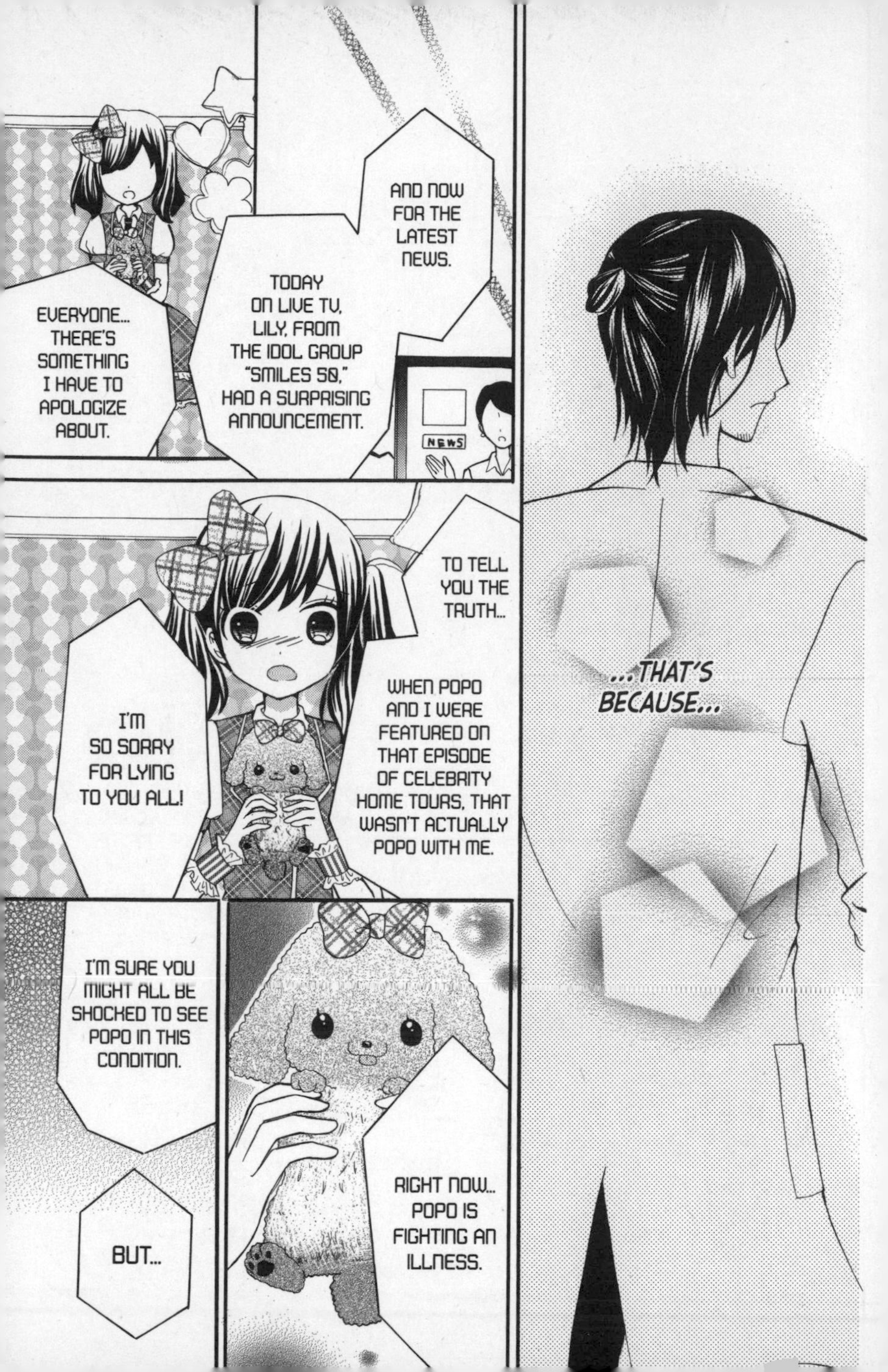
...THAT'S BECAUSE...
AND NOW FOR THE LATEST NEWS.
TODAY ON LIVE TV, LILY, FROM THE IDOL GROUP "SMILES 50," HAD A SURPRISING ANNOUNCEMENT.
NEWS
EVERYONE... THERE'S SOMETHING I HAVE TO APOLOGIZE ABOUT.
TO TELL YOU THE TRUTH...
WHEN POPO AND I WERE FEATURED ON THAT EPISODE OF CELEBRITY HOME TOURS, THAT WASN'T ACTUALLY POPO WITH ME.
I'M SO SORRY FOR LYING TO YOU ALL!
RIGHT NOW... POPO IS FIGHTING AN ILLNESS.
I'M SURE YOU MIGHT ALL BE SHOCKED TO SEE POPO IN THIS CONDITION.
BUT...

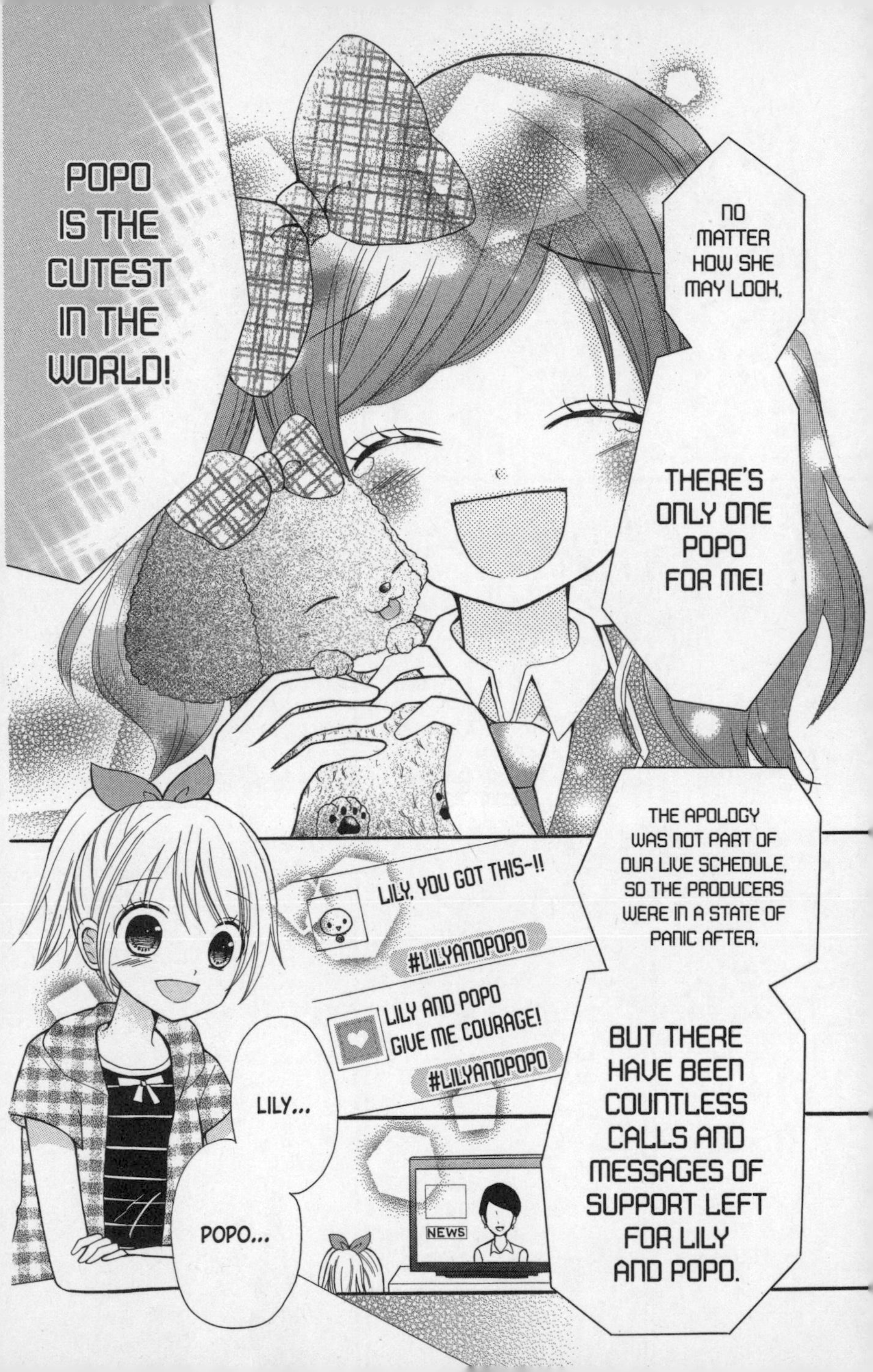
NO MATTER HOW SHE MAY LOOK,
THERE'S ONLY ONE POPO FOR ME!
POPO IS THE CUTEST IN THE WORLD!
THE APOLOGY WAS NOT PART OF OUR LIVE SCHEDULE, SO THE PRODUCERS WERE IN A STATE OF PANIC AFTER,
BUT THERE HAVE BEEN COUNTLESS CALLS AND MESSAGES OF SUPPORT LEFT FOR LILY AND POPO.
LILY, YOU GOT THIS-!!
#LILYANDPOPO
LILY AND POPO GIVE ME COURAGE!
#LILYANDPOPO
NEWS
LILY...
POPO...

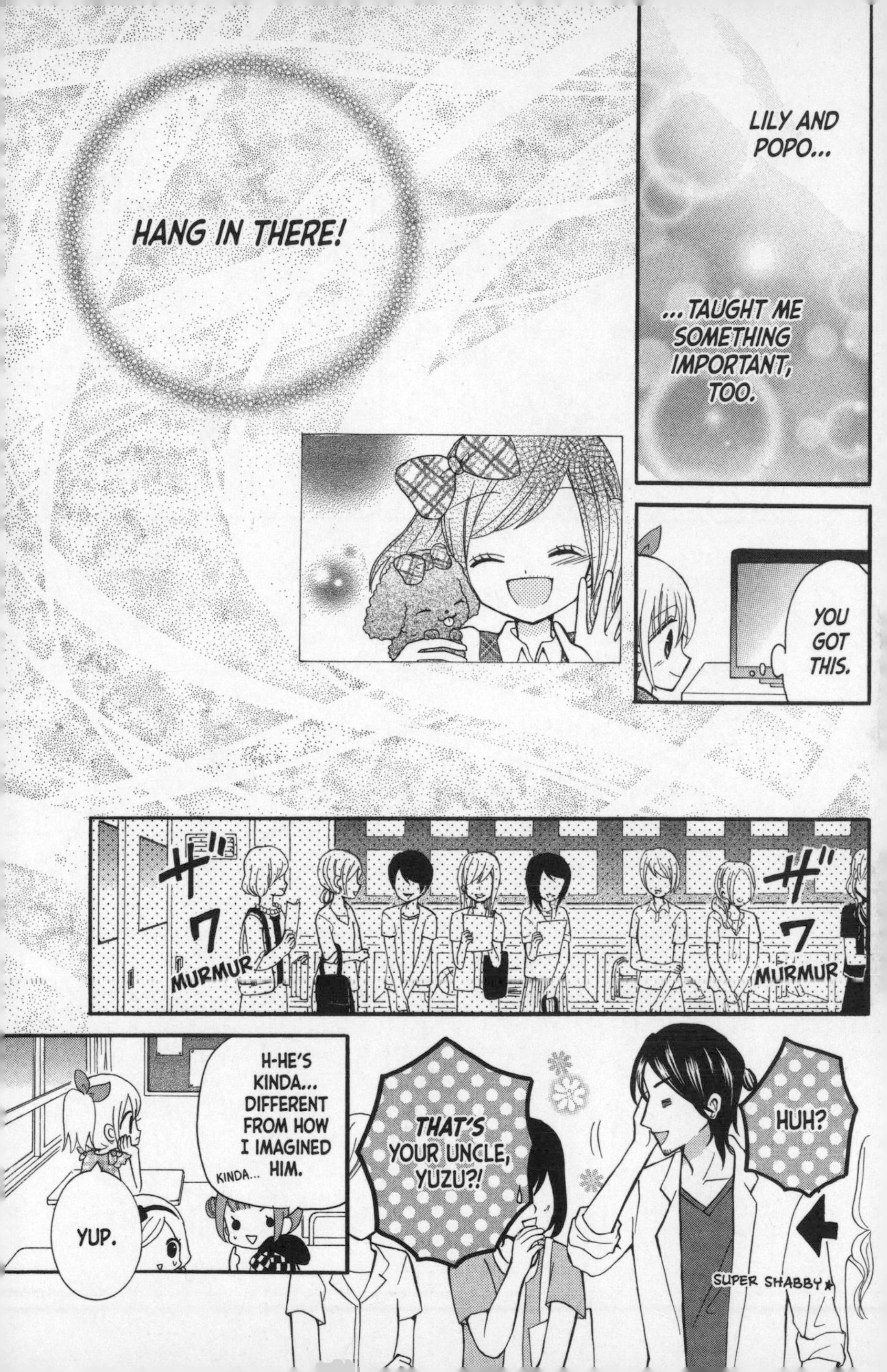
LILY AND POPO...
...TAUGHT ME SOMETHING IMPORTANT, TOO.
YOU GOT THIS.
HANG IN THERE!
MURMUR
MURMUR
HUH?
SUPER SHABBY★
THAT'S YOUR UNCLE, YUZU?!
H-HE'S KINDA... DIFFERENT FROM HOW I IMAGINED HIM.
KINDA...
YUP.

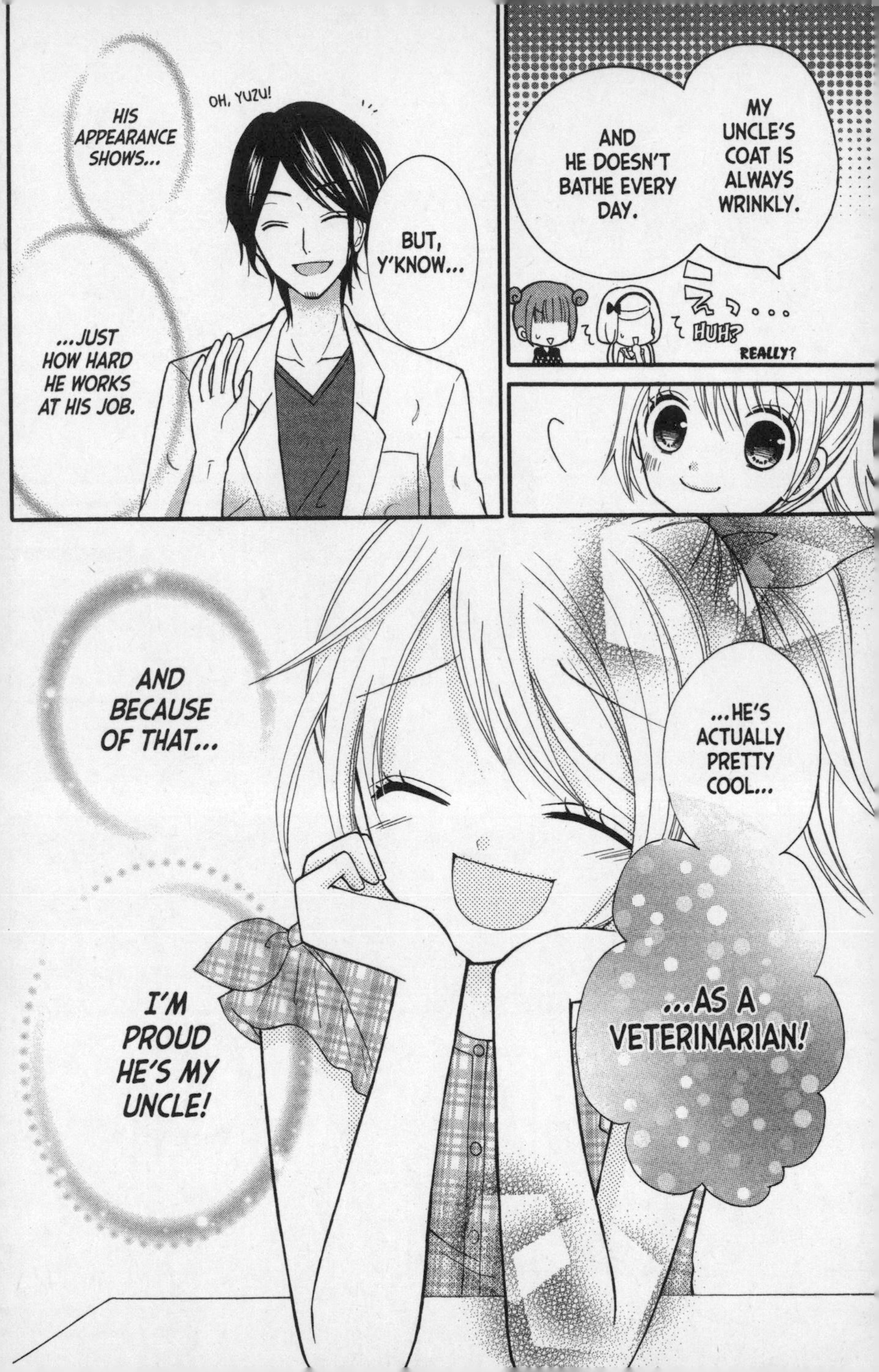
MY UNCLE'S COAT IS ALWAYS WRINKLY.
AND HE DOESN'T BATHE EVERY DAY.
HUH?
REALLY?
OH, YUZU!
BUT, Y'KNOW...
HIS APPEARANCE SHOWS...
...JUST HOW HARD HE WORKS AT HIS JOB.
...HE'S ACTUALLY PRETTY COOL...
...AS A VETERINARIAN!
AND BECAUSE OF THAT...
I'M PROUD HE'S MY UNCLE!

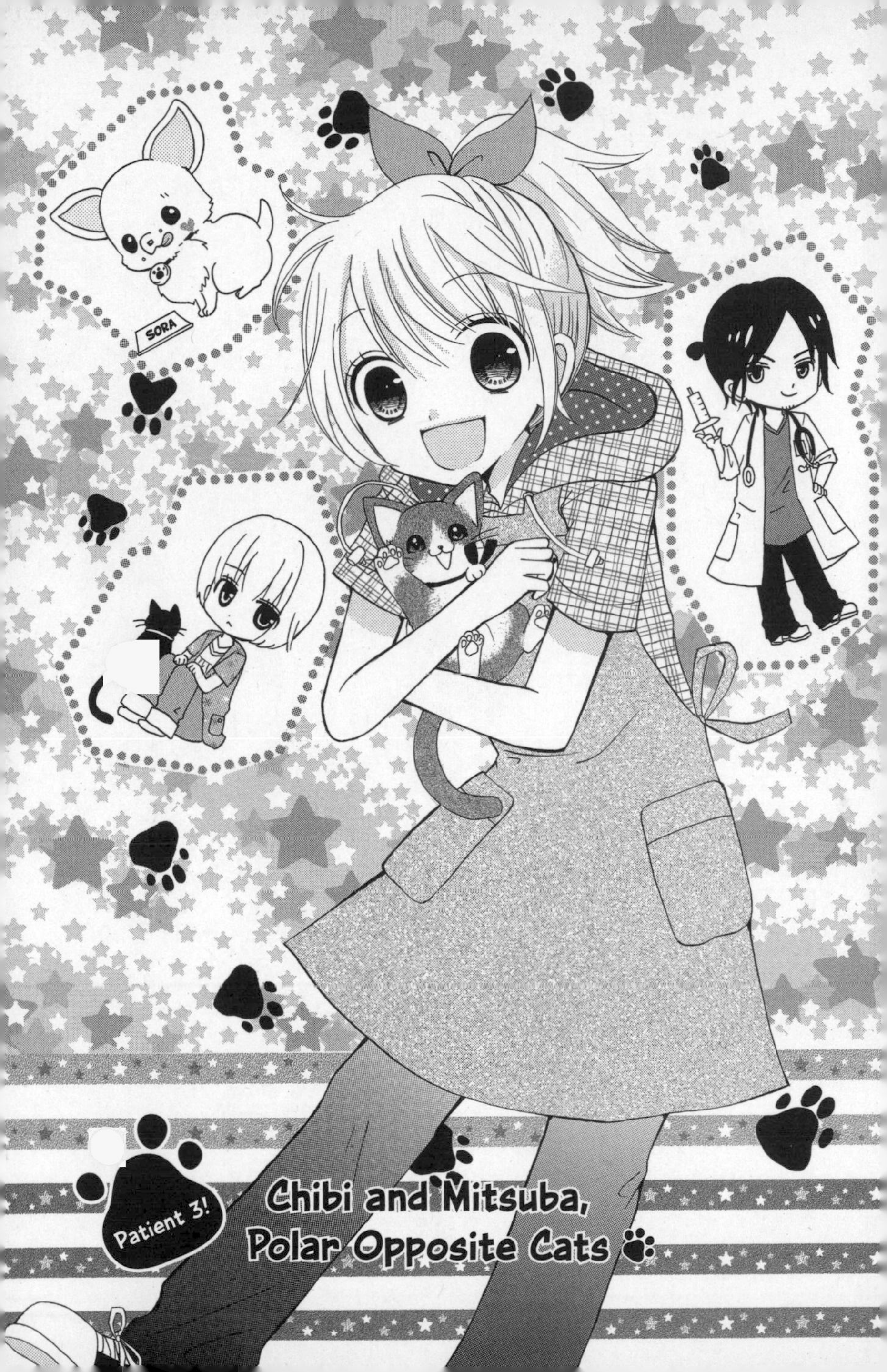
SORA
Patient 3!
Chibi and Mitsuba, Polar Opposite Cats

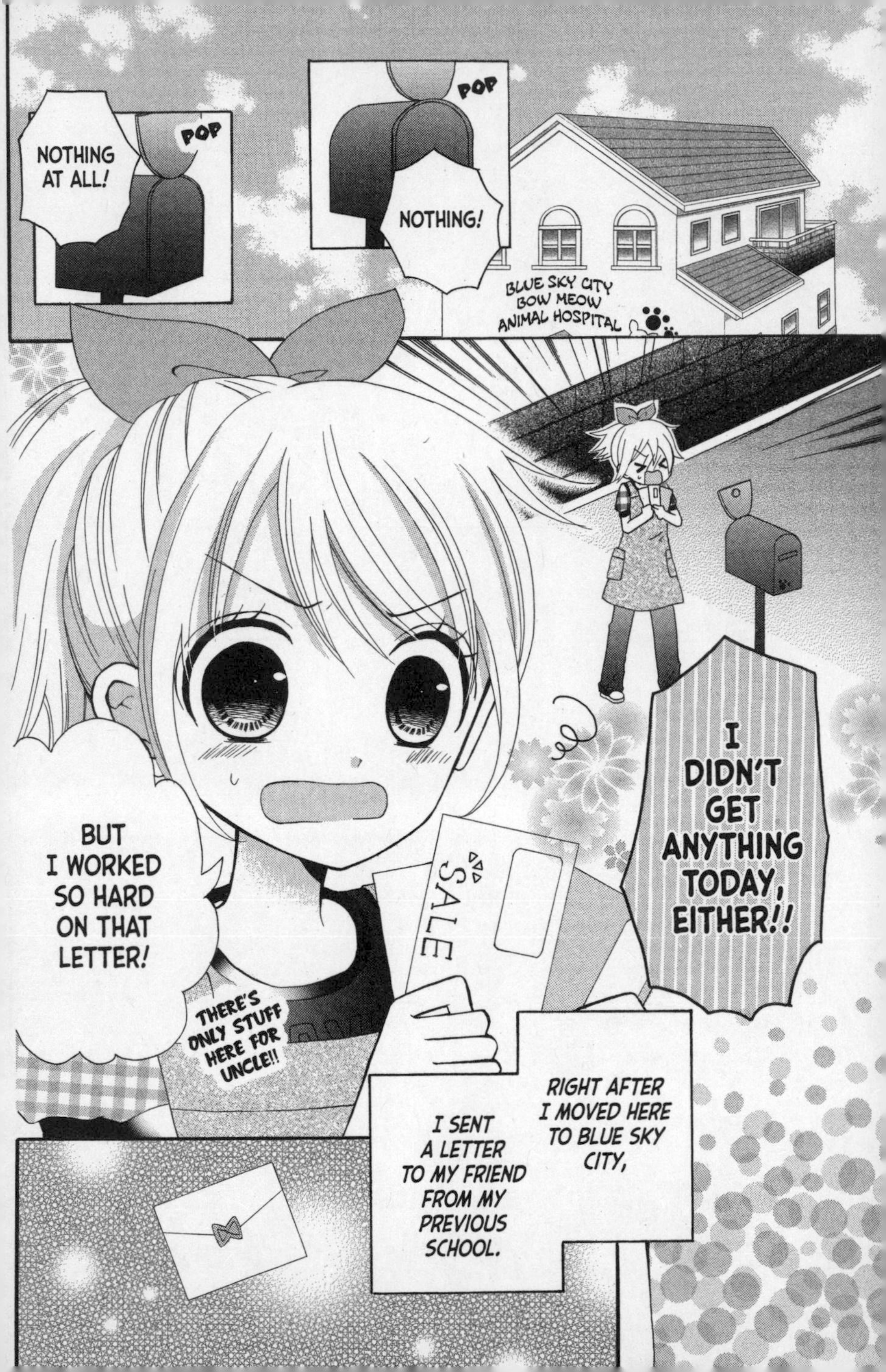
BLUE SKY CITY BOW MEOW ANIMAL HOSPITAL
POP
NOTHING!
POP
NOTHING AT ALL!
I DIDN'T GET ANYTHING TODAY, EITHER!!
BUT I WORKED SO HARD ON THAT LETTER!
SALE
THERE'S ONLY STUFF HERE FOR UNCLE!!
RIGHT AFTER I MOVED HERE TO BLUE SKY CITY,
I SENT A LETTER TO MY FRIEND FROM MY PREVIOUS SCHOOL.

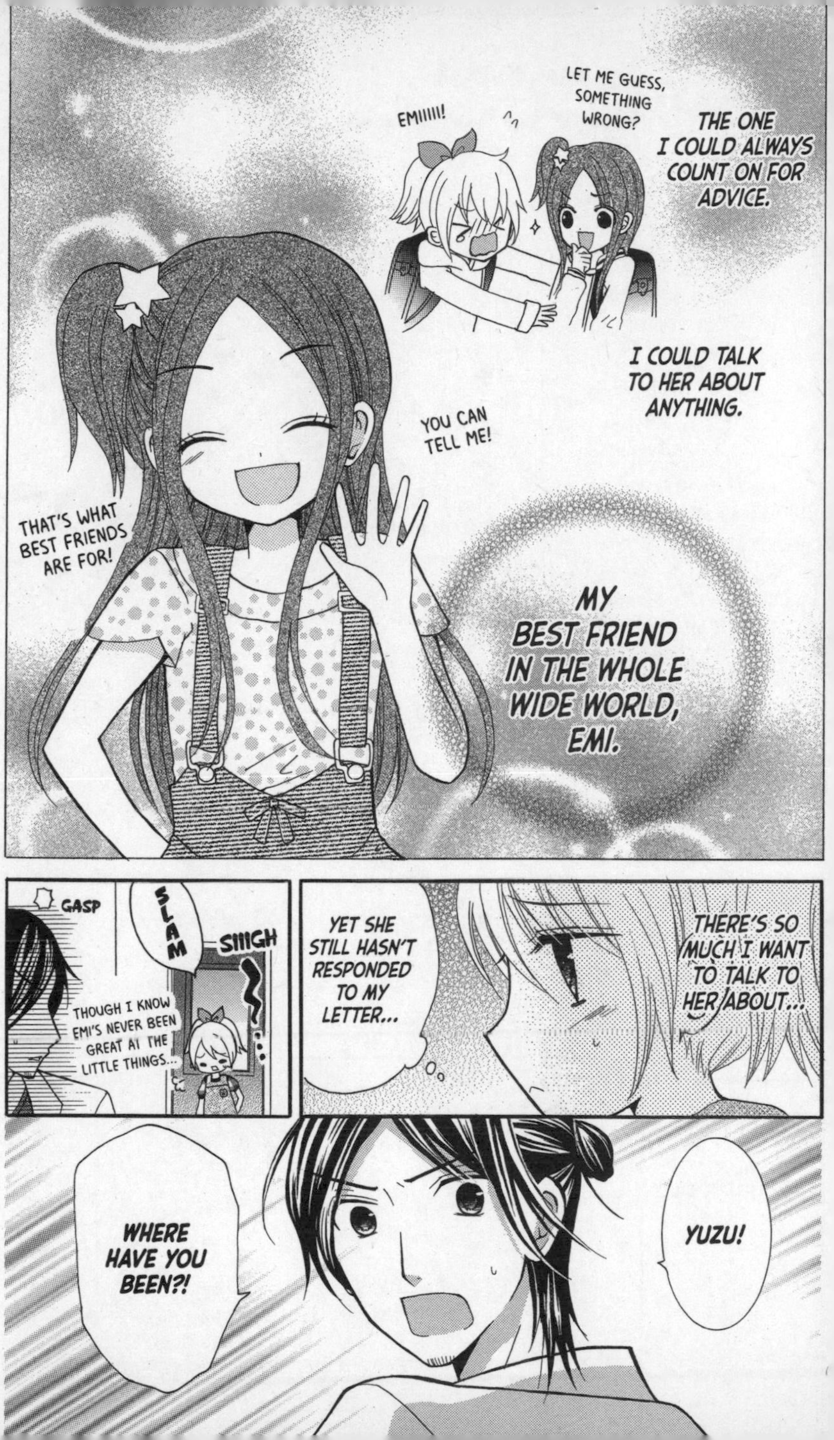
THE ONE I COULD ALWAYS COUNT ON FOR ADVICE.
EMIIIII!
LET ME GUESS, SOMETHING WRONG?
I COULD TALK TO HER ABOUT ANYTHING.
YOU CAN TELL ME!
THAT'S WHAT BEST FRIENDS ARE FOR!
MY BEST FRIEND IN THE WHOLE WIDE WORLD, EMI.
THERE'S SO MUCH I WANT TO TALK TO HER ABOUT...
YET SHE STILL HASN'T RESPONDED TO MY LETTER...
SLAM
SIIIGH
GASP
THOUGH I KNOW EMI'S NEVER BEEN GREAT AT THE LITTLE THINGS...
YUZU!
WHERE HAVE YOU BEEN?!

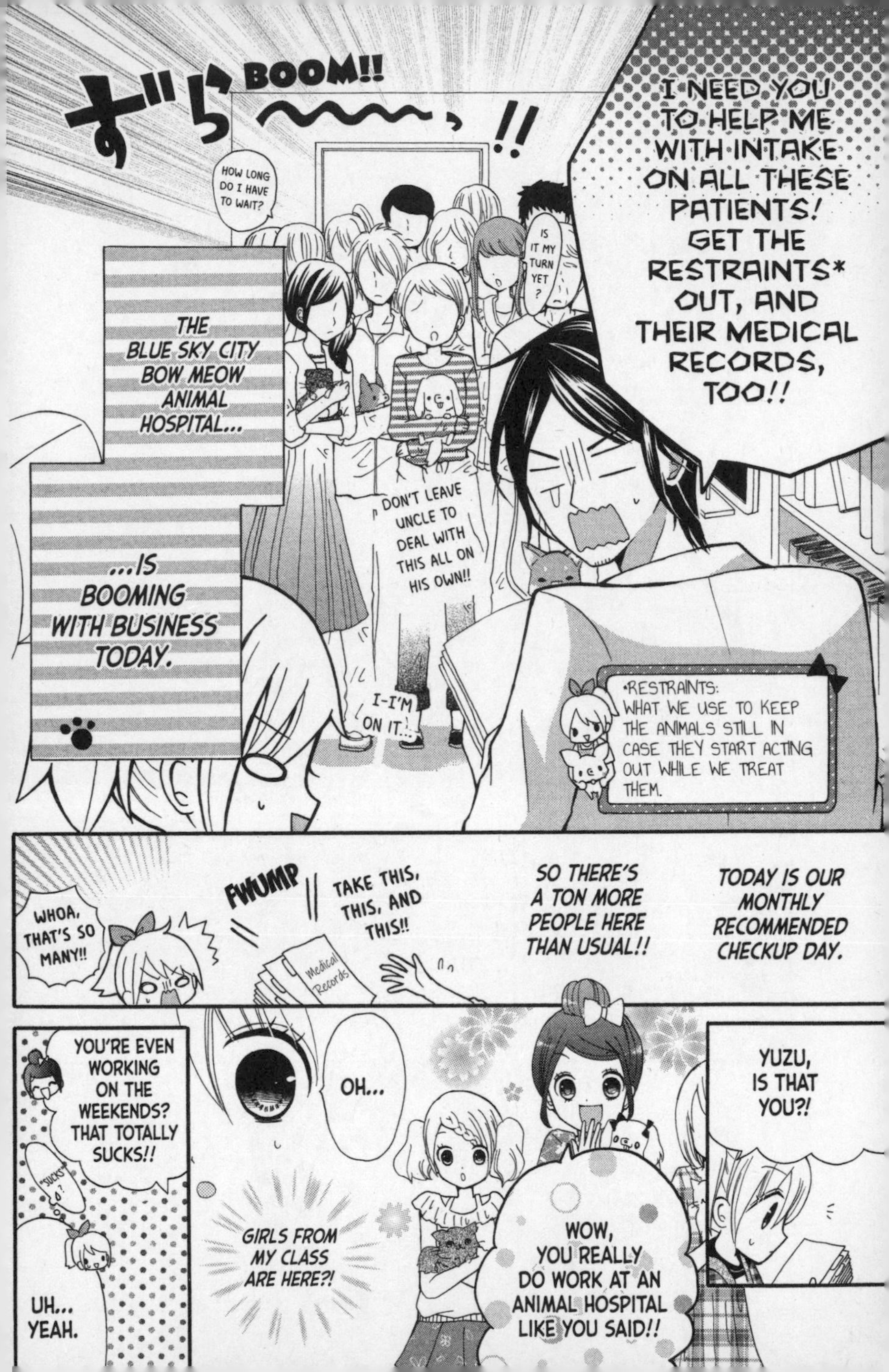

I NEED YOU TO HELP ME WITH INTAKE ON ALL THESE PATIENTS! GET THE RESTRAINTS* OUT, AND THEIR MEDICAL RECORDS, TOO!!
ずら〜〜〜、!!
BOOM!!
IS IT MY TURN YET?
HOW LONG DO I HAVE TO WAIT?
THE BLUE SKY CITY BOW MEOW ANIMAL HOSPITAL...
DON'T LEAVE UNCLE TO DEAL WITH THIS ALL ON HIS OWN!!
...IS BOOMING WITH BUSINESS TODAY.
*RESTRAINTS: WHAT WE USE TO KEEP THE ANIMALS STILL IN CASE THEY START ACTING OUT WHILE WE TREAT THEM.
I-I'M ON IT...
TODAY IS OUR MONTHLY RECOMMENDED CHECKUP DAY.
SO THERE'S A TON MORE PEOPLE HERE THAN USUAL!!
TAKE THIS, THIS, AND THIS!!
FWUMP
Medical Records
WHOA, THAT'S SO MANY!!
YUZU, IS THAT YOU?!
WOW, YOU REALLY DO WORK AT AN ANIMAL HOSPITAL LIKE YOU SAID!!
OH...
GIRLS FROM MY CLASS ARE HERE?!
YOU'RE EVEN WORKING ON THE WEEKENDS? THAT TOTALLY SUCKS!!
"SUCKS"?
UH... YEAH.

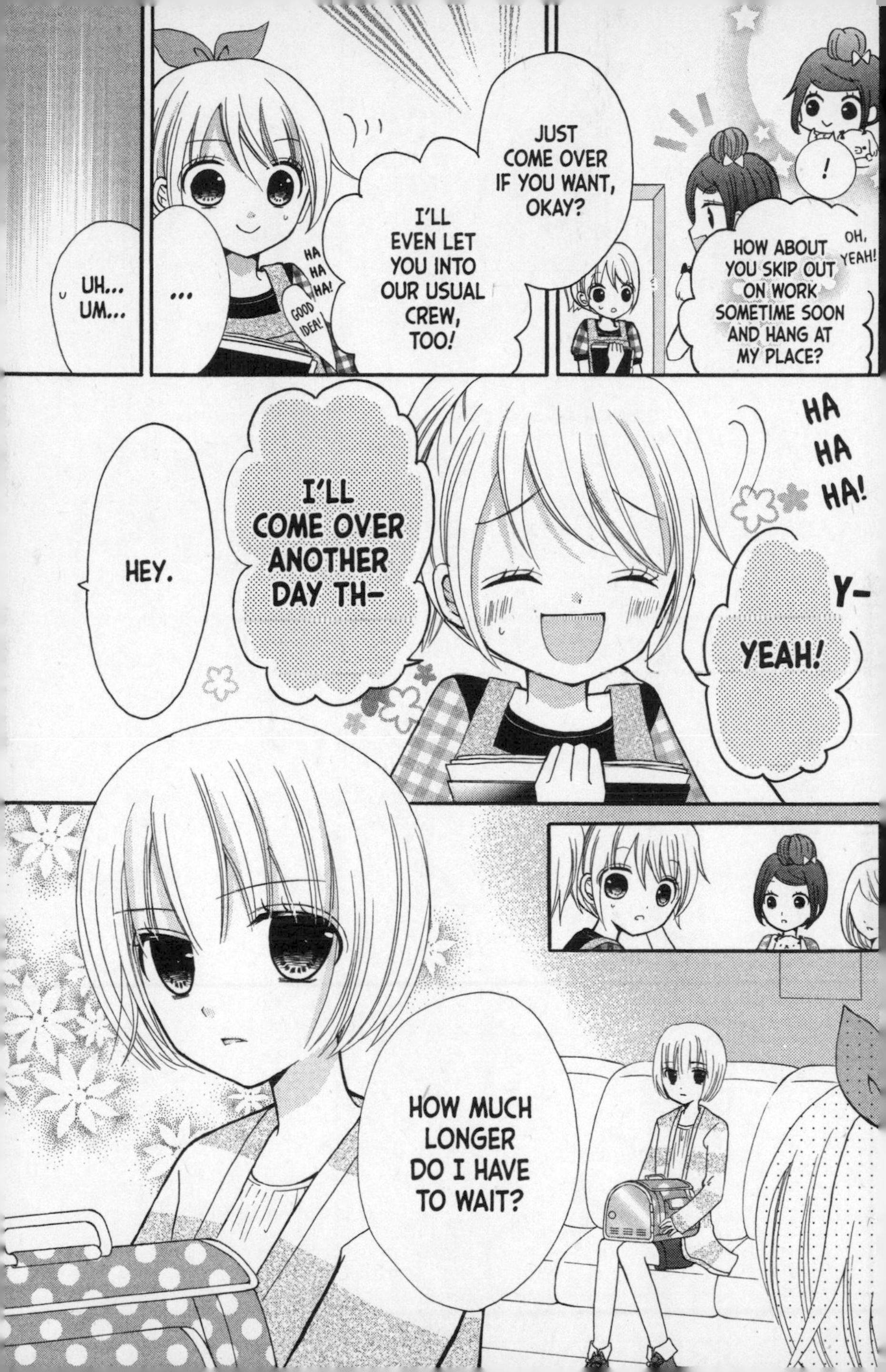
!
OH, YEAH!
HOW ABOUT YOU SKIP OUT ON WORK SOMETIME SOON AND HANG AT MY PLACE?
JUST COME OVER IF YOU WANT, OKAY?
I'LL EVEN LET YOU INTO OUR USUAL CREW, TOO!
HA HA HA!
GOOD IDEA!
...
UH... UM...
HA HA HA!
Y-
YEAH!
I'LL COME OVER ANOTHER DAY TH-
HEY.
HOW MUCH LONGER DO I HAVE TO WAIT?

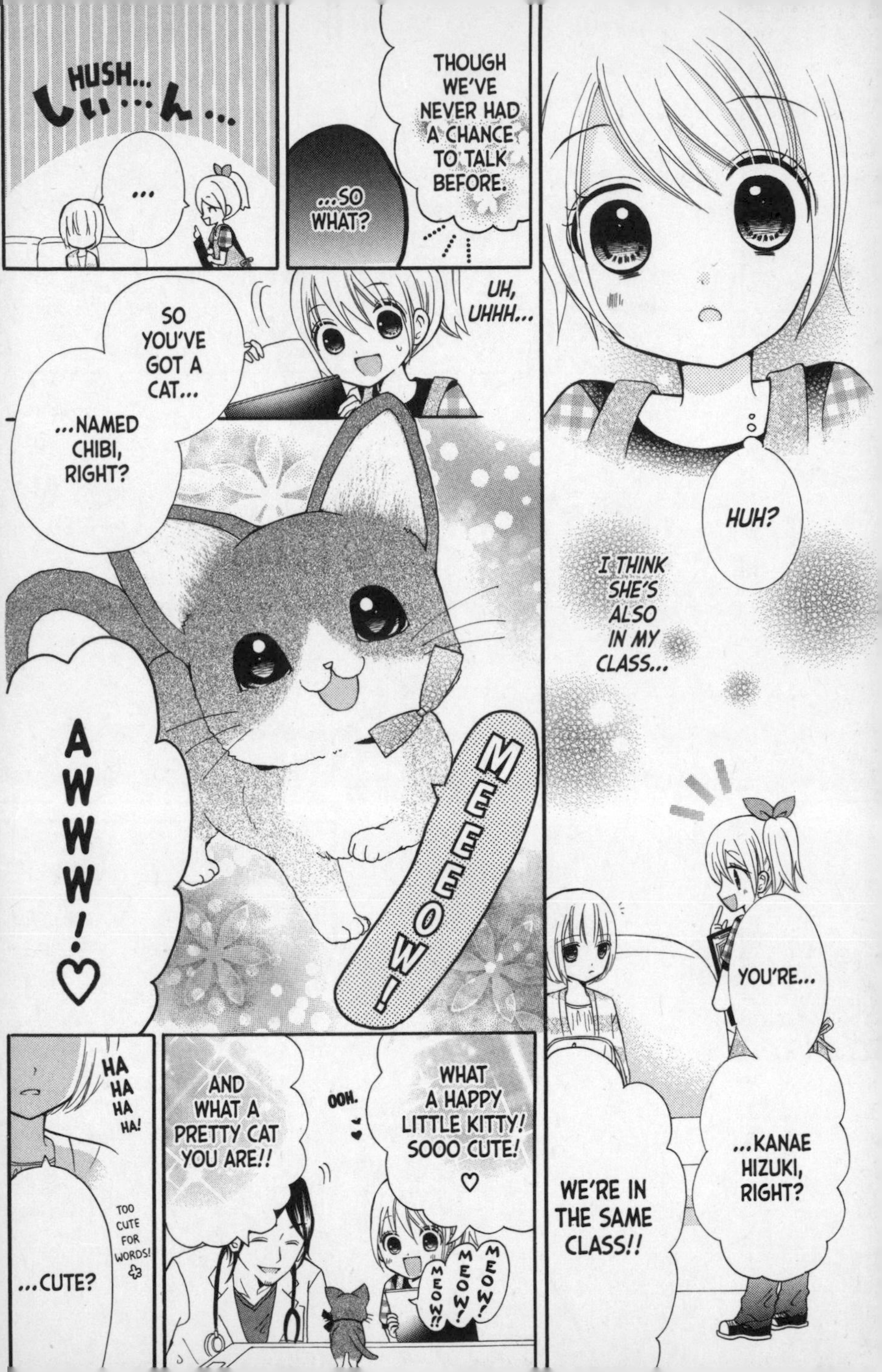
HUH?
I THINK SHE'S ALSO IN MY CLASS...
YOU'RE...
...KANAE HIZUKI, RIGHT?
WE'RE IN THE SAME CLASS!!
THOUGH WE'VE NEVER HAD A CHANCE TO TALK BEFORE.
...SO WHAT?
HUSH... しぃ…ん…
...
UH, UHHH...
SO YOU'VE GOT A CAT...
...NAMED CHIBI, RIGHT?
MEEEOW!
AWWW!♡
WHAT A HAPPY LITTLE KITTY! SOOO CUTE! ♡
MEOW! MEOW! MEOW!!
OOH.
AND WHAT A PRETTY CAT YOU ARE!!
HA HA HA HA!
TOO CUTE FOR WORDS!
...CUTE?

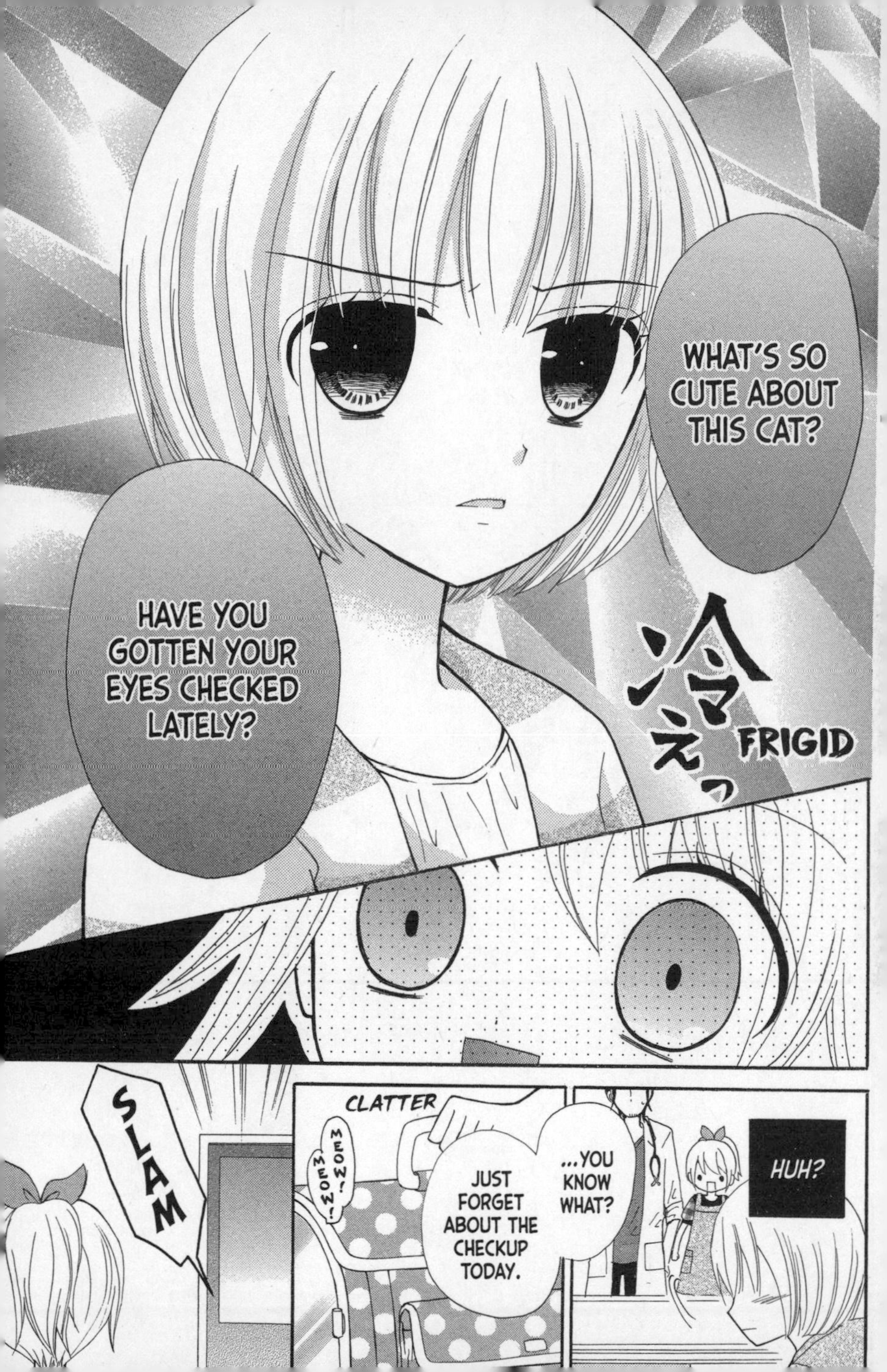
WHAT'S SO CUTE ABOUT THIS CAT?
HAVE YOU GOTTEN YOUR EYES CHECKED LATELY?
冷えっ
FRIGID
HUH?
...YOU KNOW WHAT?
JUST FORGET ABOUT THE CHECKUP TODAY.
CLATTER
MEOW! MEOW!
SLAM

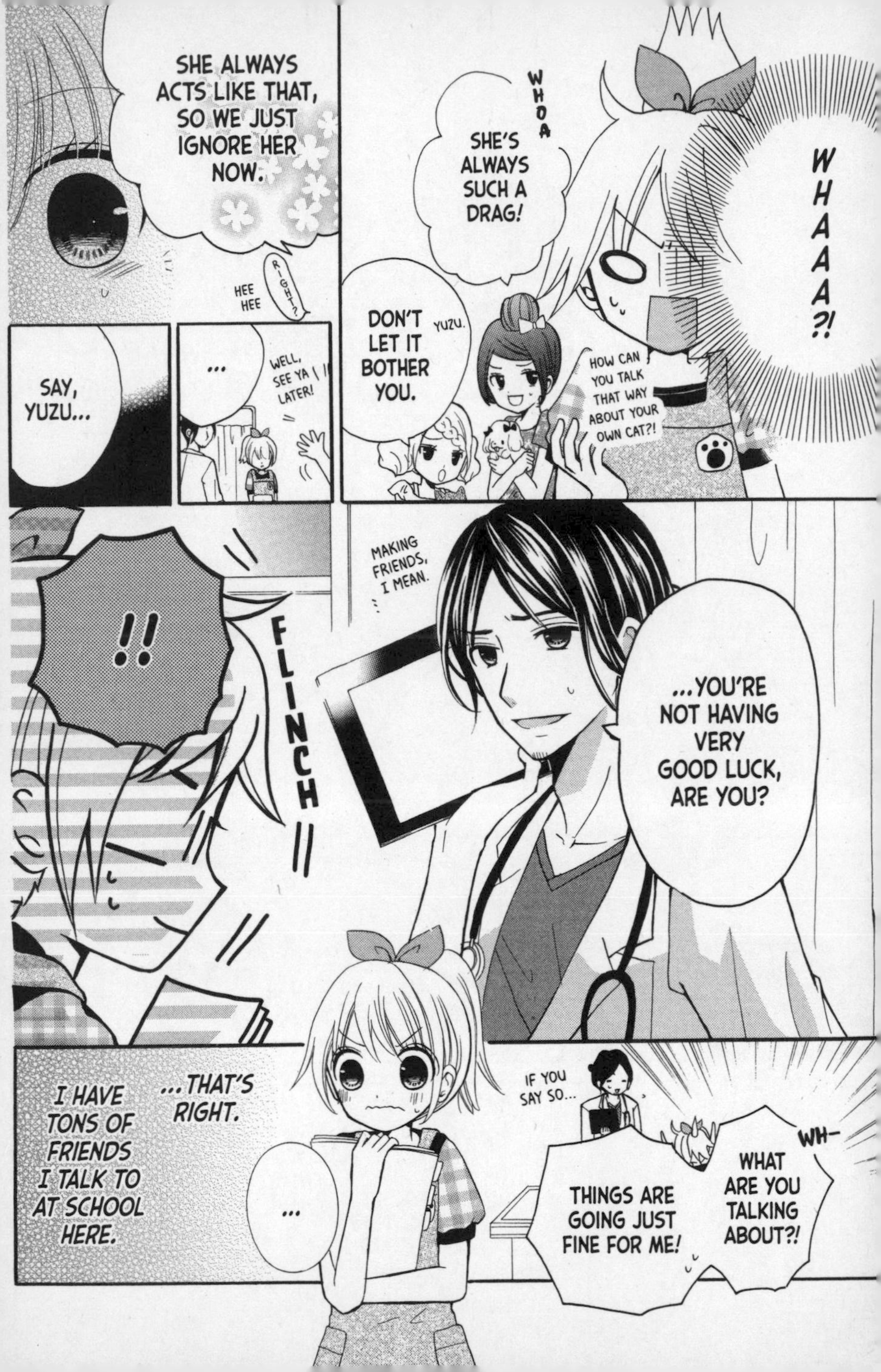
WHAAAA?!
WHOA
SHE'S ALWAYS SUCH A DRAG!
HOW CAN YOU TALK THAT WAY ABOUT YOUR OWN CAT?!
YUZU.
DON'T LET IT BOTHER YOU.
SHE ALWAYS ACTS LIKE THAT, SO WE JUST IGNORE HER NOW.
RIGHT?
HEE HEE
WELL, SEE YA LATER!
...
SAY, YUZU...
...YOU'RE NOT HAVING VERY GOOD LUCK, ARE YOU?
MAKING FRIENDS, I MEAN.
FLINCH
!!
WH-
WHAT ARE YOU TALKING ABOUT?!
THINGS ARE GOING JUST FINE FOR ME!
IF YOU SAY SO...
...
...THAT'S RIGHT.
I HAVE TONS OF FRIENDS I TALK TO AT SCHOOL HERE.

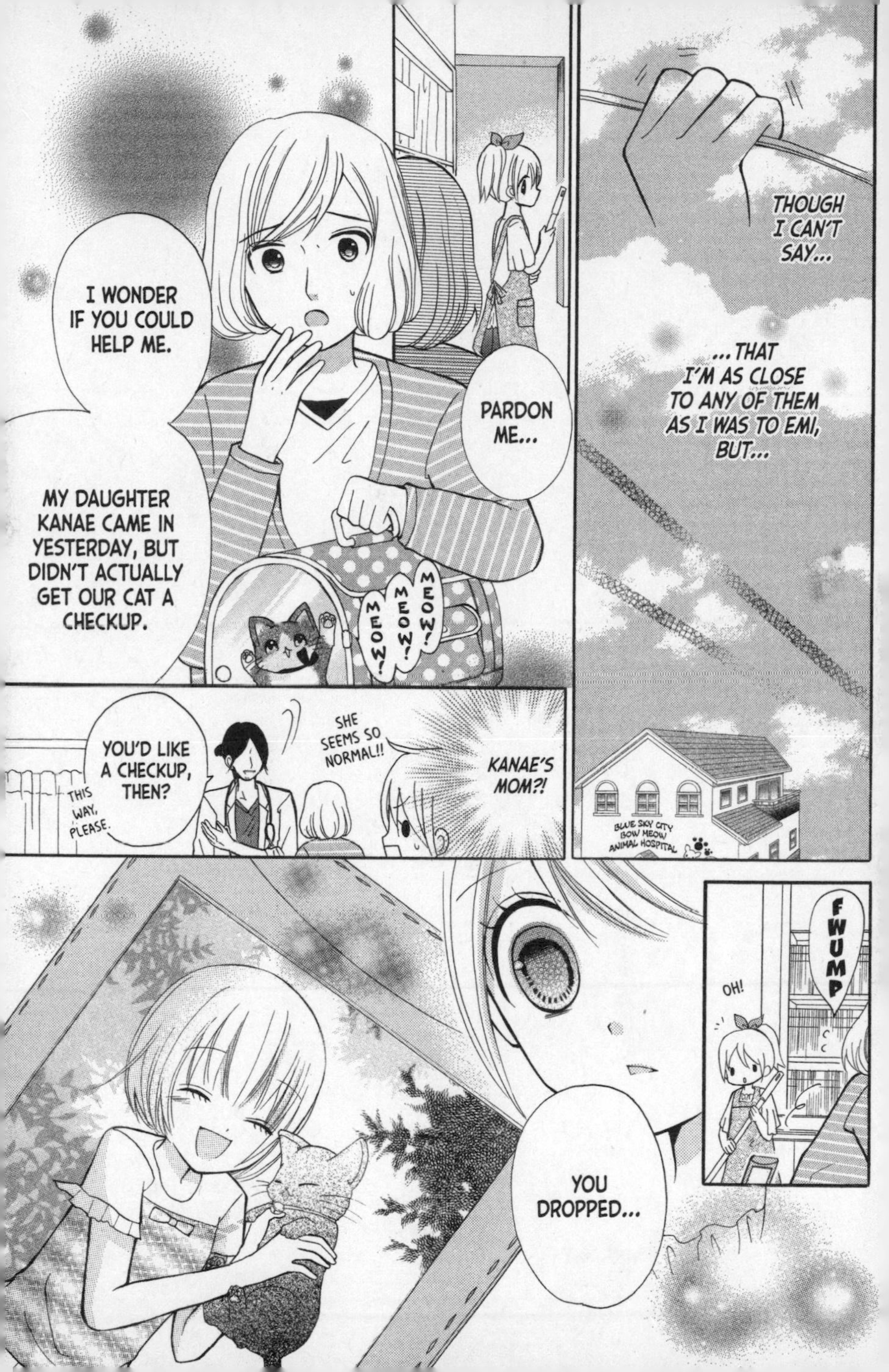
THOUGH I CAN'T SAY...
...THAT I'M AS CLOSE TO ANY OF THEM AS I WAS TO EMI, BUT...
BLUE SKY CITY BOW MEOW ANIMAL HOSPITAL
PARDON ME...
I WONDER IF YOU COULD HELP ME.
MEOW! MEOW! MEOW!
MY DAUGHTER KANAE CAME IN YESTERDAY, BUT DIDN'T ACTUALLY GET OUR CAT A CHECKUP.
KANAE'S MOM?!
SHE SEEMS SO NORMAL!!
YOU'D LIKE A CHECKUP, THEN?
THIS WAY, PLEASE.
FWUMP
OH!
YOU DROPPED...

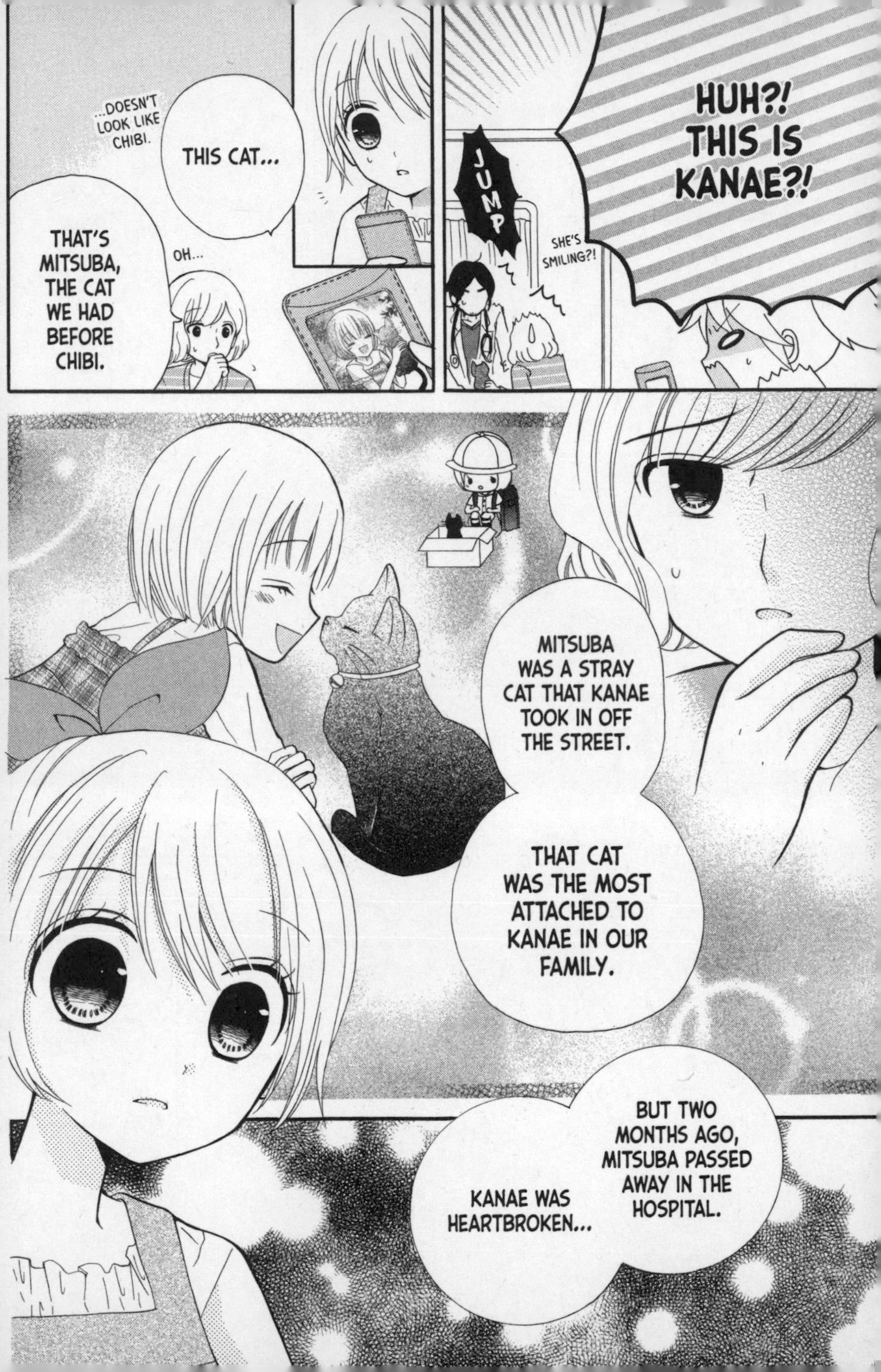
HUH?! THIS IS KANAE?!
JUMP
SHE'S SMILING?!
THIS CAT...
...DOESN'T LOOK LIKE CHIBI.
THAT'S MITSUBA, THE CAT WE HAD BEFORE CHIBI.
OH...
MITSUBA WAS A STRAY CAT THAT KANAE TOOK IN OFF THE STREET.
THAT CAT WAS THE MOST ATTACHED TO KANAE IN OUR FAMILY.
BUT TWO MONTHS AGO, MITSUBA PASSED AWAY IN THE HOSPITAL.
KANAE WAS HEARTBROKEN...

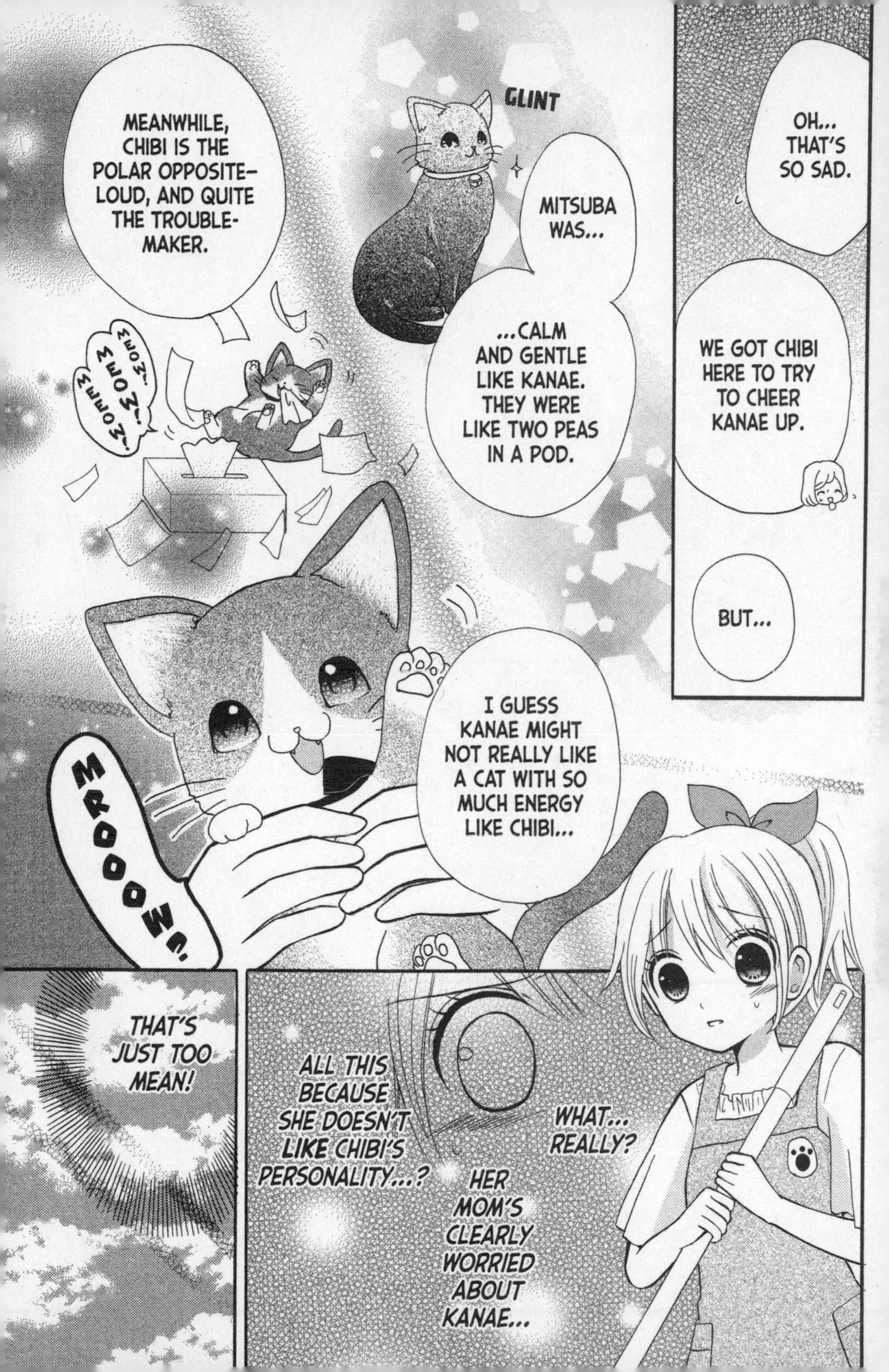
OH... THAT'S SO SAD.
WE GOT CHIBI HERE TO TRY TO CHEER KANAE UP.
BUT...
GLINT
MITSUBA WAS...
...CALM AND GENTLE LIKE KANAE. THEY WERE LIKE TWO PEAS IN A POD.
MEANWHILE, CHIBI IS THE POLAR OPPOSITE— LOUD, AND QUITE THE TROUBLE-MAKER.
MEOW! MEOW! MEEOW!
I GUESS KANAE MIGHT NOT REALLY LIKE A CAT WITH SO MUCH ENERGY LIKE CHIBI...
MROOOWR!
WHAT... REALLY?
HER MOM'S CLEARLY WORRIED ABOUT KANAE...
ALL THIS BECAUSE SHE DOESN'T LIKE CHIBI'S PERSONALITY...?
THAT'S JUST TOO MEAN!

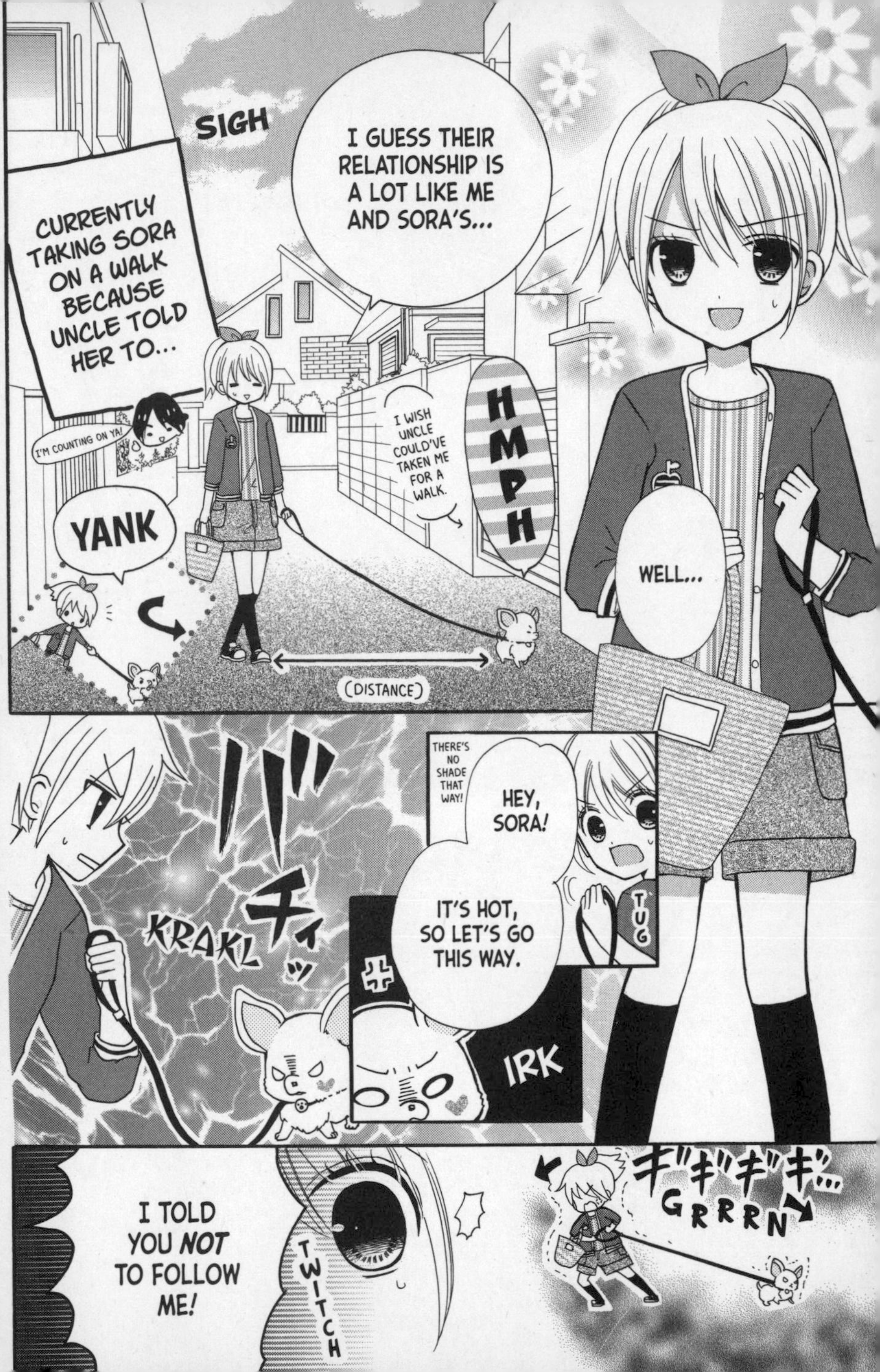
SIGH
CURRENTLY TAKING SORA ON A WALK BECAUSE UNCLE TOLD HER TO...
I GUESS THEIR RELATIONSHIP IS A LOT LIKE ME AND SORA'S...
HMPH
I WISH UNCLE COULD'VE TAKEN ME FOR A WALK.
I'M COUNTING ON YA!
YANK
(DISTANCE)
WELL...
THERE'S NO SHADE THAT WAY!
HEY, SORA!
IT'S HOT, SO LET'S GO THIS WAY.
TUG
IRK
KRAKL
GRRRN
TWITCH
I TOLD YOU NOT TO FOLLOW ME!

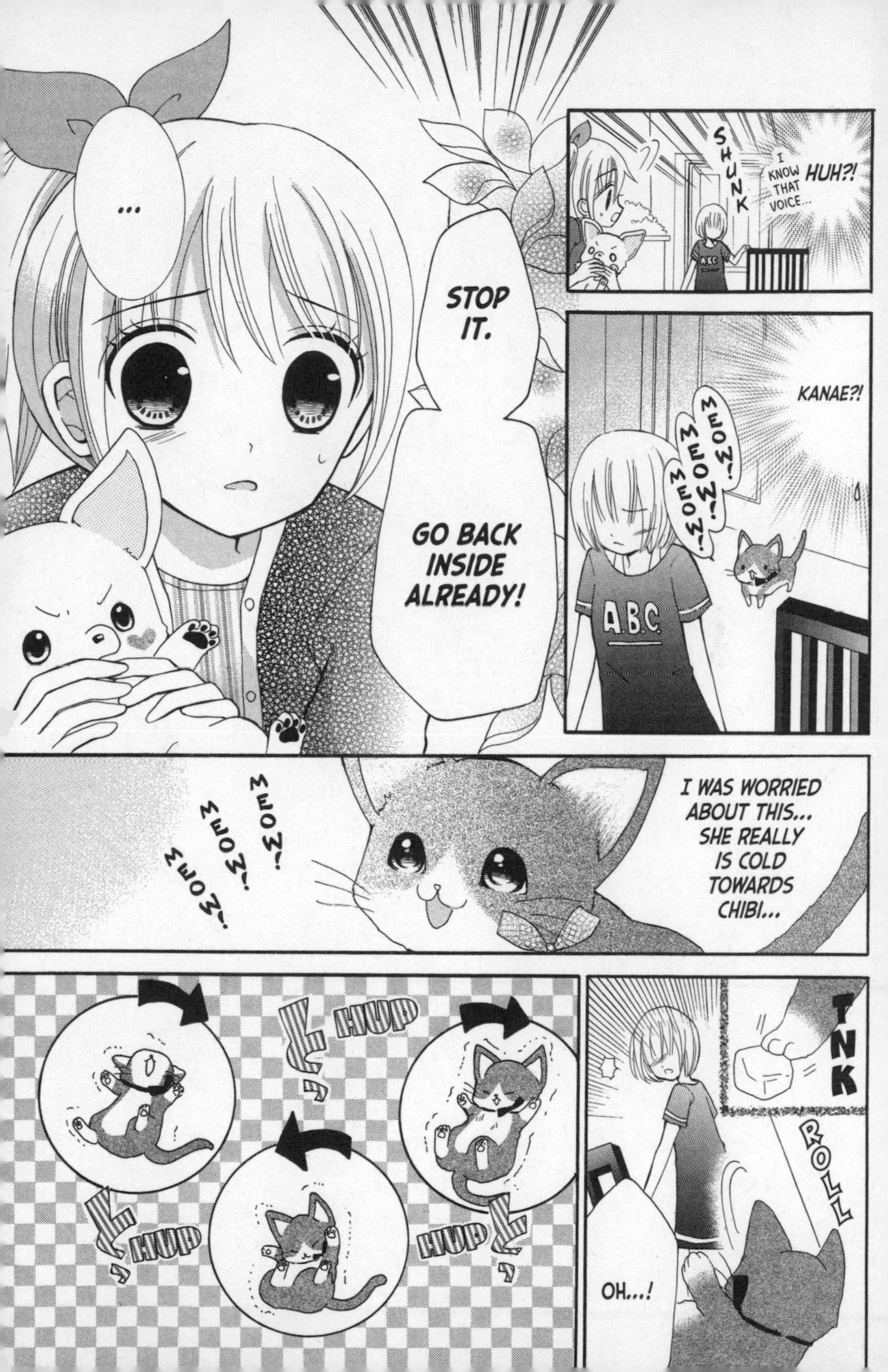
HUH?!
I KNOW THAT VOICE...
SHUNK
KANAE?!
MEOW! MEOW! MEOW!
STOP IT.
GO BACK INSIDE ALREADY!
...
I WAS WORRIED ABOUT THIS... SHE REALLY IS COLD TOWARDS CHIBI...
MEOW! MEOW! MEOW!
TNK
ROLL
OH...!
HUP
HUP
HUP

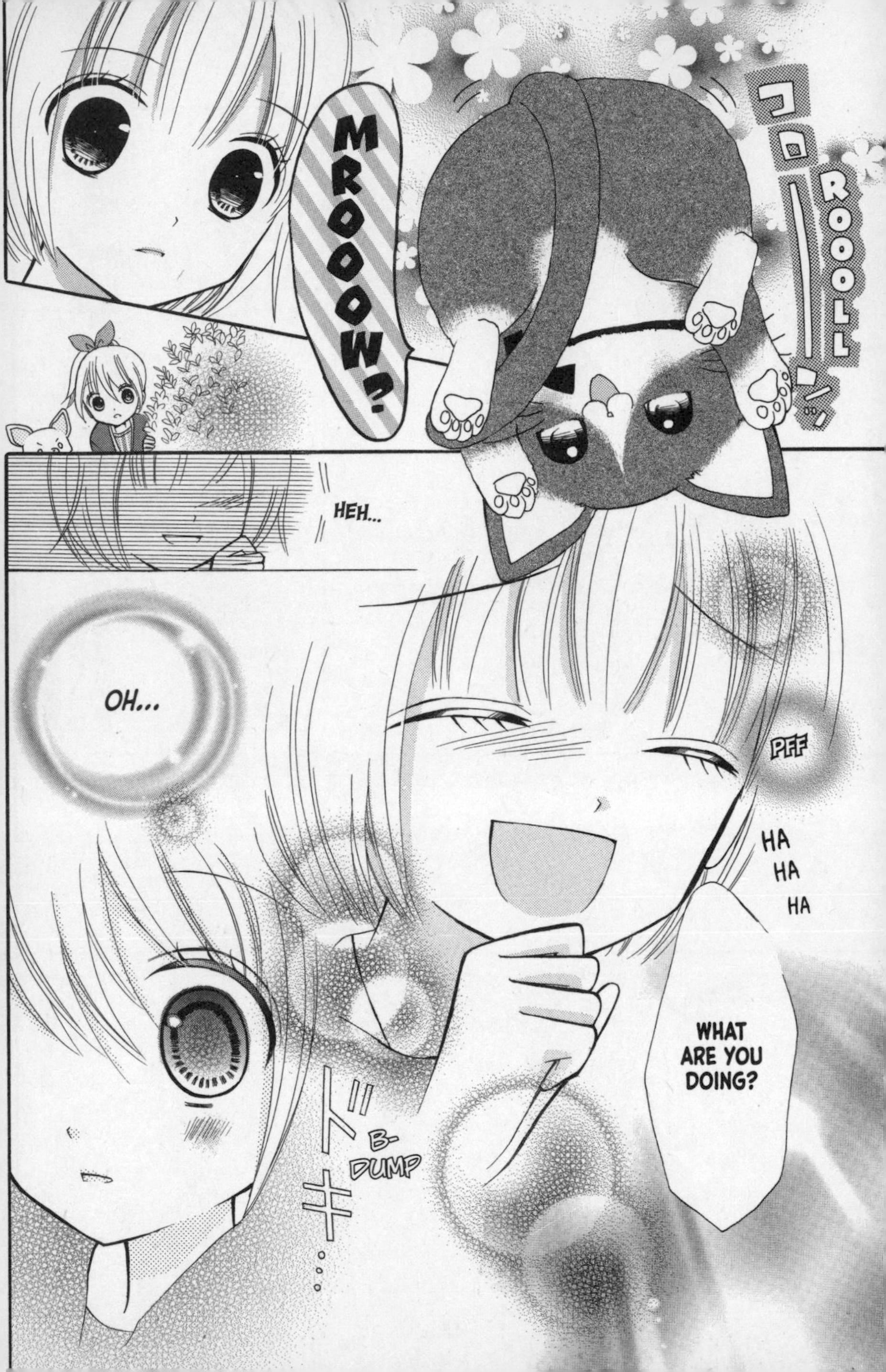
ROOOLL
MROOOW?
HEH...
PFF
HA HA HA
WHAT ARE YOU DOING?
OH...
B-DUMP

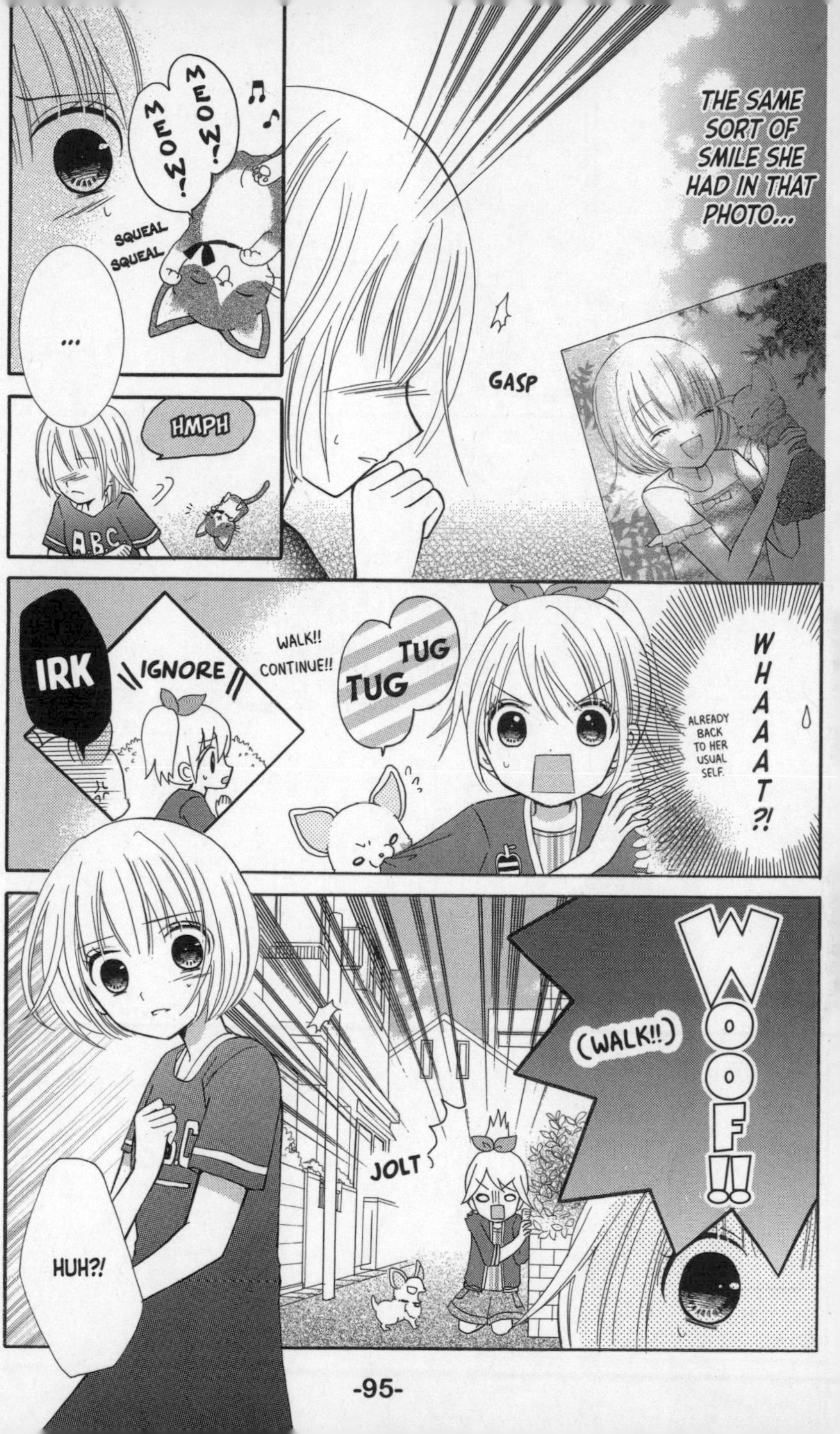
THE SAME SORT OF SMILE SHE HAD IN THAT PHOTO...
GASP
MEOW! MEOW! MEOW!
SQUEAL SQUEAL
...
HMPH
WHAAAAT?!
ALREADY BACK TO HER USUAL SELF.
TUG TUG
WALK!! CONTINUE!!
IGNORE
IRK
WOOF!!
(WALK!!)
JOLT
HUH?!

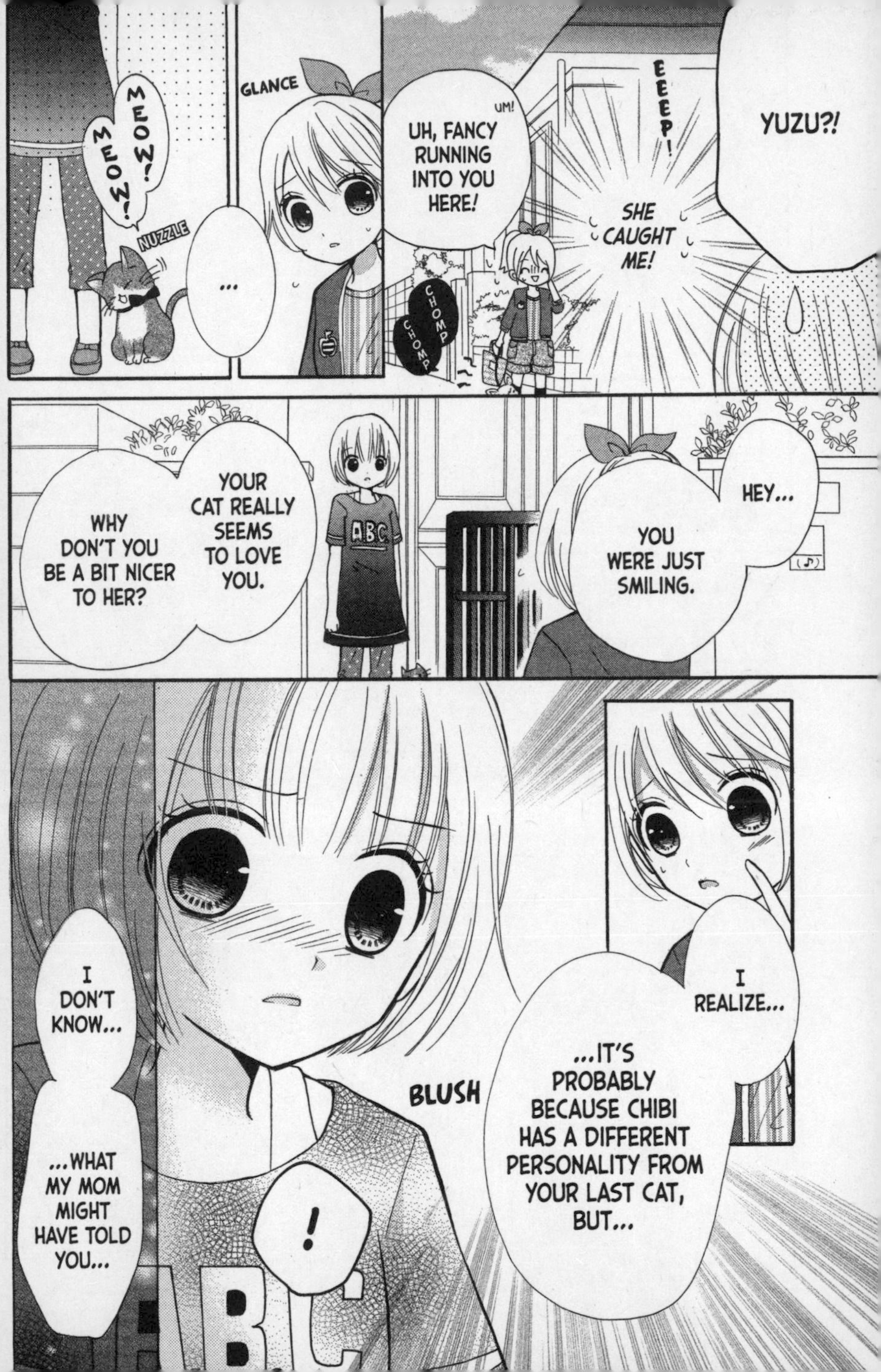
YUZU?!
EEEP!
UM!
UH, FANCY RUNNING INTO YOU HERE!
SHE CAUGHT ME!
CHOMP CHOMP
GLANCE
...
MEOW! MEOW!
NUZZLE
HEY...
YOU WERE JUST SMILING.
(♪)
YOUR CAT REALLY SEEMS TO LOVE YOU.
WHY DON'T YOU BE A BIT NICER TO HER?
I REALIZE...
...IT'S PROBABLY BECAUSE CHIBI HAS A DIFFERENT PERSONALITY FROM YOUR LAST CAT, BUT...
BLUSH
!
I DON'T KNOW...
...WHAT MY MOM MIGHT HAVE TOLD YOU...

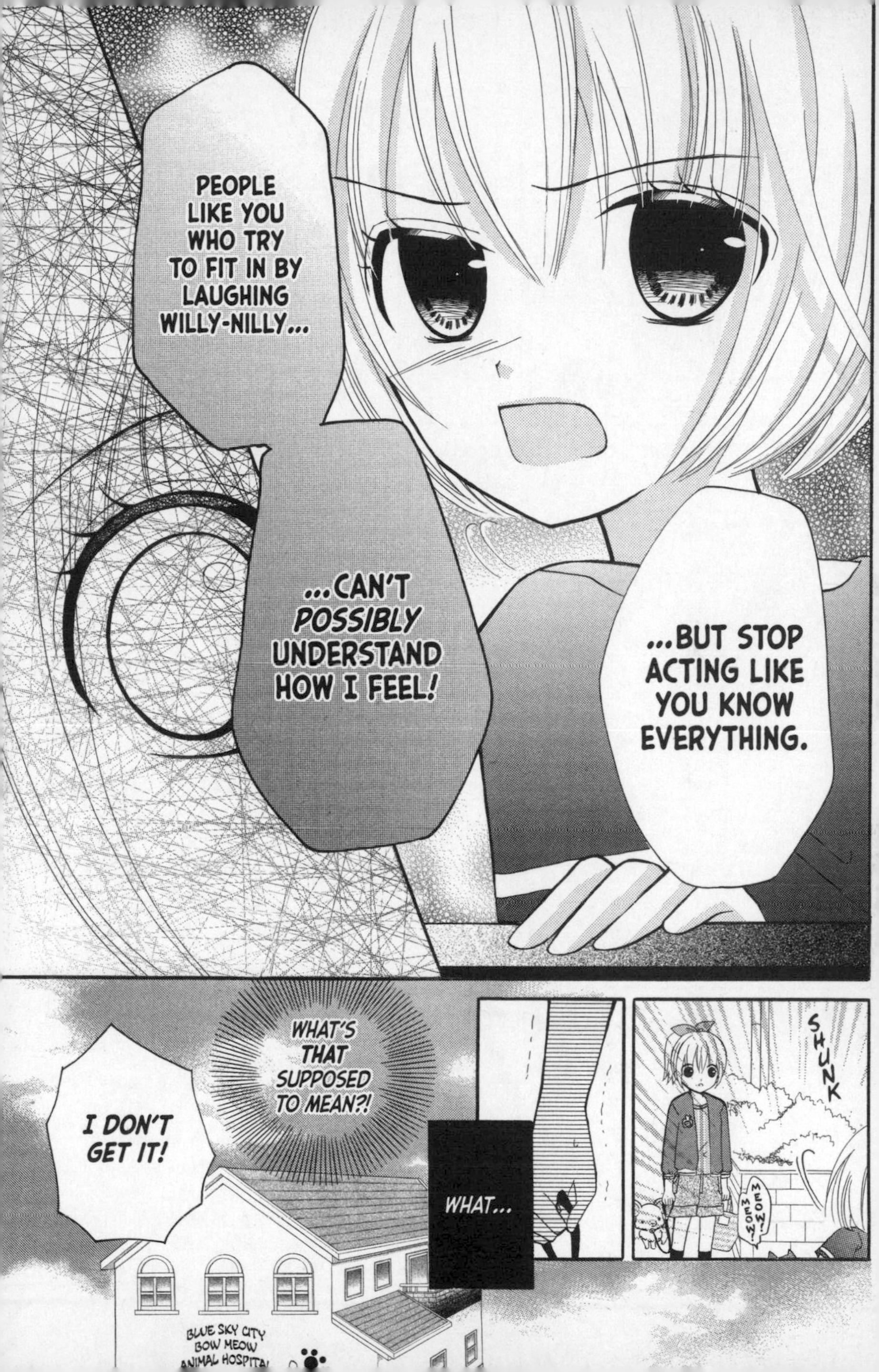
...BUT STOP ACTING LIKE YOU KNOW EVERYTHING.
PEOPLE LIKE YOU WHO TRY TO FIT IN BY LAUGHING WILLY-NILLY...
...CAN'T *POSSIBLY* UNDERSTAND HOW I FEEL!
SHUNK
MEOW! MEOW!
WHAT...
WHAT'S THAT SUPPOSED TO MEAN?!
I DON'T GET IT!
BLUE SKY CITY BOW MEOW ANIMAL HOSPITAL

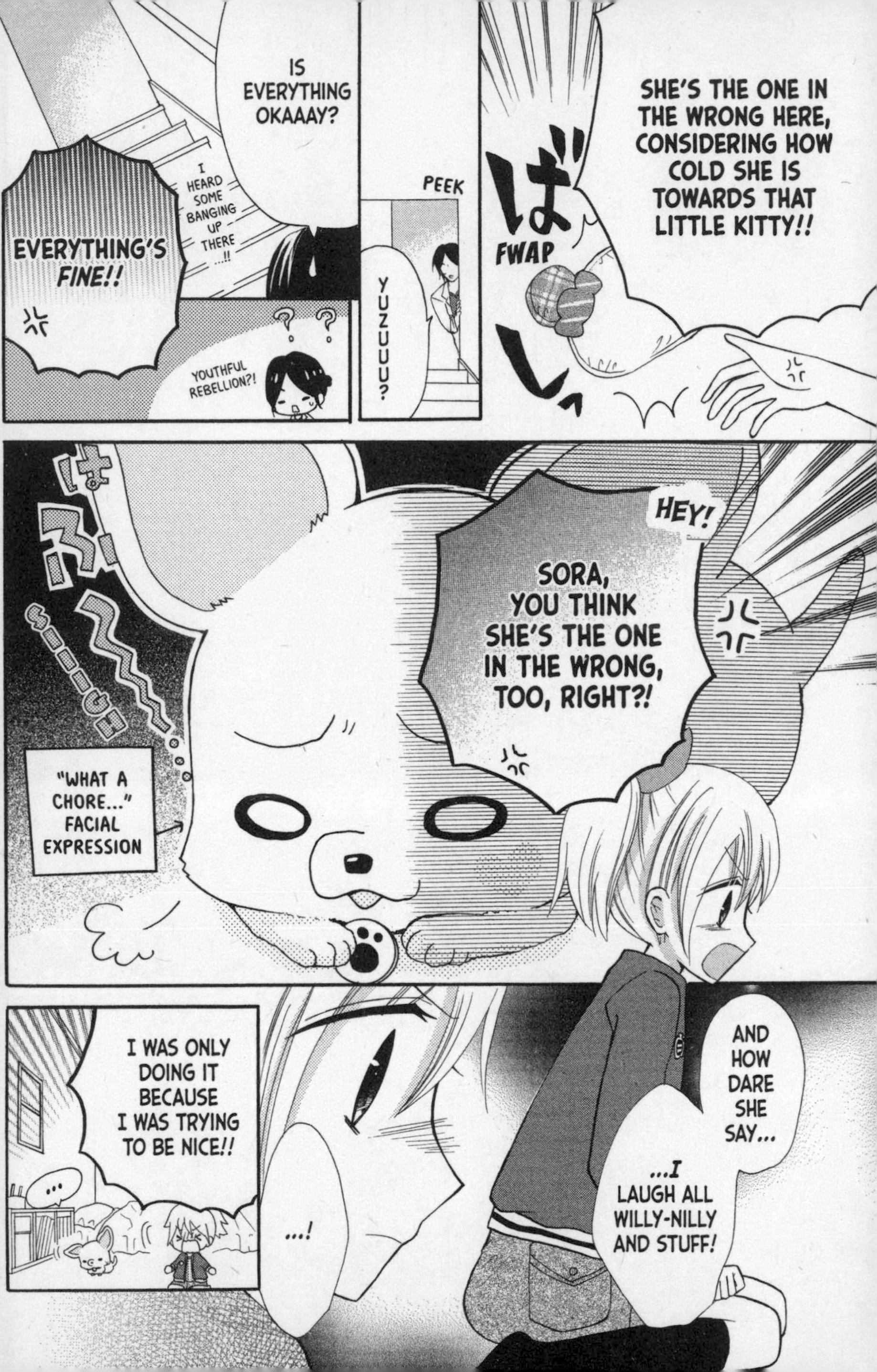
SHE'S THE ONE IN THE WRONG HERE, CONSIDERING HOW COLD SHE IS TOWARDS THAT LITTLE KITTY!!
ばし
FWAP
PEEK
YUZUUUU?
IS EVERYTHING OKAAAY?
I HEARD SOME BANGING UP THERE ...!!
EVERYTHING'S *FINE!!*
YOUTHFUL REBELLION?!
HEY!
SORA, YOU THINK SHE'S THE ONE IN THE WRONG, TOO, RIGHT?!
"WHAT A CHORE..." FACIAL EXPRESSION
AND HOW DARE SHE SAY...
...*I* LAUGH ALL WILLY-NILLY AND STUFF!
...!
I WAS ONLY DOING IT BECAUSE I WAS TRYING TO BE NICE!!
...

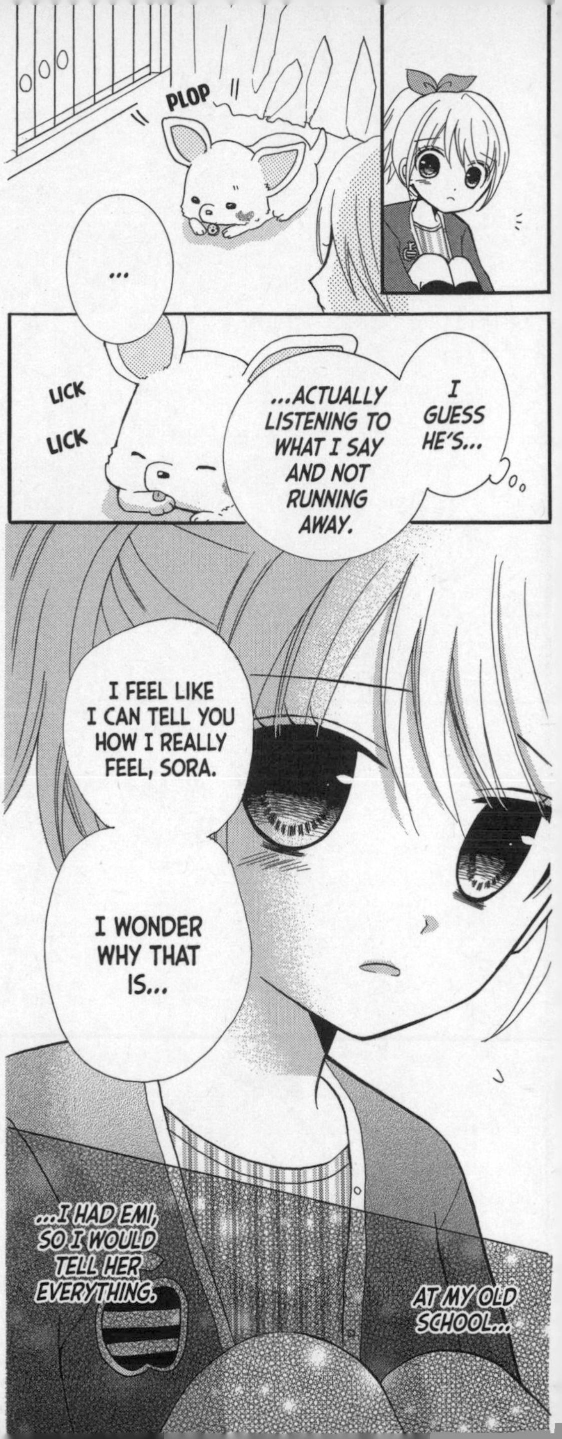
PLOP
...
I GUESS HE'S...
...ACTUALLY LISTENING TO WHAT I SAY AND NOT RUNNING AWAY.
LICK
LICK
I FEEL LIKE I CAN TELL YOU HOW I REALLY FEEL, SORA.
I WONDER WHY THAT IS...
AT MY OLD SCHOOL...
...I HAD EMI, SO I WOULD TELL HER EVERYTHING.

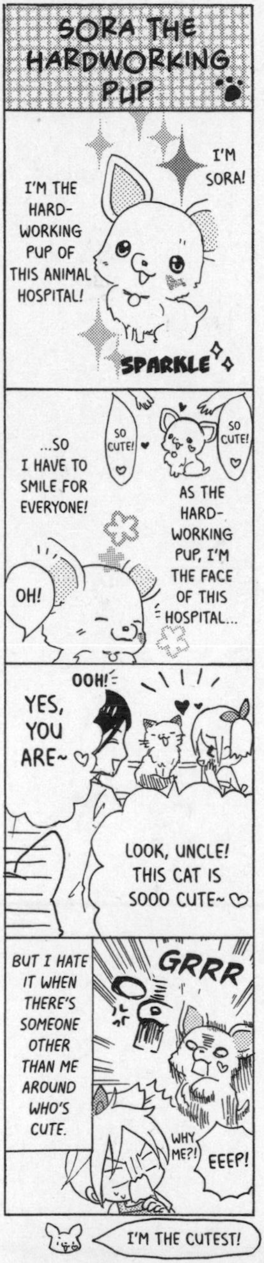
SORA THE HARDWORKING PUP
I'M SORA!
I'M THE HARD-WORKING PUP OF THIS ANIMAL HOSPITAL!
SPARKLE
SO CUTE!
SO CUTE!
AS THE HARD-WORKING PUP, I'M THE FACE OF THIS HOSPITAL...
...SO I HAVE TO SMILE FOR EVERYONE!
OH!
OOH!
LOOK, UNCLE! THIS CAT IS SOOO CUTE~
YES, YOU ARE~
GRRR
BUT I HATE IT WHEN THERE'S SOMEONE OTHER THAN ME AROUND WHO'S CUTE.
WHY ME?!
EEEP!
I'M THE CUTEST!

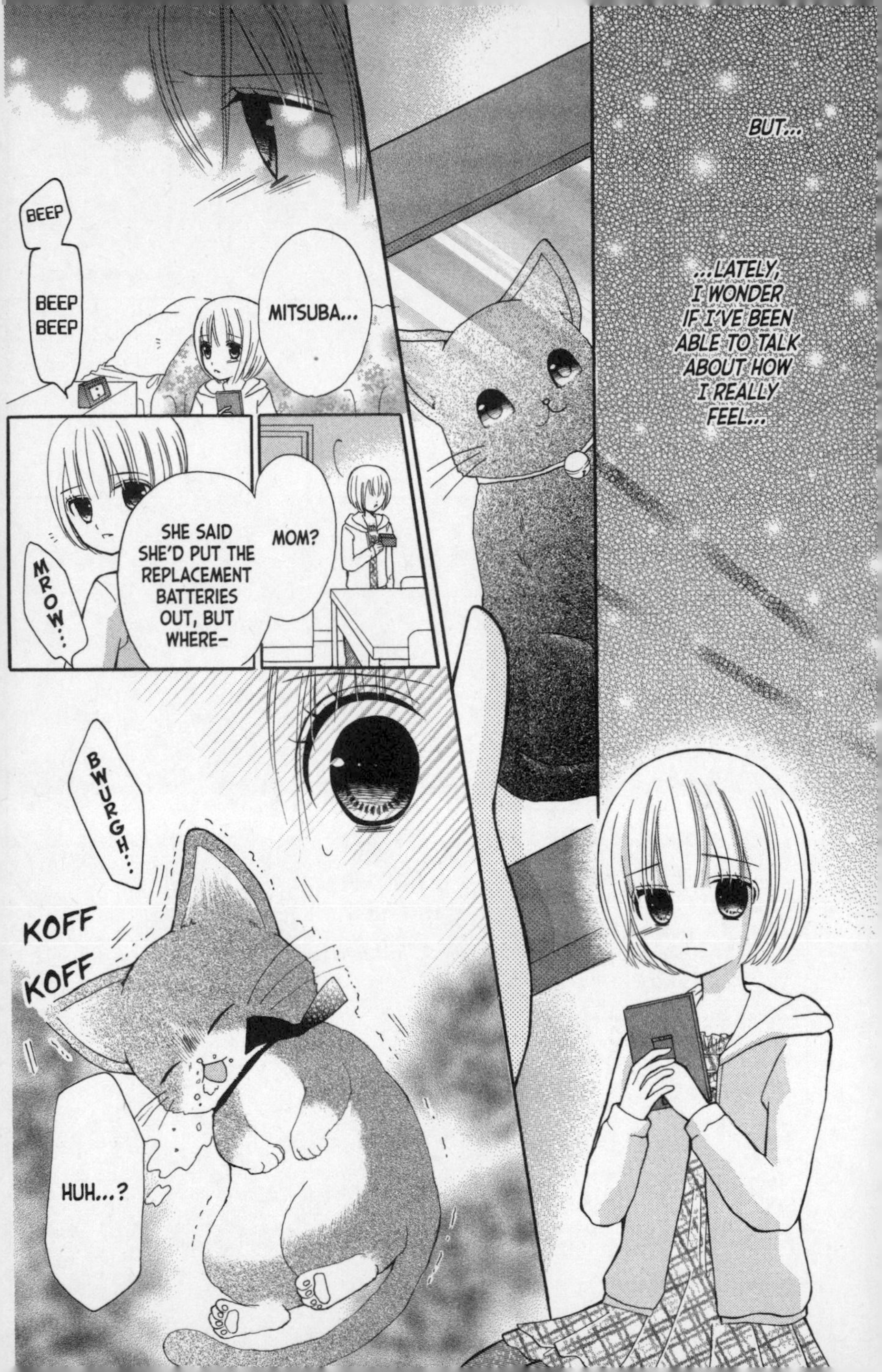
BUT...
...LATELY, I WONDER IF I'VE BEEN ABLE TO TALK ABOUT HOW I REALLY FEEL...
BEEP
BEEP BEEP
MITSUBA...
MOM?
SHE SAID SHE'D PUT THE REPLACEMENT BATTERIES OUT, BUT WHERE-
MROW...
BWURGH...
KOFF KOFF
HUH...?

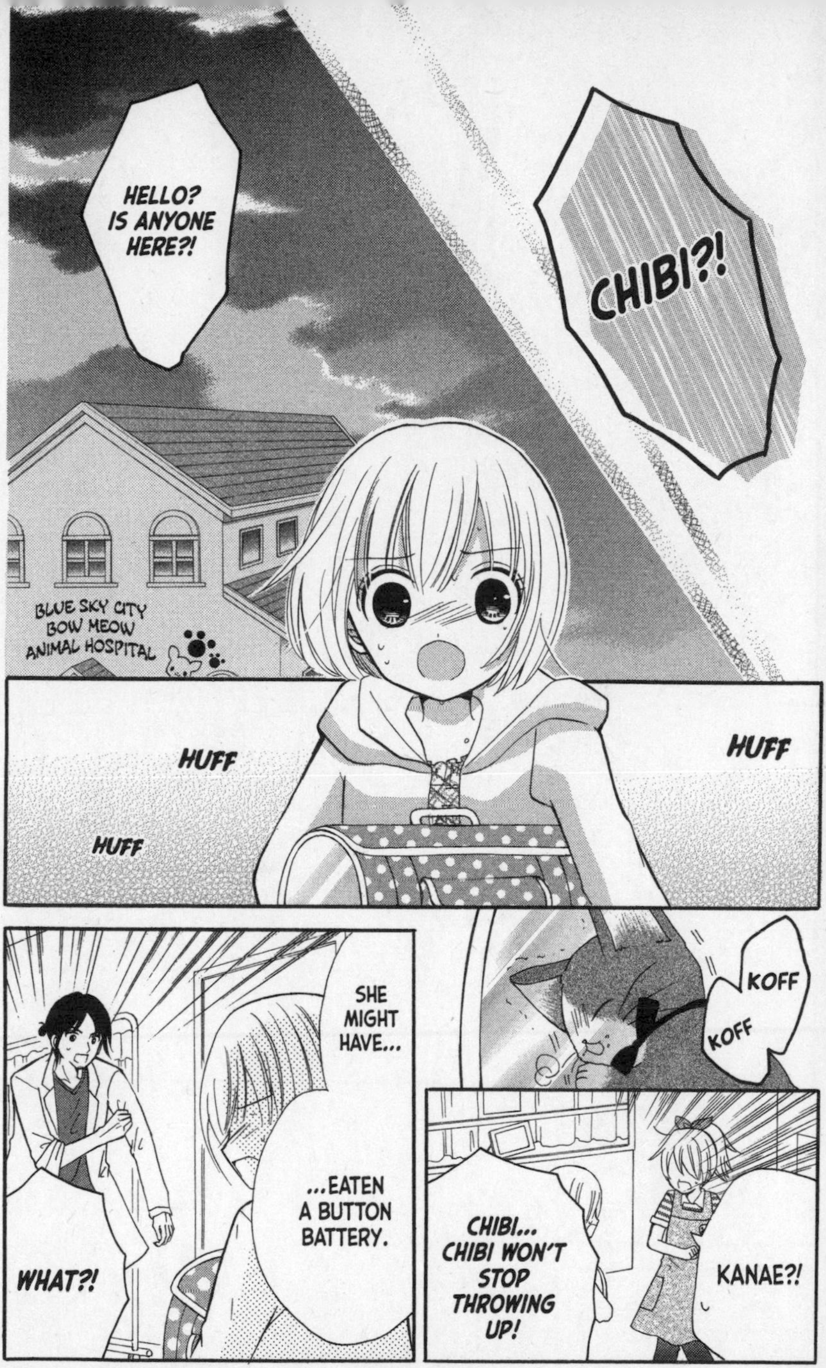
CHIBI?!
HELLO? IS ANYONE HERE?!
BLUE SKY CITY BOW MEOW ANIMAL HOSPITAL
HUFF
HUFF
HUFF
KOFF
KOFF
KANAE?!
CHIBI... CHIBI WON'T STOP THROWING UP!
SHE MIGHT HAVE...
...EATEN A BUTTON BATTERY.
WHAT?!

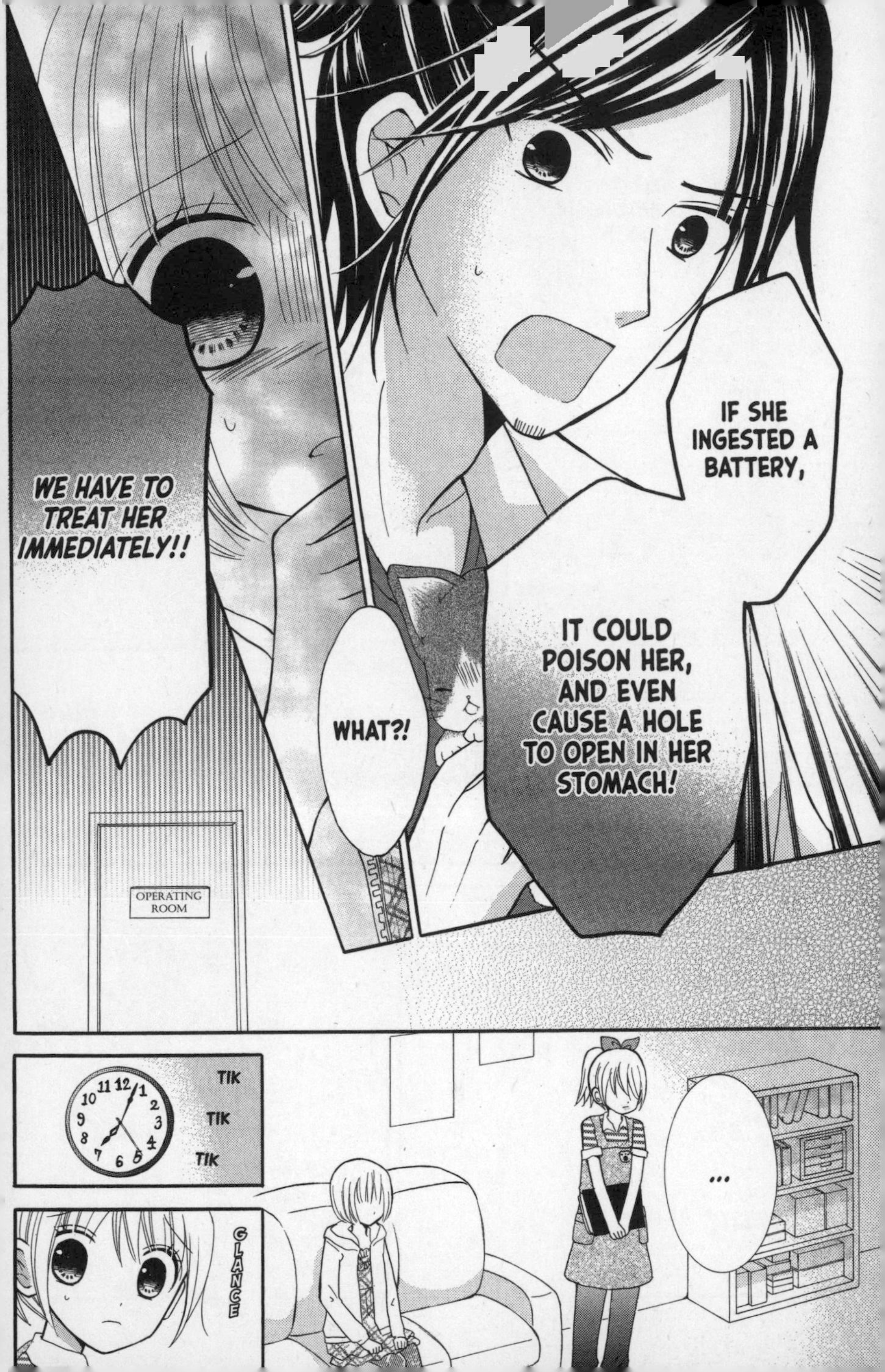
IF SHE INGESTED A BATTERY,
IT COULD POISON HER, AND EVEN CAUSE A HOLE TO OPEN IN HER STOMACH!
WHAT?!
WE HAVE TO TREAT HER IMMEDIATELY!!
OPERATING ROOM
...
TIK
TIK
TIK
GLANCE

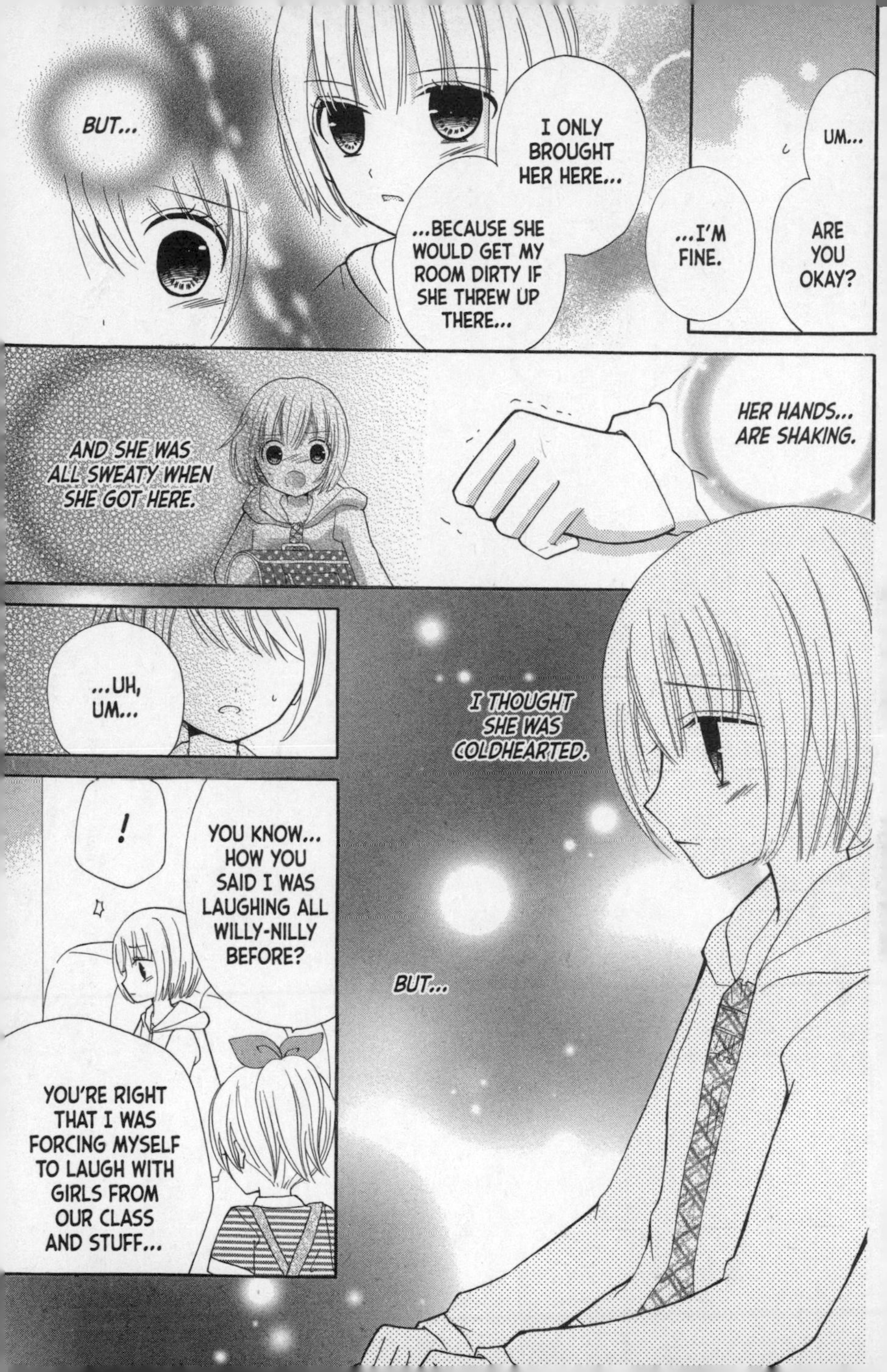
UM... ARE YOU OKAY?
...I'M FINE.
I ONLY BROUGHT HER HERE...
...BECAUSE SHE WOULD GET MY ROOM DIRTY IF SHE THREW UP THERE...
BUT...
HER HANDS... ARE SHAKING.
AND SHE WAS ALL SWEATY WHEN SHE GOT HERE.
I THOUGHT SHE WAS COLDHEARTED.
BUT...
...UH, UM...
!
YOU KNOW... HOW YOU SAID I WAS LAUGHING ALL WILLY-NILLY BEFORE?
YOU'RE RIGHT THAT I WAS FORCING MYSELF TO LAUGH WITH GIRLS FROM OUR CLASS AND STUFF...

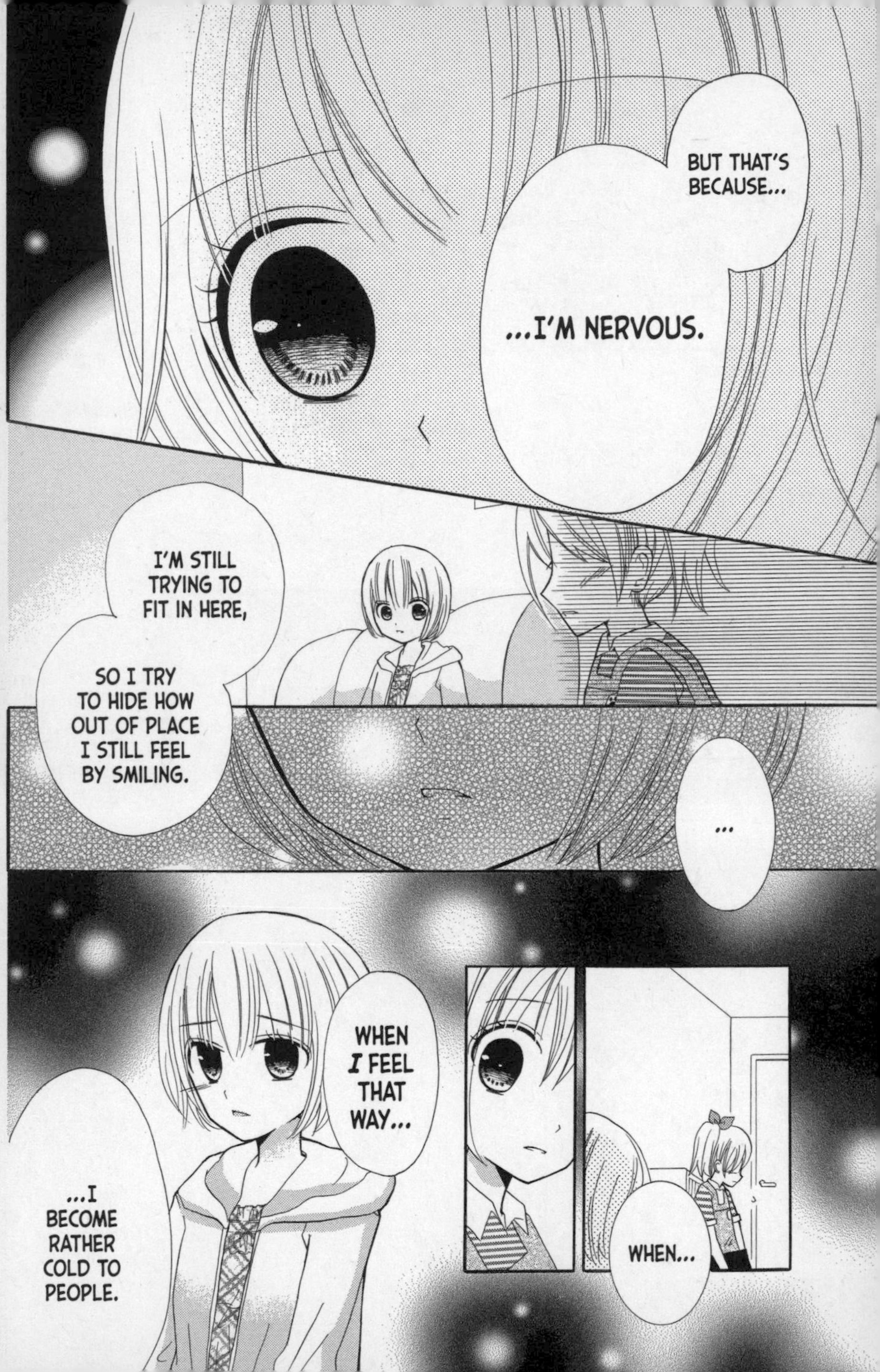
BUT THAT'S BECAUSE...
...I'M NERVOUS.
I'M STILL TRYING TO FIT IN HERE,
SO I TRY TO HIDE HOW OUT OF PLACE I STILL FEEL BY SMILING.
...
WHEN *I* FEEL THAT WAY...
...I BECOME RATHER COLD TO PEOPLE.
WHEN...

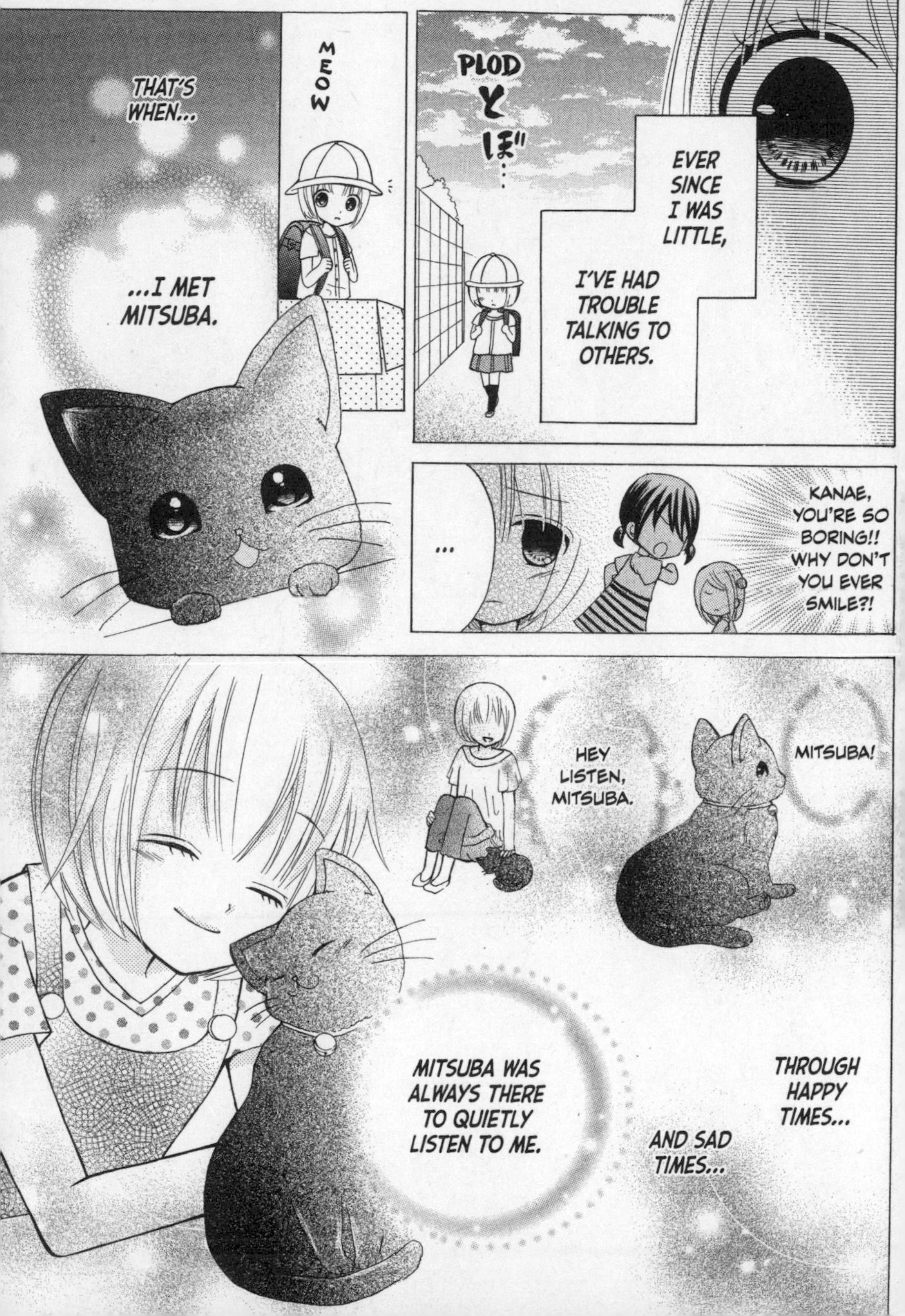
EVER SINCE I WAS LITTLE,
I'VE HAD TROUBLE TALKING TO OTHERS.
PLOD
とぼ…
...
KANAE, YOU'RE SO BORING!! WHY DON'T YOU EVER SMILE?!
MEOW
THAT'S WHEN...
...I MET MITSUBA.
THROUGH HAPPY TIMES...
AND SAD TIMES...
MITSUBA!
HEY LISTEN, MITSUBA.
MITSUBA WAS ALWAYS THERE TO QUIETLY LISTEN TO ME.

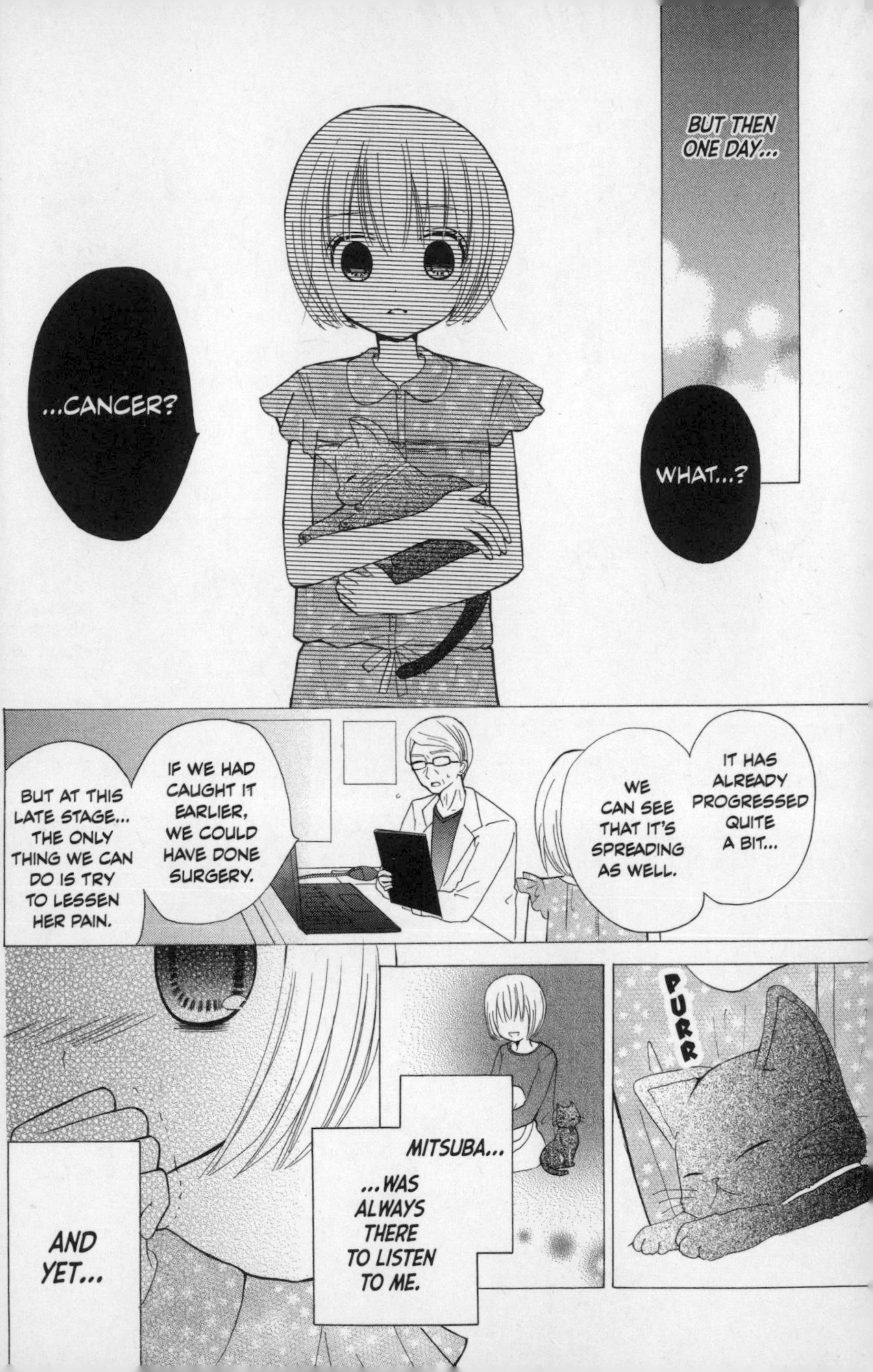
BUT THEN ONE DAY...
WHAT...?
...CANCER?
IT HAS ALREADY PROGRESSED QUITE A BIT...
WE CAN SEE THAT IT'S SPREADING AS WELL.
IF WE HAD CAUGHT IT EARLIER, WE COULD HAVE DONE SURGERY.
BUT AT THIS LATE STAGE... THE ONLY THING WE CAN DO IS TRY TO LESSEN HER PAIN.
PURR
MITSUBA...
...WAS ALWAYS THERE TO LISTEN TO ME.
AND YET...

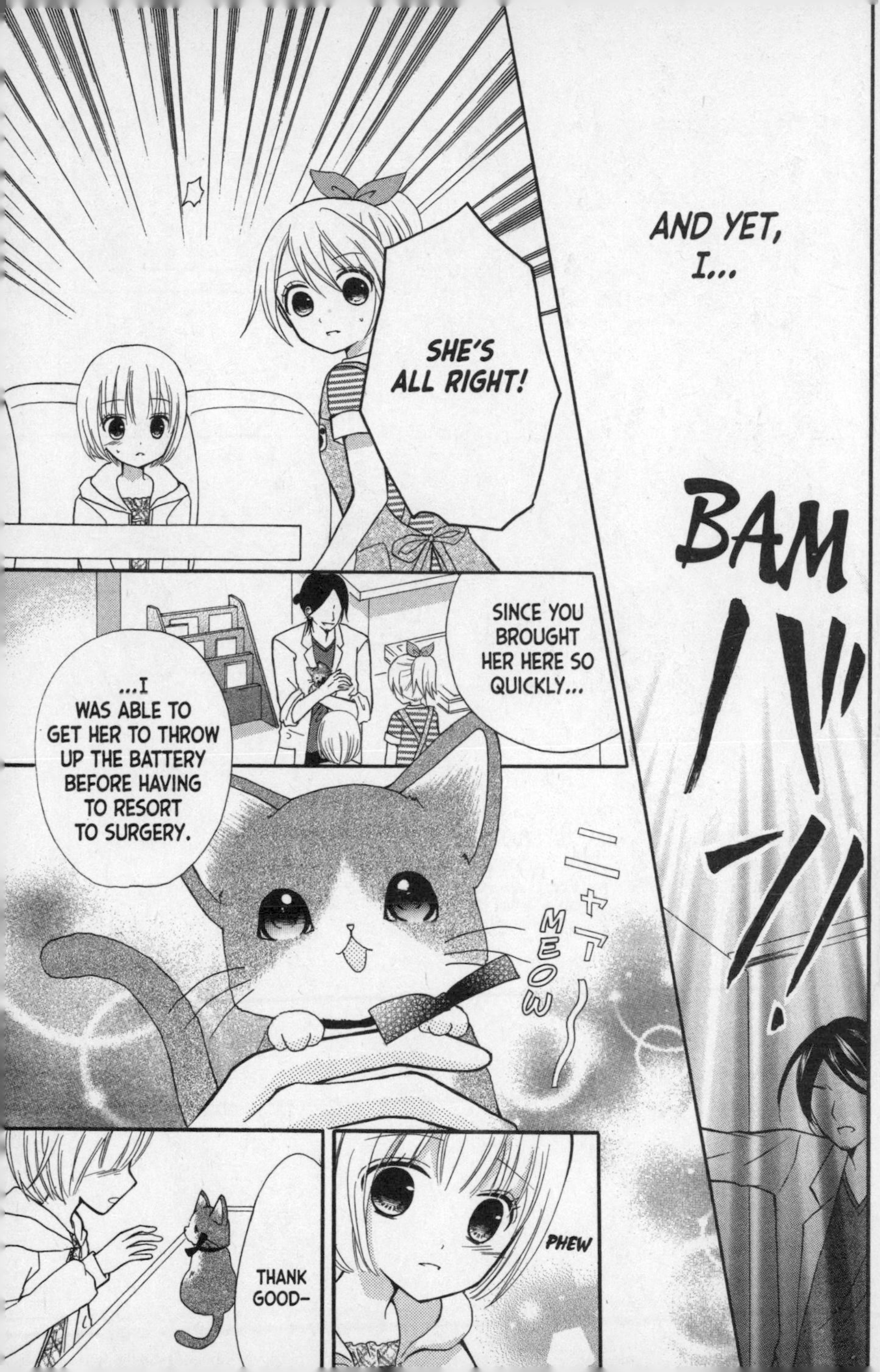
AND YET, I...
BAM
SHE'S ALL RIGHT!
SINCE YOU BROUGHT HER HERE SO QUICKLY...
...I WAS ABLE TO GET HER TO THROW UP THE BATTERY BEFORE HAVING TO RESORT TO SURGERY.
MEOW
PHEW
THANK GOOD–

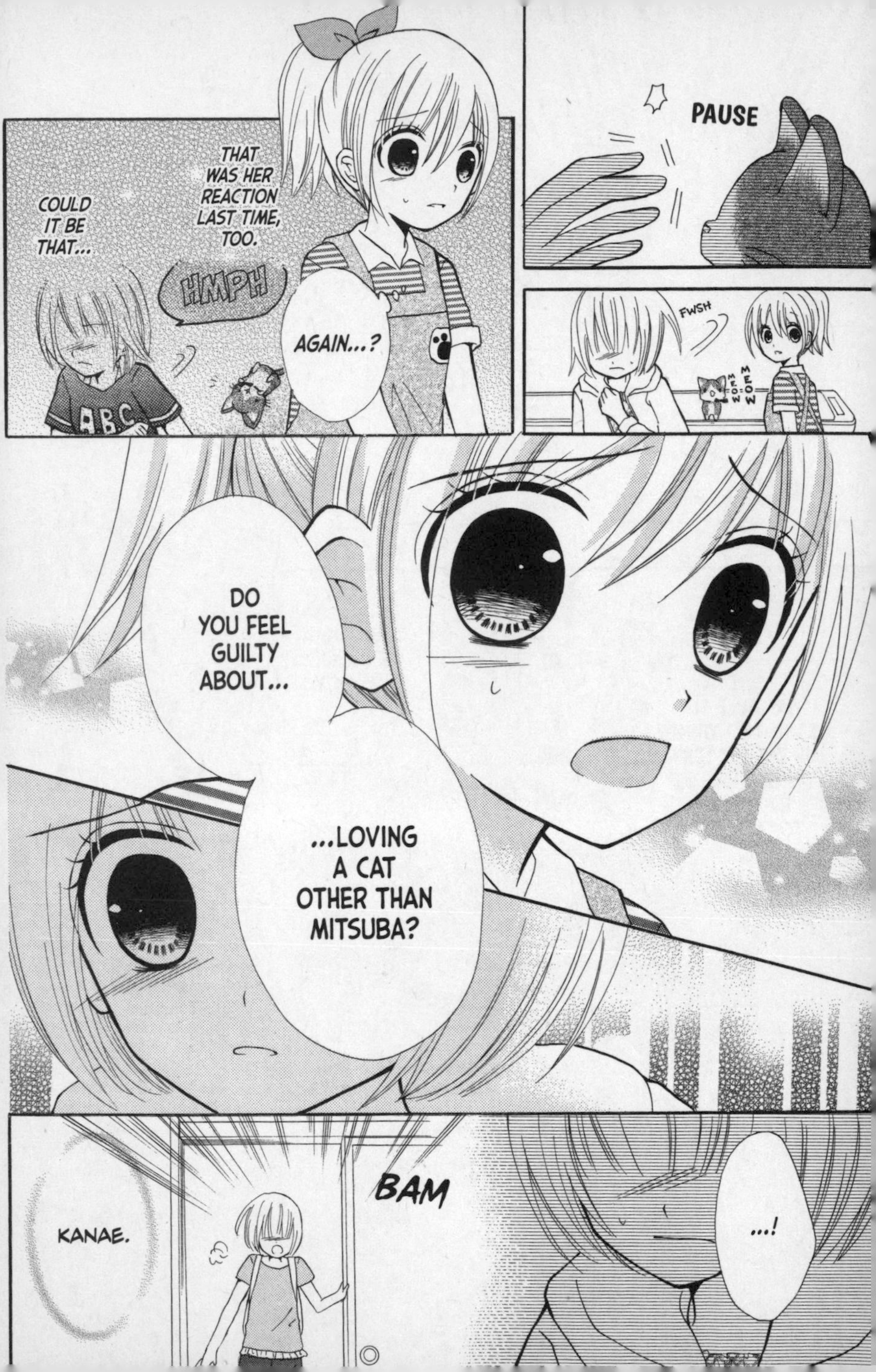
PAUSE
FWSH
MEOW MEOW
THAT WAS HER REACTION LAST TIME, TOO.
COULD IT BE THAT...
HMPH
AGAIN...?
DO YOU FEEL GUILTY ABOUT...
...LOVING A CAT OTHER THAN MITSUBA?
...!
BAM
KANAE.

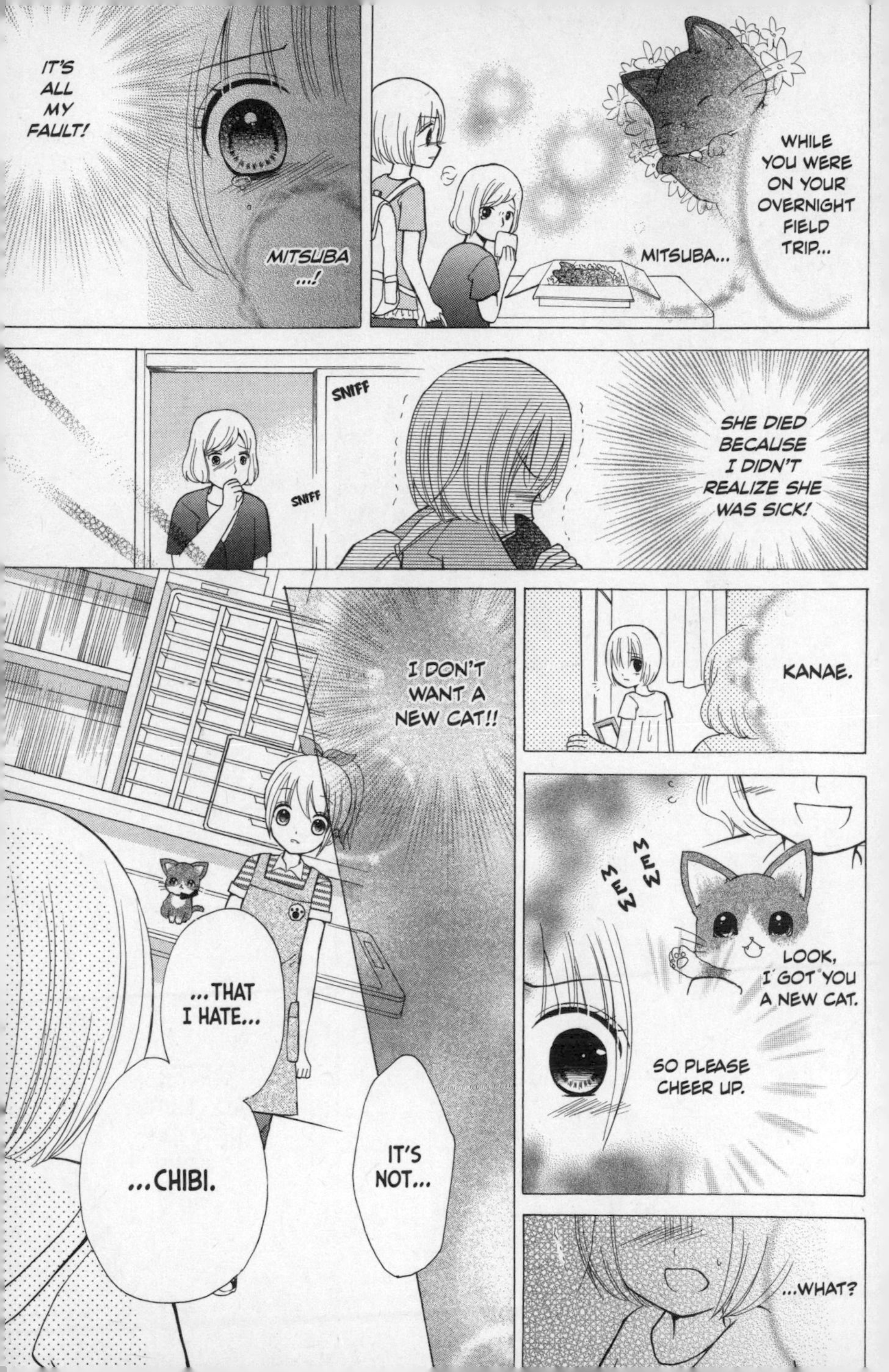
WHILE YOU WERE ON YOUR OVERNIGHT FIELD TRIP...
MITSUBA...
MITSUBA ...!
IT'S ALL MY FAULT!
SHE DIED BECAUSE I DIDN'T REALIZE SHE WAS SICK!
SNIFF
SNIFF
KANAE.
MEW MEW
LOOK, I GOT YOU A NEW CAT.
SO PLEASE CHEER UP.
...WHAT?
I DON'T WANT A NEW CAT!!
IT'S NOT...
...THAT I HATE...
...CHIBI.

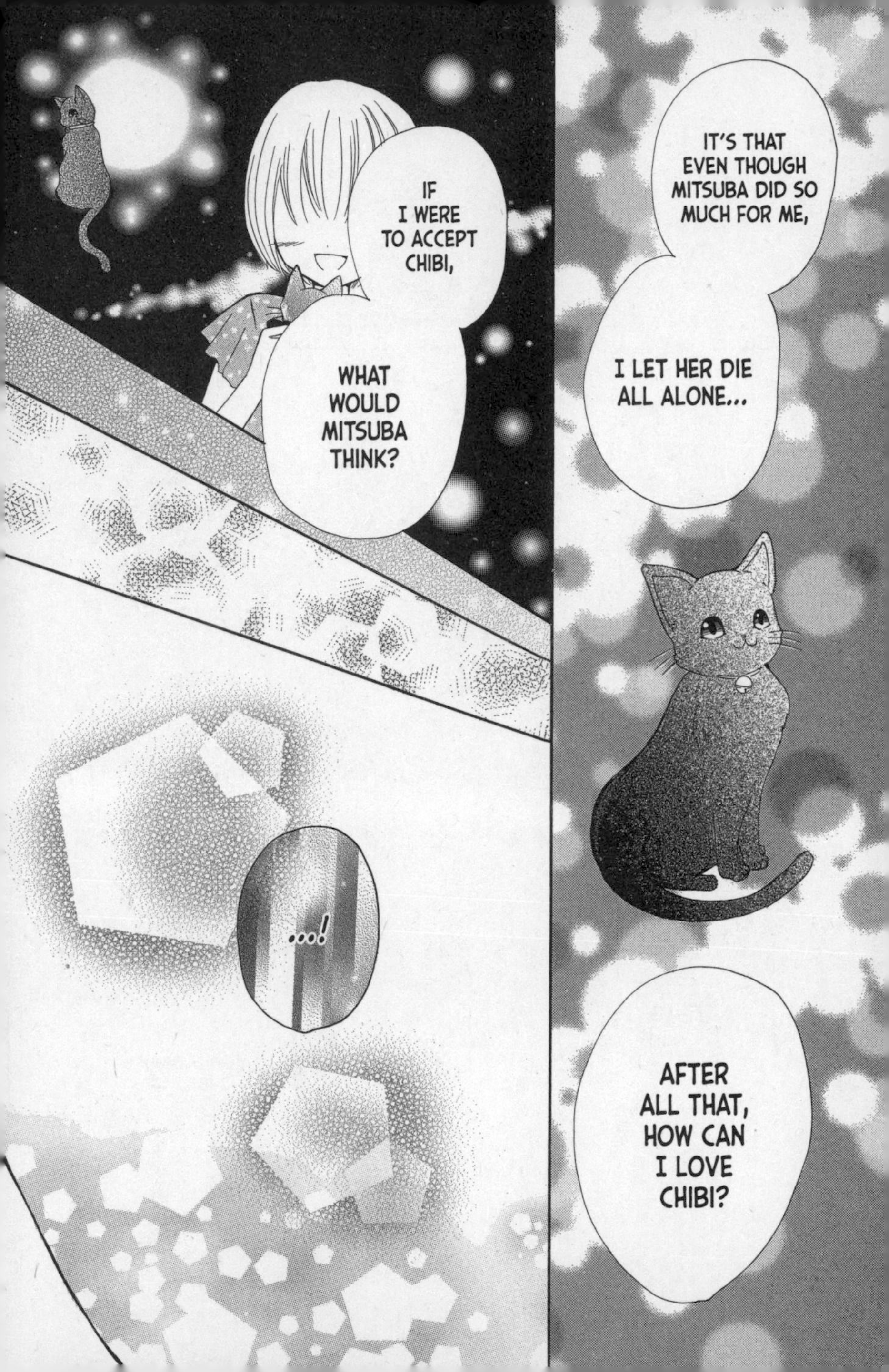
IT'S THAT EVEN THOUGH MITSUBA DID SO MUCH FOR ME,
I LET HER DIE ALL ALONE...
AFTER ALL THAT, HOW CAN I LOVE CHIBI?
IF I WERE TO ACCEPT CHIBI,
WHAT WOULD MITSUBA THINK?
...!

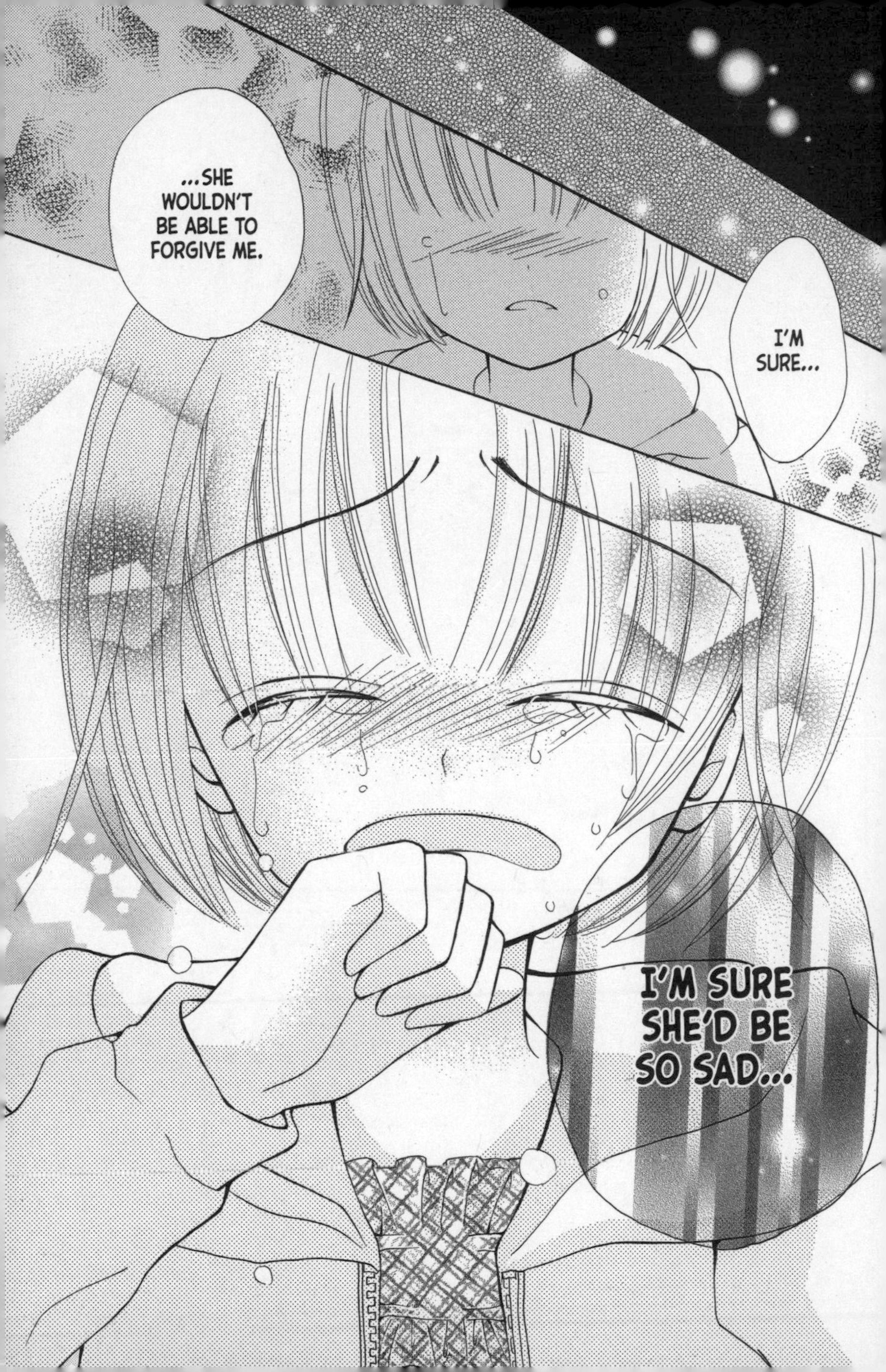
I'M SURE...
...SHE WOULDN'T BE ABLE TO FORGIVE ME.
I'M SURE SHE'D BE SO SAD...

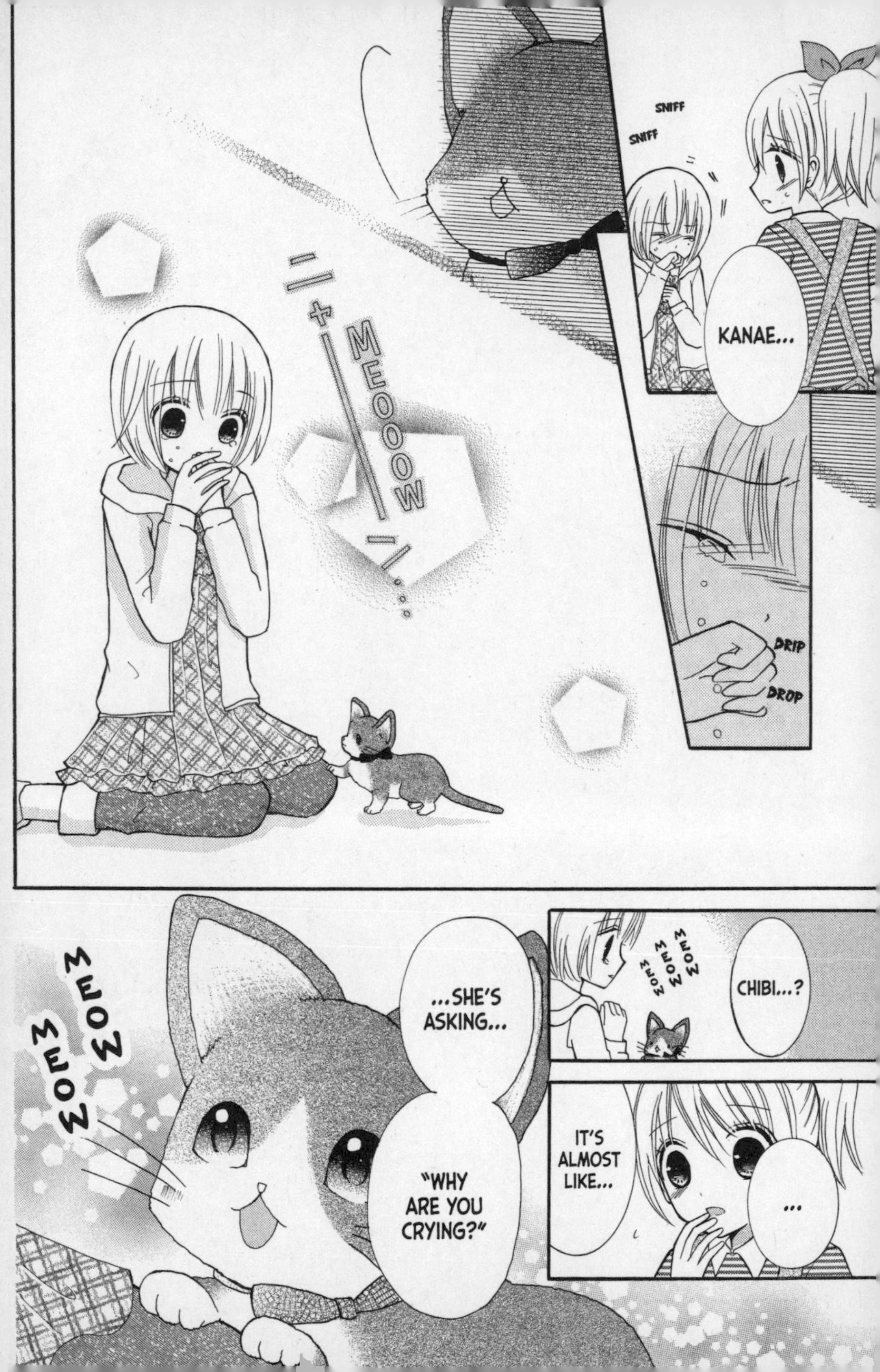
SNIFF
SNIFF
KANAE...
DRIP
DROP
MEOOOW
CHIBI...?
MEOW MEOW MEOW
...
IT'S ALMOST LIKE...
...SHE'S ASKING...
"WHY ARE YOU CRYING?"
MEOW MEOW
MEOW MEOW

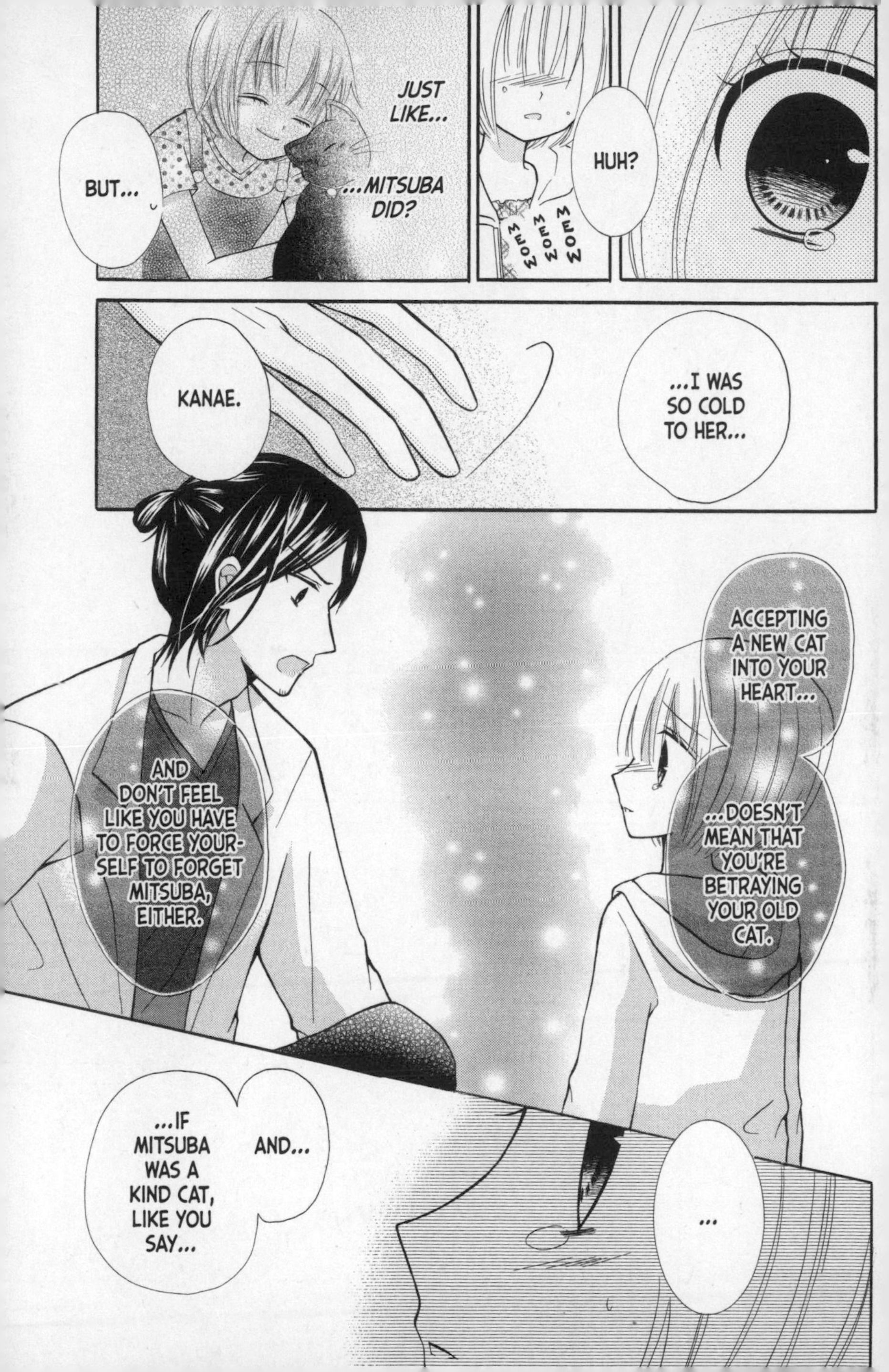
HUH?
MEOW MEOW MEOW
JUST LIKE...
...MITSUBA DID?
BUT...
...I WAS SO COLD TO HER...
KANAE.
ACCEPTING A NEW CAT INTO YOUR HEART...
...DOESN'T MEAN THAT YOU'RE BETRAYING YOUR OLD CAT.
AND DON'T FEEL LIKE YOU HAVE TO FORCE YOURSELF TO FORGET MITSUBA, EITHER.
...
AND...
...IF MITSUBA WAS A KIND CAT, LIKE YOU SAY...

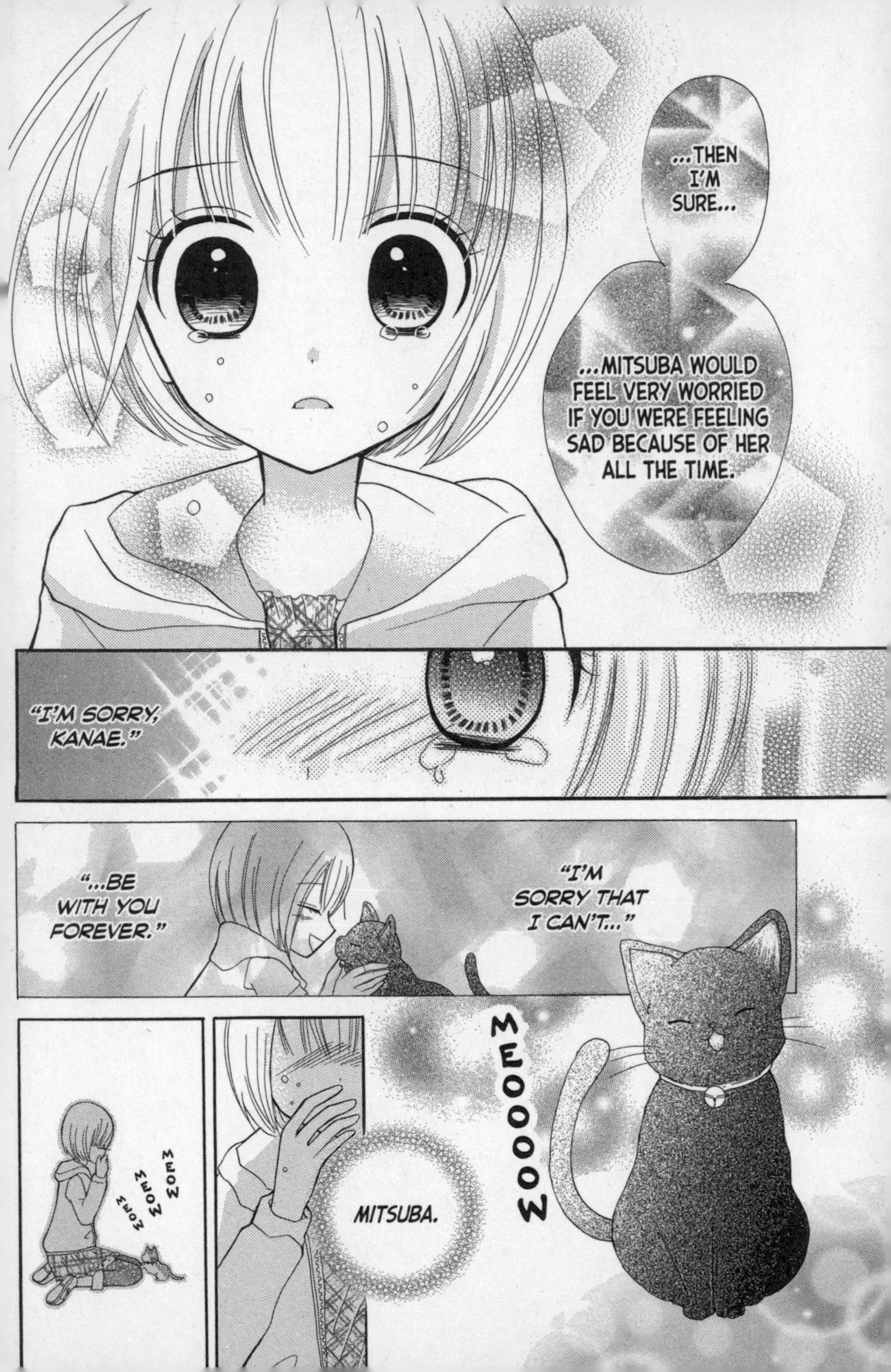
...THEN I'M SURE...
...MITSUBA WOULD FEEL VERY WORRIED IF YOU WERE FEELING SAD BECAUSE OF HER ALL THE TIME.
"I'M SORRY, KANAE."
"I'M SORRY THAT I CAN'T..."
"...BE WITH YOU FOREVER."
MEOOOOW
MITSUBA.
MEOW
MEOW
MEOW

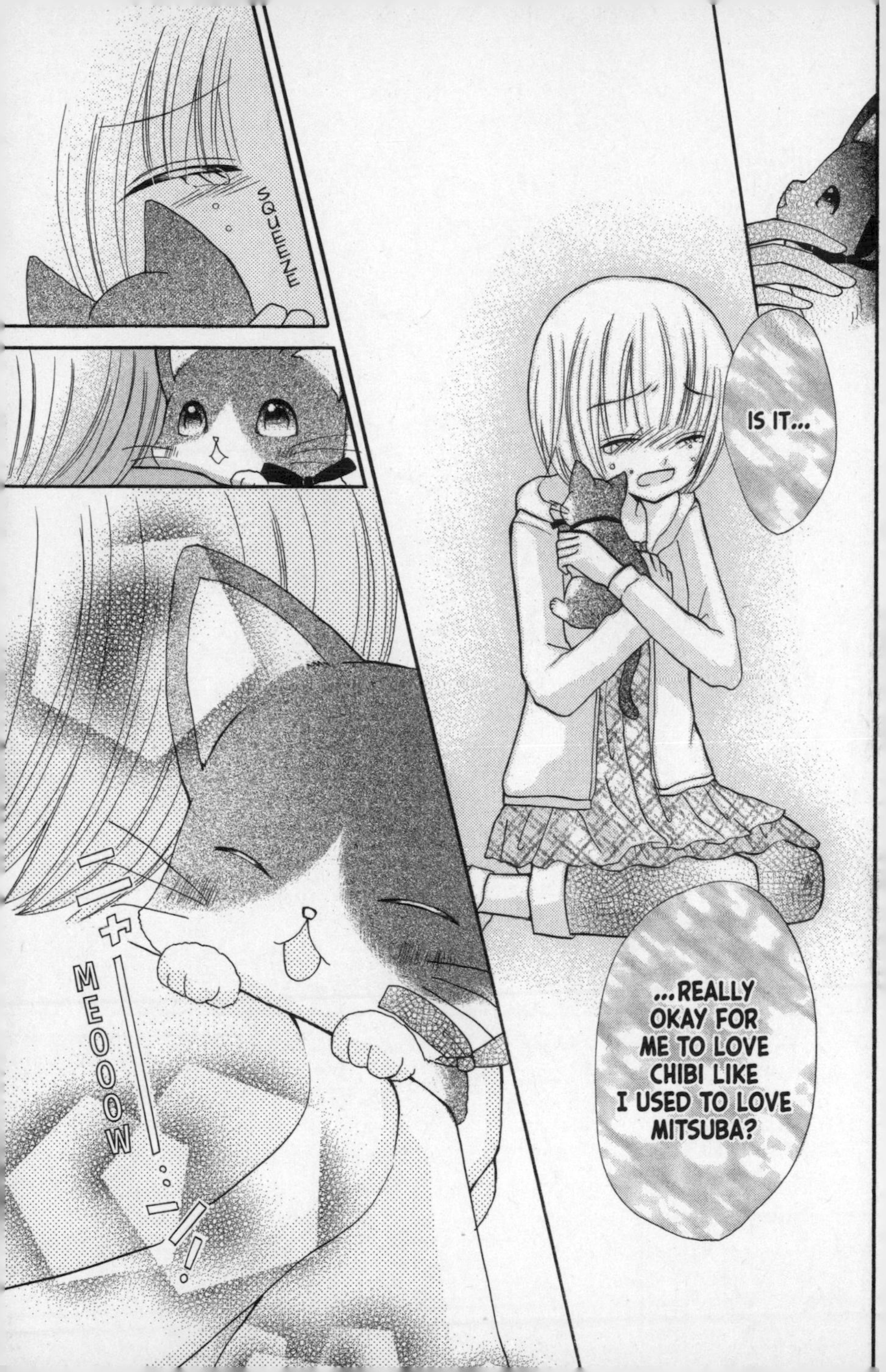
IS IT...
...REALLY OKAY FOR ME TO LOVE CHIBI LIKE I USED TO LOVE MITSUBA?
SQUEEZE
MEOOOW

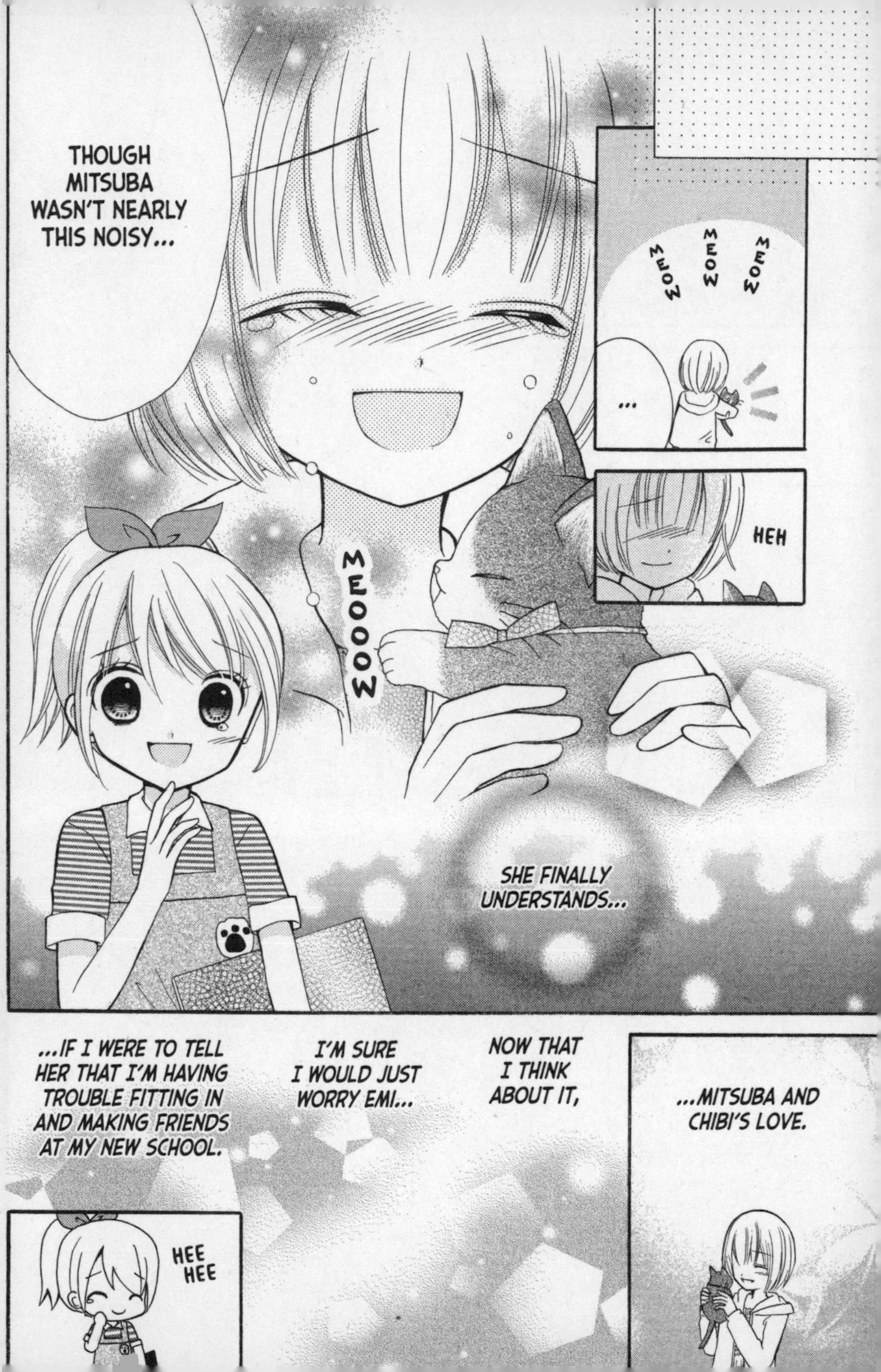
MEOW MEOW MEOW
...
HEH
THOUGH MITSUBA WASN'T NEARLY THIS NOISY...
MEOOOW
SHE FINALLY UNDERSTANDS...
...MITSUBA AND CHIBI'S LOVE.
NOW THAT I THINK ABOUT IT,
I'M SURE I WOULD JUST WORRY EMI...
...IF I WERE TO TELL HER THAT I'M HAVING TROUBLE FITTING IN AND MAKING FRIENDS AT MY NEW SCHOOL.
HEE HEE

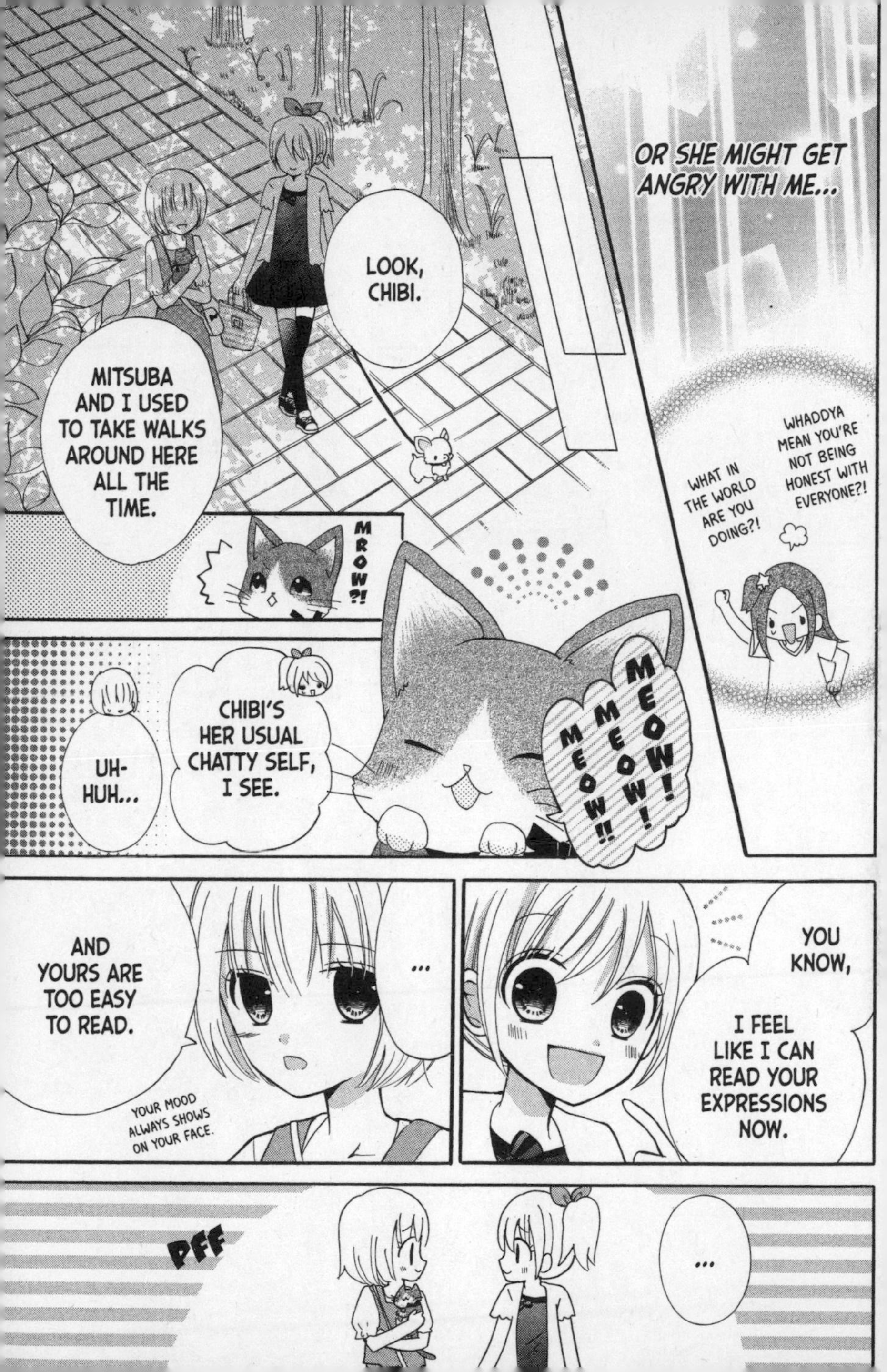
OR SHE MIGHT GET ANGRY WITH ME...
WHADDYA MEAN YOU'RE NOT BEING HONEST WITH EVERYONE?!
WHAT IN THE WORLD ARE YOU DOING?!
LOOK, CHIBI.
MITSUBA AND I USED TO TAKE WALKS AROUND HERE ALL THE TIME.
MROW?!
MEOW! MEOW! MEOW!!
CHIBI'S HER USUAL CHATTY SELF, I SEE.
UH-HUH...
YOU KNOW,
I FEEL LIKE I CAN READ YOUR EXPRESSIONS NOW.
...
AND YOURS ARE TOO EASY TO READ.
YOUR MOOD ALWAYS SHOWS ON YOUR FACE.
...
PFF

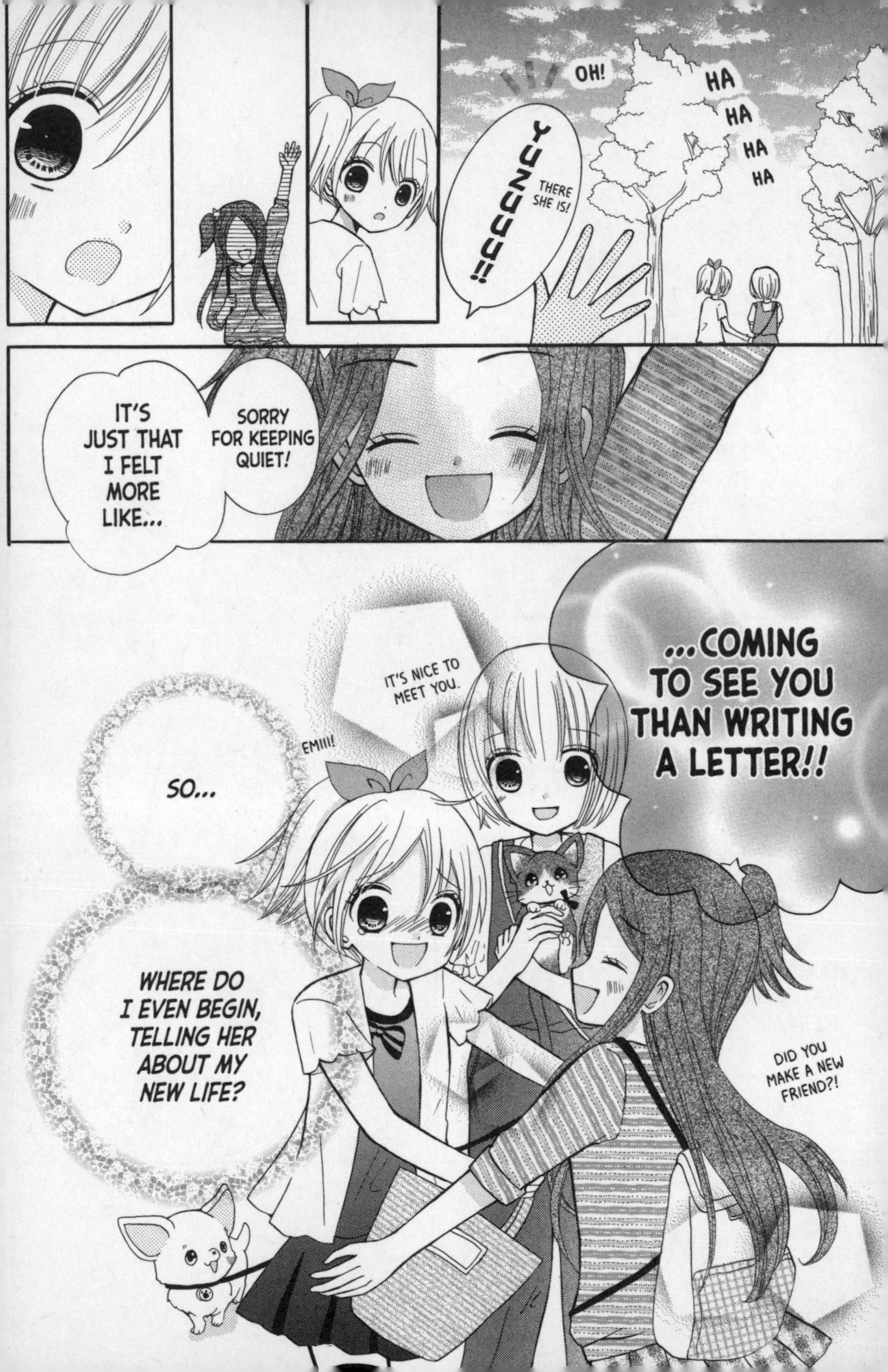
HA HA HA HA
OH!
YUZUUUU!!
THERE SHE IS!
SORRY FOR KEEPING QUIET!
IT'S JUST THAT I FELT MORE LIKE...
...COMING TO SEE YOU THAN WRITING A LETTER!!
IT'S NICE TO MEET YOU.
EMIII!
SO...
DID YOU MAKE A NEW FRIEND?!
WHERE DO I EVEN BEGIN, TELLING HER ABOUT MY NEW LIFE?

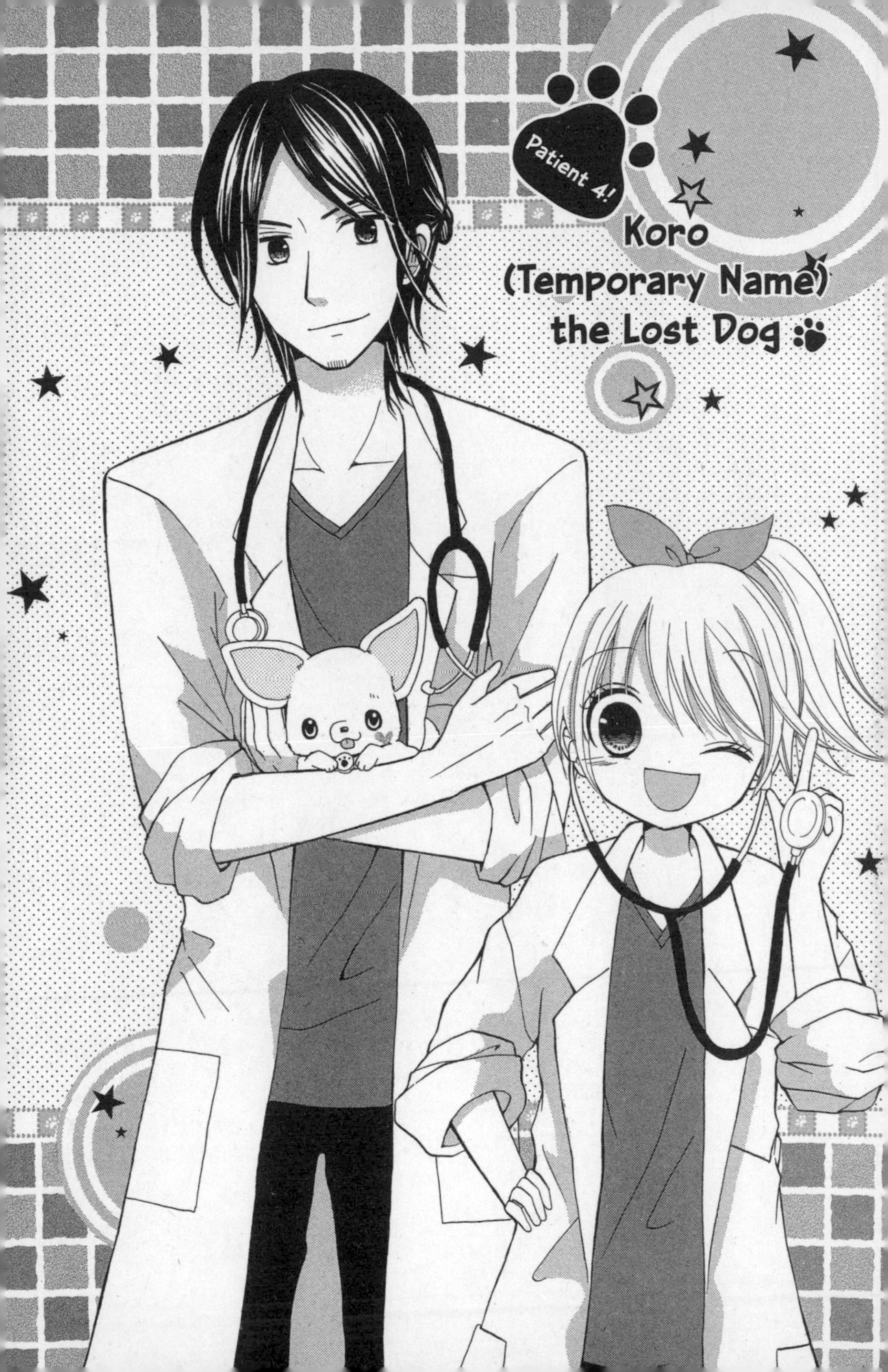
Patient 4!
Koro (Temporary Name) the Lost Dog

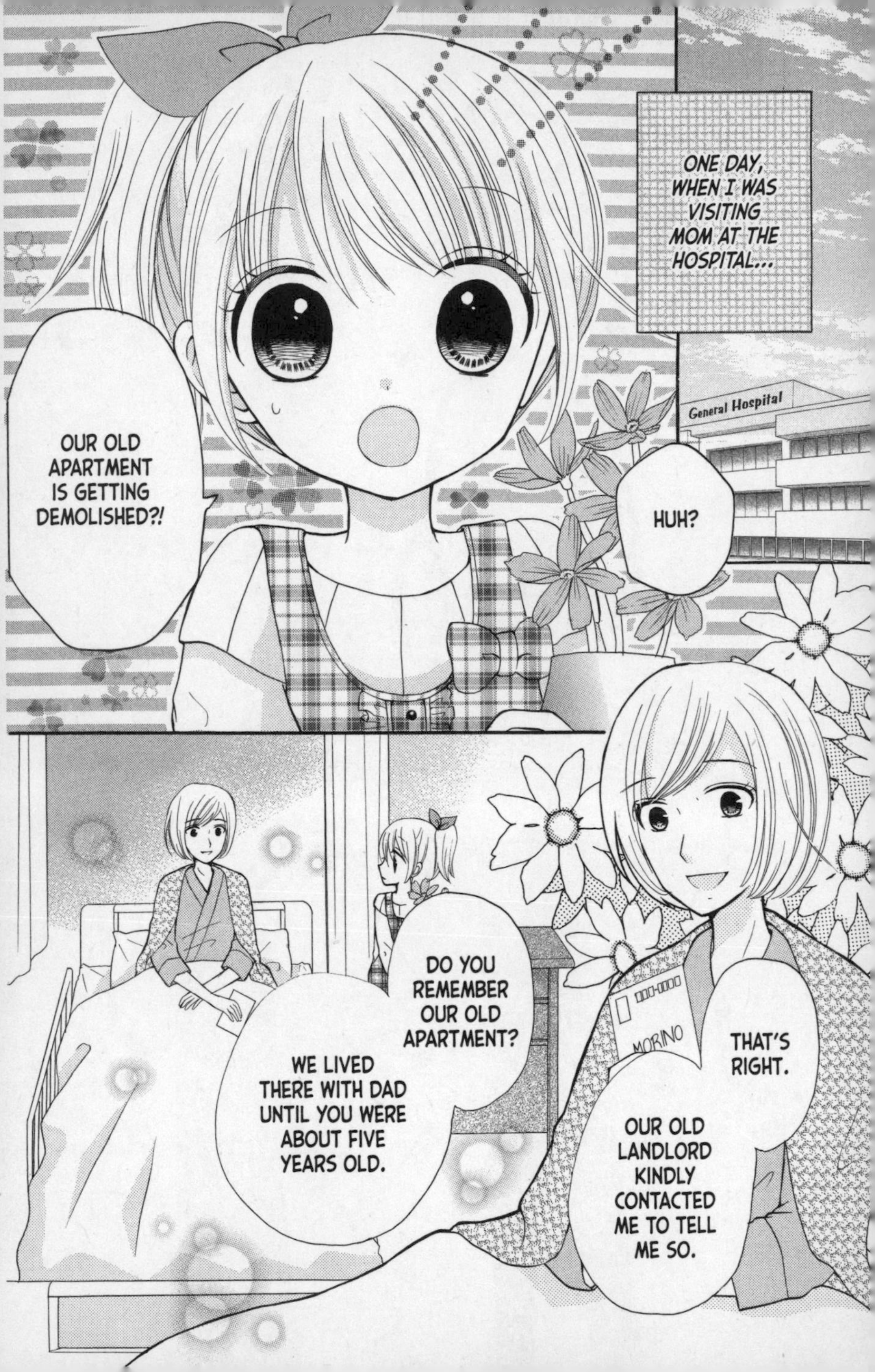
ONE DAY, WHEN I WAS VISITING MOM AT THE HOSPITAL...
General Hospital
HUH?
OUR OLD APARTMENT IS GETTING DEMOLISHED?!
MORINO
THAT'S RIGHT.
OUR OLD LANDLORD KINDLY CONTACTED ME TO TELL ME SO.
DO YOU REMEMBER OUR OLD APARTMENT?
WE LIVED THERE WITH DAD UNTIL YOU WERE ABOUT FIVE YEARS OLD.

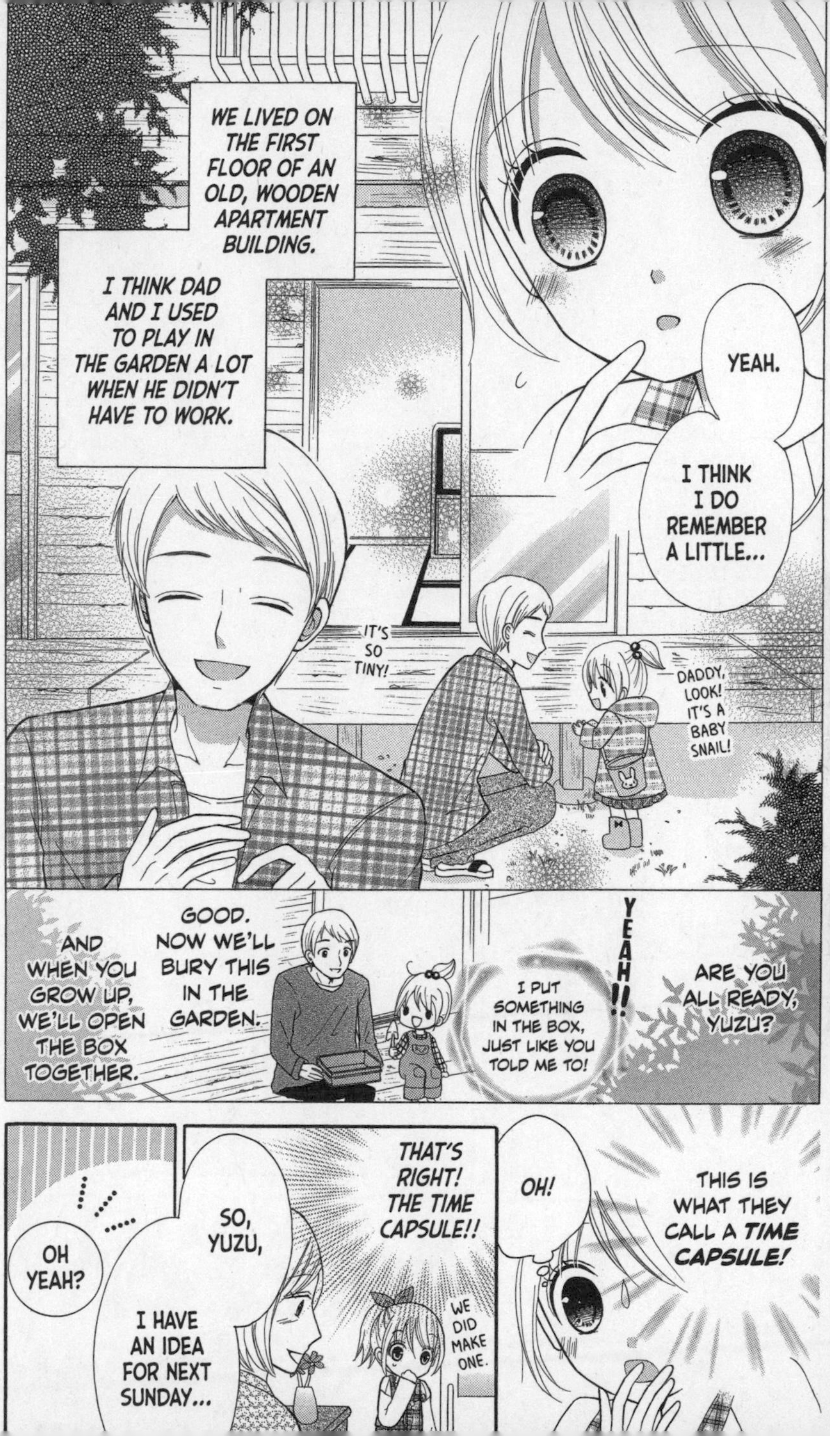
YEAH.
I THINK I DO REMEMBER A LITTLE...
WE LIVED ON THE FIRST FLOOR OF AN OLD, WOODEN APARTMENT BUILDING.
I THINK DAD AND I USED TO PLAY IN THE GARDEN A LOT WHEN HE DIDN'T HAVE TO WORK.
DADDY, LOOK! IT'S A BABY SNAIL!
IT'S SO TINY!
ARE YOU ALL READY, YUZU?
YEAH!!
I PUT SOMETHING IN THE BOX, JUST LIKE YOU TOLD ME TO!
GOOD. NOW WE'LL BURY THIS IN THE GARDEN.
AND WHEN YOU GROW UP, WE'LL OPEN THE BOX TOGETHER.
THIS IS WHAT THEY CALL A *TIME CAPSULE!*
OH!
THAT'S RIGHT! THE TIME CAPSULE!!
SO, YUZU,
I HAVE AN IDEA FOR NEXT SUNDAY...
WE DID MAKE ONE.
....
OH YEAH?

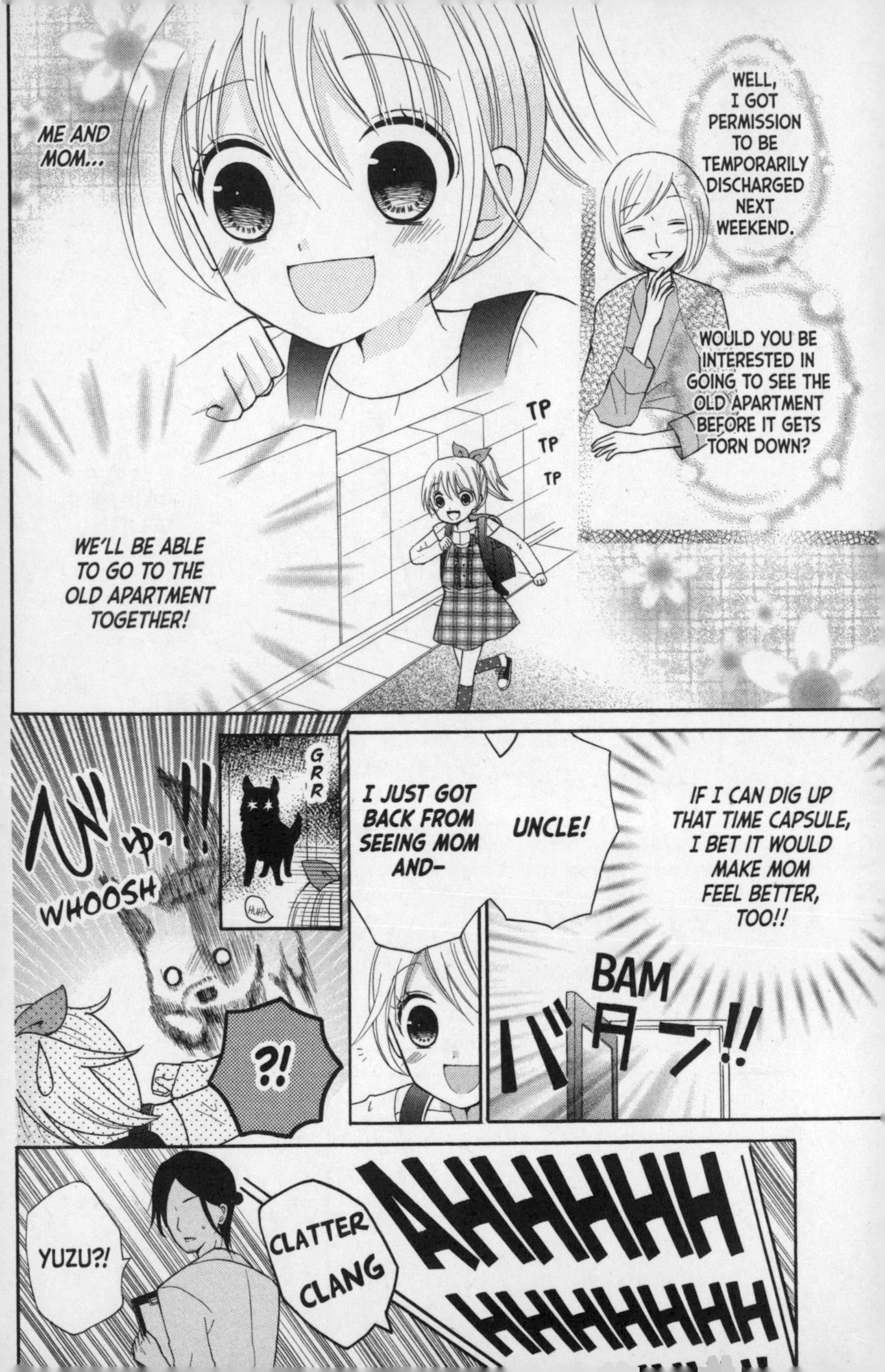
WELL, I GOT PERMISSION TO BE TEMPORARILY DISCHARGED NEXT WEEKEND.
WOULD YOU BE INTERESTED IN GOING TO SEE THE OLD APARTMENT BEFORE IT GETS TORN DOWN?
ME AND MOM...
TP TP TP
WE'LL BE ABLE TO GO TO THE OLD APARTMENT TOGETHER!
IF I CAN DIG UP THAT TIME CAPSULE, I BET IT WOULD MAKE MOM FEEL BETTER, TOO!!
BAM
バターン!!
UNCLE!
I JUST GOT BACK FROM SEEING MOM AND-
GRR
HUH?
WHOOSH
?!
AHHHHH HHHHHHHH
CLATTER CLANG
YUZU?!

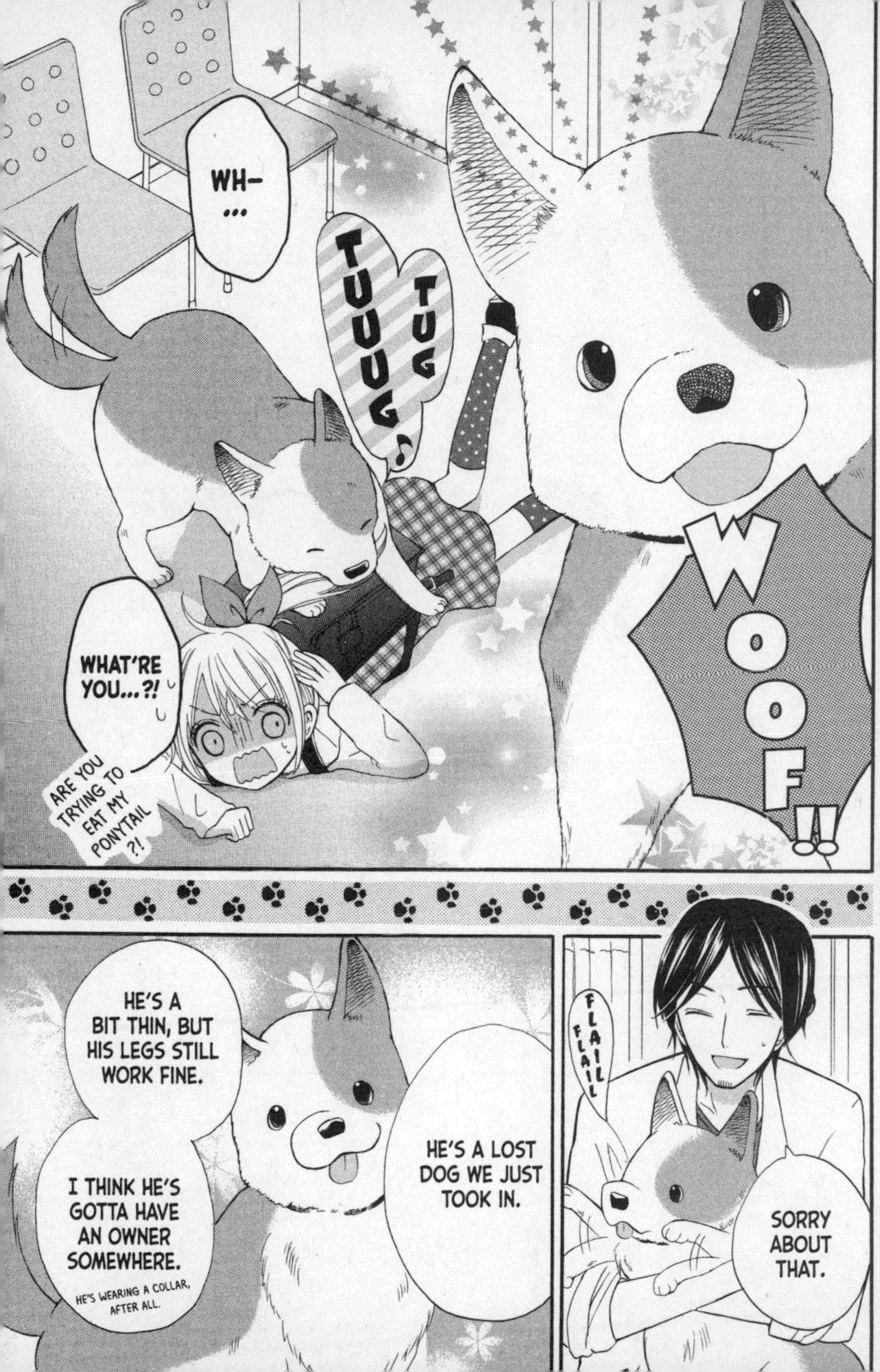
WOOF!!
TUUUG TUG ♪
WH-...
WHAT'RE YOU...?!
ARE YOU TRYING TO EAT MY PONYTAIL?!
FLAIL FLAIL
SORRY ABOUT THAT.
HE'S A LOST DOG WE JUST TOOK IN.
HE'S A BIT THIN, BUT HIS LEGS STILL WORK FINE.
I THINK HE'S GOTTA HAVE AN OWNER SOMEWHERE.
HE'S WEARING A COLLAR, AFTER ALL.

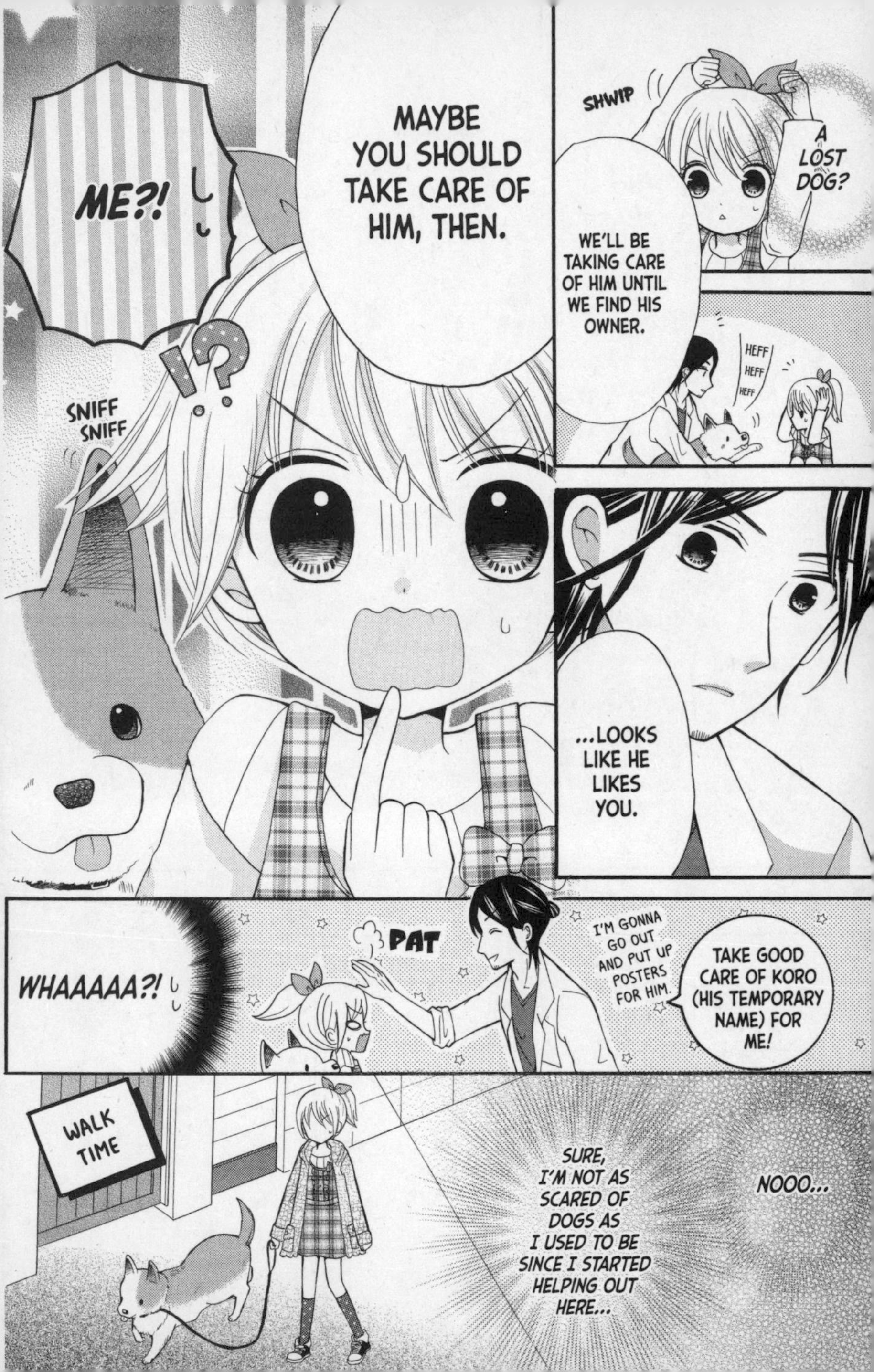

SHWIP
A LOST DOG?
WE'LL BE TAKING CARE OF HIM UNTIL WE FIND HIS OWNER.
HEFF HEFF HEFF
...LOOKS LIKE HE LIKES YOU.
MAYBE YOU SHOULD TAKE CARE OF HIM, THEN.
!?
ME?!
SNIFF SNIFF
TAKE GOOD CARE OF KORO (HIS TEMPORARY NAME) FOR ME!
I'M GONNA GO OUT AND PUT UP POSTERS FOR HIM.
PAT
WHAAAAA?!
NOOO...
SURE, I'M NOT AS SCARED OF DOGS AS I USED TO BE SINCE I STARTED HELPING OUT HERE...
WALK TIME

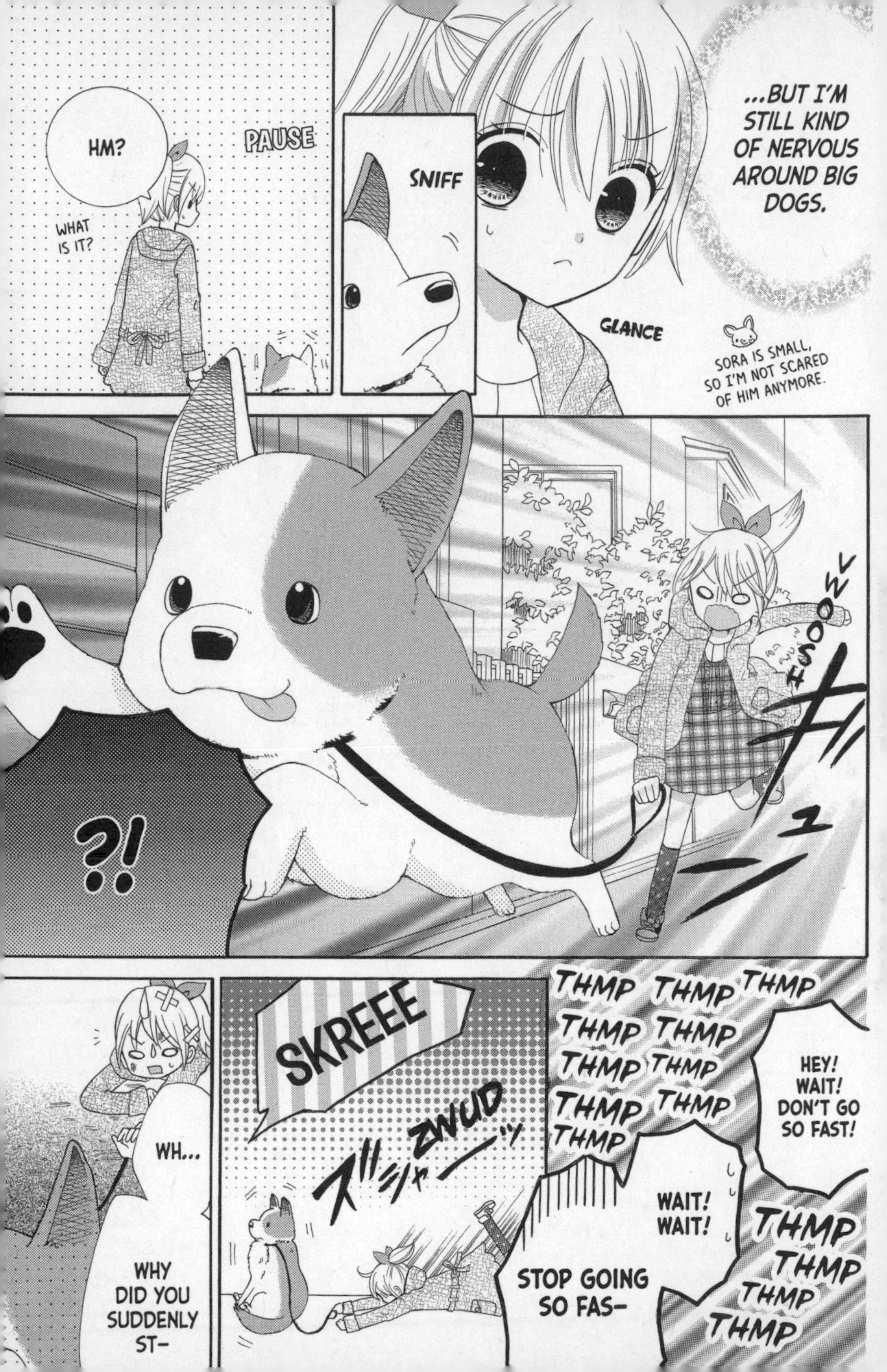
...BUT I'M STILL KIND OF NERVOUS AROUND BIG DOGS.
SNIFF
GLANCE
SORA IS SMALL, SO I'M NOT SCARED OF HIM ANYMORE.
PAUSE
HM?
WHAT IS IT?
VWOOSH
?!
THMP THMP THMP THMP THMP THMP THMP THMP THMP THMP
HEY! WAIT! DON'T GO SO FAST!
THMP THMP THMP THMP
WAIT! WAIT!
STOP GOING SO FAS–
SKREEE
ZWUD
WH...
WHY DID YOU SUDDENLY ST–

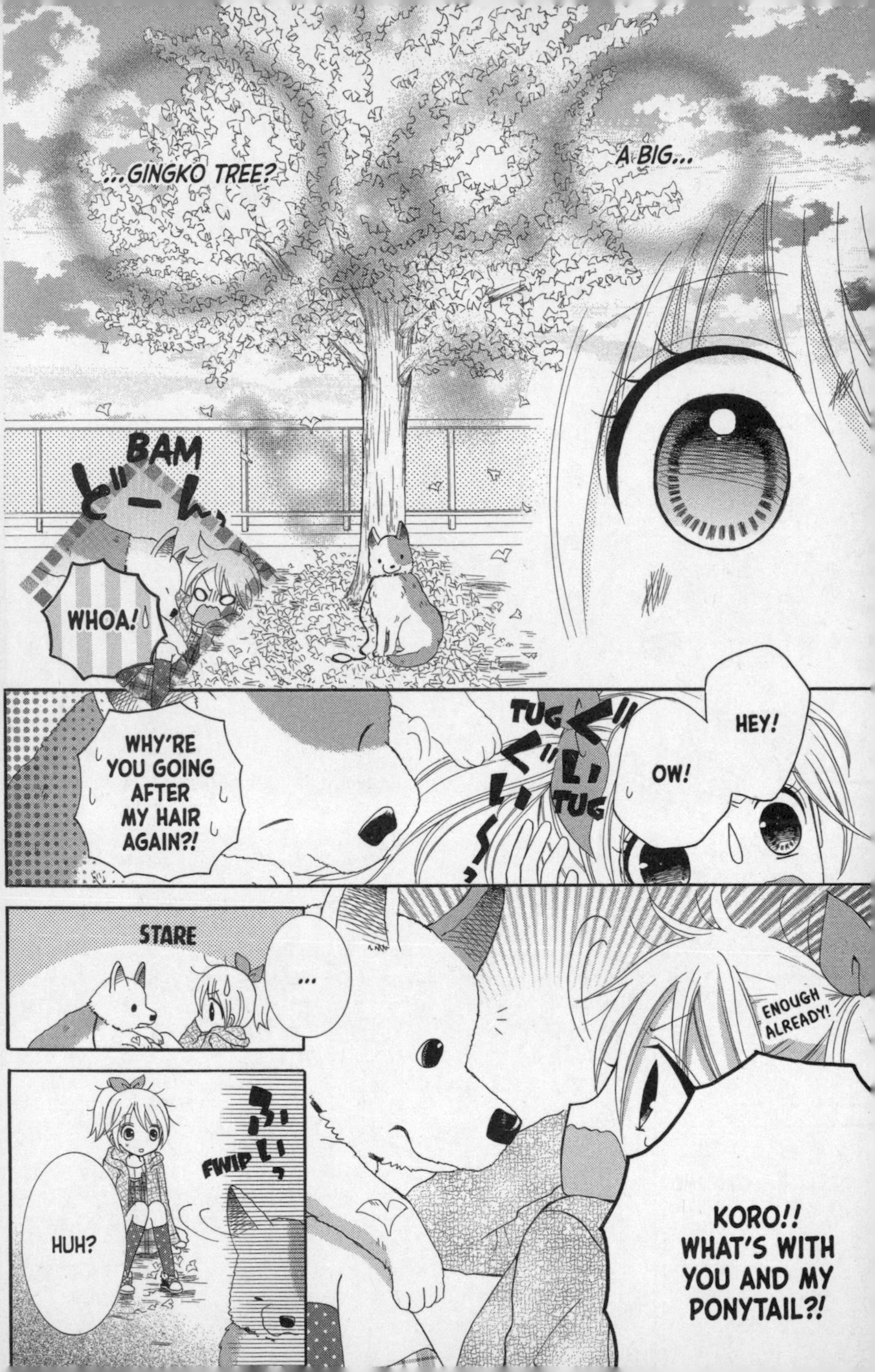
A BIG...
...GINGKO TREE?
BAM
WHOA!
HEY!
OW!
TUG
TUG
WHY'RE YOU GOING AFTER MY HAIR AGAIN?!
ENOUGH ALREADY!
KORO!! WHAT'S WITH YOU AND MY PONYTAIL?!
STARE
...
FWIP
HUH?

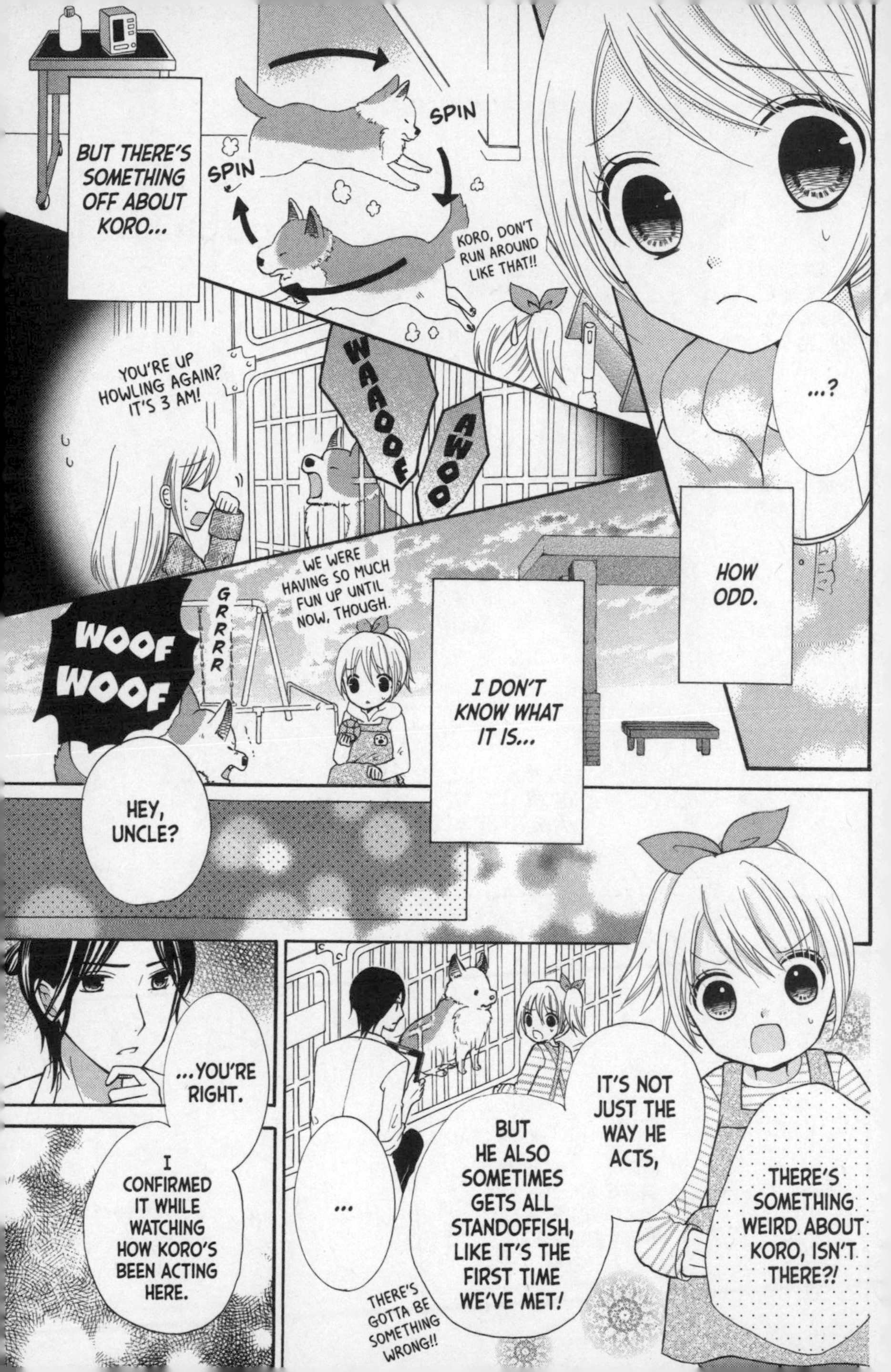

...?
HOW ODD.
BUT THERE'S SOMETHING OFF ABOUT KORO...
SPIN
SPIN
KORO, DON'T RUN AROUND LIKE THAT!!
YOU'RE UP HOWLING AGAIN? IT'S 3 AM!
WAAOOF
AWOO
WE WERE HAVING SO MUCH FUN UP UNTIL NOW, THOUGH.
GRRRR
WOOF WOOF
I DON'T KNOW WHAT IT IS...
HEY, UNCLE?
THERE'S SOMETHING WEIRD ABOUT KORO, ISN'T THERE?!
IT'S NOT JUST THE WAY HE ACTS,
BUT HE ALSO SOMETIMES GETS ALL STANDOFFISH, LIKE IT'S THE FIRST TIME WE'VE MET!
THERE'S GOTTA BE SOMETHING WRONG!!
...
...YOU'RE RIGHT.
I CONFIRMED IT WHILE WATCHING HOW KORO'S BEEN ACTING HERE.

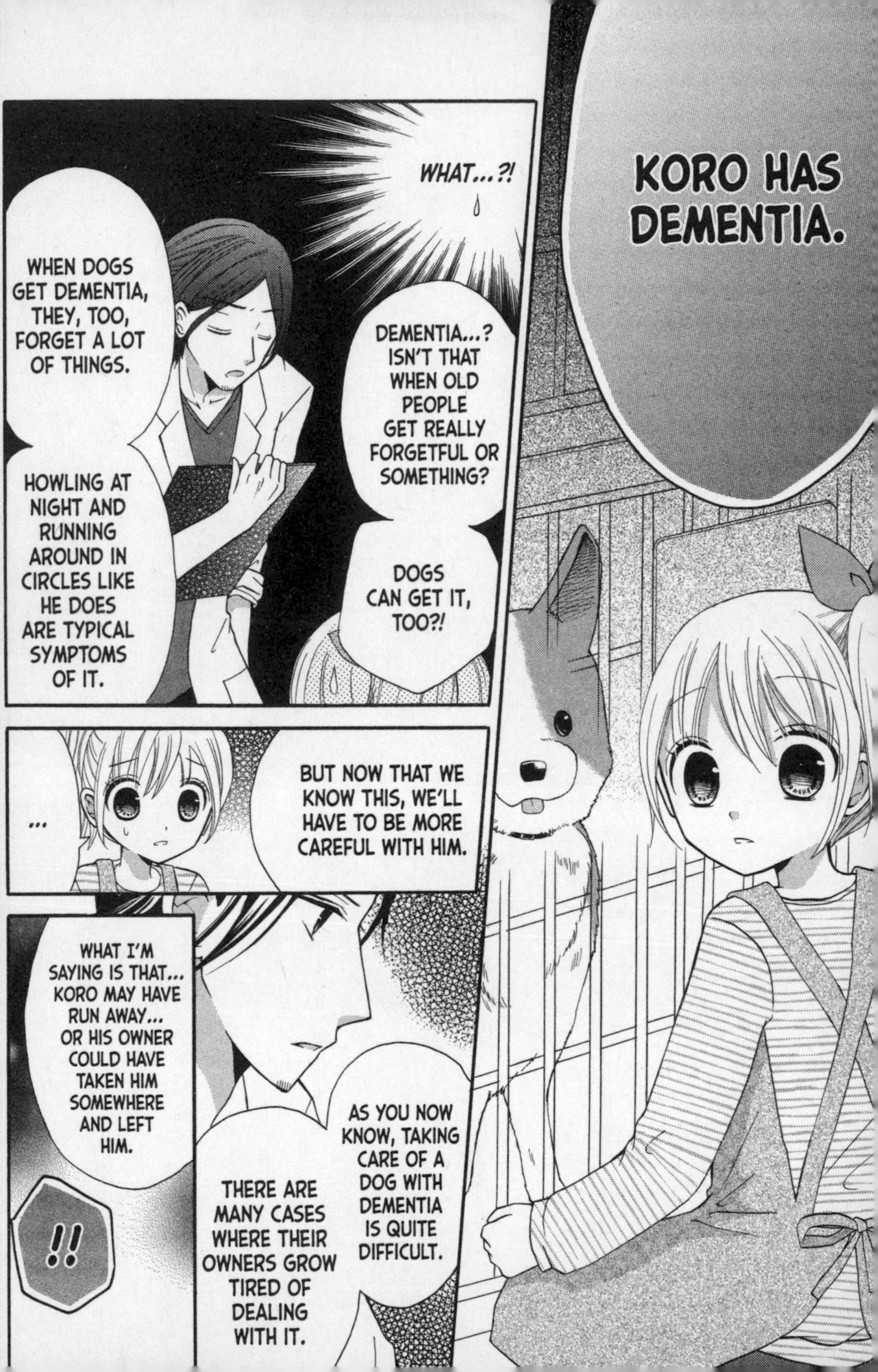
KORO HAS DEMENTIA.
WHAT...?!
DEMENTIA...? ISN'T THAT WHEN OLD PEOPLE GET REALLY FORGETFUL OR SOMETHING?
DOGS CAN GET IT, TOO?!
WHEN DOGS GET DEMENTIA, THEY, TOO, FORGET A LOT OF THINGS.
HOWLING AT NIGHT AND RUNNING AROUND IN CIRCLES LIKE HE DOES ARE TYPICAL SYMPTOMS OF IT.
BUT NOW THAT WE KNOW THIS, WE'LL HAVE TO BE MORE CAREFUL WITH HIM.
...
AS YOU NOW KNOW, TAKING CARE OF A DOG WITH DEMENTIA IS QUITE DIFFICULT.
THERE ARE MANY CASES WHERE THEIR OWNERS GROW TIRED OF DEALING WITH IT.
WHAT I'M SAYING IS THAT... KORO MAY HAVE RUN AWAY... OR HIS OWNER COULD HAVE TAKEN HIM SOMEWHERE AND LEFT HIM.
!!

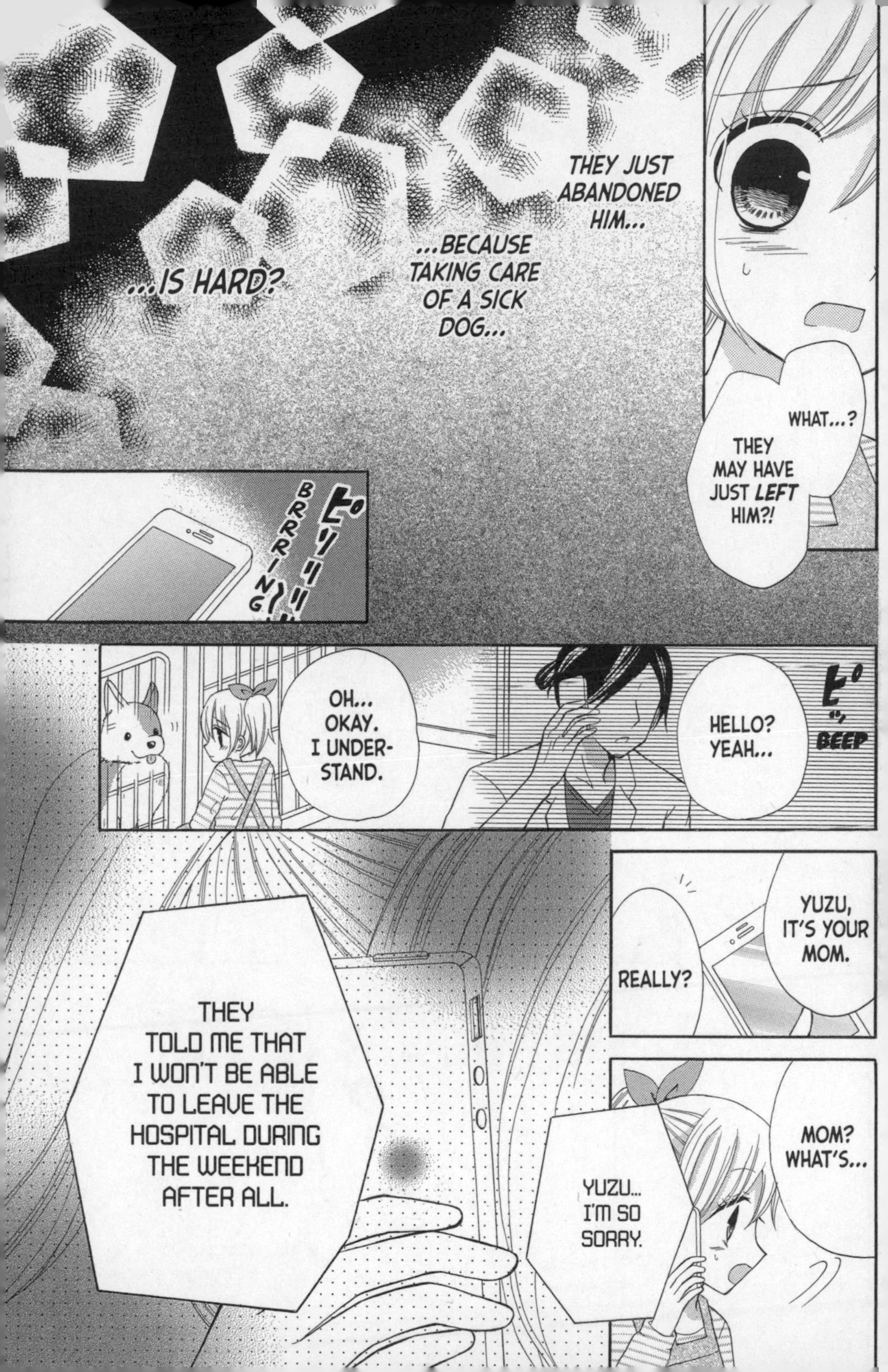
WHAT...?
THEY MAY HAVE JUST *LEFT* HIM?!
THEY JUST ABANDONED HIM...
...BECAUSE TAKING CARE OF A SICK DOG...
...IS HARD?
BRRRING
HELLO? YEAH...
BEEP
OH... OKAY. I UNDER-STAND.
YUZU, IT'S YOUR MOM.
REALLY?
MOM? WHAT'S...
YUZU... I'M SO SORRY.
THEY TOLD ME THAT I WON'T BE ABLE TO LEAVE THE HOSPITAL DURING THE WEEKEND AFTER ALL.

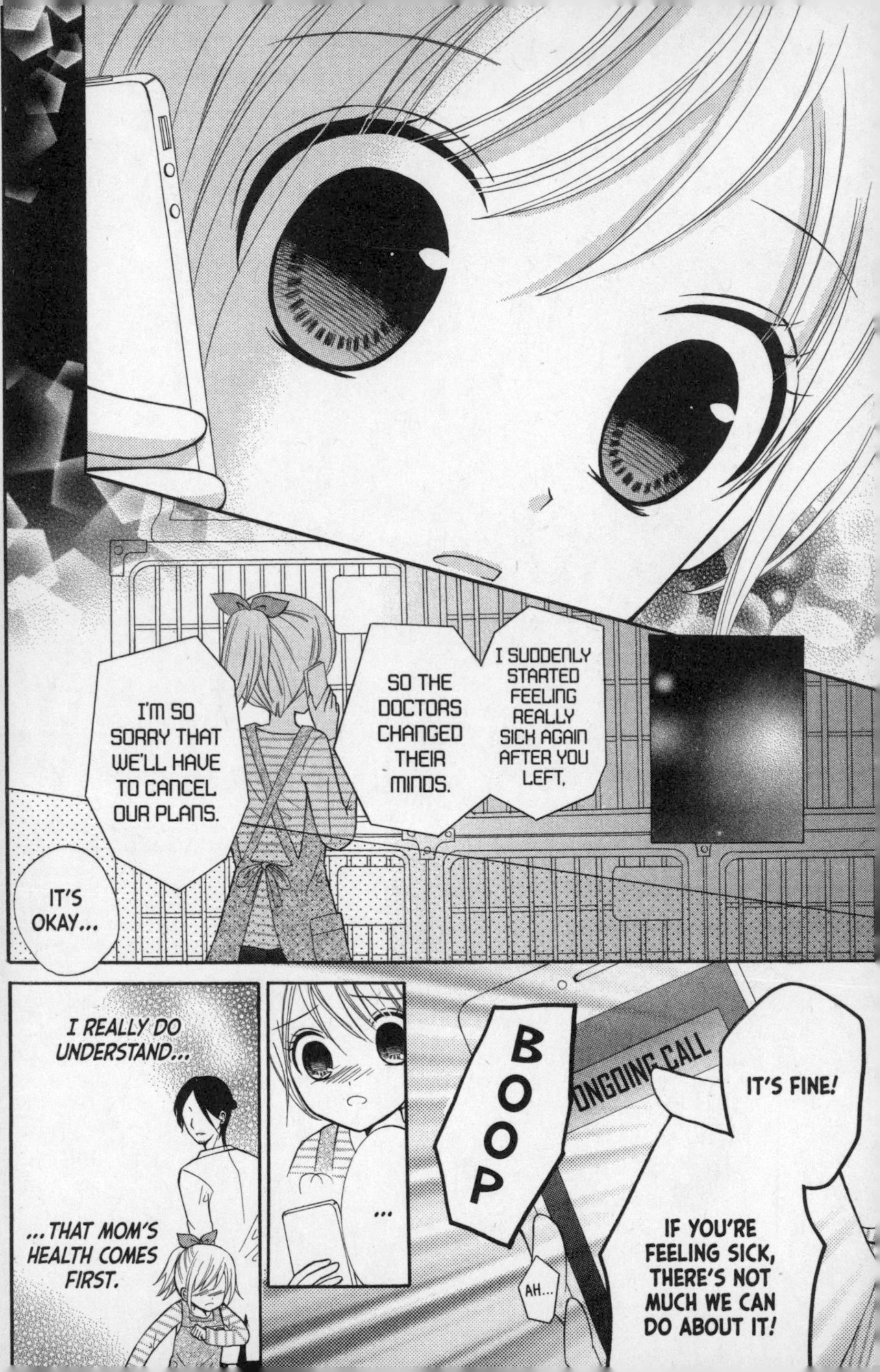
I SUDDENLY STARTED FEELING REALLY SICK AGAIN AFTER YOU LEFT,
SO THE DOCTORS CHANGED THEIR MINDS.
I'M SO SORRY THAT WE'LL HAVE TO CANCEL OUR PLANS.
IT'S OKAY...
IT'S FINE!
ONGOING CALL
BOOP
IF YOU'RE FEELING SICK, THERE'S NOT MUCH WE CAN DO ABOUT IT!
AH...
...
I REALLY DO UNDERSTAND...
...THAT MOM'S HEALTH COMES FIRST.

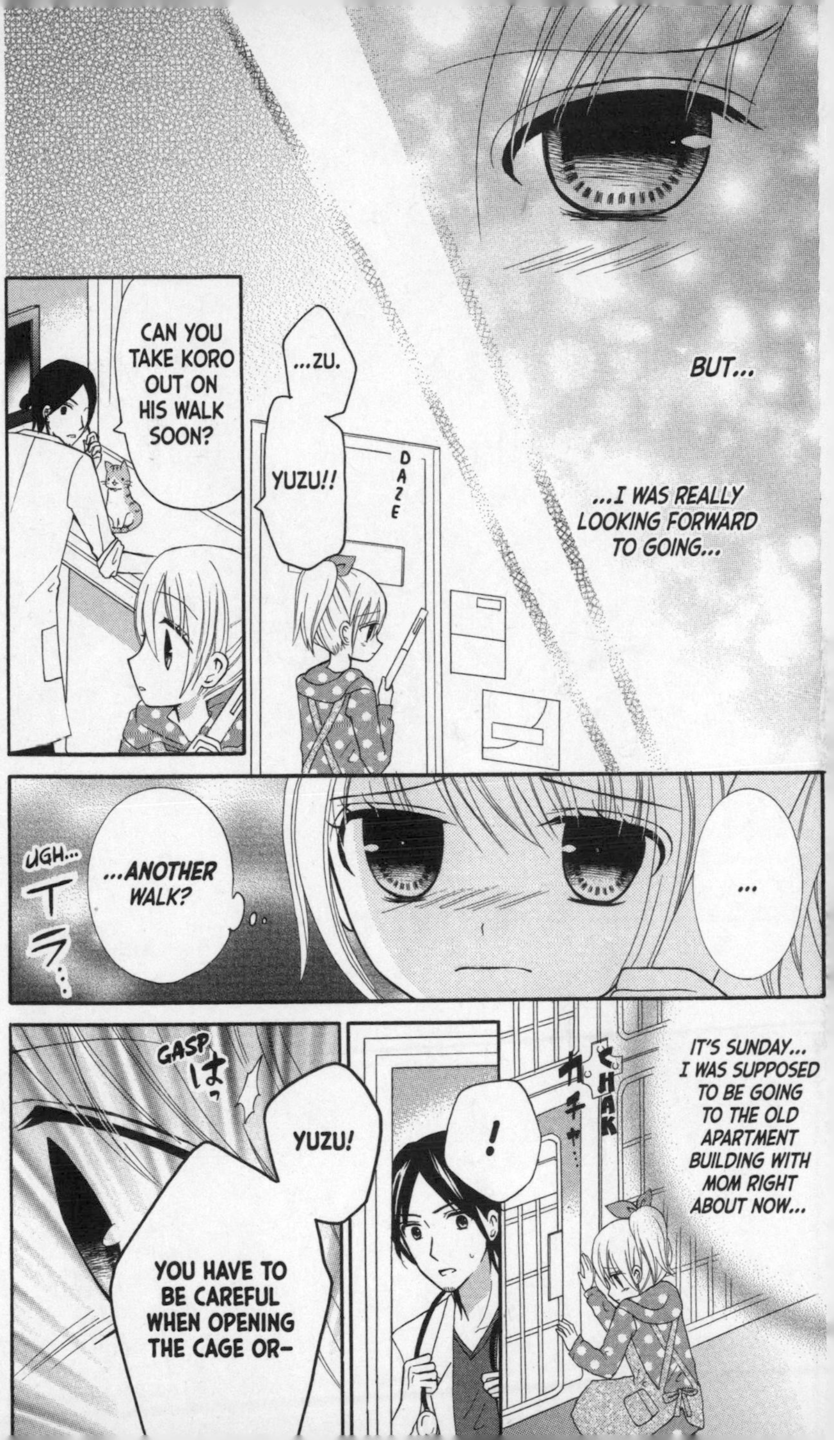
BUT...
...I WAS REALLY LOOKING FORWARD TO GOING...
...ZU.
YUZU!!
DAZE
CAN YOU TAKE KORO OUT ON HIS WALK SOON?
...
...ANOTHER WALK?
UGH...
IT'S SUNDAY... I WAS SUPPOSED TO BE GOING TO THE OLD APARTMENT BUILDING WITH MOM RIGHT ABOUT NOW...
CHAK
カチャ...
!
GASP
はっ
YUZU!
YOU HAVE TO BE CAREFUL WHEN OPENING THE CAGE OR–

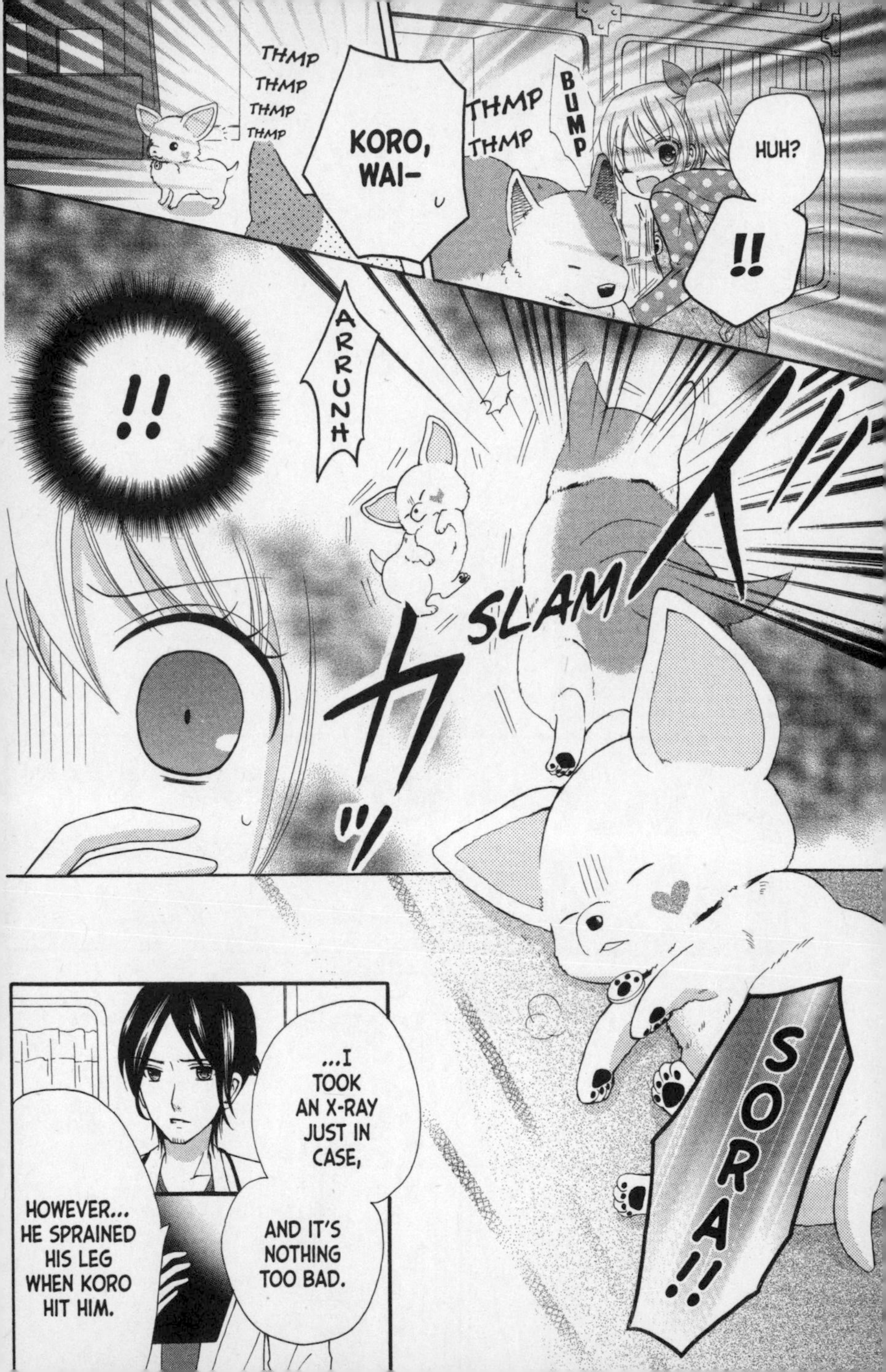
HUH?
!!
BUMP
THMP THMP
KORO, WAI-
THMP THMP THMP THMP
SLAM
ARRUNH
!!
SORA!!
...I TOOK AN X-RAY JUST IN CASE,
AND IT'S NOTHING TOO BAD.
HOWEVER... HE SPRAINED HIS LEG WHEN KORO HIT HIM.

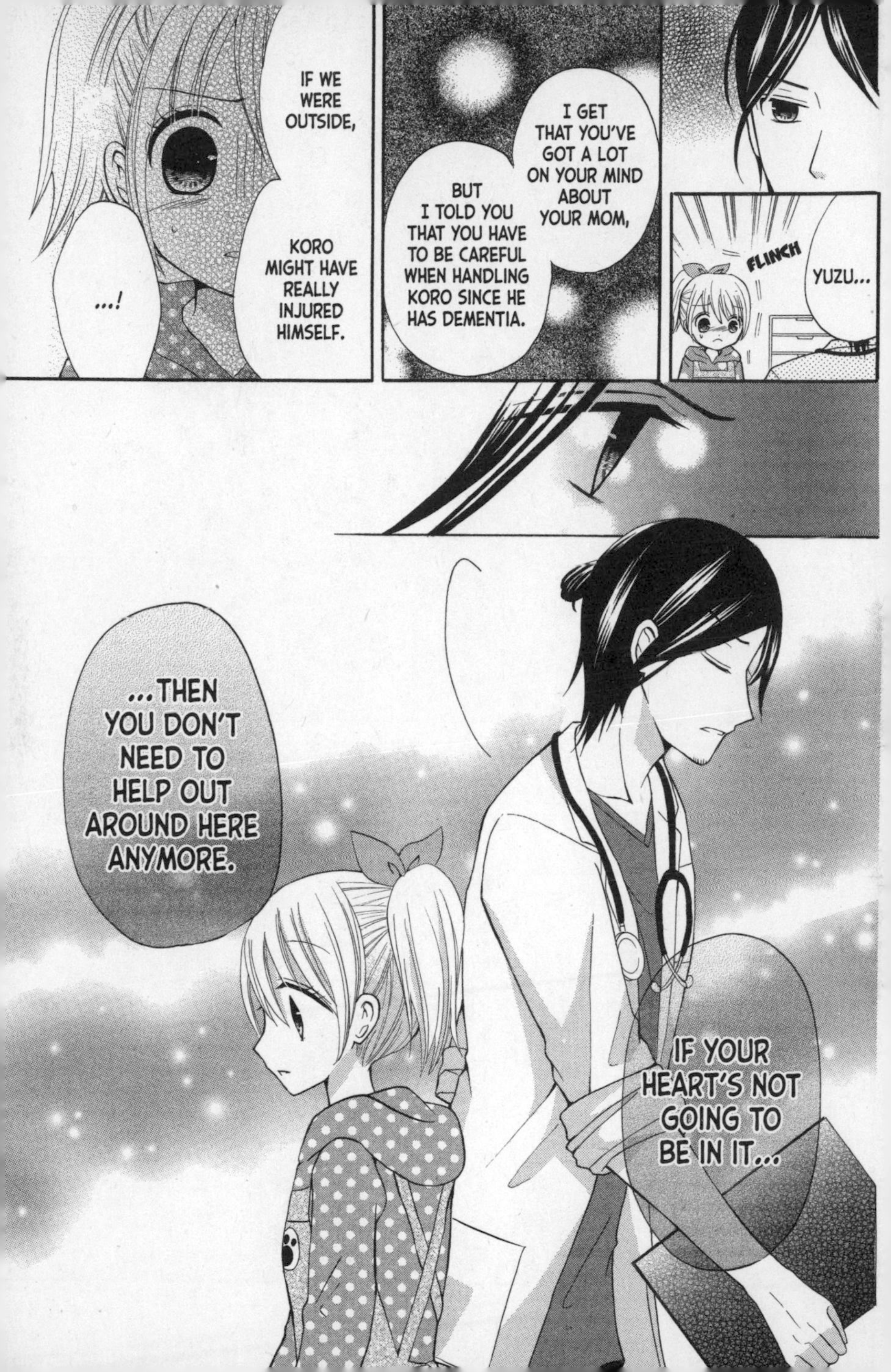
YUZU...
FLINCH
I GET THAT YOU'VE GOT A LOT ON YOUR MIND ABOUT YOUR MOM,
BUT I TOLD YOU THAT YOU HAVE TO BE CAREFUL WHEN HANDLING KORO SINCE HE HAS DEMENTIA.
IF WE WERE OUTSIDE,
KORO MIGHT HAVE REALLY INJURED HIMSELF.
...!
IF YOUR HEART'S NOT GOING TO BE IN IT...
...THEN YOU DON'T NEED TO HELP OUT AROUND HERE ANYMORE.

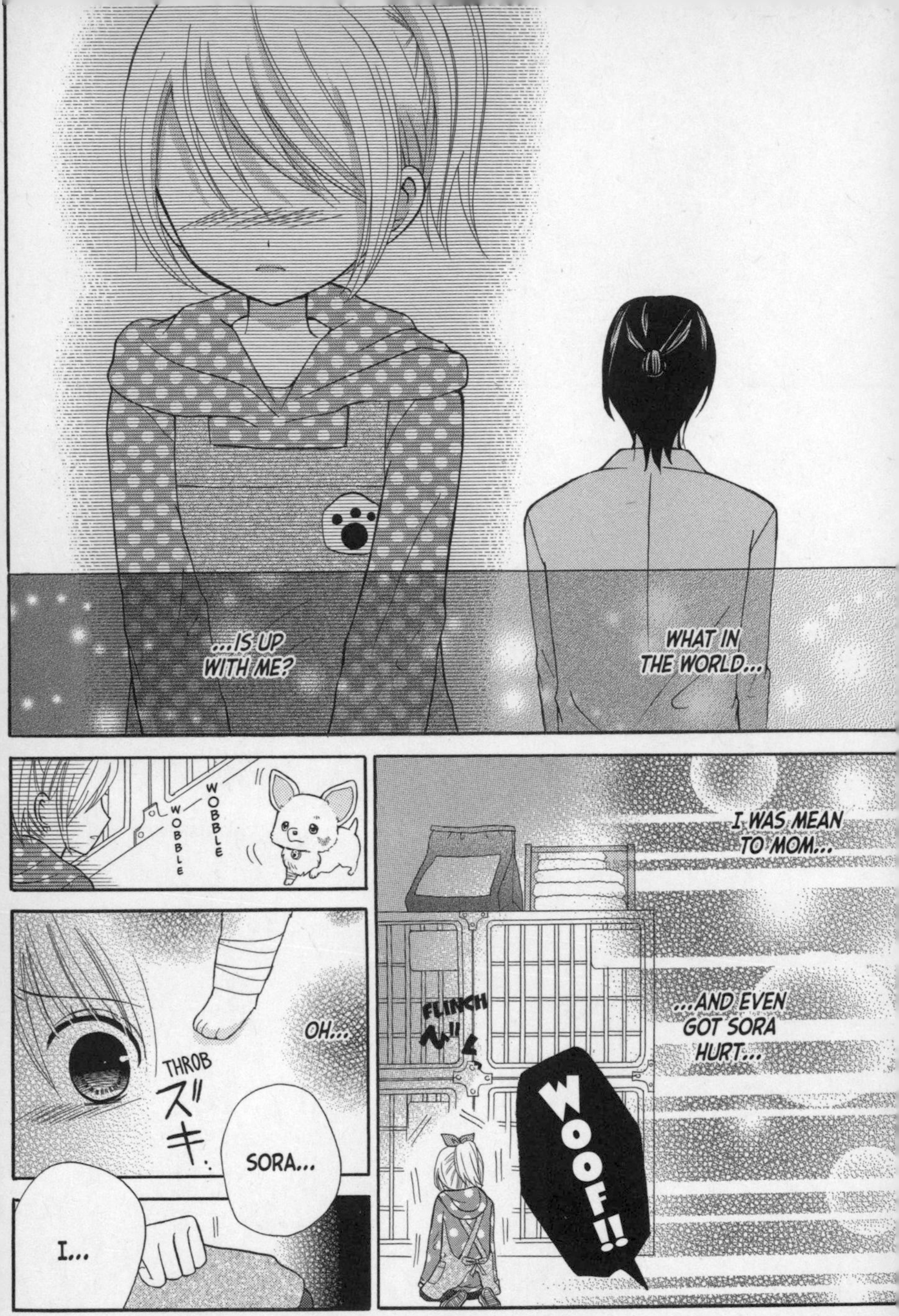
WHAT IN THE WORLD...
...IS UP WITH ME?
I WAS MEAN TO MOM...
...AND EVEN GOT SORA HURT...
FLINCH
WOOF!!
WOBBLE
WOBBLE
OH...
THROB
ズキ
SORA...
I...

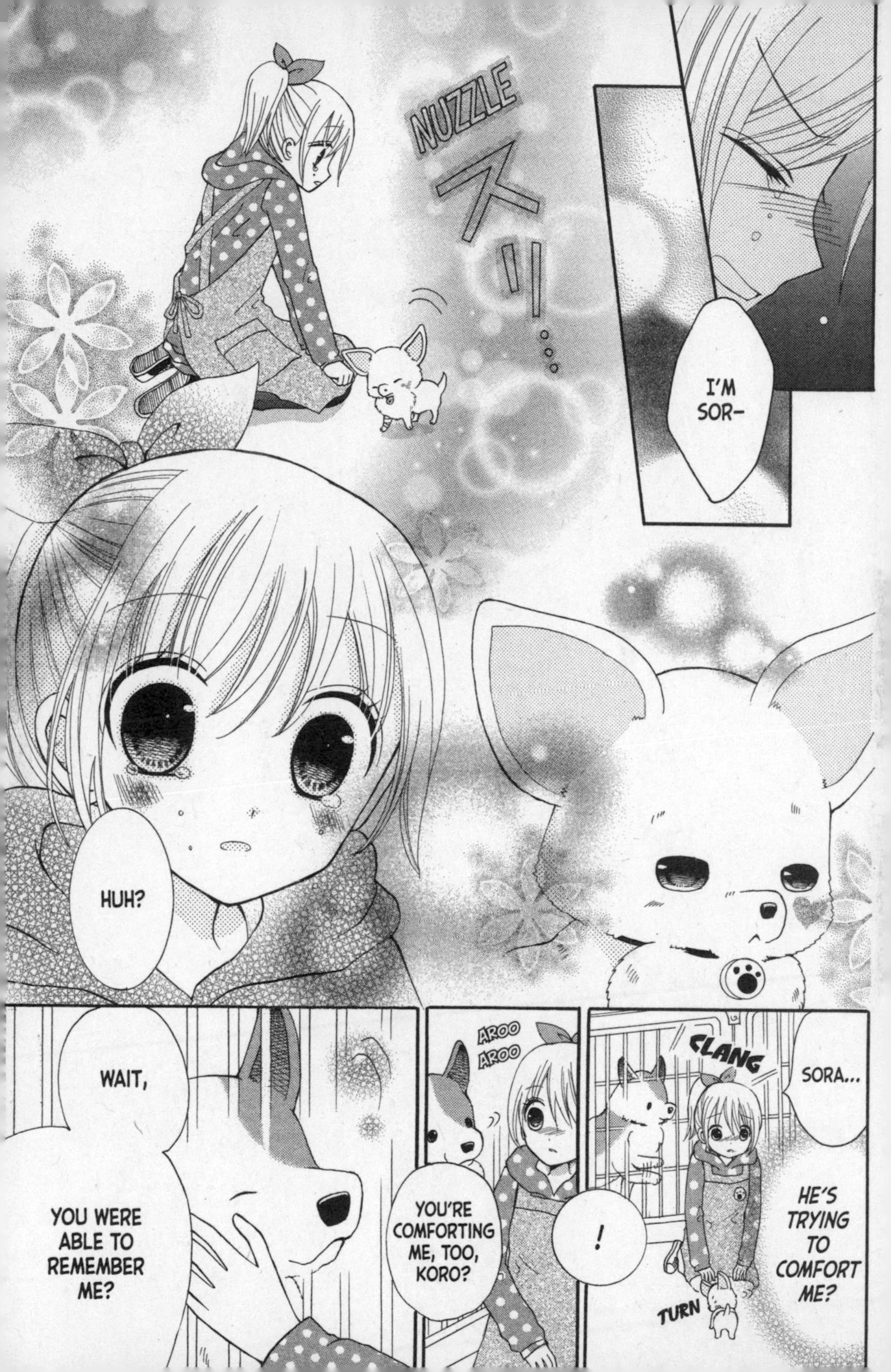
I'M SOR–
NUZZLE
スー…
HUH?
SORA...
CLANG
HE'S TRYING TO COMFORT ME?
!
TURN
AROO AROO
YOU'RE COMFORTING ME, TOO, KORO?
WAIT,
YOU WERE ABLE TO REMEMBER ME?

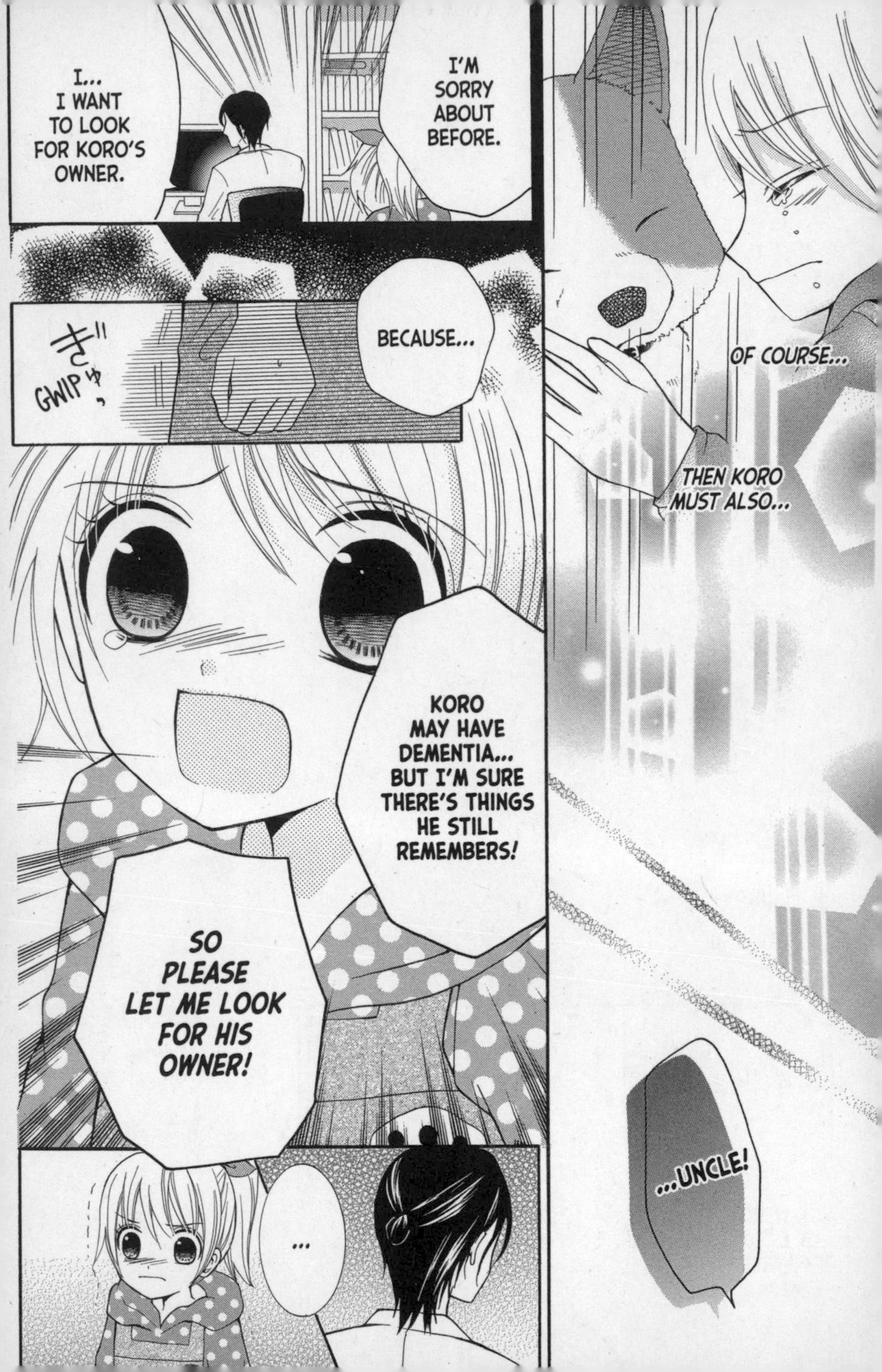
OF COURSE...
THEN KORO MUST ALSO...
...UNCLE!
I'M SORRY ABOUT BEFORE.
I... I WANT TO LOOK FOR KORO'S OWNER.
ぎゅ
GWIP
BECAUSE...
KORO MAY HAVE DEMENTIA... BUT I'M SURE THERE'S THINGS HE STILL REMEMBERS!
SO PLEASE LET ME LOOK FOR HIS OWNER!
...

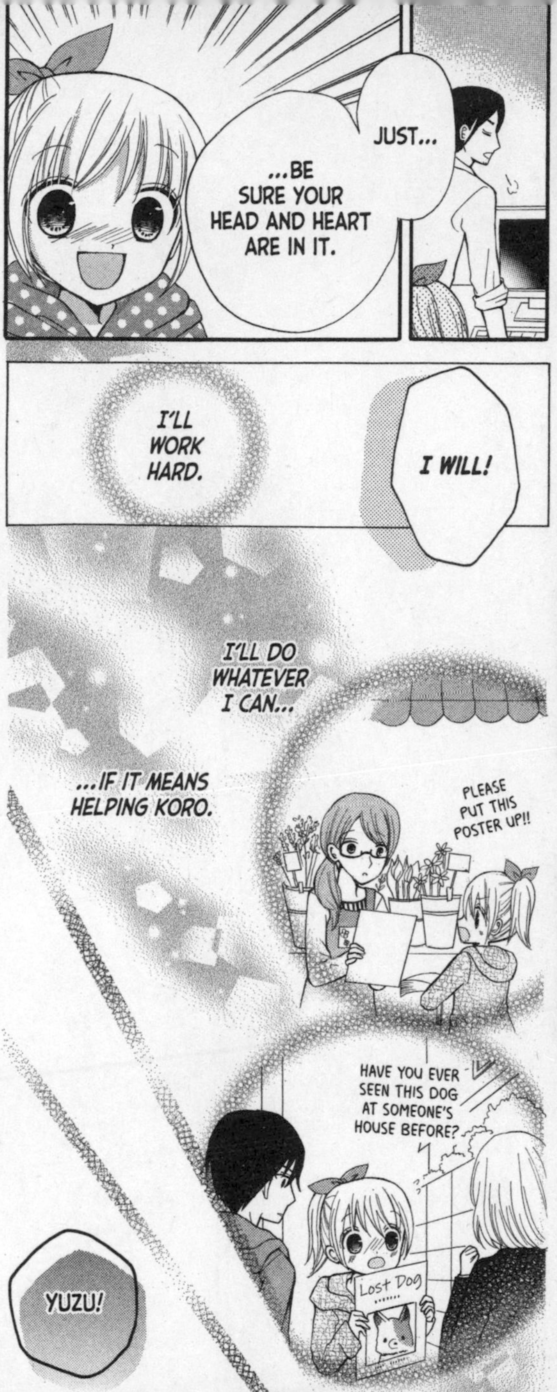
JUST...
...BE SURE YOUR HEAD AND HEART ARE IN IT.
I WILL!
I'LL WORK HARD.
I'LL DO WHATEVER I CAN...
...IF IT MEANS HELPING KORO.
PLEASE PUT THIS POSTER UP!!
HAVE YOU EVER SEEN THIS DOG AT SOMEONE'S HOUSE BEFORE?
Lost Dog
YUZU!

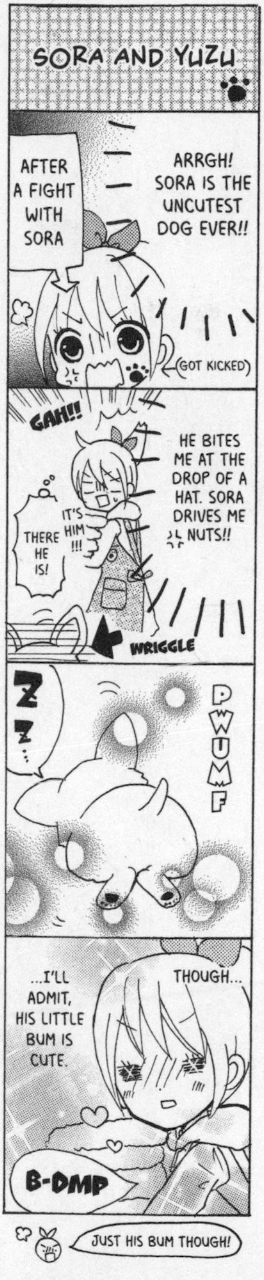
SORA AND YUZU
ARRGH! SORA IS THE UNCUTEST DOG EVER!!
AFTER A FIGHT WITH SORA
(GOT KICKED)
GAH!!
HE BITES ME AT THE DROP OF A HAT. SORA DRIVES ME NUTS!!
IT'S HIM!!!
THERE HE IS!
WRIGGLE
PWUMF
Z Z...
THOUGH...
...I'LL ADMIT, HIS LITTLE BUM IS CUTE.
B-DMP
JUST HIS BUM THOUGH!

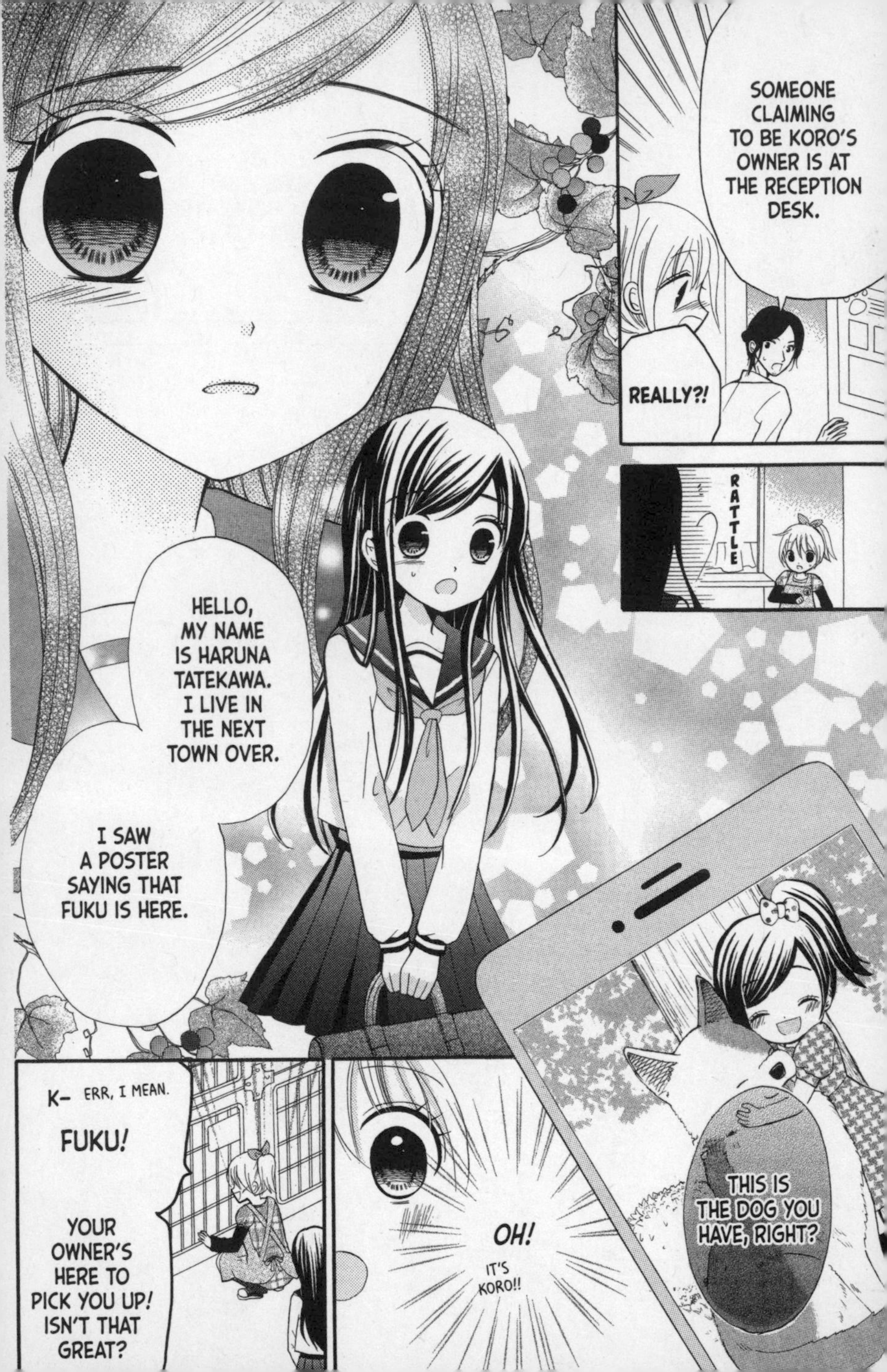
SOMEONE CLAIMING TO BE KORO'S OWNER IS AT THE RECEPTION DESK.
REALLY?!
RATTLE
HELLO, MY NAME IS HARUNA TATEKAWA. I LIVE IN THE NEXT TOWN OVER.
I SAW A POSTER SAYING THAT FUKU IS HERE.
THIS IS THE DOG YOU HAVE, RIGHT?
OH!
IT'S KORO!!
K- ERR, I MEAN.
FUKU!
YOUR OWNER'S HERE TO PICK YOU UP! ISN'T THAT GREAT?

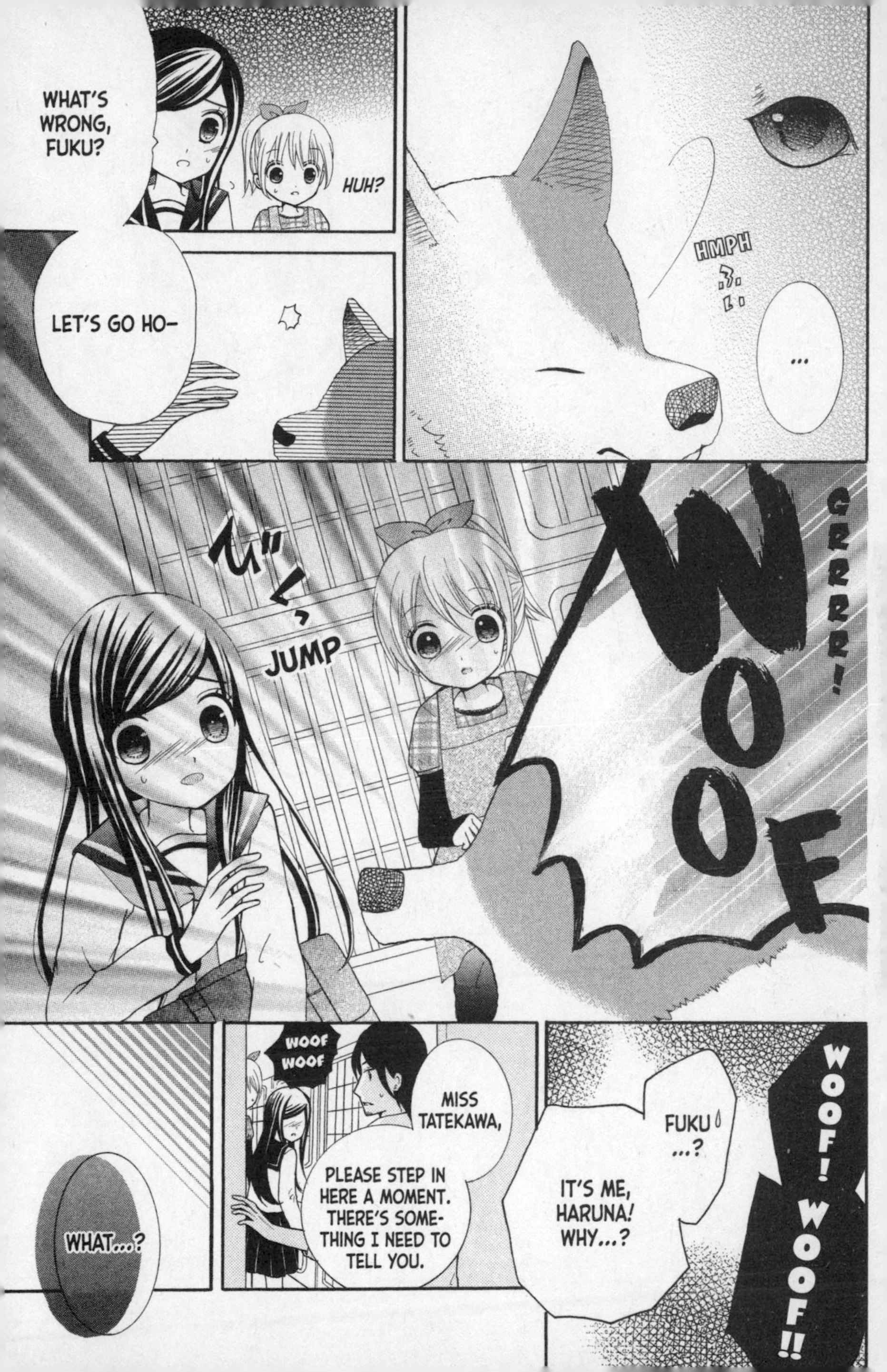
HMPH
...
WHAT'S WRONG, FUKU?
HUH?
LET'S GO HO-
GRRRR!
WOOF
JUMP
WOOF! WOOF! WOOF!!
FUKU...?
IT'S ME, HARUNA! WHY...?
MISS TATEKAWA,
PLEASE STEP IN HERE A MOMENT. THERE'S SOME-THING I NEED TO TELL YOU.
WOOF WOOF
WHAT...?

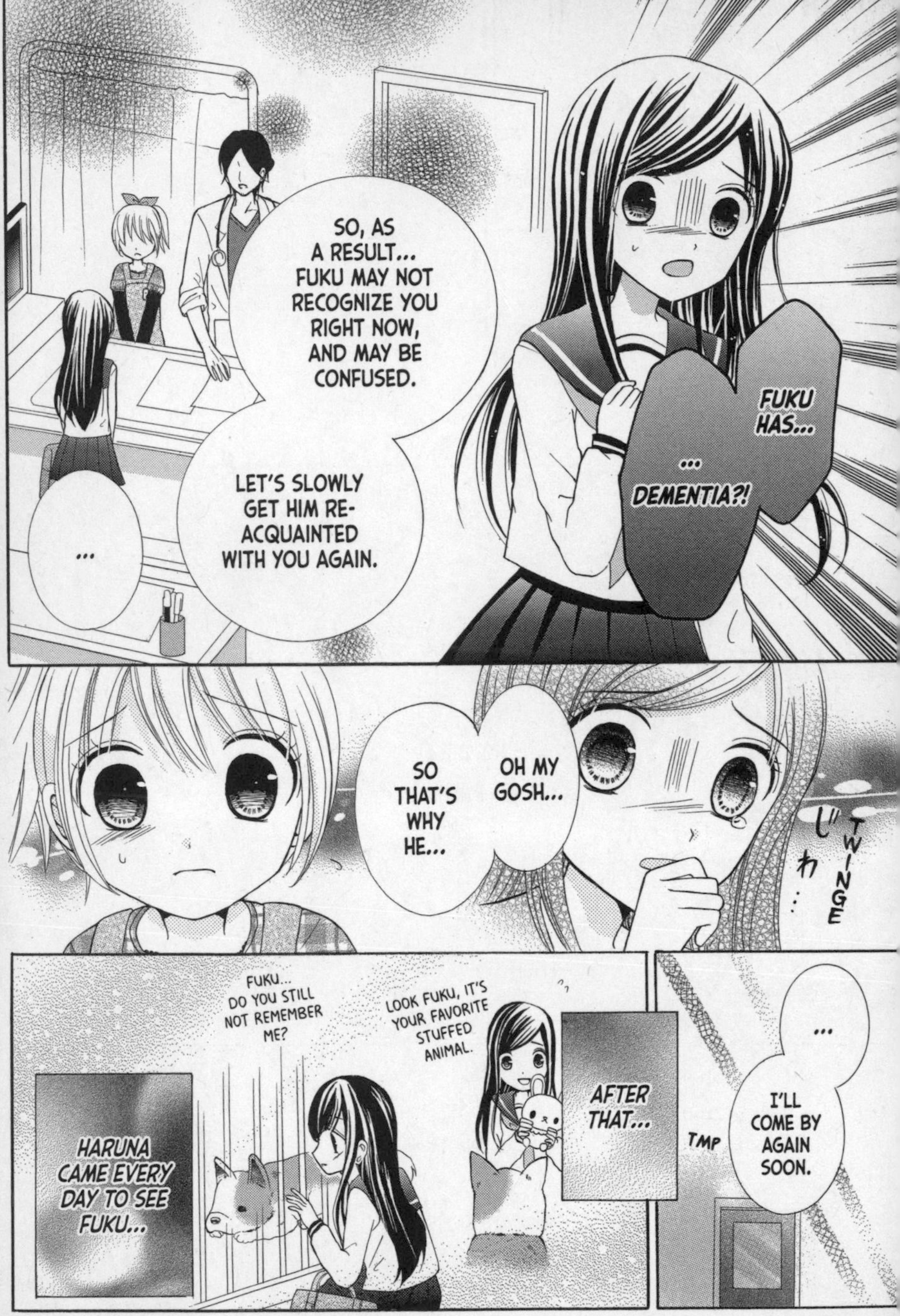
FUKU HAS...
...DEMENTIA?!
SO, AS A RESULT... FUKU MAY NOT RECOGNIZE YOU RIGHT NOW, AND MAY BE CONFUSED.
LET'S SLOWLY GET HIM RE-ACQUAINTED WITH YOU AGAIN.
...
じわ…
TWINGE
OH MY GOSH...
SO THAT'S WHY HE...
...
I'LL COME BY AGAIN SOON.
TMP
AFTER THAT...
LOOK FUKU, IT'S YOUR FAVORITE STUFFED ANIMAL.
FUKU... DO YOU STILL NOT REMEMBER ME?
HARUNA CAME EVERY DAY TO SEE FUKU...

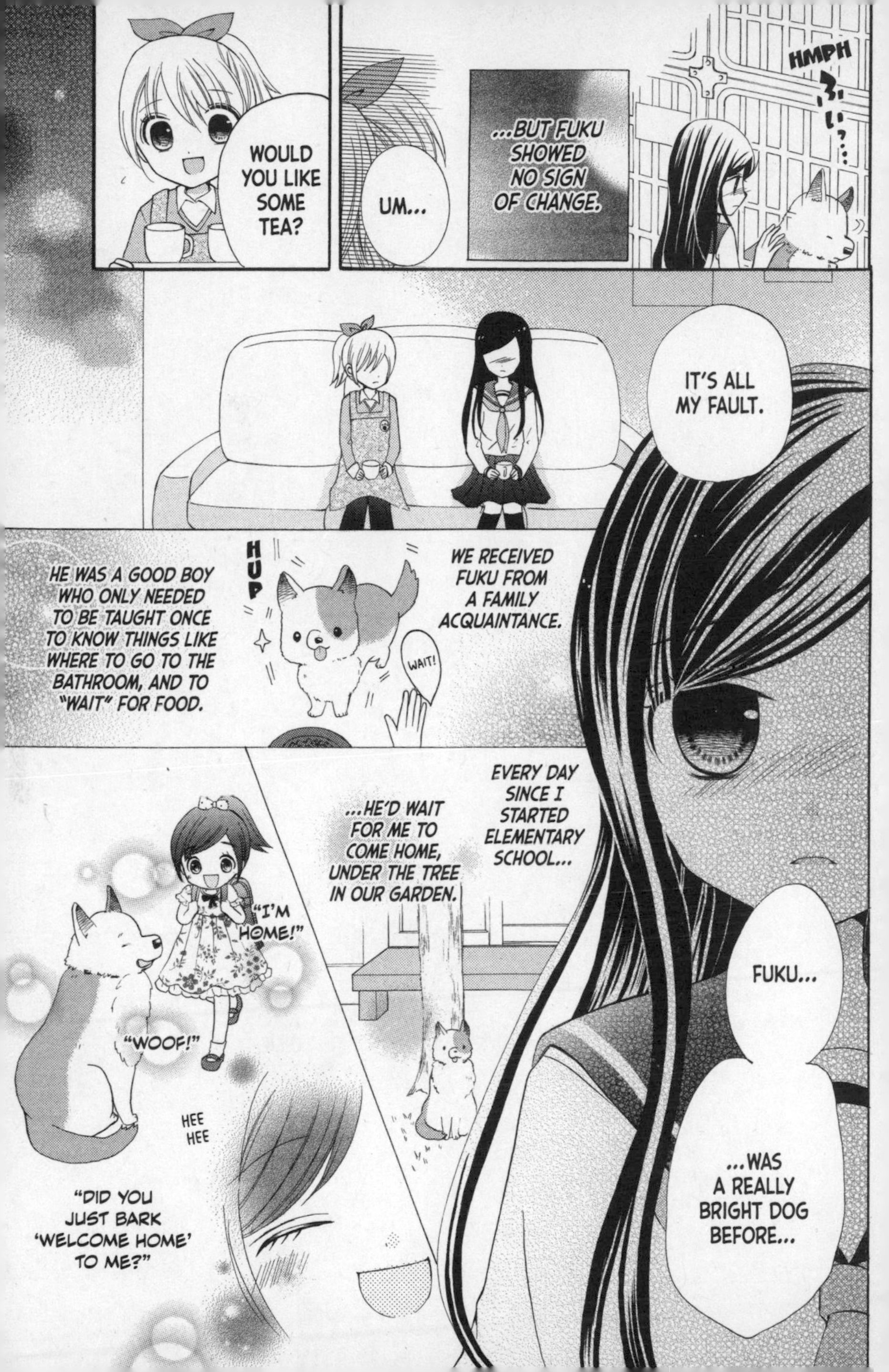
HMPH
...BUT FUKU SHOWED NO SIGN OF CHANGE.
UM...
WOULD YOU LIKE SOME TEA?
IT'S ALL MY FAULT.
FUKU...
...WAS A REALLY BRIGHT DOG BEFORE...
WE RECEIVED FUKU FROM A FAMILY ACQUAINTANCE.
HUP
WAIT!
HE WAS A GOOD BOY WHO ONLY NEEDED TO BE TAUGHT ONCE TO KNOW THINGS LIKE WHERE TO GO TO THE BATHROOM, AND TO "WAIT" FOR FOOD.
EVERY DAY SINCE I STARTED ELEMENTARY SCHOOL...
...HE'D WAIT FOR ME TO COME HOME, UNDER THE TREE IN OUR GARDEN.
"I'M HOME!"
"WOOF!"
HEE HEE
"DID YOU JUST BARK 'WELCOME HOME' TO ME?"

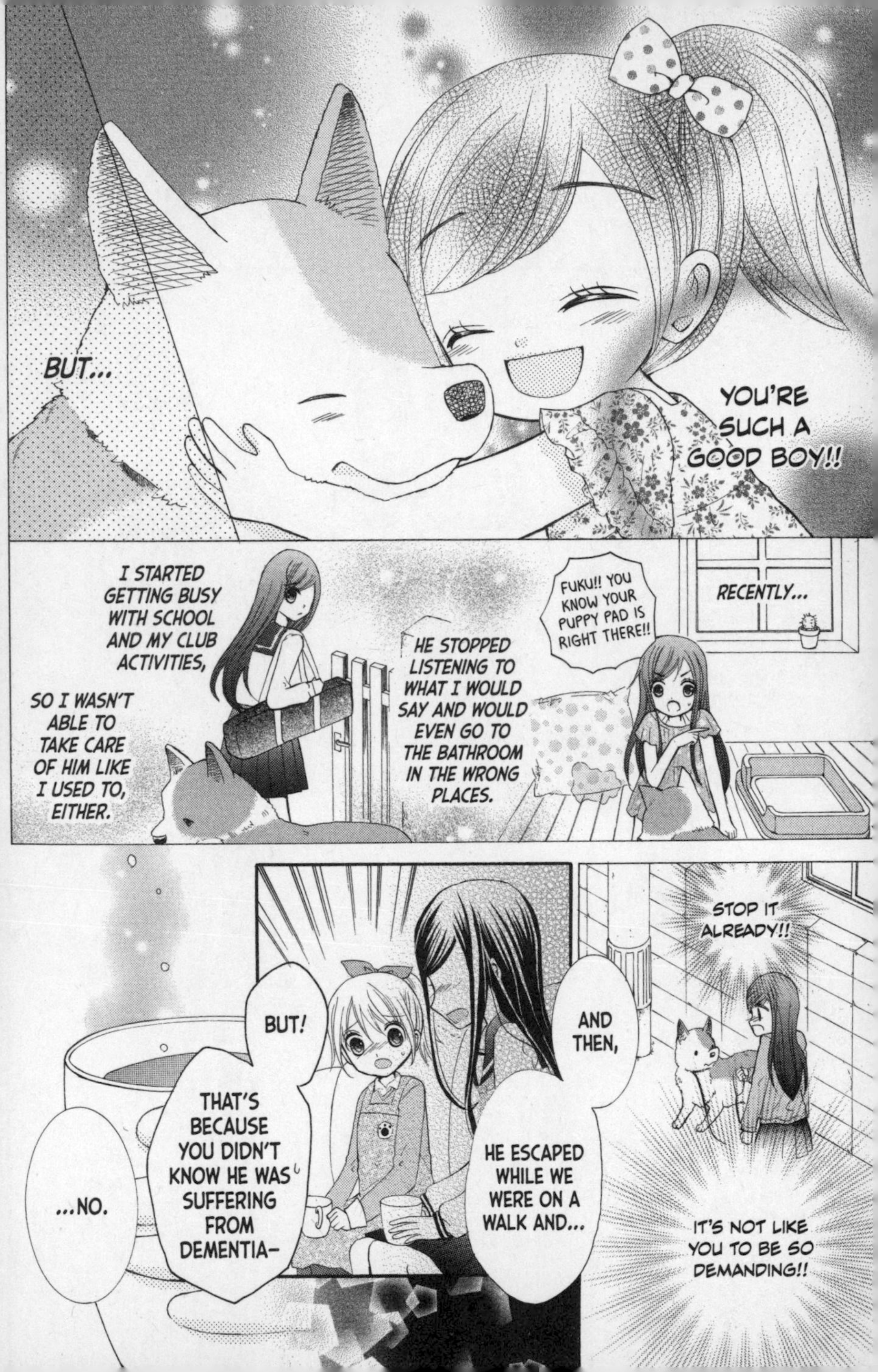
YOU'RE SUCH A GOOD BOY!!
BUT...
RECENTLY...
FUKU!! YOU KNOW YOUR PUPPY PAD IS RIGHT THERE!!
HE STOPPED LISTENING TO WHAT I WOULD SAY AND WOULD EVEN GO TO THE BATHROOM IN THE WRONG PLACES.
I STARTED GETTING BUSY WITH SCHOOL AND MY CLUB ACTIVITIES,
SO I WASN'T ABLE TO TAKE CARE OF HIM LIKE I USED TO, EITHER.
STOP IT ALREADY!!
IT'S NOT LIKE YOU TO BE SO DEMANDING!!
AND THEN,
HE ESCAPED WHILE WE WERE ON A WALK AND...
BUT!
THAT'S BECAUSE YOU DIDN'T KNOW HE WAS SUFFERING FROM DEMENTIA–
...NO.

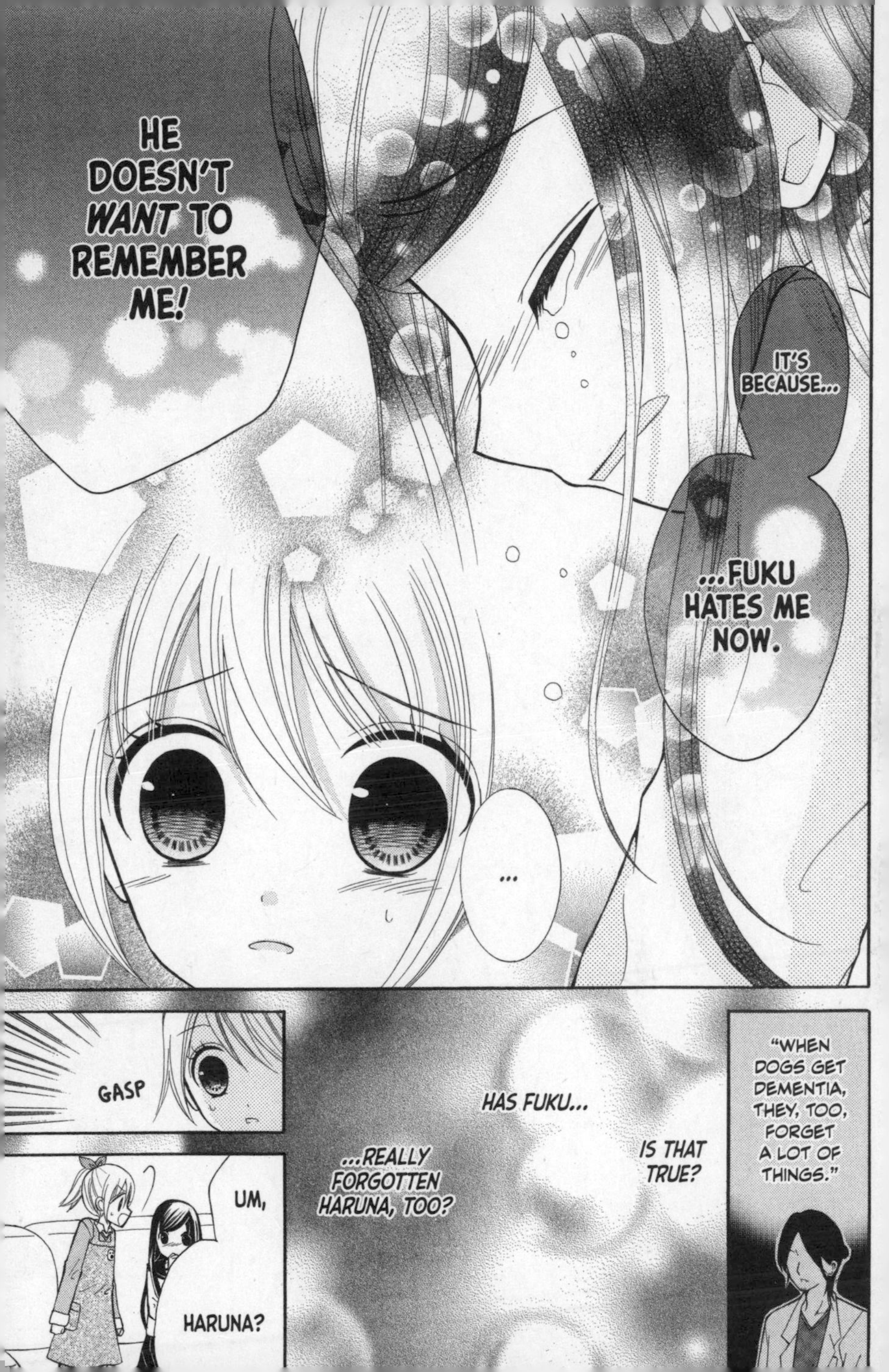
IT'S BECAUSE...
...FUKU HATES ME NOW.
HE DOESN'T *WANT* TO REMEMBER ME!
...
"WHEN DOGS GET DEMENTIA, THEY, TOO, FORGET A LOT OF THINGS."
IS THAT TRUE?
HAS FUKU...
...REALLY FORGOTTEN HARUNA, TOO?
GASP
UM,
HARUNA?

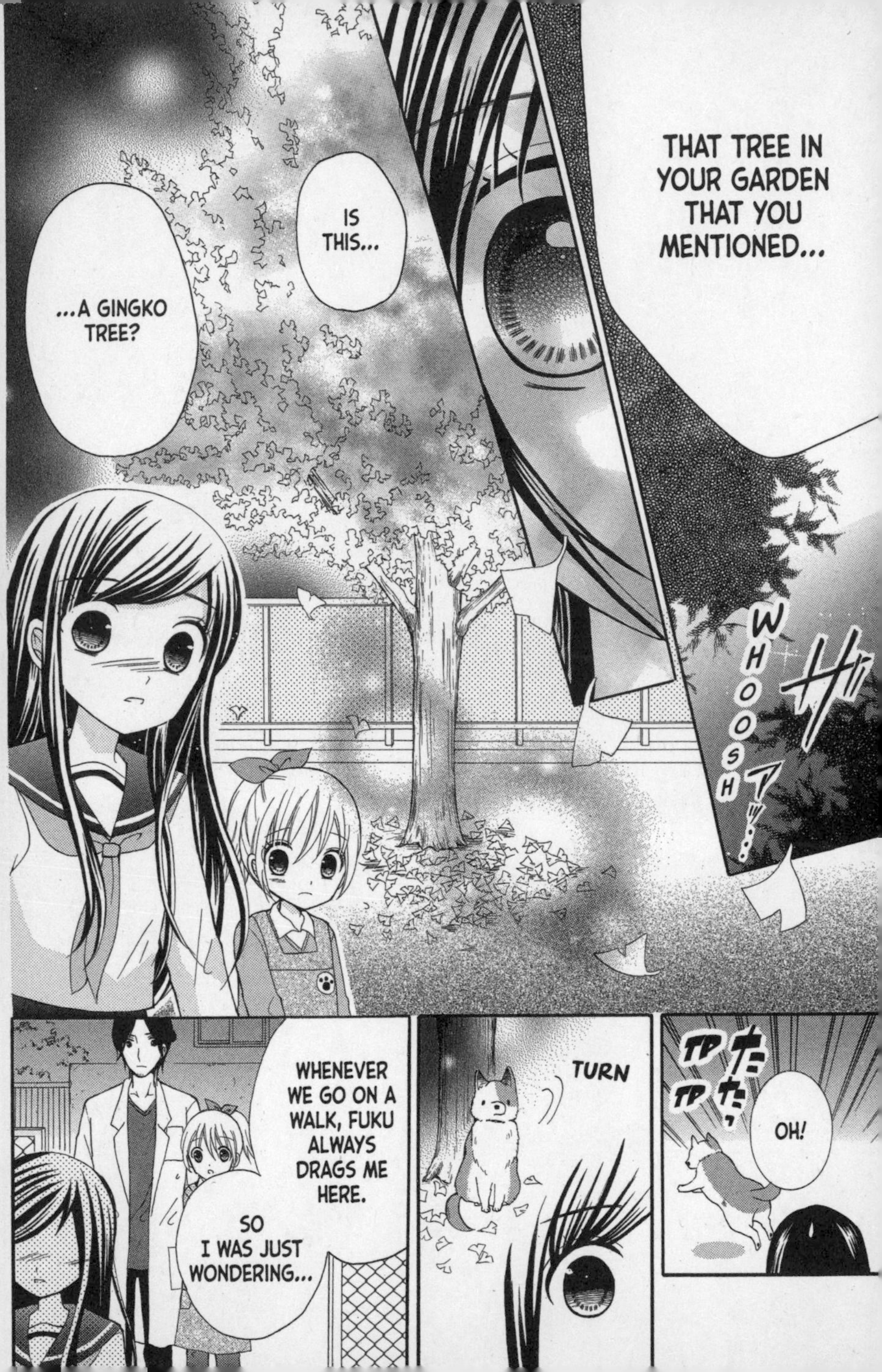
THAT TREE IN YOUR GARDEN THAT YOU MENTIONED...
WHOOSH
IS THIS...
...A GINGKO TREE?
TP TP
OH!
TURN
WHENEVER WE GO ON A WALK, FUKU ALWAYS DRAGS ME HERE.
SO I WAS JUST WONDERING...

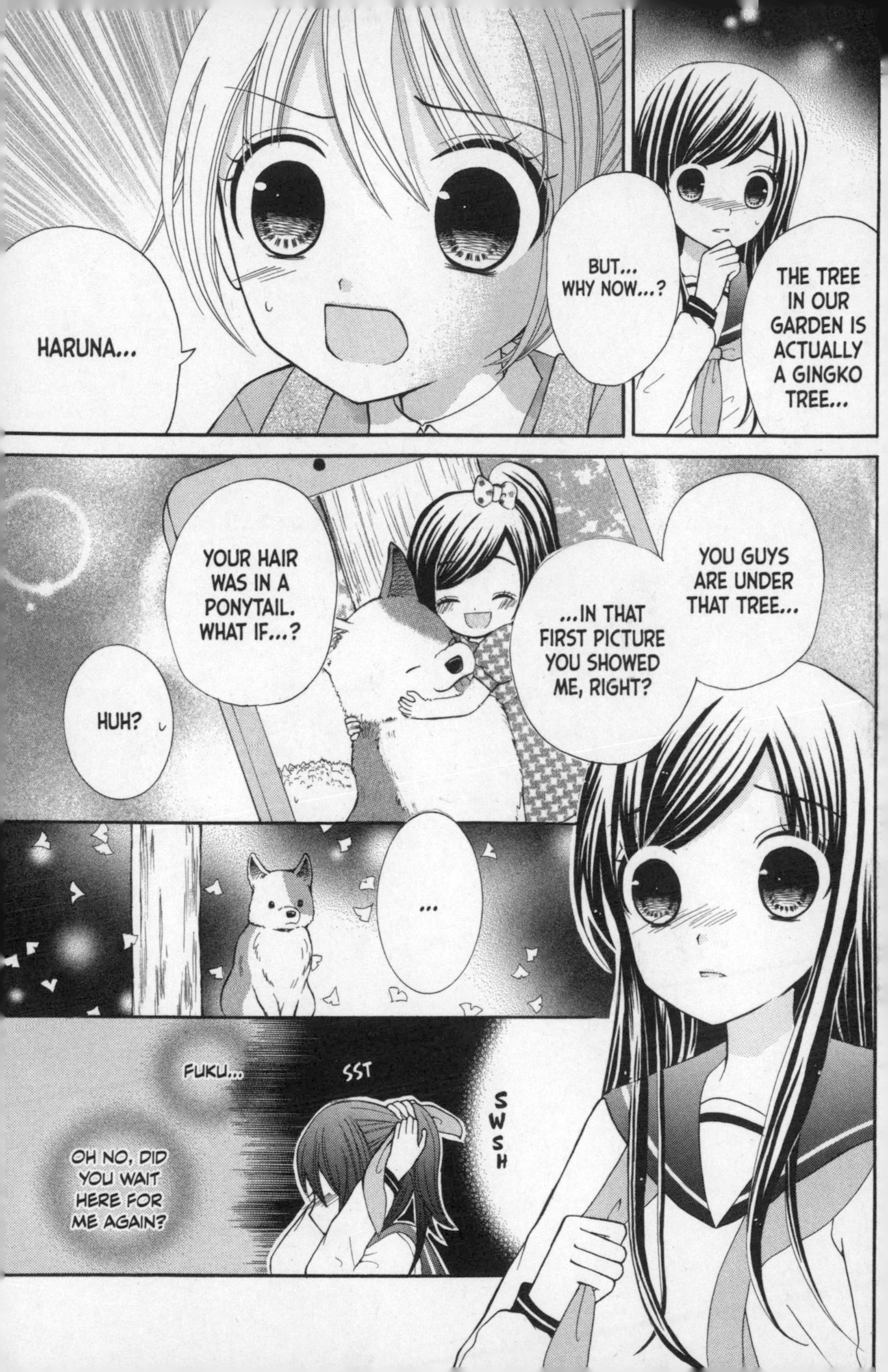
THE TREE IN OUR GARDEN IS ACTUALLY A GINGKO TREE...
BUT... WHY NOW...?
HARUNA...
YOU GUYS ARE UNDER THAT TREE...
...IN THAT FIRST PICTURE YOU SHOWED ME, RIGHT?
YOUR HAIR WAS IN A PONYTAIL. WHAT IF...?
HUH?
...
FUKU...
SST
SWSH
OH NO, DID YOU WAIT HERE FOR ME AGAIN?

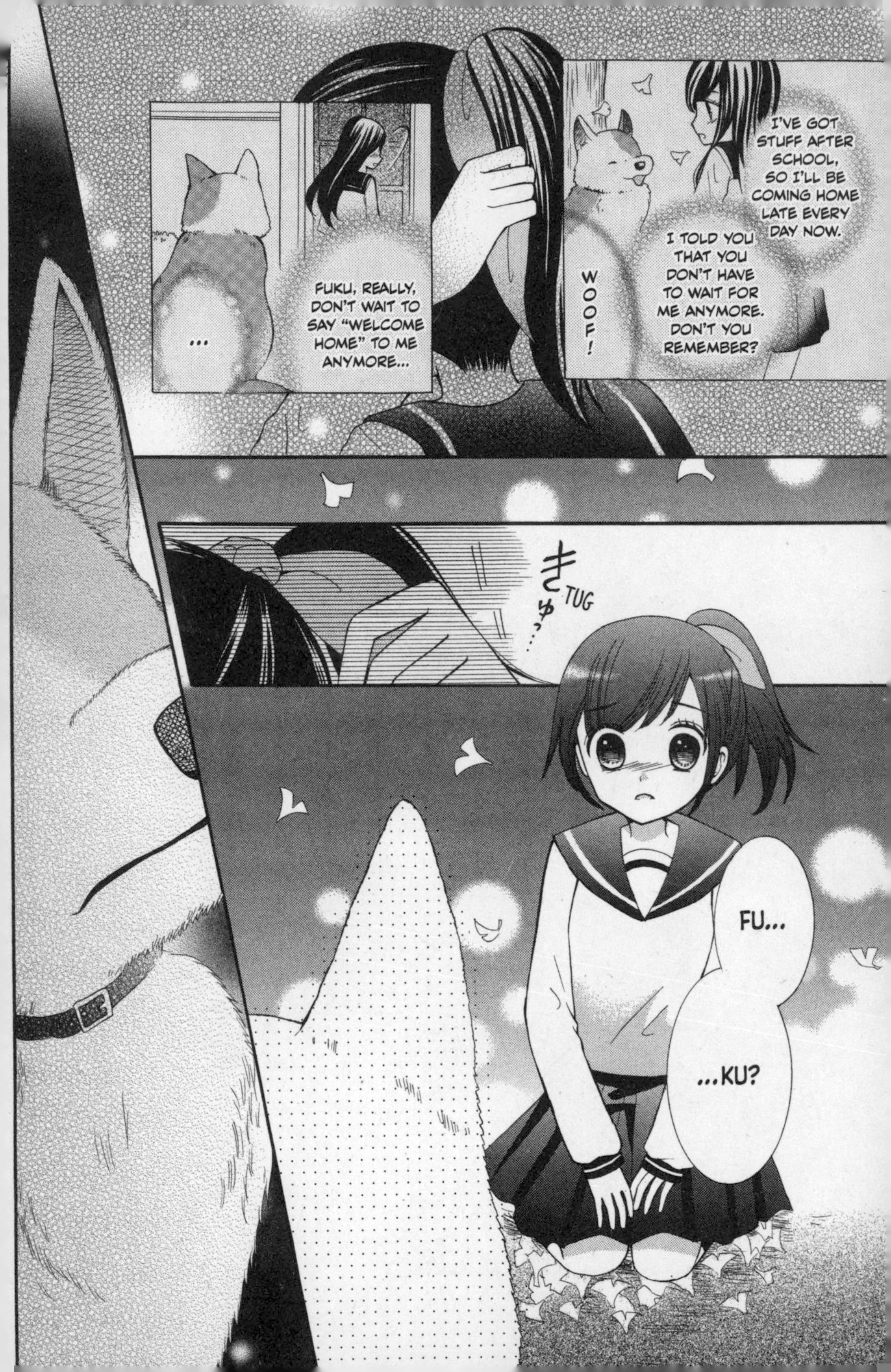
I'VE GOT STUFF AFTER SCHOOL, SO I'LL BE COMING HOME LATE EVERY DAY NOW.
I TOLD YOU THAT YOU DON'T HAVE TO WAIT FOR ME ANYMORE. DON'T YOU REMEMBER?
WOOF!
FUKU, REALLY, DON'T WAIT TO SAY "WELCOME HOME" TO ME ANYMORE...
...
きゅっ… TUG
FU...
...KU?

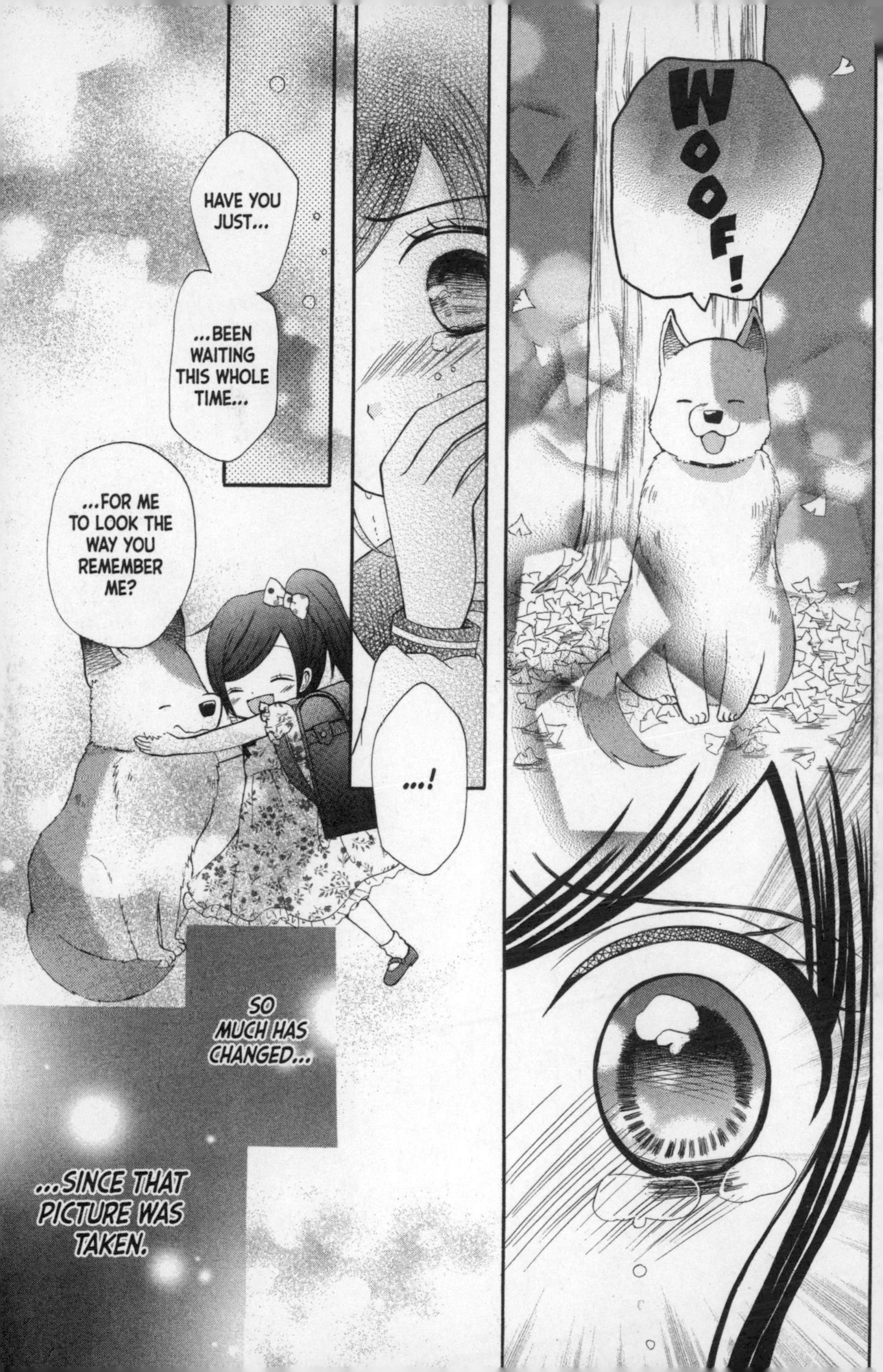
WOOF!
HAVE YOU JUST...
...BEEN WAITING THIS WHOLE TIME...
...FOR ME TO LOOK THE WAY YOU REMEMBER ME?
...!
SO MUCH HAS CHANGED...
...SINCE THAT PICTURE WAS TAKEN.

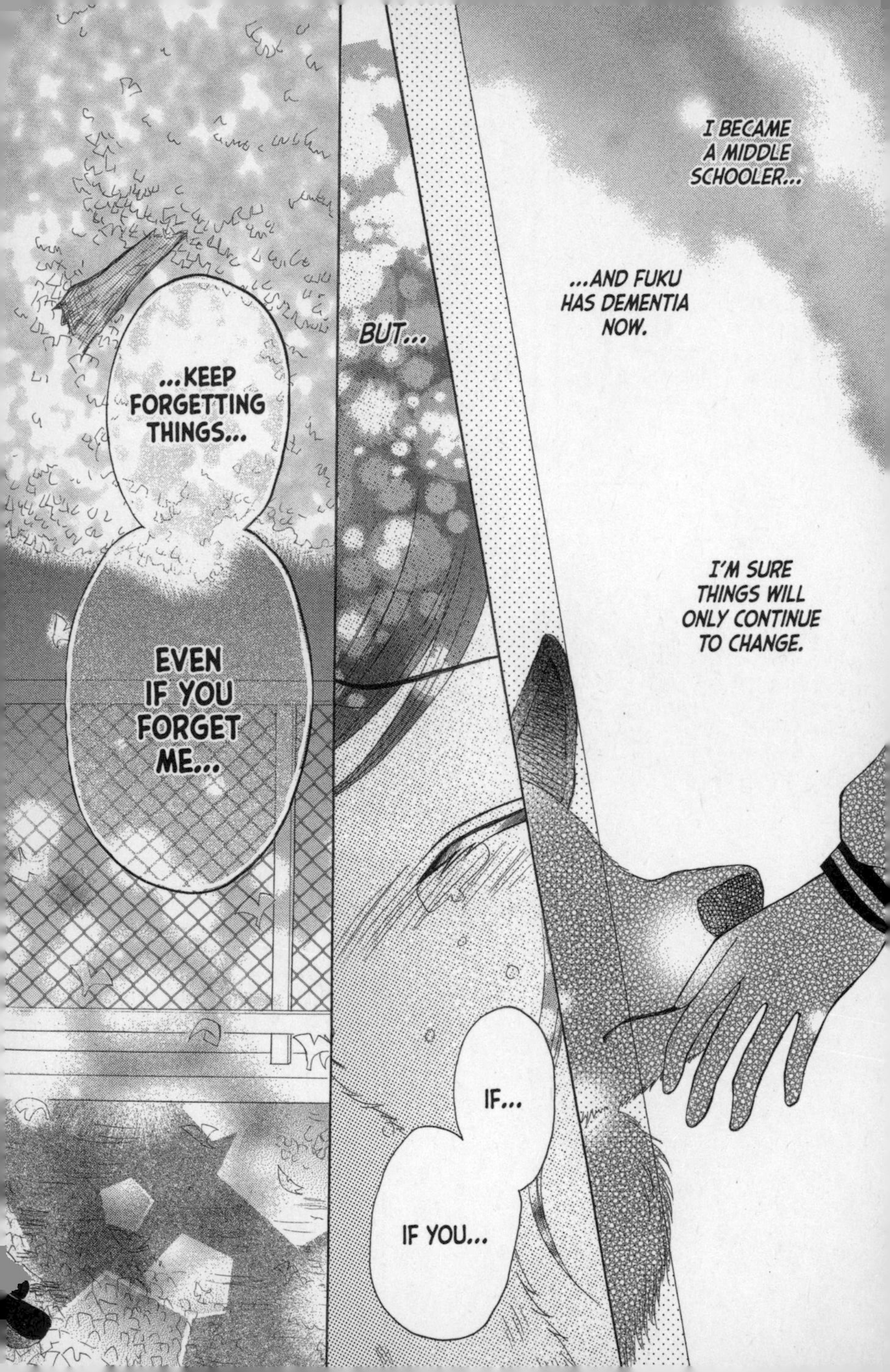
I BECAME A MIDDLE SCHOOLER...
...AND FUKU HAS DEMENTIA NOW.
I'M SURE THINGS WILL ONLY CONTINUE TO CHANGE.
BUT...
IF...
IF YOU...
...KEEP FORGETTING THINGS...
EVEN IF YOU FORGET ME...

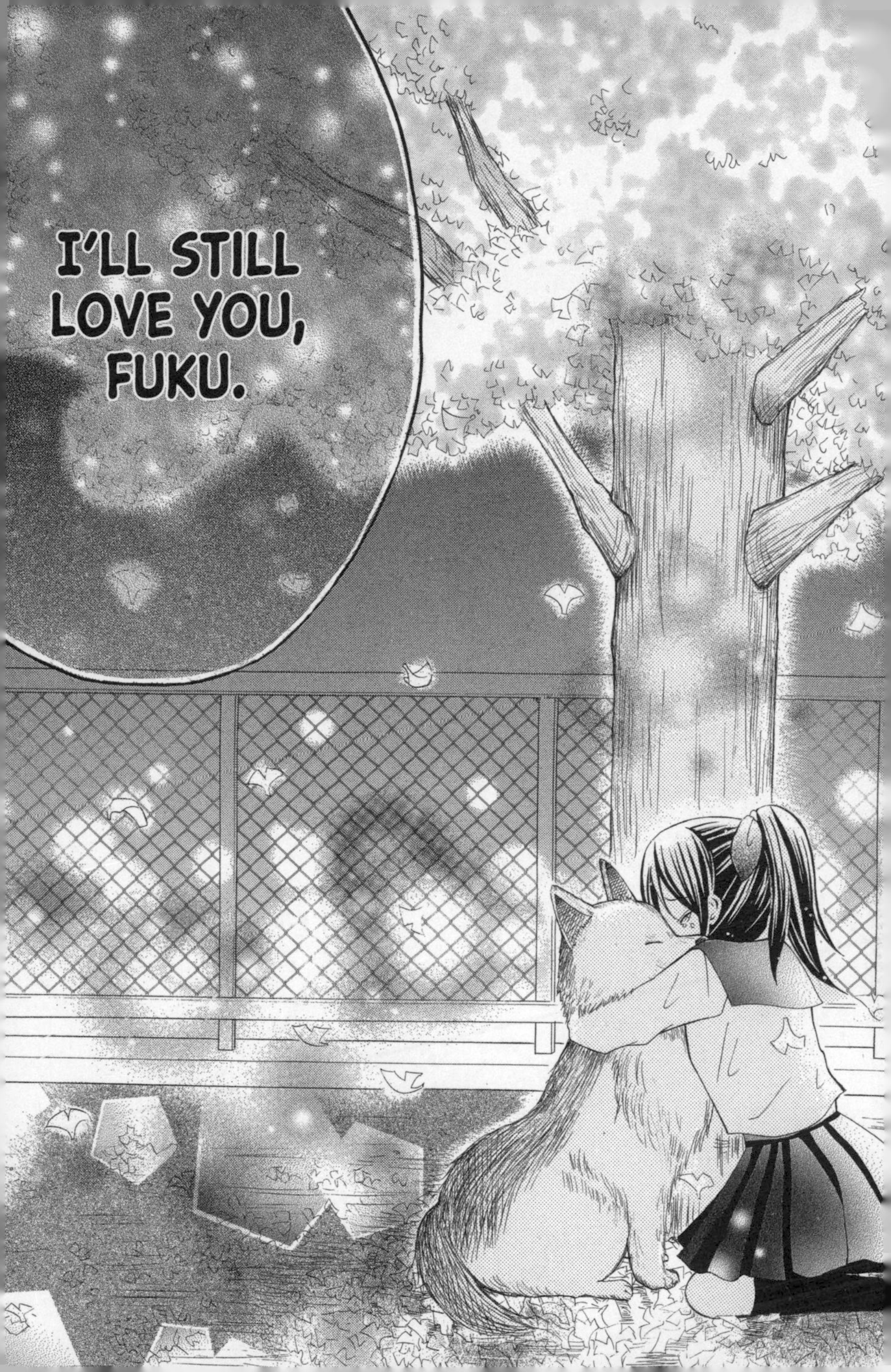
I'LL STILL LOVE YOU, FUKU.

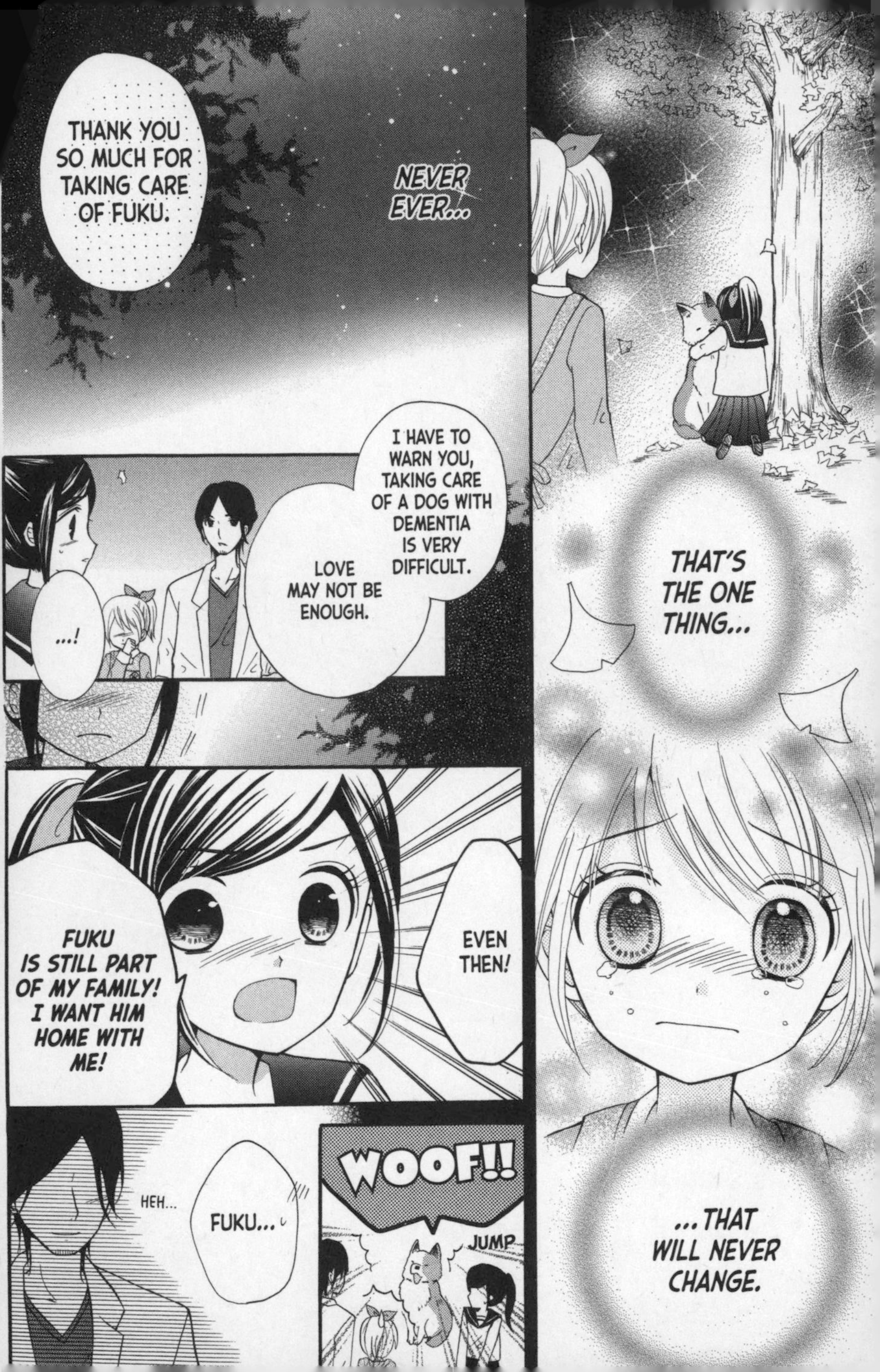
THAT'S THE ONE THING...
...THAT WILL NEVER CHANGE.
NEVER EVER...
THANK YOU SO MUCH FOR TAKING CARE OF FUKU.
I HAVE TO WARN YOU, TAKING CARE OF A DOG WITH DEMENTIA IS VERY DIFFICULT.
LOVE MAY NOT BE ENOUGH.
...!
EVEN THEN!
FUKU IS STILL PART OF MY FAMILY! I WANT HIM HOME WITH ME!
WOOF!!
JUMP
FUKU...
HEH...

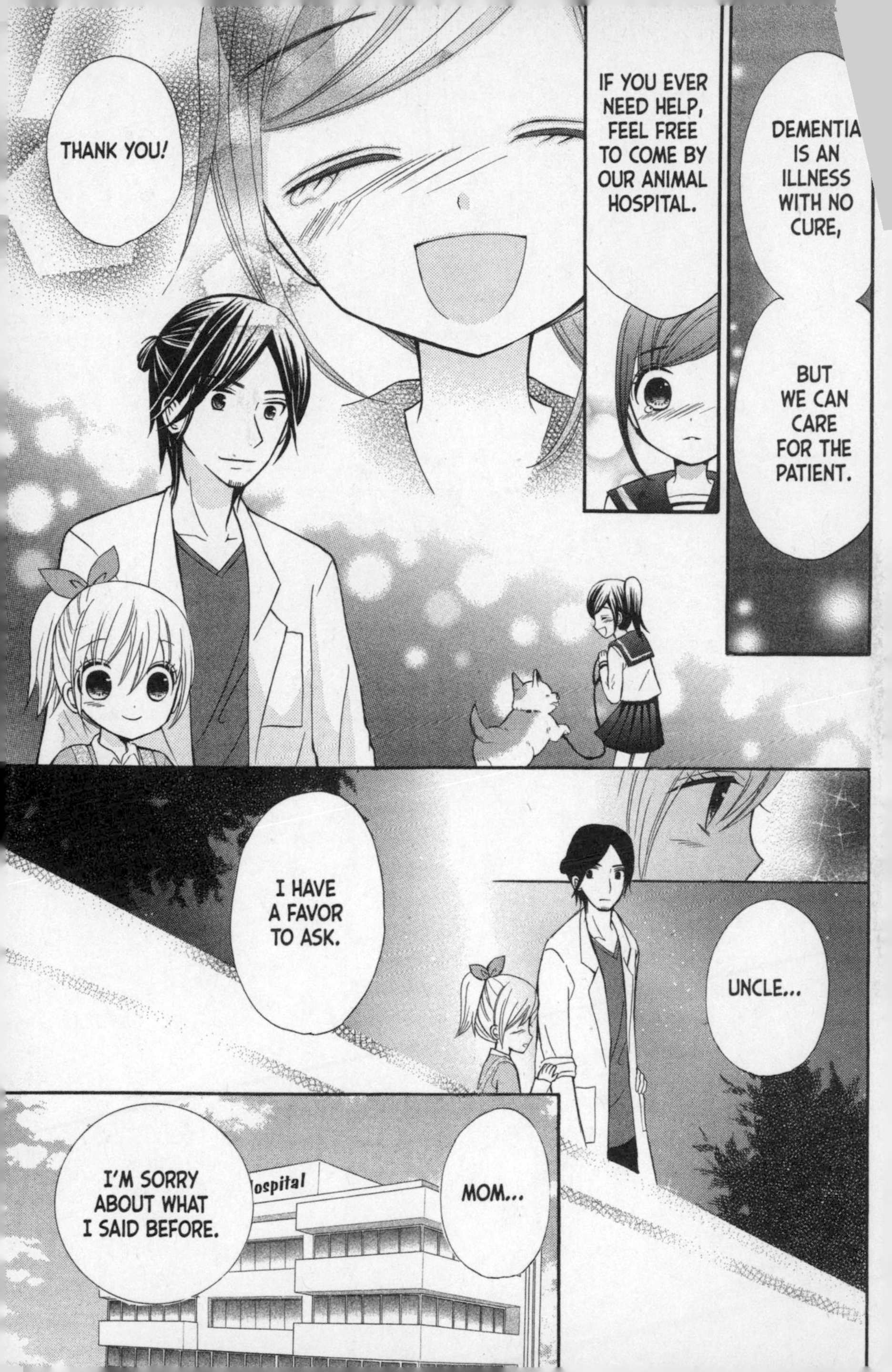
DEMENTIA IS AN ILLNESS WITH NO CURE,
BUT WE CAN CARE FOR THE PATIENT.
IF YOU EVER NEED HELP, FEEL FREE TO COME BY OUR ANIMAL HOSPITAL.
THANK YOU!
UNCLE...
I HAVE A FAVOR TO ASK.
MOM...
I'M SORRY ABOUT WHAT I SAID BEFORE.

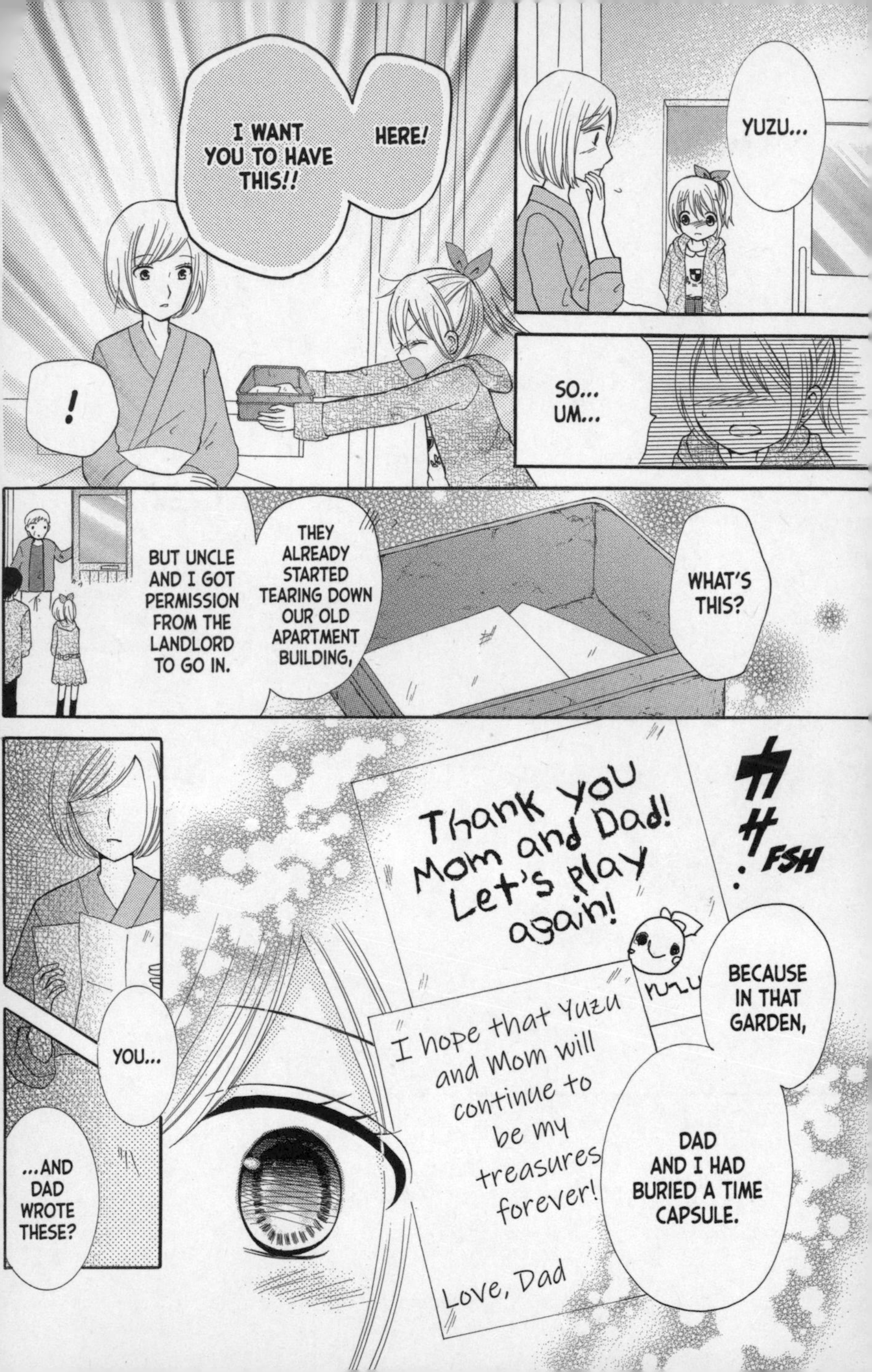
YUZU...
SO... UM...
HERE!
I WANT YOU TO HAVE THIS!!
!
WHAT'S THIS?
THEY ALREADY STARTED TEARING DOWN OUR OLD APARTMENT BUILDING,
BUT UNCLE AND I GOT PERMISSION FROM THE LANDLORD TO GO IN.
カサ FSH
Thank you Mom and Dad! Let's play again!
YUZU
I hope that Yuzu and Mom will continue to be my treasures forever!
Love, Dad
BECAUSE IN THAT GARDEN,
DAD AND I HAD BURIED A TIME CAPSULE.
YOU...
...AND DAD WROTE THESE?

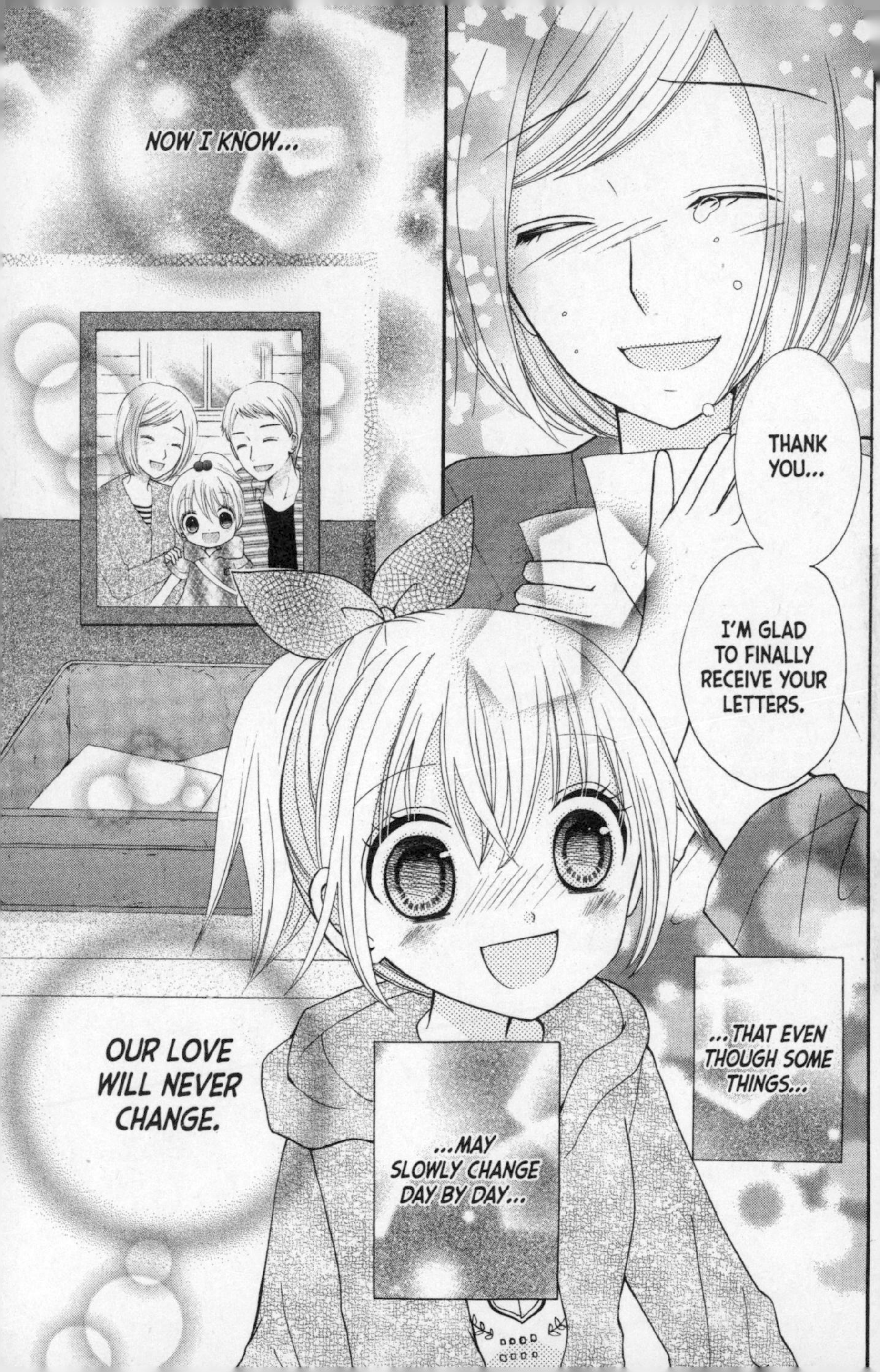
THANK YOU...
I'M GLAD TO FINALLY RECEIVE YOUR LETTERS.
NOW I KNOW...
...THAT EVEN THOUGH SOME THINGS...
...MAY SLOWLY CHANGE DAY BY DAY...
OUR LOVE WILL NEVER CHANGE.

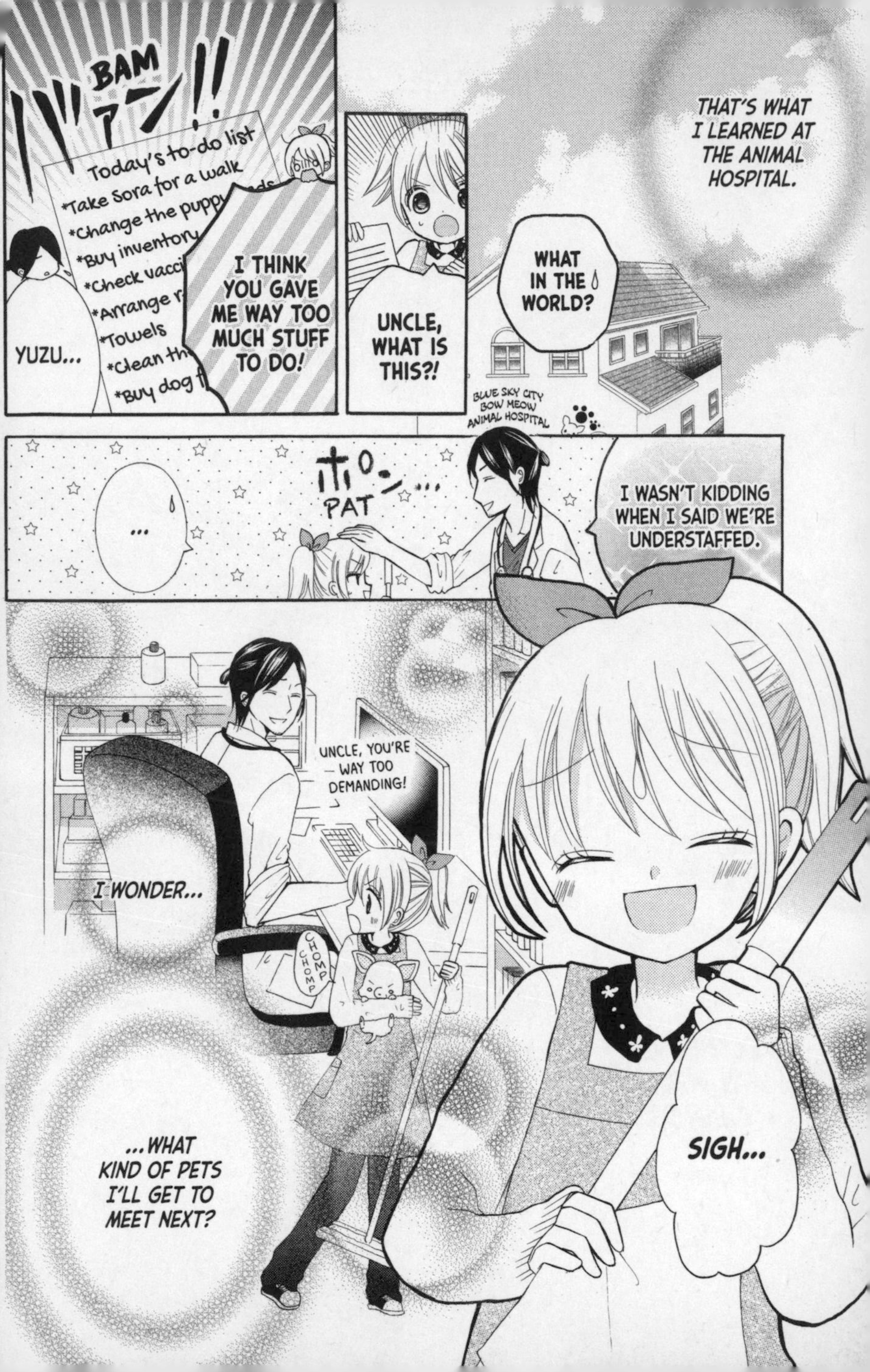
THAT'S WHAT I LEARNED AT THE ANIMAL HOSPITAL.
WHAT IN THE WORLD?
BLUE SKY CITY BOW MEOW ANIMAL HOSPITAL
UNCLE, WHAT IS THIS?!
BAM
Today's to-do list
*Take Sora for a walk
*Change the pupp
*Buy inventory
*Check vacci
*Arrange r
*Towels
*Clean th
*Buy dog f
I THINK YOU GAVE ME WAY TOO MUCH STUFF TO DO!
YUZU...
I WASN'T KIDDING WHEN I SAID WE'RE UNDERSTAFFED.
PAT
...
SIGH...
UNCLE, YOU'RE WAY TOO DEMANDING!
CHOMP CHOMP
I WONDER...
...WHAT KIND OF PETS I'LL GET TO MEET NEXT?

AFTERWORD

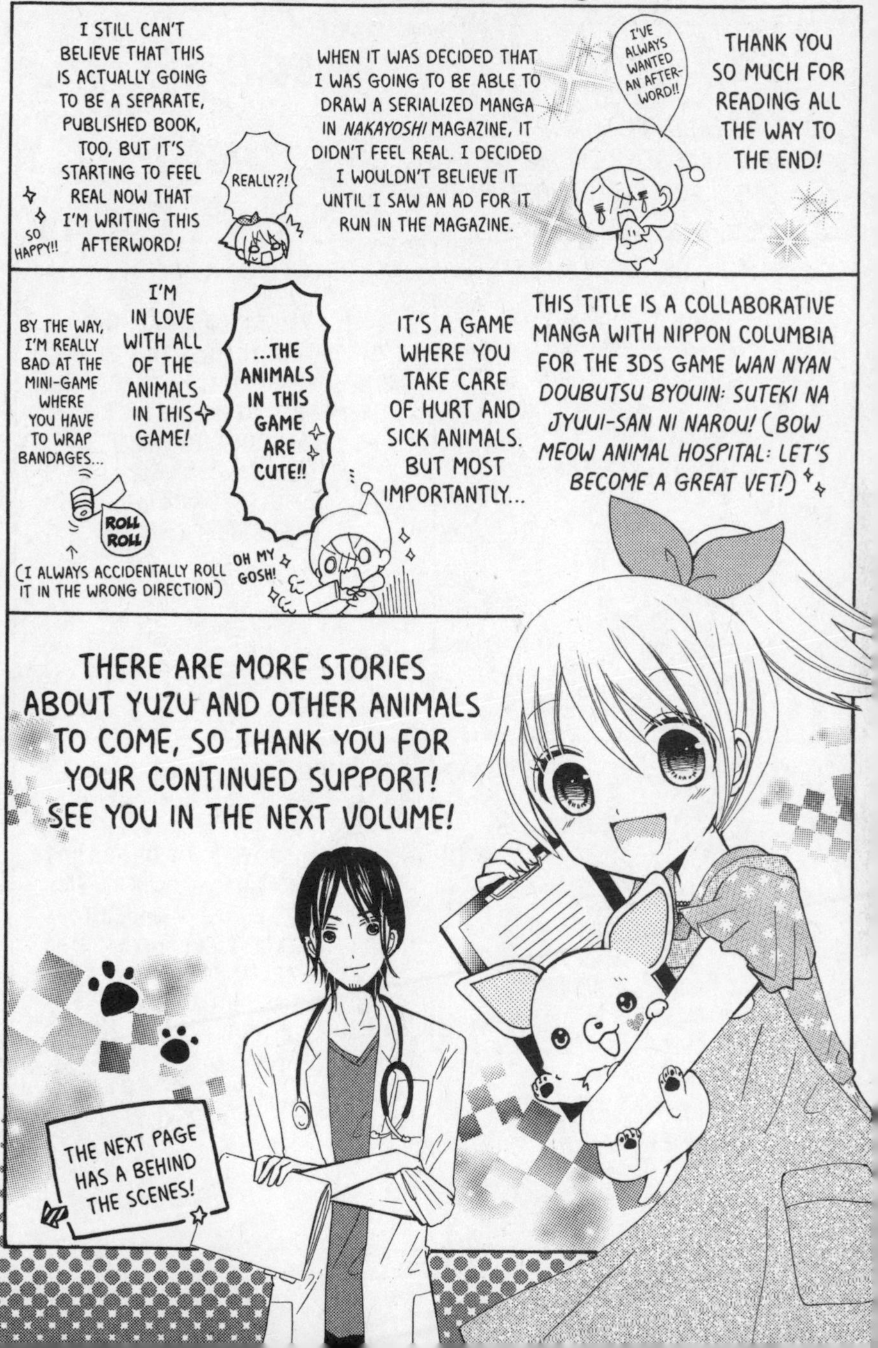
THANK YOU SO MUCH FOR READING ALL THE WAY TO THE END!
I'VE ALWAYS WANTED AN AFTERWORD!!
WHEN IT WAS DECIDED THAT I WAS GOING TO BE ABLE TO DRAW A SERIALIZED MANGA IN *NAKAYOSHI* MAGAZINE, IT DIDN'T FEEL REAL. I DECIDED I WOULDN'T BELIEVE IT UNTIL I SAW AN AD FOR IT RUN IN THE MAGAZINE.
REALLY?!
I STILL CAN'T BELIEVE THAT THIS IS ACTUALLY GOING TO BE A SEPARATE, PUBLISHED BOOK, TOO, BUT IT'S STARTING TO FEEL REAL NOW THAT I'M WRITING THIS AFTERWORD!
SO HAPPY!!
THIS TITLE IS A COLLABORATIVE MANGA WITH NIPPON COLUMBIA FOR THE 3DS GAME *WAN NYAN DOUBUTSU BYOUIN: SUTEKI NA JYUUI-SAN NI NAROU!* (*BOW MEOW ANIMAL HOSPITAL: LET'S BECOME A GREAT VET!*)
IT'S A GAME WHERE YOU TAKE CARE OF HURT AND SICK ANIMALS. BUT MOST IMPORTANTLY...
...THE ANIMALS IN THIS GAME ARE CUTE!!
OH MY GOSH!
I'M IN LOVE WITH ALL OF THE ANIMALS IN THIS GAME!
BY THE WAY, I'M REALLY BAD AT THE MINI-GAME WHERE YOU HAVE TO WRAP BANDAGES...
ROLL ROLL
(I ALWAYS ACCIDENTALLY ROLL IT IN THE WRONG DIRECTION)
THERE ARE MORE STORIES ABOUT YUZU AND OTHER ANIMALS TO COME, SO THANK YOU FOR YOUR CONTINUED SUPPORT! SEE YOU IN THE NEXT VOLUME!
THE NEXT PAGE HAS A BEHIND THE SCENES!

BEHIND THE SCENES!!

EACH CHAPTER IN VOLUME 1 OF *YUZU THE PET VET* IS A SELF-CONTAINED STORY, SO I'VE ENJOYED COMING UP WITH NEW ANIMALS TO DRAW FOR EACH CHAPTER!

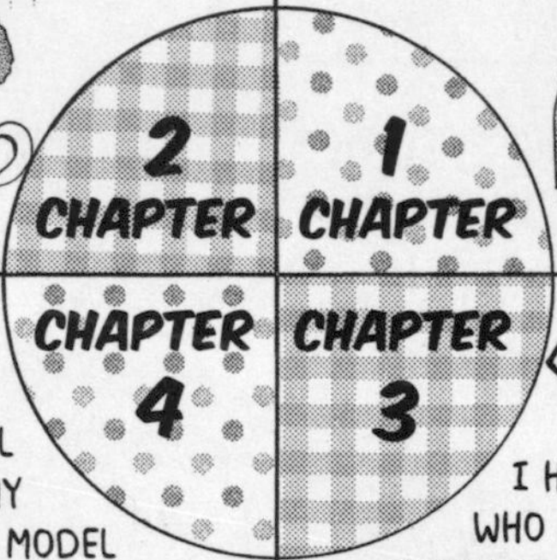

<LEON THE MOMMA DOG>

THE FIRST CHAPTER OF THE STORY AND MY FIRST TIME BEING PUBLISHED IN *NAKAYOSHI* MAGAZINE!! I REMEMBER BEING VERY NERVOUS AS I WORKED ON THIS CHAPTER. I LOVE BIG, FLUFFY BREEDS, SO I'M GLAD I GOT TO DRAW LEON FOR THE VERY FIRST CHAPTER.

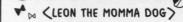

<POPO THE IDOL DOG>

THE FUNNEST PART OF THIS CHAPTER FOR ME WAS DRAWING SORA BEING JEALOUS OF HOW CUTE POPO IS. I WAS HAPPY TO HEAR THAT POPO WAS PRETTY POPULAR WITH THE READERS.

GRRR
AROOO~

1 CHAPTER
2 CHAPTER
CHAPTER 3
CHAPTER 4

<CHIBI AND MITSUBA, POLAR OPPOSITE CATS>

I HAVE A LOT OF FRIENDS WHO ARE CAT OWNERS, SO THEY LET ME USE THEIR PICTURES FOR REFERENCE. CHIBI AND MITSUBA HAVE COMPLETELY OPPOSITE PERSONALITIES, BUT I THINK IF THEY WERE PUT TOGETHER, THEY WOULD ACTUALLY GET ALONG WELL.

<KORO (TEMPORARY NAME) THE LOST DOG>

I USED AN ACTUAL GINGKO TREE IN MY NEIGHBORHOOD AS THE MODEL FOR THE GINGKO TREE IN THIS CHAPTER. I CHOSE IT AS THE LOCATION OF KORO (TEMPORARY NAME)'S MEMORIES BECAUSE THE PRETTY COLORS OF ITS LEAVES IN FALL ARE SUCH AN IMPRESSIVE SIGHT.

HEY, I'M THE MAIN CHARACTER HERE!!

SPECIAL THANKS

- IN COLLABORATION WITH NIPPON COLUMBIA CO., LTD.
- SUPERVISOR: TAISEI HOSOIDO

- EDITORS: NAKAZATO
  NAGANO
- RESEARCH ASSISTANCE:
  EVERYONE AT THE
  MOTOI ANIMAL HOSPITAL
- PREVIOUS EDITOR: SHIRATO
- DESIGNER: KOBAYASHI
- EVERYONE FROM THE *NAKAYOSHI* EDITORIAL DEPARTMENT
- ONO AND MARU THE SHIBA INU

- MANUSCRIPT ASSISTANCE: CHIRORU AOZORA
  NAOCHAN
  MEIRA ISHIZAKA
  KOUTEI PENGUIN DX
  BONCHI

I EAGERLY AWAIT YOUR LETTERS TO HEAR YOUR THOUGHTS ON THE MANGA!

ADDRESS: MINGO ITO
KODANSHA COMICS
451 PARK AVE. SOUTH, 7TH FLOOR
NEW YORK, NY 10016

FIND ME ON MY BLOG OR ON TWITTER!

BLOG MINGOROKU
http://ameblo.jp/itoumingo/

twitter
@itoumingo

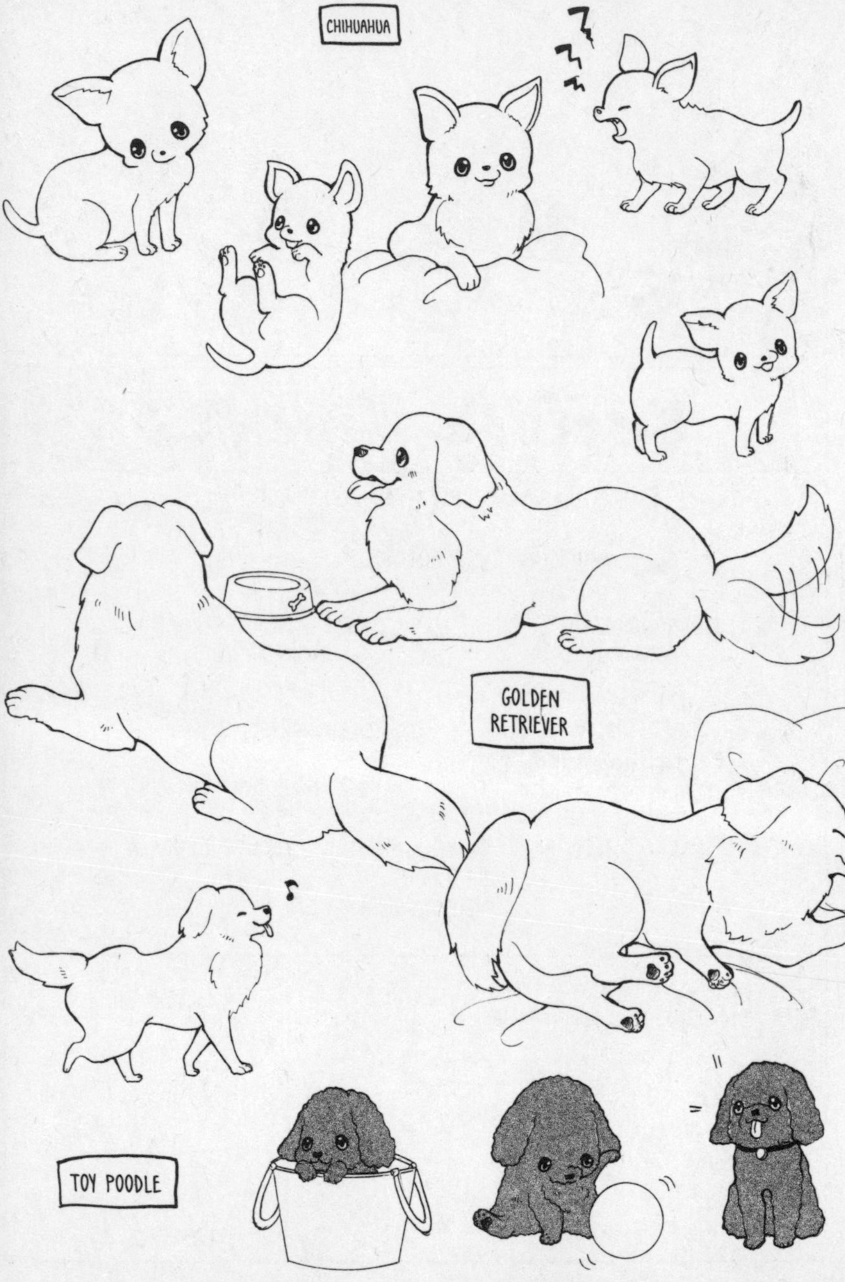
CHIHUAHUA
GOLDEN RETRIEVER
TOY POODLE

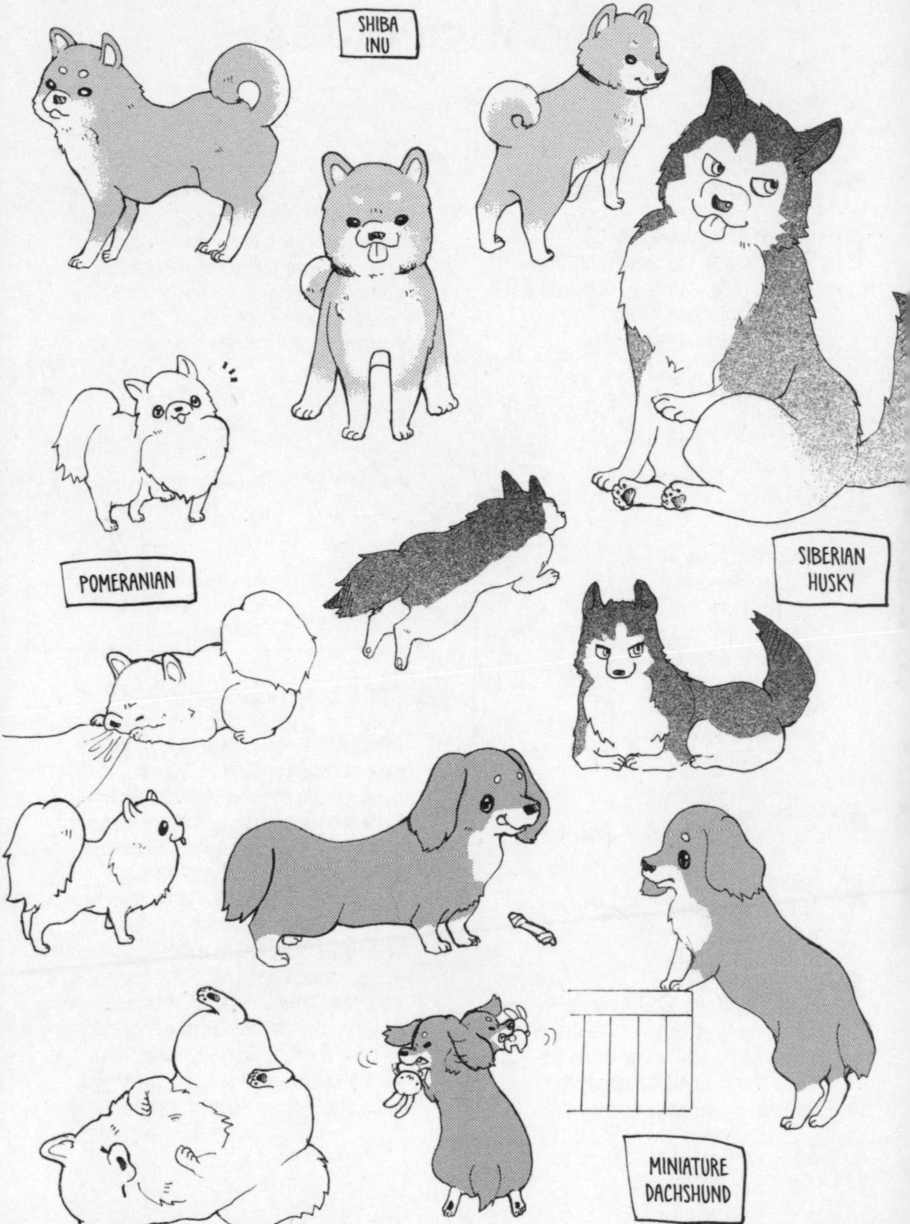
SHIBA INU
SIBERIAN HUSKY
POMERANIAN
MINIATURE DACHSHUND

Translation Notes

Sora, page 9
Sora means "sky" in Japanese.

Open House, page 46
Called "Class Observation Day" in Japan, this is a day when parents and guardians sit in on their children's classes.

> **Open House**
> *Parental guardians, please confirm if you will be able to attend.
> Yes/No

Idol groups, page 47
Idol groups are pop girl bands, often with lots of team members. Popular idol groups range from three members to even 48!

POPULAR IDOL GROUP
SMILES 50

Chibi, page 86
Chibi means "tiny" in Japanese.

Mitsuba, page 90
Mitsuba means "clover" in Japanese.

Koro, page 124
In Japan, Koro is a very common name for pet dogs. "Koro-koro" is the sound of something rolling along, or is used to describe something small and round.

Ginkgo tree, page 126
Ginkgo trees are seen often in Japan and China. They are tall and have leaves shaped like fans. In autumn, their leaves turn yellow-gold in color. They're also known as the "maidenhair tree."

...GINGKO TREE?!

A BIG...

BAM

WHOA!

Serialized manga in *Nakayoshi* magazine, page 155
Nakayoshi magazine is a monthly manga publication in Japan (*nakayoshi* means "best friends" in Japanese). Just like the author says in her afterword, *Yuzu the Pet Vet* was first published in separate chapters. For example, one chapter would be published in the magazine each month, alongside single chapters from other authors' stories. This is what "serialization" means, and is how most manga is made. Then, later on, four *Yuzu the Pet Vet* chapters were compiled into the book you're reading now!

A Kodansha Comics Trade Paperback Original

Yuzu the Pet Vet 1 copyright © 2016 Mingo Ito © 2016 NIPPON COLUMBIA CO., LTD.
English translation copyright © 2020 Mingo Ito © NIPPON COLUMBIA CO., LTD.

Published in the United States by Kodansha Comics, an imprint of Kodansha USA Publishing, LLC, New York.

Publication rights for this English edition arranged through Kodansha Ltd., Tokyo.

First published in Japan in 2016 by Kodansha Ltd., Tokyo
as *Yuzu no Doubutsu Karute ~Kochira Wan Nyan Doubutsu Byouin~*, volume 1.

ISBN 978-1-63236-941-3

Original cover design by Tomoko Kobayashi

Printed in the United States of America.

www.kodanshacomics.com

9 8 7 6 5 4 3 2 1
Translation: Julie Goniwich
Lettering: David Yoo
Editing: Haruko Hashimoto
Kodansha Comics edition cover design by Matt Akuginow

Publisher: Kiichiro Sugawara
Managing editor: Maya Rosewood
Vice president of marketing & publicity: Naho Yamada

Director of publishing services: Ben Applegate
Associate director of operations: Stephen Pakula
Publishing services managing editor: Noelle Webster
Assistant production manager: Emi Lotto, Angela Zurlo
Logo and character art ©Kodansha USA Publishing, LLC

HOW TO READ MANGA

Japanese is written right to left and top to bottom. This means that for a reader accustomed to Western languages, Japanese books read "backwards." Since most manga published in English now keep the Japanese page order, it can take a little getting used to—but once you learn how, it's a snap!

Here you can see pages 24-25 from this book. The speech balloons have been numbered in the order you should read them in.

Page 24—read this page first!

Start here, at the top right corner of the right-hand page.

Read right to left, then top to bottom.

Now continue on to the top right corner of Page 25.

After a few pages, you'll be reading manga like a pro!

Page 25—read the page on the **right-hand side** first!

Start at the top right corner for this page, too!

Don't forget to move back to the right side.

This is the bottom left-most panel, so it's **read last.**

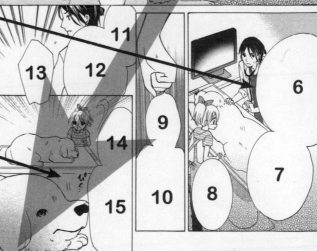

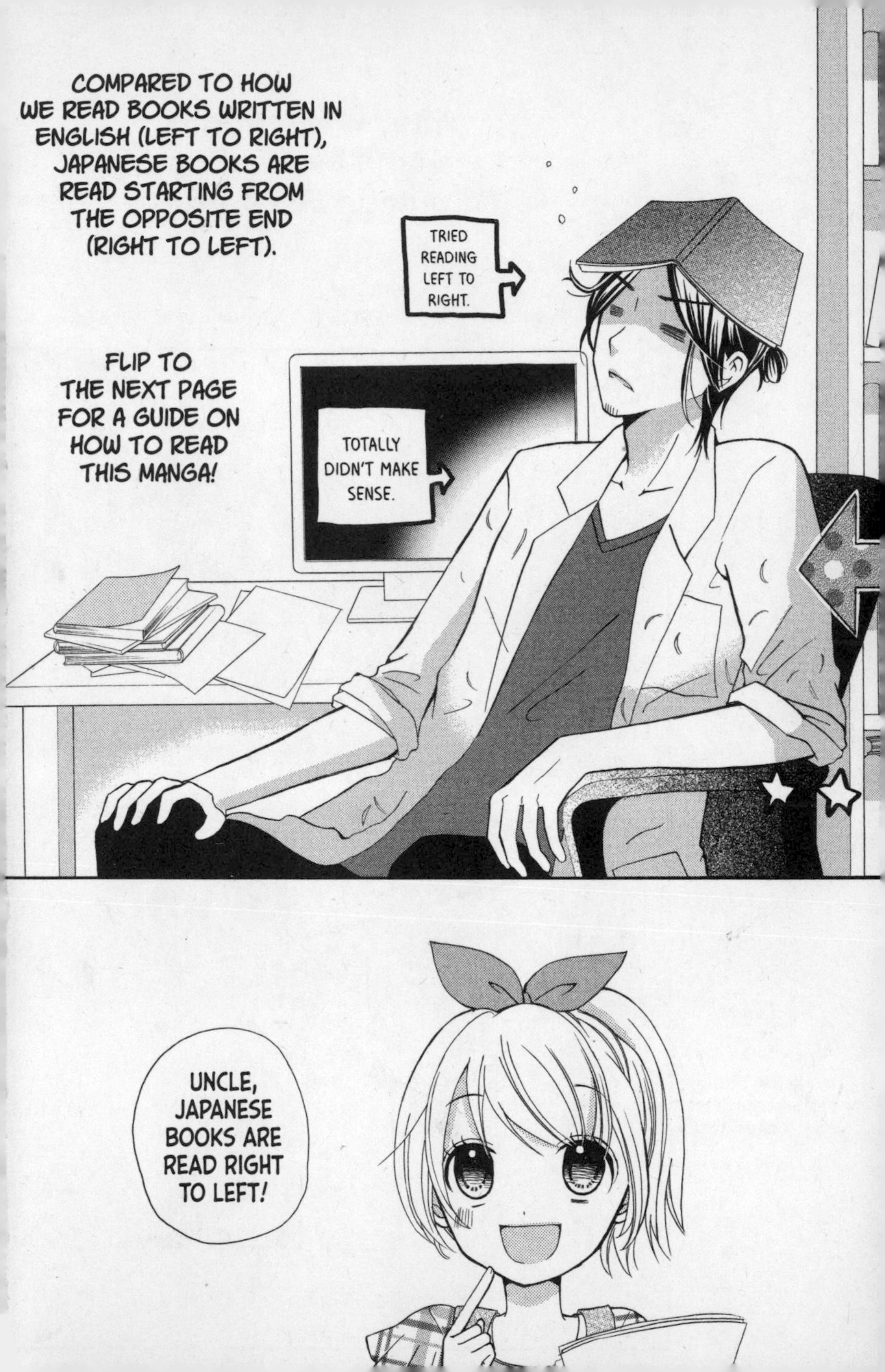
TRIED READING LEFT TO RIGHT.
COMPARED TO HOW WE READ BOOKS WRITTEN IN ENGLISH (LEFT TO RIGHT), JAPANESE BOOKS ARE READ STARTING FROM THE OPPOSITE END (RIGHT TO LEFT).
TOTALLY DIDN'T MAKE SENSE.
FLIP TO THE NEXT PAGE FOR A GUIDE ON HOW TO READ THIS MANGA!
UNCLE, JAPANESE BOOKS ARE READ RIGHT TO LEFT!